The Undaunted King
GOUDDAA
of the Arawaks and Caribs

Goudda, Son of King Aggaddaa

Book of Pillars II

Douglas Burns
and
Eddison Alric Dames

ISBN 978-1-956696-73-8 (paperback)
ISBN 978-1-956696-29-5 (hardcover)
ISBN 978-1-956696-30-1 (digital)

Copyright © 2021 by Douglas Burns

All rights reserved. No part of this publication may be reproduced, distributed, or transmitted in any form or by any means, including photocopying, recording, or other electronic or mechanical methods without the prior written permission of the publisher. For permission requests, solicit the publisher via the address below.

Rushmore Press LLC
1 800 460 9188
www.rushmorepress.com

Printed in the United States of America

Writers Diary

The Undaunted King Gouddaa of the Arawaks and Caribs is written by Mr. Douglas Burns and Mr. Eddison, Alric Dames. It is based on an original story about a time when the ARAWAKS, and CARIBS, lived under one rile in that which is today called The Commonwealth of the Bahamas.

We would like to thank all the builders and contributors to this great Bahamas. And all our friends and family and those from other origins, living in the Bahamas, making this great nation, what it is today. This book is not only a symbol of Bahamian history but a mirror into feature generations and feature builders of the Common wealth of the Bahamas.

Thanks to our readers.

Creed of Gratitude

First creed, Mr. Eddisin Alric Dames, writer and assistance director of the GOUDDAA saga, who is not only a good friend but a brother of the cloth?

Second creed, Miss Palice Lockheart from New York, living in the Bahamas, she is a writer and movie producer.

Third creed, Rushmorepress staff for their hard work on the Gouddaa saga, we thank you.

Forth creed, to my beautiful wife and family for the long hours, thank you.

Contents

1	The Gates of Murcurry	1
2	Emotional Creatures	4
3	The first Expelled to Earth	6
4	Over the celestial rainbow	12
5	Derious on earth	13
6	Even a Prince Can be Punished	20
7	Back on Earth	22
8	Back Over the Heavens	25
9	Toney Wants to See Gabby Now	27
10	The Following Morning	35
11	At Gabby's apartment	38
12	This morning newspaper	41
13	Back over the heaven's	42
14	A Secret Royal Junkanoo Invitation	44
15	Sheppard's Love for Her Brother Dicious	50
16	Secret of the Serpent Seed	54
17	Sheppard in the Healing Chamber	58
18	Dicious enters His Chambers	61
19	Meeting Prior to the First Cycle of the Wind	63
20	Sheppard Released from the Healing Chamber	67
21	Cleattius Escapes and Pay for Information	70
22	Sheppard in the Garden before the throne	78
23	Gouddaa Rides Toward the Black Forest	85

24	Sheppard Walks Among the Leagues and Bronze	90
25	Sheppard On Her Own	96
26	Absence of the King	108
27	He Knows What That Means	116
28	Fortune Favors King Gouddaa	121
29	Sheppard Revised a Plan to Go Up the Mountain	124
30	News Comes to King Libra	145
31	The Royal Convoy	154
32	Bright Skin Face Her Adversary	157
33	Sheppard Returns to the Main Hall	164
34	On the First Cycle of the Wind	169
35	Leoha Enters the Main Hall	171
36	It Feels Good to be Home	174
37	Unknown to Leoha	177
38	Leoha Meets Arrius, Bleaha, and Trottus	182
39	Traveling Distance Away	184
40	Finally Arriving at the Location	186
41	The Silence Between Them Is Thick	196
42	In the Absence of the Four Sadistic Bastards	202
43	Sadly, She Runs Away	206
44	At the Chemist's Home	209
45	In Motion of It All	215
46	Bleaha's Unawareness	220
47	It's Hot	222
48	The Difficulties	228
49	Awaken Out from Her Dream	232
50	Leoha Gets a Surprise	237
51	Into the Throne Room	243
52	The Day of the Feast of Friends	250
53	Early the Next Morning	256
54	You Must Be Well Informed	262
55	Ever Pursuant of the Truth	270
56	The Still Dark Night	273
57	King Gouddaa Black Army of Death	276

58	From Behind Leoha	288
59	Three Men on Horseback	336
60	The Barbarians	345
61	Cleattius and The Guardians	351
62	Valley of the Dust Storm	355
63	Urobeha's Visit Among the Leviathans	367
64	The Warrior at The Temple of the White Lamb	370
65	Gouddaa's Vision	375
66	Laurrennius's Flower Garden	379
67	Sheppard, Laurrennius, and The Book	385
68	Libra After Leaving Her Mother	388
69	Before the Last Great Shake of Time	390
70	The Warrior at The Great Wall	392
71	King Libra Enters Laurrennius's Garden	395
72	Gouddaa Riding on the Wind	397
73	The Lost of a Stallion the Prize of the King	400
74	The Strange Happening	409
75	To Reach the Black Forest	412
76	At Daybreak	416
77	The Head Soldier	419
78	The Strange Storm	422
79	Sheppard Back in Her Mother's Chambers	425
80	The Head Soldier and the Black Knight	427
81	The Disconnections	430

The Gates of Murcurry

After extensive traveling and purchasing of information, the Collector has finally arrived at the tomb of Old King Cole, and behold it is a magnificent sight to see. It sits surrounded by the high mountains on all four sides, in this vast valley on a platform in the middle of no man's land. Its gigantic pillars stand erecting upwards to the skies. From any view the immense width of each pillar is spectacular, truly all which has been said about them is true. The tomb of Old King Cole is truly breathtaking. Pondering to herself the structure of such magnitude, she knows it could have only been built by a lost race of civilization and later on remodified, she carefully moves in. A white mist slowly moving down the mountain accelerates coming in fast, soon it will engulf everything in the valley. She is alert, the erected Pillars are everywhere. Walking with urgency, she makes it to the middle, where she surveys a comprehensive view of everything. Encircling and enclosing around her. The white mist engulfs everything, making it most difficult to see ahead. With limited vision her warrior instincts immediately kick in, hedging against the dangers lurking in the folds and churns of the mist.

Suddenly, out from the mist, a voice captivates her attention. It is behind her, and her head tilts slightly to its sound. "Why do you seek me out stranger from the north?" Confronted, not wanting to reveal the true intent she answers, "Am only a pass a by, lost, can you kindly point me the way out." Even through the mist, obscured the voice echoes out across the pillars. She is able to identify, pinpointing with accuracy the where abouts of and what position the voice is speaking from. "You have been tracking me for some time now, Gouddiaaian, but you will die here today" Deducing it is the target she has been seeking, she can no longer hide it. It would seem all the leads she has followed have panned out. With this Murcurry has not only the upper hand but is well secured because of that information. Pictures flashback of the injured man she allowed to live back at the river days ago, he was the one who informed her. The hairs on the back of her neck stand up, as a chilling alert her, her guard goes up immediately. Her instinct spirals out of danger she needs to move.

Suddenly the pillars around her begin to turn, spinning in place, activated lengths of chains spring out at her. She is a Warrior from the Kingdom and she knows the dread of danger. Like twining serpents lunging at her, she evades them with grace a lithe of a dancer. She must get to open ground. Darting and bending away from the tentacles of live chains she runs to get out to the open ground area, but cannot. In front of her path, there are nets of chains dangerously barring and directing her steps back into the middle. Her adversary should have taken note to not underestimate her. This is Murcurry territory, full of death traps. She herself planted the traps of destruction in cunning places to ensure that none could or ever remove her father's tomb. Murcurry will kill her. She is determined to end this Warrior's life for attempting to desecrate her father's resting place. So far, the Warrior has been fortunate, but even good fortune turns sometimes.

Leaping high in the air the Collector somersaults over and again to avoid each passing danger. Her light body skills allow her to tip on spiraling chains leaping out from danger. She is being trapped in a web of chains, never the less her sophisticated leaping abilities are next to none. She is being trapped on the second floor of chains and killing devices high above the ground. Murcurry and her informer are able to see the Warrior's every movement, by looking through the green optical lens and they are pressing her. They are pushing on secret blocks within each pillar and they want her dead. The Warrior has only her instants but she has been down this road times before.

By quickly opening her Metallic hand band, unseen to the others, fallout a black marble ball of explosive might, and the Metallic band is made closed again. Leaping again to reach the edge she is met by other webs of chains keeping her locked in. The explosive black ball of might is her grantee to the outside and she uses it. Taking no more chances, she launches the black ball of might out at one of the nets of chains holding her captive. The net gives away and the pillar is reduced to rubble before turning to white sparkling dust on the ground. She is free, and again the force and power of Gouddiaaian might have been displayed. The white fog is slowly dissipating. Never has Murcurry or her informer has ever seen a display of skills like the Warrior before. The informer had also been watching the Warrior movements so intensively, even after one of his green lenses fell out of place he stayed focused blinking his one eyes envision. The slow timing of his one eyes had hindered the speed of his hand movement, allowing the Warrior a split second to escape. This Murcurry explained to him after she slapped him and still, he tries to explain "Not my false... not my false... the lens... fell aaaaaaaaaa but she two is gone. The reduced pillar which turned to white sparkling dust is left behind as a landmark should any other Gouddaaian ever pass this way it would warn them of the pending danger. Never before has Mercurry or her informer witness a reduced pillar turned into sparkling dust. They are left baffled by this.

Emotional Creatures

At the time Gouddaa arrived on earth, Prince Dicious arrives at the Tomb of Old King Cole. It is late evening, the final hour of the third cycle of the wind and Prince Dicious is where he said he would be at the Tomb of Old King Cole. Surveying his surrounding the sparkling white dust glitters against the evening sun on the ground, letting him know the Collector has already passed this way and she is long gone leaving him evidence of her being there. He knows if Mercurry is dead this place would have been reduced to ashes, he waits, not wanting to entering the pillar zone. A small caravan is passing, suddenly it stares straight toward him. Out comes Murcurry dragging behind her the chains of time. What in the hell is this he thinks to himself as she gets even closer, she stops. Throwing them out at his feet, he answers the call this is not the time for antics. Then she said. "Because I don't trust you, put them on." Walking up even closer to him with a key in hand she locks him in, hand, neck, and feet first. Then comes out from the caravan Black Synn, he steps up to Dicious and without words, he shoves into Prince Dicious chest warm clothing before staring him in the eyes, saying "You will need them, over the mountains the cold can be traitorous" Taking his words for it Dicious complies.

Looking Black Synn in the eyes Dicious hummers "So we meet again Black Synn, you should thank me for your life." With that death look of concern on Black Synn's face, he answers back "I will, you can bet your life on it." Rushing back to the backside of the wagon Black Synn signals to the on-looking driver and the wagon is quickly turned in position. Walking back toward the great Prince, Black Synn is pulling behind him a chain length of fifty feet, which he kindly attaches to the middle section of Dicious hand chain before answering "Any more thanks than this, al kill you." The great Prince says nothing more but focuses his eyes on the key in Murcurry's hand, she is only to please to oblige him. With brutal strength, agility, and accuracy, she tosses the key high into the sky, where it comes to rest on the very top of the nearby pillar that answers his question.

The great Prince is chained to walk the distance. Signaling the driver, one quick jerk from the wagon tenses the lengthy chain causing the great Prince to falls flat on his face to the ground. There he is punished with blows by Black Synn, before being whipped by Murcurry, over and again until blood spills from his mouth, still, it is not enough to kill him. Murcurry steps up to his face and with her boots she raises his head just enough to look up at her face and with a cross look she let him know "That's for sending someone out to kill me" The great Prince's head drops back to the ground. From the smile on Black Synn's face this is something she likes punishing Dicious. Words are given to move out, and for a while, the prince is dragged along until he manages to catch up on his own two feet. Mercurry from time to time would look out at his courage, impressive she thinks. The journey up the mountain is steep and coming down is even steeper. The weather in these parts can quickly change, it reminds the Prince of what little he knows of women, very little, they are emotional creatures just like the weather in these parts, one could never know what's next.

The first Expelled to Earth

When Derious first arrived on earth, he came out from the white mist staggering to gain his balance, and was hit by a car before falling to the earth. He is dazed by the hit and needs to rest for a while. The driver is a woman on her way to the Mayer private house in the country. She needs this vacation to patch up a long and overdue relationship with her boyfriend, who claims she loves her work more than him. "No, no, no she speaks getting out from the car to access the damage to the man she accidentally hit. She doesn't need a hit and runs police report added to her record. Her last accident caused her, the price of her pudding, thanks to the town Mayer, he is now her boss.

There is a news bulletin, passing over the radio warning, drivers to say clear of the fog on Highway 65, she misses both radio announcements. The man she accidentally hit lies motionless on the ground. Out of her car, she runs attentively looking over him, she is a little nervous. She is not equipped to deal with this kind of situation. By the looks of the man's strong immaculate body mask, he looks able to withstand any kind of knock, still, she can't take any chances. A knock like that, could not have killed him she thinks. His body clothing is few and the color is most strange to her. The lint-age red material he wheres is even more strange. She is too far out from any hospital, so she decides to help him up, take him to the car, and call an ambulance on her way to the country house. Her car back seat is filled with files of unexplained cases. Yes, she is the Mayer secretary, heading up to his townhouse in the country, to do a little work while on vacation. What a blow of bad luck she thinks to herself. She is young, blond, pretty, and fast past. The car she drives is payed for by the Mayer, a hot rod one of its kind. She is good at her work but even better at pleasing the Mayer after a long and stressful day at the office. The Mayer likes her, she makes him feel youthful again, something he cannot explain only that he likes it and her.

Away from home and his wife, it's the Mayer's only secret. She had it all planned to meet with her boyfriend this coming week. The files in the back seat were only an excuse used to mislead the Mayer and throw off any further employee questions. Only two of the files she is intended to work while on vacation and it worked.

My God this accident just changed her plans and maybe even her life. Quickly, by clicking a button on the car staring wheel, the passenger front seat layout flat like a bed. Struggling to get him into the front seat, she helps him to get comfortable there he falls back into sleep. Slowly driving away, she clears through an opening before being engulfed by the mist again. Reaching into her side bag, she takes out her phone, bad luck. That's not possible, she thinks "Dammit what else could go wrong." The dam phone not long come off charge. Thinking it must be because of the fog, she let it be. For a moment, she's losing her focus again on his immaculate body posture. So soon as she clears the mist, she pushes the car gas meddle to the metal. Speed is not her enemy - she is a driver and once race driver. Back then, they called her driver from hell, but those days are long gone, gone, now. The road ahead is a long drive but driving is her thing. She has been at the Mayor country house before, and she knows the way like the back of her hand.

Just before reaching the country house, her phone rings, and the car engine stop on its own, she is left dumbstruck. She answers the call, it's her boyfriend, he has been in an accident on Highway 65 but he is well. He updates her about the situation, police have stopped all cars from coming through until the fog is cleared in the morning, he must take a side street room for the night. She understands, but she doesn't get it because she left the same area two hours ago. Out from the vehicle, she rushes, digging through her handbag, in search of the house keys. Opening the house locked front door is the simplest thing this day has offered her. She throws her handbag to one side of the living room couch before rushing back to get the injured man. The house keys are still in the door lock. On opening the car passenger door, the man's eyes open, she tries to explain why he is in her car after a short while, he gets it.

With his help, she gets him up to the front door. On entering his hand accidentally hit the door closing it behind her. Struggling with extra weight is always unbalanced and difficult. On the living room sofa, gently she set him down, there he is left to rest. Into the kitchen, she rushes to get him some drinking water. Opening the fridge there is more than enough food to eats with treats. Thinking water may be a bad choice for the man, she decides wine is a better choice for the man's stomach's sake. Rushing back to the man, he is allowed to drink. Helplessly she looks over his body for any sign of injuries, so she thinks. What a body "Are you finish with the wine" she asks watching him drink. What a dumb question she thinks. As he sips down the last drop of wine, she said. "I can see no apparent injuries, al take the glass." At the time she offered him the glass of wine, she explained "It will make him feel much better." It was a fairly large glass of wine he drunk, enough to spin one's head, she never even tried to slow him down her eyes are too busy noticing his massive arms and body. Having already explained to her, he is well and just needs to gain his balance, the wine does little to help him, he falls out cold.

Thanking it's best to have him checked by medical staff, she reaches for her handbag but her phone is dead again. The evening has been most strange and daunting to her. Strangely, she remembers the keys in the door and the open car door outside. Doing what's best she takes the keys out the door and down to the car she goes. It's a new car, a hot rod given by the Mayor as a gift, and she loves it. The engine cutting out on its own earlier lingers her mind. As a once race driver, every professional driver knows their baby engine.

Into the driver's seat she ignites the engine, the car starts on less than a half crank. Raiding the engine up once, twice, three times, she turns it off and on again. The power of the engine and more is there, how, she is not sure but is willing to bet her life on it, it has something to do with the mist on Highway 65. Every race driver know the roar of their own car engine, she now senses a strange lift in the roar of her car engine and it's firing like hell. Strangely, everything works better than before. Reaching into the back seat she takes out fifteen of the files before exiting. Outside she checks the locks and doors for loss of power, they too work perfectly. She has her files, back into the house she goes the strange man is still asleep. Her nose is sensitive to smell and his smell is like no other. With only two little pieces of close like cloth on him, she sees no pockets, meaning no identification of any kind she checks, nothing. Thinking back to the accident, maybe when she hit him, they scattered out but that is too far fetched for a half-naked man, she abundant the thought.

In a strange way, on resting the files on the dinner table, her head automatically turns to him laying out on the sofa. She refuses to leave the stranger downstairs in the Mayer house alone, these days you never know who is trustworthy. Her woman instinct illumines no danger, so quickly he is helped up on his feet. He is heavy, trying to move him alone is madness, with a little help, he places his right arm around her shoulders she struggles up the stairs with him. The first bedroom down the hall is her own and she refuses to carry him any further. Across her bed, she lay him before twisting him in sleep position. It makes her remember her suitcase is still in the car back trunk and she needs to have it. The night is young, good women don't go to bed before bathing. Struggling her way back downstairs, she retrieves her suitcase from the car's trunk. Climbing the stairs again with luggage in hand is not one of her strong attributes about vacating, she makes it. On the floor beside the bed footboard, she unzips it open. A long day calls for a long and needed bath and she is ready to have one. Into the bathroom, she runs warm water in the large sonar tub, leaving it too full up on its own. Her notion is showers are for lovers only. Back in the room, she goes looking through her suitcase, knowingly she finds a matching read nightdress to that of the stranger's clothing. It's just something women do, in other words, It's a woman thing, to commemorate this strange day in her life.

The bath running water has reached its tub height, sending out a warning pitch. It cut off on its own. This is truly the age of technology at its best. Into the bathroom, she makes her way into the tub, forgetting the clothing she earlier picked out still on the bed. A worming alarm would cause anyone to forget something. Stripping off everything, she enters the bathtub, closing herself in, the bath glass doors are beautiful this is her time and space now. As she sits, she dips, the bathwater is soothing, she relaxes taking in the moment. Relaxing out at length she falls asleep, ten minutes later she woke up thinking it was all just a dream. Ball naked she walks out into the bedroom, shocked by the man laying out in her bed she screams "Aaaaaaaa" Out from his sleep he woke up, sitting up before turning his head to the naked view standing in front of him. Calmly he utters out at her screaming "I think you better stop that, it's giving me a headache" she doesn't hear him. Thinking it's not a dream, he goes on to speak "Who are you! Are you Aries!" Another name he remembered in his head.

Out from the bed, he jumps in front of the screaming naked woman, she turns and runs back into the bathroom calling for her robe still on the bed. The bathroom door is left cracked open, he passes the robe to her. "Shit, this is real" she mumbles. Now robed she come out, into the bed she covers herself within the sheets before peeping out at him. Gabby is not afraid of anyone she is very much outspoken at times. From her look's one could never tell, she can be ghetto even though she looks like a blond peach. This situation has tamed her emotions, she was thought, when not knowing what to do, stay still, and in bed there she is still, at least for a while.

The stranger doesn't remember much of his past but he is very much versatile to this new world. After a bath, he finds clothing not so much to his liking but they fit. Down the stairs, he descends with his garments in hand, into the fireplace he throws them to burns. Gabby had had a full day and time calls her to sleep. The stranger needs food, strait to the refrigerator he gets his full. The files on the table take his attention, he sits, one by one he examines them. And by mentally tapping into the fabric of time, he can see the how, the when, the where, the why and the who's. An ability he is gifted with beyond all others, in this realm on this planet. Beneath each report, he writes an accurate account of each happening, he finishes them all before morning break. His eyes are heavy, with a frequent flashback of the assurances in the reports and more a strange face of a man keep appearing in his vision, he needs to get to the bottom of it. Back to the upstairs he goes, Gabby is asleep. Not wanting to further disturb her, he settles for one pillow. Tonight, he will sleep comfortably on the bedroom floor beside the bed.

Over the celestial rainbow

Over the winter mountains Murcurry and her caravan travels, the great prince Dicious is made to walk the whole way. He is tired and needs to rest but there is no resting for one like him according to Murcurry. Old man winter has long passed him and the weather is cool now. They have arrived at the place he would pay his penance, time become his enemy. Stripped off most of his clothing his shackles remain. Tired he cannot walk any further, Murcurry orders her men to drag him to his holding place. There he is chained to the great beast of the fiends to do the work likewise. He must plow the land for the harvest and plant seeds alongside the bison.

The green vegetable in the fields serves as a diet to his strength. He is a prince from the Gouddaaian Kingdom in the far north. Why does he do it? He can have her whole family execute and all her men wiped from the earth, but no, he chooses not to go home. He learned long ago that the matters of the heart is the life line of most wars. He is his own greatest enemy, why, because he can never defeat his own heart. Murcurry hate toward him grows stronger each passing day of the wind, so much, she orders he be fed only the leftover, this he refuses. He being there to pay a debt is one thing, degrading him is another. He is a Prince, but even a Prince when hunger hit must settle with his stomach the rules of engagement is simple live or die. The great Prince wants to live and man should not live by vegetable alone. Three times a day just like the animals the great Prince eat leftover. He doesn't mind the hard work, it will give him time to think. A woman's revenge is cold, many nights to come he will doubt himself.

Derious on earth

The sleeping young lady, who brought Dirious home is awakened by the morning sun ray coming in through the bedroom window, blooming down against her forehead the bedroom window certainly gives little relief.

Stretching out her morning laziness, she remembers and her head turns, he is not in the bead. Thoughts of him being downstairs alone in the Mayor home bring a concern to her mind. Realizing she is still in her thin night robe and nothing else, out from the bed with only the top thin bedsheet wrap around her, she moves quickly. Not realizing he is asleep on the floor in front of the bed, she trips over his feet. In the motion of falling, she loses the thin bedspread to catch her fall. He is awakened by her tripping over his feet, they both steer out at each other, she is not hurt. Embarrassing she thinks, but what more could she do, mistakes happen. Knowing it's all her false this time, she gives him that down smile before saying "Hi, why is it when we meet am always most naked. Using the floor to hide her partial nakedness she stays put before going on for conversation's sake. "My name is Gabby, what's yours" she smiles. "Dirious" he answers. Still embarrassed, it shows on her face but she is strong, she can take it and she goes on "Well Dirious it's good meeting you, why don't you just stay there, al get the rest of my clothing. Slowing rising to her knees she pulls herself back behind the bed footboard before standing. Her luggage is just there beside her feet and in no time, she is dressed, G string, and robe.

Out to the middle of the bedroom floor, she walks showing herself, up from the floor he stands. "Sorry about that earlier," she said, pertaining to her tripping over his foot. "Nice fittings, you found something that fits." She response not liking his choice of fit and colors. Those last words just accidentally came out of her mouth. Gabby lives her life like there is only today but so do all women, that is why most men find women difficult to live with. It's not women false they don't think like men. It's men false they don't think like women. Trying hard not to gaze him down any further, she goes on to say "You really shouldn't sleep on the floor, could give you a cold. Al go down and gets breakfast ready" she said, pointing out her index finger toward the door. Instead of leaving, she goes into the bedroom closet and brings out another fitting for him. "These should be more comfortable for you" "Thank you" he answered as she rests them down on the bed before walking out of the room. She likes him, but how do you say to a man you nearly damn killed. I like you, even more strangely, to one who doesn't have, not one card of identification on him, he must be a fool or not, the not must be me. Into the shower he goes.

Eggs, toast, and orange just is the quick fix for any breakfast, she forgot to ask him how does he want his eggs. Bad choice of words she summons it to be, just to sexual. Back up the stairs, she goes into the bedroom, he is already in the shower. What is it about men and showers? Something, women don't understand until they get there with a man. Looking around for her make-up kit, she remembers still in the bathroom and she needs it. To shame to enter and ask, how do you like your eggs, over easy, straight up, or wet, she settles for the make-up kit.

Easing her way into the bathroom he hears her, the bath glass door speaks out to her eyes. "Dammit he's fine" and to be of good manner she turns her head away, while uttering "Just need my make up kit, sorry" Much to her surprise he gambits his words innocently "The water is warm, why don't you come in" The make-up kit drop from her hand, splattering out pieces across the bathroom floor suddenly she's not in the mood to pick them up. Standing a bit nervous and in character, she postulates "It's a hell of an idea, how often do you have them." His words are enough to make any women start running for the door, but for most lady's, I am one of them at least according to my boss the Mayor. G string off, robe on the ground, and with every step she takes toward the glass bath door, goosebumps shiver up and down her hand and across her body leaving the little of hair on her private parts standing upright.

The bath glass door open, welcoming her into his space. Stepping in, he reaches out for her, help is what she needs most now. His touch is soft as a baby butt, that she has always admired in a man. Remembering the name, he first called her, she silently puts him in his place "Am not Aries" Her tears are silent in her speak "That is what you first called me" she confirms. As her breast meets his chest, two gentle heart burns like fire, her head falls forward, there he cloaks her under the drops of shower water. Thinking back on her words he said. "It's just another name I remember. I will figure it all out soon or later" Raising her head out to him she wants to be kissed, genteelly it all unfolds. Truly, there is nothing more precious in this life, than when a true man embraces a woman. As for the shower, it truthfully holds its secrets for lovers.

If it was not for her legs giving in, she would have never said "Please take me out from here. Wet as breath, he picks her up into his arms, out they go and onto the bedroom. Looking him in the eyes, she thinks beck before whispering "You ought to smile more sometimes" she lied, correcting her word in tune she whispers "I... have a boyfriend" Her eyes close, glittering tears stream down both her cheeks. Though her last word was silent, never the less, they are in respect of Toney her boyfriend. Dirious only said, "Tell him hi for me!." Into her private space, he is allowed to enter. Making love for her has always been a challenge, she has never been good at it. The hurt, the pain the gain is always for the opposite sex but not this time, it feels so real. In silence, she opens her legs, leaving her body open and absent. From that moment on time does the rest. Even after she fell asleep, the strange happening with her legs never blanked out her mind, completely. Many will call that an after emotional effect, but for her it is real. Downstairs in the kitchen the smoke detector sound out, the bread in the toaster is crisp toast. The automatic kitchen fan kicked in cleaning the air, and the house is safe again. It is most strange when passion meets its climax, no one hears nothing.

After four hours, her brain kicks back in, she opens her eyes, close her legs remembering the toast in the toaster. Up, and out from the bed she jumps to the floor, awaking him before her legs give in again most strange she thinks. Naked, she tumbles to the floor, where she remembers the dream, it's real. She is helped up by him, strong arms right on time, and is laid to rest in bed until such time her body full function is restored. After a few quiet words in bed, she is good to go. Into the shower, she goes remembering its warm touch. Now with fewer words in her mouth, she dresses to be noticed. With the last embrace, out the room door, she goes down the stairs punching the right side of her ass. The sticking pain is uncomfortable, massaging it is her only option. Earlier, her back thigh failed her, that too is starting up again. Walking down steps, and trying to massage out a sticky uncomfortable pain in one ass and back leg thigh is not comfortable, anyway, she keeps moving knowing he is soon to follow.

It is eleven o clock, next to noon. There is no need to sample the toast, into the garbage they go. Cold eggs, microwave, in minutes breakfast is ready. Fruit salad, orange juice, eggs, toast, and hot tea, all set and ready to eat. The files at the opposite end on the table gobble her attention, they are not as she left them. She must have a look, they are stocked well and are numbered in a way only Mayors secretary knows, file closed. Quickly, she opens them, examines each, the information inside baffles her mind. She must get these fifteen files into the Mayor hand fast. It is a matter of importance and National Security. She stacks them back carefully thinking! How is this possible? Lingering thoughts run through her mind. With both hands she presses down comfortably securing, and guarding the stocked files, she is still thinking, how is this possible, names, places, time, dates, countries, years, and much more. Her concentration is broken, he is coming down the steps, her head and eyes turn swiftly out at him, heading straight toward her.

The strange look she gives, he understands. "Who are you" she questions. He walks up to her, looks deep into her beautiful blue eyes, inside are like the cosmos gloaming radiant only he alone can see. Abruptly he turns his head away, before looking at her again. "What is more important now, me or getting those files in the right hands," he asks. She is overwhelmed and impressed, she thinks her options carefully through a raise, promotion, not forgetting the millions in reward money. That tingle in her ass is back and it makes her favor his tune "Please, what did you say your last name is again? He answers "I never said but for your sake, Star" taken from her eyes. "Well Dirious Star, let's eat." At the breakfast end of the table, they both sit. That tingling in the right side of her ass strangely is gone an awkward feeling, something she has never experienced before. Pondering for a quick minute, she would like to know, where did he get that iron body from? so strong, yet tender enough to sweep her off her game even worst, right under her own nose.

It is twelve noon, on the outside. A car is pulling in pumping its horn like a mad man. She knew who it is, her boyfriend Toney, letting her know he finally made it. He is pleased to finally be off-road - the long drive can be fatigued on one's eyes at times but he has much faith in his baby the car. Like Gabby, Toney is also a car lover, the only difference is she has a need for speed. On hitting his car brakes, all four wheels locked at once, sending the vehicle sliding to a full stop. As for the dust, it will settle. His side window comes down, he is ready to fix their relationship at any cost because he loves Gabby so much though she can be most strange and unpredictable at time, she brings out the best in him and the worst at times.

On hearing the car hone "Dammit" she unknowingly said, excusing herself from the table. In a rush she grabs up the files, take from her handbag a pass and run to the outside, no shoe on her feet. Here comes his Gabby running to welcome him for the week, he is impressed. The car door snaps open, proud to see her running toward him, he takes a second look wondering "Why is she running to meet him with a stock of files clinch to her chest. Thinking to himself, "files are the cause in their relationship", women can be so unpredictable at times, he thinks.

Behind Taney's meaning of unpredictable is stupid at times, but he is here to fix that. With smiles to greet her, he began opening the car door, she runs straight into it closing it back "Dammit Gabby take your time" His smile calm things. Taney sometimes speaks like a country boy with an accent. Not fully understanding the meaning of this, he implies out to her from his car window. "Gabby! what is going on?" A little out of breath she speaks "Please Taney, take these files back to the Mayor office, place them in his hand only" Taney knows Gabby enough to know she's serious. Thinking, the long drive back, his emotions take the best of him and in few words, he yields with passion "Gabby! What in the fuck… is going on? He is an American, nothing came easy for him. The hard streets of New York could change a man Taney mellowed down after his father died, leaving him a house, his hot rod, and some money. It's not much but enough to pay bills, and eat. He needs to be careful how he uses the money, otherwise, he is as good as a poor.

Toney knows the kind of work Gabby does, is of state importance so he calms with a last deep breath. "Is this so important Gabby, why now?" Giving him her innocence, she affirms "If this was not of importance, I would never ask, believe me, al make it up to you for the last time, I will never hurt you again, this I promise." Those words bring tears to his eyes, for one year he has long wanted to hear those words from her lips. Turning his head away he hides his cry, in the tune of a higher pitch, his voice shatters "Al… do it, just hand me the files" On handing them over, he turns his head back to her, then, she said "Take this, it will give you passage, the Mayor know you, wait for his envelope, you will know what to do with it. Is your phone working? After receiving her pass, he hands over his phone. Into the phone, she puts a code and a number. From space satellite, the Mayor gets the message, package on its way. The number and code are dissolved minutes after like it was never there on the phone.

On handing the phone back over to him, his humor tassels her "Well, can a man at lease get a piss first…" "Thanks for the phone, no time for that, now." She answers back without humor. Not having a clue, she wants to keep him away, he iterates "Then can I at least have something to eat first?" "Al brings something out if you like" With a straight face and cork lip he promptly answers "Yes, al like that!" Thinking to himself, that's some way to treat your guy, he let it be. Playing it safe, she wasted no time in her uttering "Are you sure" Looking her down with eyes wide open, he simply hummers "Yea, yea, I guess so" Back into the house she runs, and into the fridge, grabbing up what food come to her hand first, before throwing them into a plastic bag, losing no time. Gazing out at her is Dirious watching from his table, the fridge door closes. Rushing, she makes a stop at his table only to say "Al be back!" and she is gone.

At the car, she shoves the plastic bag with food through the window at him, he takes it before saying "I have never seen you like this before, Gabby! What is going on?" Humoring him with her smiles, she said "This is the last time, you can be so sweet at times, thank you!" With that said, the engine starts, roaring back out at her, he calms it to reiterates. "Keep the red wine cool but open, al be back before dark. The engine roars out again, she gives space, waving out her goodbye. The deep sound of the engine rumble, thunder, and off he goes spinning tires in direction. The dry dust makes Gabby cough a little but that is short-lived. The car's new turbo boosters are in place so the trip should take him half the time. The road ahead of him is long, and the turbo car, eat the road with speed. Toney is a good drive, his baby is equipped with GPS cameras, able to see distance ahead of him in slow motion. Live monitors feed his position from space satellites. There are no speed limits out here, so he bravely challenges the road ahead.

Back in the house, Gabby finds Dirious sitting comfortably on the dining sofa. Reaching for her cellphone, it's up. A quick call to an old friend of the Mayor, all will be arranged. Beside Dirious she takes a seat, eager to know more about him, she questions.

Even a Prince Can be Punished

Elsewhere in time, far beyond the planets in the heavens, the great Prince Dicious is being pushed to breaking point. The rain brings in the cold but there is no shelter for him in the fields. He is being punished, by the rain, wind, and cold weather to the limits Murcurry want him dead. The wet soil turns to mud and he is covered with it only to be washed away by the heavy rains. There is a small group of marauds lurking around in the field, looking for anything tangible. Dicious is too cold and shaking to even realize they are close by. From the looks of things, they don't want him, he is of no value nor treats to them in his condition. They have seen this type of brutal payment before, chained and bound for seasons over eventually, most of them dies first. They have passed this way before and some are aware of the danger. They want the dry foods stock in the barn. Accidentally, one of them breaks in and his mistake costs him his life, his quick death triggers an alarm.

Mercurry, Black Synn, and her band of killers are already in place. The leader of the Marauds signal out, "waste no steel or time on the man in the field, but it's too late. One of his men miss read his signal and launches out his aggression on Dicious, luckily for Dicious the man blade misses and hit against Dicious banding chains, that along with his swift reflex save him. That was a close one, the Prince describes looking at the deep cut on his hand chain. Already, having access into the barn by the dead man, their request to steal grains is met by resistance Iron and steel meet again. Accidentally the small group of Marauds find themselves outnumbered and outwit. Not wanting to lose anymore sac of grain, Mercurry gives the orders to stop fighting. Order is quickly restored, the grains worth more than the ten Marauds lives. The leader of this small group of Marauds is shaking in his boots. He knows he and his men are as good as dead so he steps forward.

In these parts, Murcurry and her people rules. This small group of men are not killers they only want grains. Favoring their cause, Murcurry know in these parts negotiations are remembered by favor. With force and agility, she kicks a one-hundred-pound bag of grain out at the leader's chest, stumbling him back into his men, they hit the ground hard. They are not only frightened but impressed with her inner strength. While the leader fumble to get the one-hundred-pound bag of grain off his chest and on his feet again. The others beneath him struggle to move him off them, and they do. This bunch of men are not killers, only amateurs some of the others think. Embarrassed, the leader madly stands up with a cross face, that states, al kill somebody. Only two men died in this battle, plus the one caught in the trap. No death on Murcurry side, she makes it short "Take the bag with you! before I change my mind! Now go!" she points them the way out. Fumbling into each other, they are more than pleased to be let off with their heads intact, and the prize by their side.

As the group of men exit, Mercurry leaps out through an opening above to the outside and into the field, there she again looks upon her sister's killer. The Prince is at his weakest leaning over from the rain and storm for comfort, she released her side whip and she let him taste it again. Two lashes across his back, he stands upright before falling back to the ground. The great prince Dicious lies in bad shape and refuses to fight back. The arms of mercy can be cold at times, Mercurry's angry mood has no forgiveness, he is the cause of her twin sister's life, he along caused her to die. Her fury, causes her to leap out at him in anger again and she punishes him with blows still, he doesn't fight back. Yes, he is down and beaten but not dead. Leaving him as is, she returns to her sleeping quarters with nothing but more hate and anger toward him. Wine eases her pain, in it, she finds relief until morning. The inter mitt connection between Jumo, (twins) can never be disconnected nor underestimated in life.

Back on Earth

Back on earth, the space satellite had hours ago passed and extra over the Mayer country house. Gabby is in the bedroom. She has just finished painting up her toenails, pink when the call comes in. It is the Mayor, letting her know the envelope has already cross-hand and the fifteen files have already been forward and delivered to the F.B.I, in a joint investigation with National Security. The Mayor questions Gabby further about the stranger in his house. She reveals everything to him and is asked to return and meet him back at his second residence in High Hills before five the following day. If not so, he must reveal the source of his information, as he is under oath. Though he may be able to make a few calls, once he reveals the source of his information they both will be not only in harm's way but fugitives of the state. For their own safety and protection, he suggests they meet him on time, he will work out the details before then. He goes on to explain National Security can be at times brutal in its tactics, he would not want any damages to the country house.

Gabby boyfriend Toney had received the Mayor's envelope with the ten thousand dollars. Returning to his vehicle his baby just won't start, he doesn't understand the engine is dead as a doornail, even the lights. He rebuilt every inch of his baby engine and according to his calculation, not possible. It is against the law to open a car hood in front of any government establishment, it comes with a fine of five thousand dollars, up to five years in prison no one has ever been acquitted. This law was implicated a year ago after a car bomb took out half of a government building in the downtown area, the death tole sixty. After investigation, it was determined TNT was found in what is called an abundant vehicle parked on the side of the road. The news of the bombing, went worldwide because the car was registered to and by foreign affairs.

Gabby boyfriend Toney is a chancier and one who love taking chances. He would have taken the chance with Gabby pass to get out of the situation, after all, the pass is a symbol of authority diplomat community to be exact but it had to be left with the Mayor. "Fuck" he said before reaching for his cellular phone, he calls Gabby to explain the situation. She in return tells him, use the money to get his baby fix, his absents away from her, will force her an early return, she lied throwing all the guilt on him, knowing he would not be able to return. The phone call she had made, when he first left put in motion the events. A friend of the Mayer, the one they call a mad man, because of his inventions. He was able to pass Tony parked vehicle outside the Mayor's office, with a gloaming yellow light as they passed it in another vehicle, rendering all power to Toney Hot Rod, dead as a doornail.

Calling in the tow truck is not an option, wreckers work fast when something breaks down in front of government offices, it's like they are parked next door. As they hoist Taney car up onto the tow truck, he calls Gabby again, and again she explains, her return will be earlier and she will call him when she's settled. She hangs up the phone, not giving him time to further his question. The communication cuts out, he can't believe it. He tries to call back but there's no signal. First thinking, she may have hung up on him, maybe not, stranger things have happened today Taney leave it like that. Gabby takes time to explain the urgency of the situation to Dirious, which he understands and excepts, they will meet the Mayor at his private residence at the appointed time.

As evening passes over into night, Gabby and Dirious shear a few secrets over wine and dinner. After that, Gabby asks to be carried upstairs on the bed for the night. The passion of love he breeds into her space, his tight embrace quenches her taste, she passes out holding his waist, falling a sleep unto the next day.

Early the next morning Toney awakes, reaching for his car keys parked in his gate. To the outside, he goes barely awake, looking to

Douglas Burns

start his baby this day. Into the driver's seat, he makes his way, giving her the usual start of the day. The engine ignites its exhaust fire "Fuck" he shouts "Gabby! Am not for hire."

Back Over the Heavens

Elsewhere in time, Black Synn is dead out in the fields. The only person around is Prince Dicious. During the wee morning, the small group of Marauds was hijacked in the mountains. Though they revealed the barnyard they were still all killed. The second group of killers made it into the barn, on their way out the fight spilled into the field. Chain and bound Prince Dicious had to fight for his own life this time. These men were different. they were organized killers and thieves, most prepared. Dicious happens to reach Black Sin first, he hears his last and dying request. Murcurry runs up thinking Dicious Killed him and she makes him pay for it until he could no longer move nor stand. Quickly moving over to Black Synn body, he is dead. Her weapon falls from her hand to the ground. Down on her knees, she embraces him from the earth into her bosom shielding him from the rain. Her tears are testimony to the years of their friendship. Sorrows are many in these parts but when one loses a friend, who would give his life to protect her own the playground is in reverse. All around her men gathered, they too feel the loss, he was liked by many.

As she lay him down against the wet soil, something strange begins to happen, she notices his fatal stab wound, she was wrong about Dicious killing him. The rain has increased, the muddy soil is claiming his corps as if it's alive. As her men gather around, some step back so does she. Neither of them knows what to make of it. The wet mud soil claimed him, leaving a sweet smell behind. Something non of them has ever witnessed before, even still, never seen before, they don't know what to make of it. They are also the testament of his life, he was loved by them all and will always be remembered. As they begin to move out, one of her own asks "What would you have us do with the other? "Pertaining to Prince Dicious "If by the rising of the second son he is dead, burn him" Murcury said and they keep moving, much is to be done before then.

Toney Wants to See Gabby Now

Back on earth, Toney has changed his mind. He wants to see Gabby, he wants to go after Gabby, and he is already on the road. Passing through the town before hitting Highway 65, unexpectedly, he picked up an old friend going his way. He will let him off in the next town in the country beyond the Mayor's country house. If it was not for this friend, he would do it for no other. School bubbles are like a pone in a chess game, just can't tell them no like that. One quick stop to pick up his friend's girlfriend, waiting in the town diner, turns out to be two girlfriends. Toney settles to take them as far as the next town in the country. They all get in while the thunder from the engine roars out at the onlookers. The bystanders love his car and the single ladies love him. The lady friend in the back seat loves him too, what they do not know, Toney is the kind who could control both heads, that is because one head belongs to him and the other, Gabby. She gets the picture and falls back in her seat thinking, "What a wimp! a turn-off wimp!" She can't stand a man with no bolls between their legs, she calls them layovers until the storm passes. With earphones in her ear, she's ready to enjoy the long ride, she has no wary, this could only be a three sum later on tonight.

Gabby and Dirious are already on the road. Highway 65 is being challenged by two fast cars traveling in opposite directions. They are both G.P.S equip with small monitors and cameras able to revert speed down to slow motion. Coming around a dangerous curve both drivers challenge the road. There is room for one mistake but not two. The road is spacious and wide. Car monitors read each other, but they cannot see each other yet, only two red fast-moving dots coming toward each other from different directions and because of their intense focus on the road. Dirious ask Gabby to slow down a Little and she eases up off the gas throttle. An alarm goes, off letting each driver know of one another in a short distance. Both cars are high tech, they even give weather conditions on the outside. Gabby first sees her counterspart's car on the monitor. "Dammit" she criticizes. "What a coincidence, just my luck, why is he following me." She rather not Toney sees this man in her car, that would be just too much to explain. Feeling the need to speed past him, she pushes the pedal to the metal, and fly in the drive. Judging from her incoming speed, he thinks she crazy so are the others with him. Gaggy may do crazy at times, but that's his crazy Gabby, the woman he loves.

The incoming speed of her car, intrigue the passengers in Toney's car, they watch her car woosh by them. The after-effect rocks Toney's car, he hit the breaks sliding the car to a complete stop facing the opposite way, in the middle of the highway Gabby is gone. Thinking to himself "She didn't even notice me." That's just not possible. "What a hot road both girls in the back answers? For them, it's like a high. Thinking again to himself, he hit once the steering wheel "Fuck, what is going on, with that Gaggy again." He doesn't understand. He put the car back in gear and spin her around in Gabby's direction, the girls in the back seat favor out at him "If that was your girl driving, she's with another man" and out loud the other answer "I think she did it deliberately?." Their remark angered Toney's attention, and he answers them back viciously and deliberately "Fuck you, fuck you." Together they answer him back "Fuck you" Then the first bimbo answers again "She did it not to be seen." From the front seat, the boyfriend turns and answers his girlfriend back, to settle tensions in the air. "Darling, don't speak anymore, al tell you when to speak, ok" and with a smile out to him she nods her head, indicating yes before answering "Yes, darling." Now, that's the kind of a woman every man would love to have, so he thinks.

Hitting the gas throttle, wheels spin in direction again, the car hit the road at high speed and the girls love it. Fuel-injected, twin-turbo, ignites the road ahead finally arriving at the crossroads into the next town. Toney informs his friends, buses in town are on each hour. Coming down the road there is one now, they get out, the girls look at their watches, on time. It is sunny and Toney's friend wonders "Why is it always shady under crossroads?" Thanks and congratulation are short live, the bus arrives and they get in, they each take a seat. From the bus window, people stare out at Toney's Hot Rod, most children in these parts never get the chance to see a Hot Rod in action. Toney displays a spin of wheels for the bus passengers. Most of the children love it and off he goes on the road again. He cannot catch up to Gabby anymore, she is too far gone. The evening sun tips down on the road, giving everything that orangery look, never the less, Toney challenges the road and she's a beauty as her tires grip for speed.

Gabby pulls in the Mayor's driveway, five to five, his front door opens and he comes out to greet her while his wife remaining standing in the doorway. Time to meet the Mayor she whispers out to Derious before getting out of the car the Mayor greets her with a hug like old friends do while whispering in her ear, "Be good" she repeats "you too", before focusing her eyes on his wife standing in the doorway. Lola, he shouts turning his head out at his wife, you remember Gabby, from the office, the secretary. Waving out to each other, Darious, walks up to the Mayer, while from behind the Mayor's wife shout "I have always wanted to meet her so beautiful is she. Gabby presents Dirious saying "This is the man, Dirious, Dirious Starr. With a handshake, a formal introduction is made while Gabby runs over to meet the Mayor's wife, introduction but the ladies are made with a bright smile. The Mayor Speaks, "Well Derious, do come in" the Mayor said pointing out his hand the way. Together they all enter the house and the door is made closed.

On the inside, the Mayor's wife suggests Gabby come with her to the Kitchen to pour out wine for the thirsty travelers while Dirious and the Mayor continue into his study there they exchange few more words.

Back in the kitchen, the wine glasses are full "Would you like to carry them in?" Gabby suggests looking around at the amazing kitchen decoration. So swiftly Lola grabs her, slaps her, and strongly shoves her against the kitchen sink before placing her other hand on Gabbys Mouth, muffling her scream. Gabby is shocked, her tears relax down the side of her face, draining her make-up, then Lola speaks "Don't think I don't know, Slut! So quickly Lola's persona changes and she go on sadly to say "Please help me, he's taking those blue pills, I can't keep up, he's gonna kill my front because of you." Shocked by Lola's honesty, Gabby slowly embraces her while she lets it out in tears. Q at the moment Gabby confesses "Am so, so, sorry." Shaking out her head to Gabby, Lola step back, head up she looks into the eyes of youth and spoke. "I think it was my false for pushing him but he couldn't do it without you, thank you for bringing him back, and am sorry for hitting you, you're okay aren't you?" Gabby nods her head out up and down. Stepping apart Lola turns to the full glasses of wine and reiterates "Take in the wine, al bring in the other two" Their happy smile could not be more appreciative walking to the study.

    They could hear the men speaking, they enter silencing the conversation, the men's heads turn to notice them as each is present a glass of wine. Looking at both ladies they wonder, what did take place in their absence, it is Gabby make-up and their glossy eyes give them away, the Mayor beacons "I see you two have gotten acquainted" With a smile, Gabby answers "It feels like I know her for some time now." The Mayor buys it but not Derious. Turning to his wife he said "Darling give me a minute al be out soon" She knows the routine "Good to have met you, young man" and she waves out her goodbye before leaving the room. The Mayor made a short call then turns back to Gabby and spoke. You must go straight to the Embassy that's the American Embassy, ask for Mr. Kevin Rodreggus, hand this to him, he will handle the rest, go now. On receiving the key Gabby expresses "Thank you Mayor al never forget this" smiling back to her the Mayor said "Thank you Gabby, but where do you go from here" Gabby grantee "Al called." Derious and the Mayor shake hands, on that note, the Mayor said "You have a gifted ability, they need you. Finishing up the wine, out the door they go into the car speeding off. The American Embassy is a distance away, during the ride Gabby fixes her make, Derious don't even question it. Instead, he questions

Gabby on the outcome of things, she could only answer so much until such time they finish the Embassy.

Back at the Mayor's house, he is back at his desk, the wine glass is shaking off the desk, he catches it in time realizing it not what he thinks, small earthquake then it stops. Routing out to the front door his wife follows like he expected Toney's car. He is searching out Gabby, the Mayor explains she left for the Embassy then to home. Off he goes, blasting out the Mayor's yard destroying private property, plants, and grass, the Mayor only grumbles out at him disappearing to the main road. His wife walks up beside him "What should we do? What a mess" he answers "Call in the gardener then meet me in the bedroom. Stunned by his response, she put her hand between her legs and run into the house, speaking "Gabby, al kill youuuu!

At the Embassy Gabby and Dirious are in a meeting with Mr. Kevin Rodreggus. After the introduction is settled Mr. Rodreggus goes on to say "Here is your passport and reward money, a check for thirty Million dollars Mr. Starr. As for your accommodations, settled for a lifetime in the downtown President's hotel, it's also government-owned with its own government bank downstairs. The department of investigations could use a man like you. I hope you would consider it even as a private contractor. It took law enforcement years and nothing on those files, you filled in all the blanks. Al likes to ask, who are you, but we have already passed that. My card is in your envelope should need be and good luck. Dirious in return thank him and out the door, he and Gabby go.

Gabby has never been so happy in her life before. From there to the bank, they go. Along the way Gabby explains more about how the banking system work even though he knows, it will still be explained by the bank teller, Half of everything belongs to Uncle Sam. In the bank in front of the teller, he orders fifteen Million given to Gabby, the happiest day in Gabby's life. She hugs and kisses him all over. The bank teller is a man tired of seeing millions pass through his hand and not one sent is given to him. Gabby is very outspoken at times but she is blond, that the upper hand. She orders the teller to deposit fourteen Million in her account and make out a manager check for one million, she whispers out the name to him.

The manager check is made in the amount and passed over to her in an envelope, she opens it, read it and seal it.

The bank teller is hoping to have a favorable tip, so for smalltalk, he clears his throat, Gabby looks at him and he kindly asks "So Miss Gabby, what are you planning to do with all that money? She answers "Well, aaa, not work for another cock-sucker for the rest of my life. I paid my dues on my knees I pray, thanks to you Dirious she smiles out at him before turning back to the teller" she goes on to say "Al go and help my family and friends out from this rat race. The world out there cares little about us, we were fucked before we were born. The teller is so impressed with Gabby's free tongue of speech he forgets to mention his tip, out the door they are gone. The engine starts and off they go in the opposite direction to do some serious shopping for Dirious. Toney's car just passed another Embassy, he had forgotten to ask the Mayor which Embassy so he must now pass them all, no Gabby not even her car. Considering his options after passing all the Embassy's he settles to wait it out at Gabby's apartment in his car there he cut the engine off, lean back in his seat with eyes closed. Dirious has finished shopping but Gabby has just begun, he entertains her, My God women do shop till they drop, Gabby car back trunk is full to the top with family and friends' gifts and much more. To Derious's hotel, they go with porter services at the door. Dirious purchases and two bags of Gabby are left with the bellman, to the front desk they walk. Through government agency information is passed by the fingertip of the computer keyboard, check you in no question, swipe cards are given to enter each room and to the elevator, they go.

As they walk holding hands along the corridor their room is in view. The door is made open and they enter followed by the bellmen who goes on to explain more about the room accommodations. Gabby thinks he taking up too much time so she tells him. "Do you ever just shut it, get out!" And he runs out from there closing the door behind him.

This is no ordinary living accommodation. To stay in a place like this one you must have over Ten Million in the bank. The accommodation is equipped with a swimming pool and ideas the average person never thinks about. Toney must have dosed off because it is dark, the engine starts, and off he goes home for the night. After bath Gabby dresses in her new outfit and Dirious is ready. Downstairs they go, Gabby looks so beautiful, her blond hair sparkles under the lights and her earrings match so well with the color of her long dress, her shape is lean and means for any man to want, she is elegant so is the man she's with, as for her tongue that remains to be seen though she knows when to switch it on. This night belongs to Mr. Dirious Starr and her. Entering the luxurious restaurant, they are greeted then seated.

For a minute Gabby sits back in her chair and thinks "This could not have been possible without the accident, who and what is manipulating the destiny of us all, Gabby is not religious, but she does believe something is out there. The night is warm and romantic, the dinner, good is an understatement, top of the line. A romantic walk after dinner is every woman's dream, she stopped him by the hand, turn to him and kiss him before saying "Thank you" he accepts. Moving to continue the walk she suggests "You don't speak much do you?" "Only when it's important." He answers. "That's quite" She smiles before saying "I had enough walking, let's go back to the room." The pain in Gabby's ass never troubled her anymore, must be the money. They say money stops pain, she is pleased with that.

Now back in the room, silence speaks through their tongues, the amber kisses of each embrace lead them closer to the bed. By removing her dress straps his finger slip the zip, letting her know he is there. The dress slides down from her body to the floor and she disrobes him before herself. In a touch of passion, the bed graces their presence, again in her space he is allowed to enter. This night is different because her screams and tears are fluttered with her emotions. It is late and loves grace, she is asleep.

Toney is not so well, his anger about Gabby avoiding him speaks to the damages to his china and porcelain ware smash on the floor. The noise and the use of abusive language have awakened the neighbor. They never liked him because it is a resident but with that thunder hot rod of his, only the children in the neighborhood find favor in him, not the old folks, they want him out. The police are called in and Toney explains "It's only a simple domestic matter between him and his girlfriend" he just had to take his anger out on something, better it be on his own goodies. Toney kindly thanks them for arriving on time before he decides to burn the house down, bad choice of words, they take him on the ground of potential Arson, danger to himself and the neighborhood. At the police station, he runs into his grandfather Sargent Bethel. He explains the situation and the report is a dump. He is offered an apology with an explanation" Not much as been happening on the late-night shift, and this is the time of year cops are looking for promotion and higher salaries and again sometime the men do get restless and Toney is off free. Having to walk back home, lucky for him another police car is passing and one of them know him. "Thank you, Jesus," he made mention getting into the back seat, his police friend response back, you could get locked up for using that name. Emitting out his feeling Toney describes "What in the hell is this world coming to, al keep my mouth shut, you know.

    The police car pulls through the corner and Toney is allowed out in front of his home, the Police car keeps moving. Walking into his driveway he could feel the neighbor's eyes lurking him from their open window curtain, out loud he shouts "Fuckin neighbors…. With his house keys in hand, he knows what needs to be done after the cleaning. Toney loves Gabby and would never, ever rest a hand on her, only if provoked.

The Following Morning

Gabby awake eleven the following morning she could never forget this night. The living quarters come with their own cook's breakfast, lunch, and dinner all set out buffet style. The owners never have to clean nor wash the accommodation, they think of everything, even Dirious shopping close and shoes are all in their place, shopping bags and all, what service to die for. Out the tub Gabby dresses, make up and all, into the kitchen she enters. The breakfast buffet is still there and she helps herself before taking a seat opposite Dirious at the table "Good morning she speaks watching him enjoy the mixed glass of fresh fruity juice. Then he said "Had a few calls this morning from government agency, they all want me on board. Finishing up her eggs she questions "And?" And he answers, "Am more of a private person" "Then you should do the private thing" she answers" "Look at this" he said reaching down and showing out his drawing. It is a picture of a man with a long beard he looks like some kind of a Viking Warrior. Who is he, she asked finishing up the glass of juice? "An image in my head. If I was looking for someone where would you suggest I go first but not just anyone" Gabby answers "Mug department downtown in police headquarters, they would be able to help you, better still, you did mention not anyone so I suggest you start with the church, on second thoughts he looks like a priest. Ask the front desk to mail it for you to Vaddician they would know or not." Thinking through Gabby's suggestion he concludes "Good idea, I think al just do that and wait for the outcome. Resting it to one side of the table Gabby shares. "After all you do have it named, so do that man exist? I hate those people in Vaddician they hide behind their robes, untouchable"

Staring at her nibbling on a french piece of croissant their eyes meet, so smoothly and abruptly she commands "What..." And on that direct note, he intrudes "Why do I feel this is our last meal." That stuns Gabby, unaware she knocks over the side water glass, stands up she steps away from the table. Looking out at him her tears tell her story "Not possible she thinks sagging her head left to right. "Do you read minds?" She asks as he gets up from the table to meet her. "No Gabby, only body language" he recites "Impressive, you are good and your special, given a special gift, that could be frightening at times you know, you read my mind. "Where will you go, Gabby." He asks "Home, home to my mother, my family, I love you, but you could never be mine, I need to find me, this is not me, this is what the world made me. I owe you so much, you could say I owe myself Fifteen Million times over and if you could take it now, am willing to give it so freely. With a sad smile on Gabby's face, she goes on to admit "Yes, I look the part but truly am confused and broken, this world would do that to you, it tamed and broke me but you, your good, even in bed your good. Stopping here before she goes any further, he clears her words "No Gabby, it's not that am good, you just had a lot of bad hurt and pain. Not wanting to admit her guilt she could never lie to him so she smooths things out "Yes your right but I could never admit it. I feel I belong to you, where ever this road leads me, even if am married with children, should you call, I will come to you and give myself, it may sound foolish today but tomorrow we all still have a price to pay.

Concern by Gabby's hurt and pain, he again interjects "It doesn't have to be this way, Gabby. Crying out to him he reaches out to her and in his embrace, she graces her words "I know no other way." On his lower chest, her head drops, and there, Gabby expresses cry and cry and cry. There is no guarantee in her words for him, she may never come back this way so he remains quiet. Pulling away she break his embrace to be free.

In all Gabby's life, she has never given endless respect to anyone, not even her own mother. Looking up at him she reaffirms her words "Thank you Mr, Derious Starr" On her knees she kneels giving him the utmost respect before standing upright again, off she goes running toward the front door. This breakfast is finished, never again will this time with Gabby come again. Forged in his mind the time of moment, bind in his heart this memorable moment. Leaving the breakfast table toward the bedroom, on the side table there is a card, he picks it up to read the labels, It Gabby card with all her information tabled.

At Gabby's apartment

It wasn't until that evening Gabby arrived at her apartment, after gathering and packing a few things in her small rolling suitcase, downstairs she goes to her Landlord office. On entering the fat out of shape, bad taste, open gate Landlord office Gabby walks up to her desk and question "How much do I owe you" Struggling to stand up she tilts to one side behind the desk, still shoving pizza down her throat, with the poor presentation the fat Landlord speaks "Plus… late… fees…" before drinking down a full can of soda, nasty Gabby pitched to herself.

It is disturbing to see one like her neck, shoulders, waistline, hips all in one straight line. Where is her feature, who will want to love her? For small talk sake Gabby hummers "That stuff will kill you, you know." The Landlord stops eating, tills upright, look at Gabby, and outright said. "I don't like skinny bitches coming to my office, next time you should read the sign on the door before entering. Unaware Gabby turns her head at the door behind her and sees nothing but white papers. Turning back to the Landlord, as to say, what sign, the Landlord continues "Discrimination is an offense, keep your personal opinions to yourself." Gabby is no hush, but she chooses, she's quiet while the Landlord pulls her file. Thinking, never upset your Landlord will work to your advantage. With a bad taste in her mouth and crunched lips the Landlord shares "Who are you again and what apartment are you in." Gabby complies "Number ten upstairs at the end" The Landlord remembers this room and said "Oooooo, ooooo, the Mayor usual drop in to pay ahead of time, he said it's his outside daughter place and keeping it quiet will be appropriate, you are the daughter? your father is very generous" somewhat surprised to hear the news Gabby's eyes move from left to right wondering "What in the fuck is she talking about, Gabby says nothing but "So how much do I owe." The Landlord again affirms "Like I said, "The Mayor has been very generous to us. Not willing to say much more Gabby asserts "Well am leaving the apartment, everything in it is yours. Smiles come to the landlord's face, her happy smile couldn't be more appreciated "Please tell your father thanks" Gabby takes hold of her suitcase handle pulling it along as she walks out the door.

Walking back toward the out-front Gabby makes her way toward her car, surprise again. Toney's car is parked facing hers with a short distance in between. He had entered with new modernization made to the engine, the engine can be silent at a push of a button. Out of his car, he walks to meet Gabby leaving the car door to close on its own. Blocking her way slows her steps, she stops. "You look like your leaving town, Gabby" he speaks. Without a smile on Gabby's face, she tells "No Toney! Am leaving you." That's disturbing for him to hear, sagging his head side to side he need not explode now. Expressing his anger pleasurable he waves the calm out at her "Gabby, what in the fuck is going on with you? Who is he?" he shouts. Missing his Q, he calms again, she knows him, ruffs around the edges at time, women like that at times you know but this time it was different "I have to go Toney. I already gave you my words, I will never hurt you again."

Like all men slow at times, Toney finally gets the picture "So leaving me is your way of never hurting me again" She makes a few more steps and again he blocks the way. "Just tell me Gabby, who is he?" Noticing her frail look of concern, she wastes no time in her utterance "I wish I knew, there are some things in this life that doesn't add up or even make sense, this is one of those. Flashing back on how stress can be manifest in so many different ways, he is at a loss with Gabby but he must say it "I don't understand that type of fuckin talk Gabby "he shouts. Wasting no time Gabby asserts her words with assurance. "It's the only way, Toney. I don't love you anymore, what do you expect from me, Toney" He answers "To be with me, Gabby, what is so hard about that." He questions.

Reaching into her handbag she pulls out an envelope and shoves it into his lower abdomen. The shove cuts his breath, he leans forward and she goes on to say "Take it." With suitcase handle in hand, she rushes past him. Eager to know the continence in the letter, he quickly opens it while she shoves the suitcase into the car back seat before taking to the driver seat. Toney cannot believe his eyes, a bank manager checks with his name in the amount of one Million Dollars. Her car door slams close, reminiscing the possibility's his reward makes him shouts "We can start over, Gabby…." Engine starts, she knows he will follow so to stop him, with engine force she gears the car up and slams into Toney's car head-on. He can not believe what Gabby just did slam into his baby front on. Sadly, holding his hands upon his head he is in disbelief of Gabbys actions. She reverses spinning in the direction and off she goes, gone with the wind. On that note, Toney anger takes the best of him and he cries out "Fuck you Gabby, you here me, fuck youuuuuuuuuuuu…"

Quickly he moves to assess the damages done to his baby, busted front end, radiator spilling out antifreeze all over the parking lot, not good. The hard bang frightened the landlord so she called the police. Luckily for Toney the same patrol unit dropped him home was in the area, they answered the call first. With little explanation, he is again let off and no police report is filed. Toney calls in the tow truck but this time it's different because he doesn't have to feel like a millionaire, he is a millionaire even if it's without his Gabby. Still, the sad circumstances gleam in his heart.

This morning newspaper

One-week later Dirious Starr's picture is in every News Paper, Magazine, and top news for resolving fifteen unexplained government files. The news goes viral worldwide and every idiot with an unexplained situation begin calling for help. By the hundred and thousand, they call willing to pay top dollars. The demand for his help is so great the manager of hotel Presantaa offers Dirious free office space in the downstairs. Dirious had become a private entity working alongside law enforcement. He had attempted to reach Gabby by phone but failed due to Gabby not answering. Three months later Dirious is worth Fifty Million and more. The Hotel Manager is worth Thirty Million thanks to the agreement he and Mr. Derious Starr had made

Dirious had taken time to make a few calls and he locates Gabby's Mother who explained because of his generous gift Gabby used it to give her family and close friends living accommodation with the best of amenities. They all owe their success to Gabby but not one helped her but her own mother. She is in rehab, cocaine addition, and she is afraid for her daughter's life because she has two Million Dollars left in her bank account to play with and her daughter's only friend is the white lady as we call it here. Derious is saddened by the news. Gabby is now living in another state.

Back over the heaven's

Over the rainbow, the loneliness of summer, winter-spring, and fall has long passed. It is the ninetieth Cycle of the wind and Prince Dicious has been given better food treatment because he had explained Black Synn last dying words out to Murcurry. He remains shackled in his chains. It is mid-day under the second son when Murcurry showed up dressed like her sister with a blade secured behind her. The length of the chain holding him allows him five feet behind her stand. Standing face to face he gets the feeling today is that day. The memory of her being dressed like her sister reflex, taking him back to a time their lives were filled with joy and happiness. He is brought back when she throws out the key to his shackle at him, it falls at his right foot. The air is quiet and a slight breeze moves across the earth as she speaks "Does love have an age Great Prince" "Neither do hate." He answers watching her in silence. Yet again she asks, "How can I face tomorrow Great Prince when today is all I have." Her formal words of respect alert his instinct to assert "Given this day, how can you face your tomorrow." She understands now from his words there is but one way out and takes it. So, tell me, Great Prince, how fast are you Dicious? Thinking of his odds, he could never pick up the key, unshackle himself before she strikes but he could try to avoid her Swift Blade but for how long in his condition, he will get injured. And should he attack first he may be killed, he will not be responsible for her death and that of her sister. It would defeat the course of him coming. So, he waits for her to make the first move, as for him getting the key is vital.

Surprise to hear her say "Pick it up" he slowly picks it up. Again, surprise to hear her words, she confesses "Because apart of her still lives in me she wants you to know. No one could never have the part of me I gave you." Jagged by her words, so swiftly she unleashes her Blade from behind her back out at Dicious throat while bluntly uttering "Al kill you" knowing he must revert his leap. And with swift death from her Blade Mrucurry slice through her own throat before falling to her knees "No... no... Dicious shout leaping to her rescue, catching her in his arms before she hits the earth. With her last breath she reaches out her finger touching his face glutting "You... are a good man and would make an even better king. Forgive me prince Dicious for all the harm I caused you. Murcurry passed away in Dicious arms.

The Great Prince Dicious weep so much over Murcurry dead corps, he never realizes the whole crew of her men, family, and friends all kneels around him at the loss of their great leader and his freedom. The news had long gotten out the man shackled in the field is a Prince from the far north, Gouddaaian Kingdom. And they all stayed on their knees in respect to him until he rises and unshackles himself. They all knew it was not his false for the death of Murcurry sister and in a way, they resented how poorly he had been treated but orders are orders when they come down from the top. And the Great Prince Dicious stayed on with them and he teaches them how to bill a great nation with rule and order. And he teaches them how to make the most of their harvest and that everything can be used for something. And on the rising of the third eclipse of the moon, the Prince said his goodbyes. And as one people to become one race together they wish him fear well. His hair has grown long and with a beard, no one will recognize him. He is built out from the test of time, strong as the oxen and buffalo in the fields, his direction is now north.

A Secret Royal Junkanoo Invitation

A chariot is moving with stealth speed towards Queen Sarraha palace when she receives secret unannounced royal news of her father. King Gouddaa is on his way to visit her royal palace. Quickly a royal order is dispatched stating her royal convoy along with her royal Junkanoo guards, and her entourage of royal Junkanoo dancers shall accommodate the welcome of her father from the gates of Darr into ther royal palace.

Behold, it is a moment of spectacular and wonderful to see, Junkanoo conch shell horns of many different sizes and shapes, rhinoceros horns carved with african symbols, cow-bells, with amazing sounds, colors, and shapes, buffalo cowbells, goat skins drums, in different colors, size, and shapes. Elephant drums of various components shapes and sounds, zebra flutes, folk-lore dancers, Junkanoo dancers, male and female, sons and daughters, brothers and sisters, children in costume parade out from the house of Queen Sarraha. Happiness heightens colors in the festivity of joys anticipated, the synergy combines creating an elation and euphoria of consuming sound which shakes with vibration the mighty under pillars of the under earth. A collage of fusion encompasses all, dazzling eyes and senses.

King Gouddaa's royal coach approaches the royal palace. It is at the commencement of his arrival that Queen Sarraha releases a platoon of innocent and pure royal virgins to greet him. It's contagious, the bursting excitements, they pour out awaiting him with enchanted awe. Many remember all of which they had born from childbirth about King Gouddaa's wisdom. In a show of honor and respect with the highest regard, they bow.

King Gouddaa steps out from his royal coach to a picture-perfect setting, three hundred virgins dressed in red and pink sheer silk garments, have taken their positions. Fifty royal virgins of incomparable beauty and stature run to surround each side of him allowing only for Gouddaa's two Superior Guards to follow four paces behind. The remaining four guards stand down staying behind to secure the grounds ready to protect his royal secret coach. Three hundred virgins have lined the pathway leading to his daughter Sarraha's royal throne. After the three hundred virgins had looked upon his face for the first time, suddenly they all turned their heads to him, and simultaneous in one tongue and one breath, they all said. "Aa-da-gouddaa!" which means (Father Bless Us).

Greatly amused King Gouddaa is touched by the fanning attentions and unforgettable beauty surrounding him. The sight of such beauty leaves a searing impression not easily dismissed. Upon entering the palace, his eyes quickly roam around the inner palace foyer at his daughter's amassed wealth, wall drapes, and vibrant colors of deep rich purple, silver, red, and gold. Behind him sultry whispers distract his attention with affection his eyes grace approvingly the royal virgins for a second time, turning he spies his daughter expectantly watching him sitting high and mighty on her throne.

There she is, regally attired she is dressed like a bride adorned for her husband. The diadem of her Junkanoo crown sparkles in colors of emerald, diamonds, and blue sapphire, and green pearls. As Gouddaa reaches the first step of her throne, Sarraha herself is surrounded by thirty of her own mighty men. Queen Sarraha stands up suspending all movement from the seven hundred, the room stills, everything comes to a sudden stop. Gouddaa is fascinated by her purple and red sheer silk clothing and at that moment he had forgotten the child she once was. Wishful foresight reminiscent of the past now beholds the woman she has become standing high upon the throne and he wishes he could have taken her back in time.

On taking her first step down from her throne, the three hundred virgins exit in silence. With each step down from the throne to meet her father, royal subjects vacate as if they were never there. By the time she has reaches the last step of her throne, even the thirty mighty men have exited without being seen. Until only what remains is what he sees, his daughter Sarraha. Queen Sarraha, now has rule over one-quarter of his mighty kingdom. And to her father she said. "Father welcome." Stepping down to the ground, she embraces him first with a kiss to his cheek, before falling to one knee and standing upright again. Gouddaa implies his wishes looking back at his guards, "Guards, be at ease!" They understand and leave to post themselves outside the door, standing close by.

Now alone with her father, Sarraha looks to him, "Father did you not receive all three of my requests? And why is it that you haven't answered me?" Gouddaa looks at her. "Daughter! It is because all of your requests are likewise the same and it is for that reason they were denied." Appropriately chastised, sullen with pout Sarraha gives him that most disappointing look of hers, which reads, I am hurt. "Father, my kingdom is yours to command. I only ask that you allow Derious, to freely return home. All though he is my brother, his long exile has bruised my heart and I do miss him. I know, you wish not to discuss him but It breaks my heart father." With that, Gouddaa becomes concerned. He looks sternly to her cutting and abrasively he responds "Daughter, this is not the time nor place to discuss such matters but if it is of any comfort to you. Yes! I have long known of your love toward your brother, Derious, and for what my eyes have beheld here. I can only hope that soon you will grasp my meanings."

A blush touches Sarraha's cheeks, bashfully she turns to him, in the complexity of emotions. This was not turning out the way she thought, tactfully pulling back she again said. "Father, though you are pleased to see me, behind your image you look so sad. All of this I have done only to welcome you. When I was a child, I once said to you. If I am to surrender my life, it would and should be surrendered only unto you and, you father in return said that such faith or cleverness should indeed be rewarded and I have truly been rewarded as Queen over the one-quarter rule of your mighty kingdom. And I rule this part of your kingdom with nothing but love, father."

After hearing her expressed words, he rephrases his intent. "Daughter, you have always taken my words out of context. I come just to say, I must leave for some time and your sister Libra shall be visiting soon. As you already know, she sits on the throne until my return." Sarraha bluntly retorts her dissatisfaction not very much liking that particular sister said, "Father, though you love her more than I. She is not welcomed here and will never be as long as I sit on my throne." Composed Gouddaa does not allow the disparities verbalized by his daughter bait concern in his heart, he replies, "That is exactly why I have come. To remind you that though you speak for one-quarter of the kingdom. She speaks as I do for the entire kingdom. There cannot be an inner war."

This was not what Sarraha expected, it was obvious she found conflict in observing this request. Not clearly and fully understanding her father's implication Sarraha takes offense, in agitation, pacing she moves away only to return. To him she again said, "Have you also told her that father? There cannot be an inner war!" Her flustered condition and strained statements further indicate that she did not fully grasp his meaning. Reiterating for clarity, "Daughter, I have entrusted to you the power of rule, not because I can, but because none of your other siblings were ready at that time. You alone stepped forward, and it is for that reason alone, you are where you stand. Remember my words daughter, there cannot be an inner war." Consumed by contentions of her feelings towards her sister, Gouddaa words burn her. She has always believed her father found better favor in his daughter Libra, whom she very much dislikes. Sharply she retorts with seething venom, her tone disturbing him, "She is not smarter than I. She has just only decided to stay beside you, father. I can run your Kingdom much better than she and should you not believe me father, just you ask her to step down and announce my rule."

Moments of pondering her strong words leave him wanting. To her, he responds again. "Daughter! In the balance of time is recorded everything which, is, was, and shall be. Can you understand this and can you decipher its meanings, now!" She looks at him while considering his question. And in a still and calm motion, she said "No Father, not at this time, but she is a riddle specialist. Why don't you ask her first?" And to her surprise. He spoke. "I already have! And to know that all things are recorded in the timing belt of life gives one the abilities to withstand the times ahead. You say that you rule with nothing but love, but there are perilous times ahead of us. The danger is real, and it is a must that you be ready."

These words move her, a little more cognizant of the urgency now, it registers, finally. She looks to clear things up. And to him she said. "Father, did you say peril, and dark days ahead, as in war?" Again to her surprise and chagrin. He said. "Yes daughter, yes." Hot tendrils of fear prickles throughout Saharras limbs like a fever. She is the one who is afraid of war, death, and destruction does not realize she has stepped in even closer to him. It's enough for her to concede her position." Father, should that be the case, then you have better leave her at rule until. But how is that possible? Are we not at peace with the other nations, Father! Are you well? Are you starting a war? Am I in danger? I don't want to die! Tell me, father, why must you leave again! Is it because of mother?" Gouddaa, not wanting to further frighten or alarm her gives her the truth, awakening her to the harshness of reality ahead.

Gouddaa expands more to Sarraha's confidence "Yes! Her life now depends not so much on my safe return but the medicine I must again retrieve from the Black Widow, herself." And she while feeling his concerns said. "Father! Why must I feel like this? Please don't think am only able to rule in virtuous and good times. And how soon must you ride again father?" He explains, "On the next Cycle of the Wind. I shall ride once again into the Black Forest for the widow will accept no other but me." Anxious now filled with anxiety she senses his disturbing pain. She again moves away, only to return. "Father, I don't wish to say safe return so please feast with me as a token of your safe return." He agrees, nodding his head. Then out from his pocket, he pulls out a small silver object, without her seeing he drops it on the marble floor. On hearing the high sonic pitch released from the dropped ball the two superior guards again enter. The sonic emitting ball rings a tune, which only means something to Gouddaa guards standing on the outside.

Queen Sarraha walks her father into a second hall where he is greeted by two of Sarraha's advisers. On Sarraha's, orders a feast is carried in by eight mighty men. After she and her father had taken their seat. One hundred virgins enter dancing around the colossal table, depositing plates and decadent morsels of succulent and savory treats in abundance before them. Once again, the great king is dazzled by the hundred beautiful virgins. The one hundred virgins all come to a sudden stop and all together and in one tone of voice, they all again said to the mighty king. "Aa, Da, Ra, Da Gouddaa." Meaning "Father we wish you well." And after everything is in place, Sarraha, lifts her wine mug and she gives thanks for her father's safe return and so did they all. While Gouddaa looks on he orders that his remaining four bodyguards still on the outside guarding his royal coach, be brought in at once and it is done.

And the virgins ply the six superior bodyguards with wine and food. Each time their wine mug depletes, each is refilled again in consumption, lust grows. Everyone is feeling merry all together the superior bodyguards lift their wine-mugs unto the Great King Gouddaa to his safe return. Gouddaa, stands up for all to hear. And out loud, cries out. "Drink! Drink! Superior bodyguards, for this, is a spear of spears (day of days)."

This is a spear of a spear, a twilight hour like no other, Sarraha, goes on to request her father. In a display of skills, a challenge is issued between four of her Mighty Men against four of her father's superior bodyguards of his royal coach. King Gouddaa obliges her, but not before reminding his superior bodyguards, that they are invitees. They understand his meaning, and again he stands up, and with all mugs raised, Gouddaa, again cries out, "Let the display of skills begin!" Although joy and happiness show on his face, in his heart remains resolved just knowing that his own life may now have to be given to save that of his wife, Laurrennius. After having had his fill, Gouddaa gets up and quietly gives orders that none are to follow. Walking outside he vanishes in the inky darkness of night.

Sheppard's Love for Her Brother Dicious

It is the night before Dicious and Leoha were set out to destroy the Black Scarlet and the Black Widow. Feeling the spear of time, Dicious's youngest sister Sheppard has a compelling need to be with him. She loves him. There may not be another chance nor opportunity for her to say her goodbye's so she comes up with a plan to fulfill her desires.

The three Evening Suns are setting on the outer plains of the Kingdom as Sheppard walks toward the hidden pathway leading to her brother's chambers. Coming straight towards her, Sheppard walks into an unusual face. As the lady approaches, Sheppard looks over her unique garments intrigued. When the lady gets within range Sheppard extends a comment of compliment "Splendid garment!" The Lady is also surprised to see Sheppard in the hidden passageway and heading in the very direction she just left. The Lady surprisingly only said. "Thank you."

While they cross beside each other, Sheppard becomes jealous, this woman shouldn't be here. It's not that Sheppard hasn't heard about the women Dicious entertains in his chambers. The maids' gossip. They talk about a woman called Urobeha. This passage is reserved only for royalty in urgent matters of the throne. Originally the escape route was designed not for commoners to know or use so this woman could have only been invited by none other than her brother. The added fact that the pathway leads only to and from her beloved brother Dicious's chambers gives Sheppard reason to pause. "Stop where you stand stranger! I shall ask you only once! Are you Urobeha, and have you just come from my brother Dicious Chamber, and did you seduce him?"

The beautifully dressed lady stops, and as she turns to look Sheppard down, she knows who she is. There aren't many who don't know of Sheppard's status as princess in the house of King Gouddaa. Urobeha has no problem showing her respect, what she finds objectionable is the barb-wired tongue of Sheppards' bad attitude and rude manner. Unlike Sheppard. conservatively she decides for other reasons to keep calm. And to the Princess. She said. "Yes! I am she and even if I have seduced your brother, what concern would it be of yours? If you love him! I could only suggest you tell him, young Princess." Urobeha takes Sheppard off guard with her direct response and candid observations, very much touching to matters of her heart. Strongly Sheppard exclaims, "What makes you say that? Let me suggest, you choose your words carefully Lady." Urobeha discerns Sheppard's words to be not only demanding but that of a Serpent Seed, cunning and deceiving.

Urobeha is not dismayed by the accusations, something about Sheppard appeals to her. "Besides it being written all over your face. His heart is caught up with his sister Aries, just like your heart is caught up with his." This incenses Sheppard even more, how dare she have such an audacity to speak to her like that. The lady she is facing words just as decadent, declaring her to also be a serpent of the seed. She is one, and upon meeting Sheppard nothing she would rather like than to teach Sheppard a lesson in better manners. And to the lady Sheppard again said. "I so much despise women like yourself and if I had it by my command. Women like you! I would have stripped and thrown into a dungeon of naked men to enjoy."

Urobeha thinks about the abused privileges of royalty and how they take advantage of power through position If it was not for Sheppard being a royal princess, Urobeha would have loved to smack her across the face but, she holds her hand but not her tongue. "Is that what you think of all women in a splendid garment?" Urobeha's answer surprises Sheppard for a minute, Sheppard ponders how could the lady had already seen straight through her, be so discerning. So, she decidedly changes her approach. And again, to the young lady, Sheppard said, "Tell me! Are you not the sister of Meiha?" Again Urobeha responds, "Yes, I am she!" Sheppard goes on to say. "Your sister has chosen to stay beside the Holy Mother, but I must ask you? Please tell me, did he see you? Did he look at you? I want him so much to look at me for the woman, I now am."

Sheppard is not only naive and young but desperate for love and innocent. Her quick change of attitude touches Urobeha, heart. It is there Urobeha, realizes Sheppard's insecurities are a misrepresentation of her inner self and it does not define her true nature. Unable to conceal her emotional conflicts any longer about her brother Dicious, in the outburst of tears, springs the truth of her feelings. Urobeha, upon seeing and realizing how innocent Sheppard truly is, in a more caring tone says, "You should go and tell him, just how you feel. Yes, you should and yes! he looked at me!" So attentively, Sheppard said. "Then why did he not take you?" Keeping things in perspective Urobeha, said, "I never said that he didn't take me." For a third time surprise registers on the Princess's face by the lady's words. To Urobeha, the Princess quietly said. "I am sorry. I guess I did read you wrong."

To enlighten the young Princess understanding on how the heart and mind don't always work as one to her Urobeha, said. "When he looked at me, it was with his eyes and not with his heart. At first, I had trouble figuring it out, I knew something wasn't right. It wouldn't matter because later he confided it all even before I asked." Sheppard slowly absorbs her words, stepping to the opposite side of the lady, with admiration for her clothing shining in her eyes. Sheppard is persistent, she then said, "Then could you tell me! How could I make him see me with his heart and not with his eyes?"

Urobeha, lips twitch bemused, "A man such as he, I don't think you can!" The point is mute but still, this does not discourage the young Princess, Sheppard will not be denied. Captive to her emotions she leans more to the serpent side. And she said, "Then what can I do? I so much need him to see me, no longer as his little sister but as a woman, the woman I now am. And again, am sorry for the way I first approached you." Urobeha had long accepted the Princess's apology. So, to the Princess, she said. "So am I. You are still young and there is a splendid and bright beauty about you. Come, let me whisper something in your ear. Sheppard, being eager to know and to learn, leans over her ear to Urobeha, and in her ear Urobeha whispers, "Tell me, does this pathway have ears?"

Sheppard smiles knowingly because she so understands the meaning. She shakes her head no, in Sheppard's ear Urobeha, further whispers, words of the serpent seed, a silent pact and truce is declared as they both laugh out becoming good friends. Urobeha, advises Sheppard how to get her brother Dicious's attention, and should it fail, she could always visit her home town, where the men are all guaranteed cowards. Sheppard not knowing what to make of such news, listening even more, more attentively to words of the serpent seed. She accepts the words with relish, thinking no harm could be done. Each walks away in the opposite directions and then things started to change quickly.

It isn't until the following late afternoon Sheppard goes to act upon what Urobeha had whispered to her. Secretly she sneaks into her brother Dicious's chambers, not knowing if he's there or not. To her surprise, he is there sitting at his studies. Sheppard's heartbeat races at the sight of him.

Secret of the Serpent Seed

The moment Sheppard enters his chamber Dicious's instincts tell him someone is present and will soon reveal themselves. He does nothing until they show their face, recognizing it's not a threat. He continues making battle plans for him and his Warlord sister, Princess Leoha. The urgency has magnified due in part to the short time remaining before they both ride out to the Black Forest to finally take out the Black Widow and the Black Scarlet.

Drugging his wine is the first step to seduction. After Sheppard has drugged the bottle of wine, she brings out a full mug to him. With his back turned he already knows it is she in his chambers. So, he spoils her surprise. "Sheppard! I know it's you." And he continues his writing. From behind him, she hands over the full wine mug specially prepared to his liking. He takes it, having full trust in his little sister and before he could question her about being there, she said, "I come just to say my good-byes before you ride out again, and I also came to drink with you." He takes the full wine mug from her, drinking deeply he leaves only a little for her to finish as they would so often do. Handing the wine mug back over to her, it accidentally slips from her hand spilling to the ground. The shattering mug causes him to look up breaking his concentration to better focus on her.

Quickly getting up from his studies to see if all is well with her, he is surprised by the beauty of her sheer silk garments of red, purple, and green. For a moment, he just has to stop to admire her bright beauty that matches so well with her garments. Now standing surprised, to her, he said. "why are you dressed like that?" At first, she says nothing but approaches him, while showing out her beauty to him, in hopes that the drugged wine would take effect quickly. Sighing he looks over her innocent beauty. Now face to face calmly with sultry tones coyly Sheppard said, "Just so that I may drink from your cup and say my goodbyes." Bold yet innocent it makes him wonder how best he could deal with the situation, without harming either of them. Better to help his little sister ultimately, sacrificing himself to the cause he opens his arms to her and said. "Sheppard, come into my arms."

The comfort of peace enfolds her yearning falling weightlessly into his tight embrace. And to him, she whispered, "I just want to be shield by your love alone. Please- help me." Gracefully, tears of joy roll down her cheeks, because in his embrace is where she's long wanted to be. The comfort and warmth from his body heat the glow of her bright skin and she smiles out, just to know the wine has finally kicked in. Soon she will be able to help him to his bed-chamber but the strength of his embrace does not waver or weaken, he is still undrugged to her surprise. "Sheppard, you are so important to me, but there is something I must now do and I will be back later." At his words, (be back later) a spark shivers down her spine that makes her wonder. . . why isn't the drugged wine taking its effect on him? In disappointment with herself, she begins to pull away from him causing him to release her. Speedily stepping away from him, while looking him in the eyes, "Maybe you should have another cup of wine."

Running back to the wine table quickly she pours out another mug of wine and rushes back to him. He kindly accepts her offer by taking the full mug of wine. Resting it onto a side table causes her to maneuver taking charge again. Once again, she takes up the full wine mug and she offers it over again to him. Her persistent behavior becomes noticeable. "What is it about wine? Why do you want me to have so much of it?" She begins to realize her mistake and tries to cover it up. Smiling out to him gently, she said "It's just that I too need a bit more."

He offers the wine over to her. "Then please do have one with me." Not to further alert him of anything, she replies, "That would be too much for me and I do prefer you drink first brother." He pulls the wine mug away from her and again rests it onto the side table. She becomes further exasperated that he did not see the full picture, stepping up to him she smacks him viciously across the face. Stunned, why? Strictly and directly to him, she said "I poisoned the wine!" His eyes take notice of the spilled wine on the floor, and the black colored wine tells him she is speaking the truth. And again, to her surprise. He said, "I know."

Quickly she said, "Then why did you let me give you the wine, knowing it had been poisoned? He says nothing. "I put enough poison in that wine to take down a bull." He's disappointed by her behavior she turns her head down. "I am fully immune to that kind of poison, but you shouldn't have." Sheppard employs antics of the Serpent plan not wanting him to further distrust her, she falls to her knees before him so regrettable, she cries out "Brother, please forgive me and if I must be punished, I will rather be punished by your hand but just let me say. I meant you no harm. I only want to be with you. I am so lonely and I only want you to love me and am sorry for hitting you. Am I so wrong for wanting to be loved by you alone?" Knowing, he is as much responsible as she, he allows it to rest, time is not on his side. "Sheppard, you no longer have to explain this! Let's just forget about it but still, I must leave. You already know! I and Leoha are soon to ride out into the Black Forest, and the undaunted task ahead somehow frightens me. Please get up."

She knew he would forgive her. "If getting up is all that you ask. then I will comply." Arising from her knees so gracefully "Please, Dicious, may I stay, just for a while longer, until your return." He is the brother of her choice, looks at her "It is I Sheppard, who must leave and I can only promise you, that after this battle is over. I shall take you to see far beyond these lands but please no more of those wine tricks. She gives him, a sorrowful pout, wishing it could be now. He returns a smile with a tilt of his head she knows all will be well. "I promise." He turns to leave, "Dicious! Would you have me clean this mess up?" Stopping to look back at her. "Just leave it and I shall take care of it on my return." This makes her smile out to him. Walking away he leaves his chamber not realizing, what his and his Warlord Warrior sister Leoha, chances are of returning home from the Black-Forest.

The Undaunted King Gouddaa of the Arawaks and Caribs

His beautiful little sister Sheppard, marches into his massive sleeping chamber drawing comfort in the way his room smells. Inhaling masculine scents of sandalwood, vanilla, and lemon please her. Cozy comforts enamor a sudden urge to cuddle herself among the many pillows laying out in his bed. Removing all of her garments she crawls onto his bed. The beautiful little sister Sheppard falls into a deep sleep.

Sheppard in the Healing Chamber

Not soon thereafter Sheppard falls into a slumber, the Warrior Warlord sister, Leoha, is in search of her brother Dicious. To further discuss their battle strategies on the soon to be mission she calls out to him over and again only to find he is no longer there. And just when she is about ready to leave her brother Dicious's chamber, her warrior eyes take notice of the dark-colored wine on the floor. She knows from its dark color - the wine is poisoned.

With honed warrior instinct, to let her know of any pending dangers still present in his chamber she studies the room. Alarmed, she wants to know, who could want to do such a thing, knowing the outcome is death. She is now most alert, her nose detects a sweet fragrance, the air is hot and occupied telling her someone else is in his chambers. The odd sweet smell disturbing the room's synergy has a lingering trail that leads her straight into the sleeping chambers. There is a young lady naked and asleep in her brother's bed, her long hair conceals most of her face. Leoha can not recognize the young lady and figures, it best to get out. Quietly in retreat, the young lady upon the bed turns to better comfort herself, exposing her face.

Leoha, in disbelief, is rooted to the spot, because it is her youngest little sister, Sheppard, laying out naked across their brother's bed. To be certain of her eyes, she moves in even closer. Without warning to Sheppard, Leoha madly grabs hold of her long black hair and drags her from across the large bed onto the floor. Awaking to hell Sheppard is screaming out from her sleep for help but no one can hear her due to the density of the doors of the chambers and its massive walls.

Leoha smacks Sheppard, over and again. Each time Sheppard falls to the ground, she tries to reach for her clothing, but each time she is deterred by another forceful blow. Leoha, screams out, "What are you doing here? You little…." In an explosion Leoha's, anger consumes her, she continues to smack and throw Sheppard hard against the thick walls. Beginning to bleed out her swollen mouth her face starts to become distorted from the forceful impact. And still, Leoha would not stop punishing her. Sheppard cries out over and again to her Warlord sister to stop the beating but the Warlord sister's strength is just too much for her alone to overcome. Weaken and pained by the blows she still is unable to clothe herself. "No!. . . No! Leoha! It's not, -what- you think! Let me ex. . ." Each time Sheppard tries to explain, she is thrown across the floor over and again.

Furious Leoha blasts Sheppard, on how the in house rules of engagement must be followed. Leoha always had an aversion, never really liking her adopted sister Aries. Aries seduced both of her two brothers Dicious and Derious into hating each other. This caused the dismissal and exile of Derious, from the kingdom by the hand and incantations of their own father, Gouddaa. She could not allow it to happen again, so she punishes Sheppard for not respecting the in house order of rules. Harsh and cutting Leoha cries out at Sheppard. "You-! You- are nothing but another Aries! I thought better of you, is this, why I place my life on the line to protect you and the Kingdom? Your sweet life is given to you by persons like your brother and me! The love between brothers and sisters is not acceptable by the laws of the father! It is not! Do you hear meeeee!"

Badly bruised and injured Sheppard can do nor say anything. It is Leoha's fear of meeting face to face in battle with the Black Widow, that drives her to accidentally takes it out on Sheppard. From the floor, she again takes hold of Sheppard, and she tosses her again against the wall, Sheppard falls onto the floor without movement. To compound matters for worse, Leoha pulls on one of the chamber secret cords, and comes running in are the six guards now on duty. After greeting Leoha, she gives the orders "Now take this one down into the dungeon and chain her up against the dungeon walls until such time." Hesitantly they reserve to move, resistant to the Order and unknowing origin of circumstances encompassing the woman now lying unconscious and bruised on the floor. Leoha cries out, "Now!"

Quickly, two of the guards each take hold of the unconscious young lady's two hands and drag her out into the front Chamber. Leoha, follows partway, they coming to a stop before parting separate ways, one of the guards said, "Princess! What name shall we log her in as?" Not wanting to further deal with the matter or unwanted attention, to them she said, "As you wish, just take her out," Naked and badly injured Sheppard, is taken and dragged down into the lower Dungeon, and there she is left alone chained up against the Dungeon walls unconscious. Now when the guards first came in Dicious Chamber, they were a bit hesitant because no one had gotten passed on their watch which didn't account for the unconscious woman now chained to the dungeon walls.

They did see Prince Dicious leaving his Chambers, but because Leoha is a Princess and a Warlord one at that, they dared not question her orders. Sheppard had entered her brothers, Chamber through the secret passages and unannounced by the front guards so they did not know of anyone being in his chamber. Her long black hair, draped over her face, and facial bruising causes the guards who dragged her away, not recognized her to be Princess Sheppard. So they all did as ordered.

Dicious enters His Chambers

It's much later when Dicious on entering his chamber notices things are much out of place. He remembers Sheppard's last words. Upon entering his bedroom room by the looks of things all thrown around, he knows something violent has taken place. Out front, he goes, and after questioning the front guards, he can paint himself a full picture. Straight away he goes down and into the lower dungeon and he finds Sheppard chained and strapped against the dungeon walls. He orders the gatekeepers to release her at once and should the news get out about Princess Sheppard, they would be held responsible. The two gatekeepers do as ordered and together they help unchain her.

Dicious removes most of his clothing to cover his sister's nakedness. Sheppard is taken by her brother Dicious and is placed into one of the healing chambers to begin her quick recovery. In and out of consciousness she can still sense his presence beside her. With the little of her remaining strength, she summons up enough to get his attention, before the top lid is closed. With a weak breath, she whispers, and he hears her with concern he looks into her eyes and said, "Sheppard! I am so, so, sorry but you will soon again be well. Just you hold on and get well!"

Crying, "Why me brother? It is I who wants so much to see you and now you are finally here. I wanted you to see me robe-less, and now I am. I wanted to drug you just to have my own way with you, but it is I who has been drugged by the mind of Urobeha. Leoha, had her way with me, just like I wanted to have my way with you, and I would have so much loved it. Is this destiny? Is love destines by the Gods?! Tell me, brother. What is the greatest love of all and when you find out? It would be that love which I have for you." The sincerity of her words brings tears to the mighty Prince's eyes and because of her courage, he could say nothing but wish her a speedy recovery. There is no more to say to her or his Warlord sister, Leoha because it was high time, he and Leoha, get riding. "Please little Princess, please say no more of this and focus on getting yourself better. Please do it for me!"

To encourage her to keep up her good morals and courage, he smiles out to her wishing there was more he could do. She exclaims her state, "When my eyes were open, I was blind and now that they are bruise shut, I am still blind. What is my lesson and what have I learn? Only that love can be so cruel and brutal at times." Little Sheppard cries out to him and he tries to calm her but cannot. The keepers of the healing chamber come running in, they give him the cue that she must be put under to sleep, he agrees. One of the keepers walks up to the control panel within minutes a white mist is released covering the topwater. Sheppard is made to sleep and the top lid is closed.

Dicious knows the routine of the healing chamber, leaving her in good care he walks away. Now above all Dicious other siblings, it is Sheppard he loves the most. Under an oath made long ago with his mother Laurrennius, he promised not only to watch over Sheppard but to guide and direct her pathway in the ways of becoming a great princess. The news of Sheppard's brutal beating by the hands of her own Warlord sister Leoha travels through-out the walls of the kingdom like a wildfire. None dare to question the Warlord Princess on what had caused her to become so violent, vicious, and brutal toward her youngest sister. Though it is never mentioned by the Warlord Princess or her brother Prince Dicious, it remained not a hushed topic among the different ranks of the guards.

Meeting Prior to the First Cycle of the Wind

Meeting before the first cycle of the wind, Leoha and Dicious did not engage in conversations about the bruised Princess Sheppard. Focusing on the up-coming task to destroy the Black Widow and Black Scarlet is his only objective. On the rising of the third moon, which is the first cycle of the wind, they ride out to meet destiny. The ride is long. Along the way, Leoha makes a stop to retrieve herbal leaves in the area as Dicious continues. The herbs once eaten will increase her strength and size. She catches up to Dicious sometime later, who rides at a slower pace. Together they ride hard on the wind across the great open plain until they reach the outer limits of the Black Forest. Into the Black Forest, they enter and there they separate themselves.

Leoha engages in battle with the Black Widow as does Dicious with the Black Scarlet. They are both defeated, in ways far beyond their own courage. Leoha is left to believe she had escaped on her own, not ever realizing the Black Widow plot allowed her to live and leave. Infected by the touch of the Black Widow on her way out from the Black-Forest, she walks straight into the Black Scarlet, who demolishes her. The great Warlord Princess, not wanting to surrender nor die at the hand of the Black Scarlet is made to fall on her knees before her. Mercy is granted unto her along with the secret to heal herself and knowledge of who the Fifth Element is - the

White Guardian of the throne. She has word also that the house of gouddaa will fall.

Prince Dicious is speared as well from death because of a secret he and the Black Scarlet shared. On his way back to the kingdom, he enters through the deep forest because of its unknown secret passages back into the kingdom. Just as he is about to exit the deep forest, he is attacked from behind by an intruder. The intruder Blade injures him, making a stand he is still able to defend himself when given the chance, and the moment comes to the intruder, Dicious said, "Stranger! Who are you? And why me? And why now? The stranger stands unrecognizable due to the veil across the face. The Intruder cryptically replies "The head of the tempest is most powerful" Dicious, recalls the words, they are his own once spoken by him to his brother Cleattius. "Cleattius, don't we both fight for the same cause?!"

Cleattus unveils his face before his brother to show Dicious, he is not afraid of him. He has been away in his studies for some time and has much improved his fighting skills. He wants his brother to pay for the humiliating defeat he suffered and endured by his hand. It's retribution time, with disturbing malice, Cleattius, face twists and contorts in a snarl to his brother Dicious, "I was badly injured by you and I made it. Now let's see if you can make it. Cleattius dropping the veil attacks his brother with his new skills and it is there Dicious, feels his brother's wrath. Cleattius shows him no mercy, and the great and favorable Prince Dicious is beaten down in shame. Looking to teach the favorable Prince an eternal lesson Cleattius takes his right arm and he drags his battered body across to a nearby old tree trunk. Laying Dicious out on the forest floor, on an old log, he rests his brother's right hand and raises his Blade to sever it from his body.

Concealed there is another Cleattius who did not see observing the match of wills and strength. Before he can act, he is stopped by an incoming dart that grazes, marking his face. Had he not moved out the way in time there is no doubt the person has skills, he would be dead. This not only angers him but challenges his newly acquired skills. He is eager to know, who is there but before he could gain his balance another veiled face steps out from behind one of the nearby tree trunks.

To Cleattius the veil face intruder said. "If you continue, I will kill you!" Cleattius recognizes and realizes the skills of such a person equals that of his own, be wary this is a formidable opponent. To the veiled one, Cleattius says, "I do not quarrel with you! Just stay out of it!" To his surprise, the veiled face stranger replies, "You do now!" Bound in frustrations of denial, satisfaction still evades his triumph. He recognizes the hand to be that of a woman but it's not enough to tell who she is. He knows one with such skills would not stand down so easily, so to find out more to her he said. "I believe in knowing who the enemy is before doing battle with a total stranger."

To him, she said "That's your business! Mine is only in giving him safe passage." Who is this intruder? Wanting to further understand her reason. To her he again said. "Who is he to you? We have an old score to settle and that's none of your business!" Undeterred again to his surprise. She said, "My business is getting into other's business. could you understand this, because now I do have a score to settle with you?" Cleattius confidence tests the boundaries again he said, "If you know who I am, not even your tongue couldn't save you. You talk big lady! But it's your death so save your breath.

Prince Cleattius makes his stand for battle as does she. As she draws out her Blade, others emerge from behind the tall trees. Out comes, a platoon of mask archers, all their arrows aimed at him. Swallowing hard, by the looks of things, he realizes he is far outnumbered. To the great Prince Cleattius, the veiled one gives him, an ultimatum, "Live or die?" She didn't have to say it twice. Cleattius had long recognized the odds were against him and before she could say die. He is in the wind, long gone, disappearing through tall bushes and trees leaving behind him the badly injured Prince Dicious. Finally, the moment of uncertainty has past allowing me to take a calming breath. The veiled face intruder walks up to the badly injured prince, laying out on the forest ground dropping to one knee beside him. Readjusting her veil to one side of her face to her the great Prince Dicious, she smiles out. Dicious, "It's good to see you too and I have been in a better position, you know. Thank you again, family matters can at times be disturbing."

To him, she said, "You should save your breath, Prince. Just don't let your father know about this. I don't think he would like me threatening one of his royal sons." They both smiled out to each other, she again veils her face moving away, out to the others she said, "Don't just stand there, take him and hurry." These are the unseen guardians of the Northern Forest they all know and protect the routes of the secret tunnels and passages into the deep forest that lead into the kingdom. Shroud in mystery, secretly they take up the injured prince back into the kingdom. There he is placed into the same healing chamber which he had ordered his sister Sheppard to be placed into.

Sheppard Released from the Healing Chamber

After the first cycle of the wind has passed, Sheppard has been released from the healing chamber before her healing time is complete by none other than her sister Libra, the King. And on the opening of the chamber door, Sheppard falls out to her knees. She is still weak and trembling from the cold air. but with a little help from her sister Libra, she is made to stand on her own. Libra seeing her discomfort, removes one of her robes and covers her sister, not only from the cold but also from her nakedness. Then she summons the female keepers of the healing chamber to fetch warm clothing to better comfort Sheppard.

Sheppard is somewhat surprised to see Libra there because she had expected her dearest brother Dicious, to be there first. Dazed not yet alert, she doesn't realize Libra has seen that uncomfortable look shadowing Sheppard's face is not only due to the tight-fitting robe. Sheppard reserved the right to remain silent because Libra also sits on the throne and to stay in favor with the King. With a discerning tone, Libra said, "What bothers you further at this time, Sheppard? Sheppard realizes the dual position her sister holds not only to her sister but also to the King. She gathers and composes her options, to her sister the King. She said, "Do I have to?" Libra's smile asserts her disposition in its official capacity out to her, "I rather you do."

Sheppard knows the rules, punishable by death for lying out to the King. She spoke. "Well! well, when I first fell to the ground, my vision was a little blurry, and I. . .aaa! Well, I was expecting Dicious. Libra, wanting to be certain of what Sheppard had just said look at her scrutinizing the content of her response, Libra, "And you what?" Sheppard outright confesses, "Well I thought you were Dicious. Is he back? is he?" Libra, is surprised by her words, the audacity, with judgment speed she draws back her hand and smacks Sheppard hard across the face. The force of the strike cracks her thin skin causing her to bleed out from the side of her mouth. And to her. Libra said, "You better save it! That is not what you should be asking at this time. Listen well, little Princess. Love is not the answer to every question nor is it the key to open all doors. And though love is the only thing we may have to freely give and share! Do not abuse it! Let me not have to remind you of this again."

Sheppard is surprised she has displeased her sister her quick reaction stuns her. Snide, warm, and cunning her eyes narrow to slits, staring glaringly down at her sister with a direct and sharp tongue, "If I cannot freely speak! It would have been best you leave me in the healing chamber, until Dicious, arrives. So now, will you hit me again?" Libra shakes her head confounded by Sheppards will to love their brother Dicious, "No, but I hit you because Dicious won't!" Sheppard standing with her back facing the entrance does not take notice of the two-chamber keepers returning with her garments before they reached them. To Sheppard Libra said, "Your clothing is here!" The keepers show their respect out to the King and the princess therein are they dismissed. Libra receives the clothing, handing it over to Sheppard. Sheppard goes into the changing chamber and when she emerges, even the King has to admire the splendid colors of her clothing which matches so well with her glowing bright skin.

From her sister's smile, she can tell she stands in favor of the King. Sheppard walks up to Libra and hands over her sister's tight robe, "Thank you! Please, don't take what am about to say out of context, but I don't understand your every meaning at times. I don't even understand myself at times, sometimes I only wish I could comprehend and understand the meaning of things you say. I know it's for my good but please be patient with me. I sometimes wonder what makes us so different from the commoners. What's makes us

Kings, Princess, and Prince, and not them?" Libra upon hearing Sheppard's words and her concerns, "Come walk with me."

Together the two sisters exit the healing chamber room and down the long hallway, they begin to walk. Libra goes on to say, "You know Sheppard, we are what we are and as a Princess! You must learn to live by your words or die you must, by them." This is not what Sheppard expected Libra never showed much love towards her before. Now would be a good time to clarify this with her sister, "I, aaa. I always thought you never liked me!" Libra knows at times she is misconstrued to better clear her mind from such negative thoughts it's important poor choices of words do not color the tone of her conveyance to Sheppard, "They are your own words! What is there in you for me not to like? Yes! I may have been jealous of you at times because of Dicious! But to say dislike- is a strong choice of words. Don't you think?" Sheppard, "So tell me! Are you saying! I should try and forget about what Leoha did to me. If I do that! You tell me. What question should I now ask myself?"

Looking to further elaborate words and understanding. Libra said. "There is no such thing as one question. You should first ask all questions from the heart then, your mind. Your body is now healed and it's left to you and you alone to heal your mind. As for your question! Maybe if the role of the commoners and the Princess were to change and reverse, then you may better be able to understand. I tell you this because all eyes of time prepare today for your tomorrow. If you can decipher this, then the journey ahead may not seem so far fetched. You have to excuse me. I just remember I need to get back but, should you further need me, come later into the halls of the crown so that we may further talk." Libra takes her leave of absence, while Sheppard stays on for a minute contemplating her sister's last words.

Once Libra is out of sight, Sheppard moves toward the outside gardens and there she breathes in that long and needed breath of fresh air. There she begins to marvel at the way she now feels, so different after being released out from the healing chamber. And while she marvels at the beauty of her father's garden, she begins to understand what her sister had once told her about the after-effects on one's body after being rejuvenated by the healing chamber and how it allows one to better tap into one inner self and hidden ability's.

Cleattius Escapes and Pay for Information

Cleattius has escaped from his encounter back in the Deep Forest. In secret, he returns to the kingdom. Looking for information on the stranger who had slightly injured him, he is told by a high-ranking friend that only the King and a few others are privileged with that kind of information. His friend explains how the skills of those knights are unequal and unmatched. The knight never wanted to kill him otherwise he would be dead and as for the archers, they are never to be underestimated. Cleattius takes his friend's advice, but he needs more information. On he goes to a few of his personal informers but he is again told very little. Frustrated and displeased, after all, he is also a prince who believes in his entitlements. Nothing, no information should be held away from him. Even after using up all his playing cards, he finds he is still no closer than when he first started.

He won't stop until he finds what he seeks. Again, he leaves the kingdom to search elsewhere in a faraway small town for answers. Their information is valid for a price and anyone buying is welcome. The seventh prince travels like a commoner until he finally arrives at the place. Walking in he makes one stop at a small group standing beside the door putting out the word for all. Morning light now cloaks the sky when he walks to the last empty table in the inn. The tiny inn is full to its maximum with eaters, drinkers, and others looking for something or nothing but a good fight. Taking a seat, he is offered wine by the server before she walks off. Shortly after getting settled, he is approached by a lady with her face partially covered. Taking a seat just beside him, facing the opposite way, to throw everyone off she speaks out. To convince the others, she requires a quick boot fix, in a show of irritation she removes the right boot adjusting it for a better fix. Secretly, to Cleattius, she said, "What's your need and can I be of help?" Cleattius responds, "Nothing much! Just a few pieces of information."

From his garment, he takes out a gold bar and rests it on the table in front of him, when she sees the amount, "What's your question?" "You mean your friends at the door didn't tell you? I had words with them coming in." The lady answers, "She is one of the elite knights from the North." Quickly Cleattius, said, "I already know that! You will have to do better than that! I need a name?" She goes on to say, "Better known as the Collector! she is also an expert with the Blade, a war Knight of the Kingdom, protector, and commander of the thirty-first division archers. She lives in the Deep Forest but none of us here really know what she looks like, her purple veil keeps her secret While she places back on her boot Cleattius, said, "Take it!" Quickly she removes the gold bar from off the table securing it within her garments. To Cleattius the lady whose face is partially covered speaks, "You already know who my friends are. Hope to see you again!" She too, moves like the wind, leaving him only to spot her from behind. In the crowded room between moving bodies, he sees her meet her friends, together they all walk out.

The food server is back to take his order and off she goes. Coming through the door, the beauty of a woman enters, her unique proportions command the attention of all eyes. Perusing the room, she searches for a free table but there are no open spaces. The only available table space is besides Cleattius. Steady she walks making her way through the crowded room towards him. He watches her approach, grazing the back of his thumbnail against his bottom teeth he bites down, she's so close he could touch her. Kindly and ever so sweetly to Cleattius, she speaks, "Please, kind sir. All of the other tables are full and taken and I won't be very long may I?" Cleattius can't help being one who adores from time to time, the extreme beauty of women.

Extending his open palm towards space she desires he obliges her the opportunity, "It's a pleasure, please do" She sits as he asks her, "Lady if you don't mind being asked. Why would someone from your class enter a place like this? Things in here could get ugly at times for one like you?" Smiling at his words, at first, she says nothing. Again, he asks, "Is there something so wrong with my question?" Looking down she raises her view to his eyes, "Not at all! but why did you say someone from my class? It sounds like I shouldn't be here or better still not belonging here." He quickly tries to correct his words. And with a smile to her. "No, no. I didn't mean it like that." To his astonishment, she said, "Then how do you mean it?" Cleattius, "Definitely not like that!"

The lady is not immune to her own charms or its power, knowing the effects most beautiful women have on men in these parts. She decides not to back him into a corner but straightens things out before he goes any further. "My mother owns this place and at times I come to visit." Her words are not only a surprise but it clearly defines why she feels no concern being there. Transfixed for some strange reason, he keeps looking at her eyes, and the more he looks the more her eyes remind him of someone. He can't place the feeling he knows the depths unsure he leaves it alone.

Knowing, he may have spoken too fast, he decides to make up for it. "Please excuse my tongue, I did not know, let me make it up to you." He calls for another cup of wine, the server pays extra special attention to her while pouring it out for them both to drink and enjoy. She kindly thanks him as the food is brought in and placed down on the table. The server gushes over every serving detail, overemphasizing, and she sees his kindness, to him she again said, "Thank you." Cleattius raises his cup "Toast to my apology?!" After they had drunk he calls for more plates and shares his meal with her, together they enjoy the moment. To her again he said, "You can call me Cleattius." Sweetly she replies, "My name is Starr." Cleattius, "Well Starr! I am only passing through and it is good to know one such like yourself." Again she smiles at him, "You don't have to flatter me but thank you again. I do stay close by but I have never seen you around before. Are you a traveler of purchase?" He, not wanting to reveal himself, smiles, "Let's just say! It's not one of my usual stops."

The Undaunted King Gouddaa of the Arawaks and Caribs

Outside a young lady peeping in calls out with a high-pitched voice to Starr, "Starr! Starr! It's me! Am here!" Her friend also captivates Cleattius's attention, Starr waves out her hand to her friend signaling her to come around through the front entrance. Rossa gets the message, Starr's attention then turns back to Cleattius, who is watching everything. To him happily, she explains, "That's my friend Rossa. She's coming in to join us. If you don't mind?" From what Cleattius, has seen of Rossa through the window, he surely doesn't mind. Both girls share a unique similarity in beauty, what more than that could he want. "Please- allow her!"

Rossa quickly moves around to the front entrance where she enters. Three drunkards are staggering on their way walking out. She takes not much notice of the first two passing, until, the third one obnoxiously belligerent, walks directly into her pushing her harshly to one side. The commotion causes the other two to look back. Without a warning to the drunk, she retaliates leaping to the air kicking him hard across the face. The other two find it funny and they laugh out at him. In order not to lose face among his comrades the drunk attacks Rossa. The fight spills out into the open street. The man is inebriated and Rossa doesn't care to waste any more time with him. Disengaging from the fight she leaves him staggering side to side still poised for more opposition.

The other two come over to them. One of the two Drunkards yells at her "Stupid woman! Why don't you stay out of the way? You ought to show us more respect." Rossa has always found reasons to dislike men of this nature they are lewd and cruel. The disrespect fuels her to act once more at the ignorant swine, she kicks both drunkards simultaneously across their faces angering them further. Fortunately, one of the in-house fighters see everything and he comes flying out to her rescue, bringing things quickly to a stop.

To the pretty Rossa, the rescuer said, "Lady they are drunk! Why don't you just forget about it! They had a lot to drink." To him, Rossa, exclaims, "Tell them that!" Rossa, already had the last say when she kicked both men across their face. The in house fighter figures that is enough before someone really gets hurt. In retaliation, the two Drunkards push him aside and the battle resumes one against three. Rossa is an excellent fighter even in their inebriated state she

73

finds the three Drunkards fighting skills are worthy. The in-house fighter re-enters the battle again to equate a balance.

Starr on the inside is unaware of the strife Rossa faces outside. Sitting at the table with Cleattius, concern creases the contours of her face, aware looks with anticipating search for her friend who should be here by now. Why has not Rossa shown up yet? Persons gather to the windows, with spectators growing others gravitate to the scene happening outside. Foreboding dread grips Starrs innards it may have something to do with her friend. Cleattius sees her concern, he too figures whatever is happening outside may have something to do with the lady's friend Rossa. To be of assistance to the rare and beautiful woman before him, "Please, let me take a look! Be right back! He excuses himself from the table and walks to the front entrance, where others have gathered.

Yes, Rossa is in battle, alongside another fighter dressed like a warrior. The in house fighter with all his experience is badly hurt and injured by two of the Drunkards. Falling to the ground he chokes on his own blood, the odds remain three to one. Altogether pronounced the three Drunkards feats grow more, showing a wide range of abilities and skills. Prince Cleattius finds the odds against his new friends not welcomed. Leaping into action giving Rossa, a helping hand together they teach the three Drunkards a lesson in a good manner. Suddenly a shift in tide turns as the three Drunkards begin to fight back as one unit. Cleattius is hit by one of their potent darts, Rossa is almost down.

Starr not seeing Cleattius return, walks out to the front. On seeing both her friends injured and in trouble, urgently she knows what she must do. Cleattius is bleeding and losing blood but she has a plan. The eldest of the three she recognizes. She is known in these parts, from time to time, for a handsome sum she secures contract services. Cleattius needs not to know more about her than necessary. Quickly to bring things to a stop, she runs over to the drunkard in charge. Throwing herself into the fight, she allows him to hit her. Stumbling to the side with twist and flex, she pulls into him, up close secretly showing out a symbol of authority, it gets his attention. Very much familiar with the symbol he brings his men fighting to a stop complying with the silent request they moved out.

Starr and Rossa collect, taking hold of the injured Cleattius. Together they take him back to their dwelling place. Two moons later Prince Cleattius awakens. His eyes flutter opens to roam the ceiling in the space where he now lies. Eager to know where he is and how he got there? His nose guides his eyes to a table prepared with waiting food. He is hungry. The beautiful lady he had met back at the tavern is sitting and eating at the table. Slowly he begins to sit up, holding his throbbing head, while feeling his chest. To the young lady at the table, he said, "Oh my head! Tell me how long was I out?"

Elated, to see the injured Cleattius up and recovering, Starr looks over at Clettius, "It's good to see you're finally back! Though the dart had only scratched you, they can be lethal at times!" From the table, she picks up the dart showing it out to him, before allowing it to drop back to the table. "So, what kind of dart is it?" Returning to her meal it's obvious the meal spread out, is enough food for both of them, and he is famished. Starr knows Cleattius needs to gain back his strength, nurturing and caring for him this far. Indicating to the object resting before her, "It's right here on the table! A sleeping dart and not so vital! Your food is waiting. . . Why don't you come on over?

Slowly getting up from the cot, he looks around for his missing garments. Awkward, Starr smiles to herself, Cleattius is naked, vulnerable, and exposed. The way he is moving around the bed covering himself, she could tell he is much concerned. Slowly he stumbles to the eating table and sits. Reciprocating his hospitality, she serves him eats, and drink, as he had done with her back at the tavern. He smiles out to see himself, positions reversed. To remind her of it, he said, "I have seen this situation before." Reminiscent of the moment she understands his meaning. They both smile out to each other.

Starr confides to him, "You don't have to worry. Your secret is safe with me and as for your clothing they are in the back and will be dry soon." Mollified, his concern about his concealed symbol of authority relaxes somewhat. "So, you take a look." Looking at the beauty as she sits gracefully, looking at him. "I had to, to see better the wound but you were not badly injured. I think it must have been that strong wine that took its toll." They finish their meal.

Rising, Starr goes to the back and outside to the line, where she retrieves his clothing and Royal Seal. On handing them over to him. She said. "Here are your things. Your seal can only bring death to me. Yes! Out here everything is for sale, but I would never think to take it." Receiving his clothing, once dressed, he walks back out and over to her. "I owe you so much. I have never met anyone like you before and I would like to see more of you and I think it is high time I get moving" Curious, Starr prods, plying Cleattius with small talk, "If you don't mind me asking! What brings a prince to these parts? Vaguely breathing a sigh, no closer to his goal than when he started with a blank stare on the horizon he replies, "Answers! Just seeking answers." Bemused, smiling out to him innocently, she said, "But you are a Prince. What answers could one like you, need in this place and can I be of use?"

This vendetta with his brother Dicious has led to many consequences and ends, "Just an old score and I rather not bother you further with such trivial matters." Receding her position, she does not want to impose being nosy. "As you wish my Prince." Reminding her of what he earlier tried to mention, "So! Can we meet again?" To his surprise, she agrees, "Yes! That would be nice and I would so much love that, but we both live in different worlds. You are a Prince and I am a commoner! I could never truly fit in your world, but should you ever be passing this way again, please do stop in and if you should ever need my assistance my home is yours, my Prince!" Prince Cleattius, finds favor in her, "Please don't call me that." Perplexed a bit at his chagrin, "Then what shall I call you Prince?" Returning her smile, "Just call me Cleattius! And we are now friends." Grabbing him under his arm she places hers, "Well now friend, let me walk you out."

In no time he is fully dressed, together they reach the front door of the house. Starr opens it, looking down the street Rossa is running towards her home with a gift for the Prince. Before Rossa could arrive, Starr pulls herself back to the inside to Cleattius, "My friend Rossa is on her way here and she has with her something of yours!" Wanting to know just what that could be, eagerness takes the best of him. Playfully pleading to her, "Let me have a quick look." Moving aside she allows him to look and Rossa is there. Stepping to the outside Starr follows Clleattius. Rossa stands with her eyes bright with anticipation she hands over to him the straps to his beautiful stallion.

Rossa confides, "I have never met a Stallion I couldn't ride. This one is the first and is so late." Cleattius is pleased to see both of them. To Rossa, "My! This is a surprise, seeing both of you. He can be a little stubborn at times." Stroking the horse's mane, Rosa looks at Cleattius, "It's a lovely animal and one to be admired. Back then, I did not get the chance to say thank you for saving me. My name is Rossa, and I already know who you are." Cleattius turned to Starr, in question? Wide-eye Starr looks back at him nonchalantly replying, "Well! She did change all of your bandages." The Prince could only smile at her words, turning back to Rossa, he tells her how brave and thankful he is for her and Starr's assistance in aiding him in time of need.

Leaping to his horse, there is much more he would love to say to both ladies apart from each other but now is not that time. Looking down from his horse at both ladies standing warm, beautiful, and posed. To Rossa, he asks, "The Stallion! How did you know?" Rossa and Starr look at each other, then back at him sitting on the Stallion. Prepared to leave, Rossa pays compliment to the horse attributes, "Even though I could never ride him. He is most discipline, much more than our horses." Rossa is a lover of animals, gently she pats the magnificent beast on its head, as to say goodbye to sweet beauty. To Cleattius. She asks, "So, Will we ever see you again, Prince?" To be assured they do, he pulls out from his lower saddlebag, two royal passes from the Kingdom. Handing them over to Rossa, "Please take these. It will give both of you safe passage to see me when and where ever I am.

Rossa kindly receives them with a bright smile of thanks, she moves closer to Starr. Cleattius looks into Starr's eyes with an unspoken word of promise, we shall meet again. Rossa tells him, "I shall cherish it until we meet again." Turning his horse, he slowly rides off. Never did he know or realize Starr, is the very same warrior he is looking for. The same one who stopped him from severing his brother Dicious's right hand in the forest.

Sheppard in the Garden before the throne

Sheppard is in the gardens exploring her body's new feelings after being released from the healing chamber. She has a lot on her mind, thinking it through, she is still at a loss about things, her sister Libra said. Making her way into the hall of kings, there is Libra on the throne. The atmosphere and the look of things are somehow different from that of her father's rule. The orders of the guards have multiplied and so have their weapons. Though she disapproves of many changes, she understands with this new rule comes new change.

The King takes notice of Sheppard standing to the side. Giving orders for all further matters to be resumed in three lengths, meaning (three hours) she removes her royal crown resting it to the side. The royal guards remove it to lock it away. Ascending from the throne, Libra walks down to meet her youngest sister Sheppard. "I have noticed you looking around. Do you disapprove of my taste?" Right away. Sheppard said. "No, no, not at all! Is father gone?! I did not get to tell him goodbye. Libra studies Sheppard's countenance "Neither did I! But come and lets us have a little chat." Sheppard nods her head.

Out from the king's hall, they walk until they come to a spot suitable for a private conversation. Both sit Libra asks, "Now Sheppard! What bothers you so?" Disoriented feelings of detachment plague Sheppard cries out, "Since my recovery from the healing chamber. I feel so different. My head! So many questions in my head, not enough answers in my mind. Please help me! Libra, looks at her, little sister. "You must give yourself some time. The chamber affects each person differently but like I have said. It will soon go away along with the pain, then you will better understand.

To further help Sheppard, calm herself Libra grabs her, "Look at me Sheppard and concentrate on my finger." Libra raises her hand out in front of Sheppard's face. with one finger stretched forward, she rests the finger between Sheppard's two eyes and slightly presses against her skin until she comes to a calm, then Libra removes her hand. Where there was once a shaky haze of fog now clarity, and focus have been restored. To her amazement in relief, Sheppard feels like herself, "How do you do that?. . . Thank you!"

Libra has never questioned her ability to perform feats such as this, and it's not really relevant right now, her sister is troubled. "I don't really know but enough about me. Tell me little sister what bothers you so?" Sheppard takes in that deep breath not knowing where to begin. "Please, don't think I don't care, but I! well. . . Can you tell me more about, where are we all from, and why are we so different from the commoners? What makes us kings and queens and rulers and them not?" The entitlements of divine birth is a matter of high understanding of the purpose of life. Libra, after hearing her sister's many concerns, can only wonder. Where does she get it all from? This more than likely is a side effect from the healing chamber.

Libra tries to slow down the secession of questions, "Well, I do wish you a speedy recovery, but that's a lot of questions in such a short time and the answers are not that swift. It could take me generations and that amount of time, I just don't have. So, let me just ask you a question and pending your answer. It may be the start you are looking for and the beginning of seeing things from different sides. Now listen well before you answer." Sheppard, shakes her head, Libra continues, "Did you choose to be born in this family? And do you know of any commoner or non-commoner who have?" Without further thought, Sheppard said, "I think, I now understand." Libra, did not expect her to understand so swiftly, to be sure Sheppard is free from doubt again to Sheppard, she asks her to explain what she does understands. "Sheppard! Please do explain what you understand?"

Her mind has cleared, steady now, out bluntly, in the obtainment of more knowledge Sheppard seeks even more crucial explanation that will enhance the substance of her being. "Yes! I believe I now do understand. You have just moved weight from off my heart and my head but my mind still has questions and I would like, you to continue. Please do tell me more!"

By Sheppard's mention of the weight of her heart, Libra does not doubt the Princess's enlightenment. Upon seeing her eagerness to learn and know more about the ancients, Libra elaborates. The annals open, ventilating to the young princess how once her father Gouddaa, instructed her in the enchanting scriptures of knowledge. The intriguing subject relaxes her, as it eases the consciousness of her mind. Absorbed in the long and overdue lessons of the enchanted ones Libra weaves the historical lineage of the ages as it was conveyed to her. One consolation, while in the end, it may break her endless nights of having little sleep or none at all, it does give her something other to consider.

Libra goes on - according to the seventh books of pillars, the very first set of the Gouddaaians who lived on this planet, lived without rule and laws as you know of it. They were a group of peaceful people much taller than the average Gouddaaian is of today and a much stronger and mightier race. They lived in peace and harmony with not only each other but also with the land and everything which surrounded them. They were giants, they lived to be nine hundred and more full cycles of each of the three moons, which turns around every first Sun.

Products of the existing environment, their children developed attributes of telepathic ability. Not only could they mentally move objects with a thought, but they communicated with the trees of the land and the earth, to bring forth more fruits in the harvest. The oceans provided in abundance for their needs when mothers' childbirth was plentiful in the land and more food was needed to sustain them.

After the nations of Gouddaaians had multiplied in great numbers, they divided themselves over the land. Keeping the intergalactic rule of all things, was good because the earth and the generations multiplied copiously in numbers. Others came down from the sky, making themselves look and act like us, but they were different. Unlike the giants and us, they possessed the ability of mimicry to shapeshift at will to look and act like anyone. They were not welcome among the giants, hiding among us, they still do today as Gods. They infiltrated some of the smaller races of Gouddaaians, with wicked motive and intent they afflicted our perfection. Changes began to take place, infected by malice, we began to turn on each other and many like us became evil.

The Gouddaaians, giants were fooled, giving to them their sons and daughters in exchange for higher intelligence. They were wrong, the young women and men they gave to them were assimilated. True to their nature, shift changers altered the state and conditions of their minds releasing toxins into the bloodstream that ignite rebellious consequences. Through interaction others were affected in different ways, alienating many of them from their mothers and fathers. The ones taken by them much later, bare children of their own. Their mother's births were no longer peaceful but excruciating, painful, and complications magnified provided even greater challenges. Many young mothers screamed out losing their minds, some died in childbirth. Others killed their own unborn because the natural link of nature had been altered, broken by the sky people. The children, half Gouddaaians, half people from the skies, babies' skin were no longer dark but bright. Their eye color was that of the sky and they were born so beautiful that their mothers were told, they are to be called children of the rainbow, children of the sky.

To their sons and daughters, shapeshifters gave the power of dark rule. They made what remained of the pure Gouddaaian, race, slaves in their own land. Much as it is today their children evolved to become men and women of renowned authority. For a minute Libra pauses, turning to look she finds Sheppard is disturbed by her words, tears stream down her face. Concerned Libra asks Sheppard, "Sheppard, would you like me to stop now." Softly she responds, "No, no, I need you to continue, please do." Libra goes on to say. "So many generations of peace among Gouddaaians mentally vanished and by the time the ancient Gouddaaians, realized, who and what the people from the sky came to do and what they were truly up against. They were already blind slaves to the new generation of a rule.

And mother earth broke off her connection with the Gouddaaians, and they became a lost race of people, and they lost all their natural ability's and we are their decedents. Half Gouddaaian, half people from the sky and in our new genetic code, lies the power to rule and dominate others, where ever we may go."

Sheppard cries, reaching for her sister Libra hugs her comforting her to remain strong. Libra gives all the love and caring any mother would give to a loving child. Sheppard comes to calm once again, pondering what has just been explained, "Why did they come here?" Libra shrugs her shoulders, "Why does anyone go or come elsewhere?" Sheppard answers her own question, "To find what is needed." The more questions, the more answers are required, "What did they need from us?!" Resolved to the defiant circumstances which are their plight in life Libra holds her head high, "Chaos, and havoc but the stronger part of us as Gouddaaian somehow prevails, because those who came from the stars were never Gods, but life forms with an agenda for their own survival."

Sheppard is still confused, asking, and answering all the right questions doesn't always prove to be satisfying. Unrelenting to this new information there is so much more to know, "But here we have a lot, so how could their need be pinpointed to just one or two things? That would be most unlikely and just impossible. Don't you think?" Libra knows this is much to decipher in one sitting, but she does her best to clarify, "It depends on what you are talking about. But impossible is just a lack of one's belief. Would you not say?" Sheppard insists, "Make me understand."

Libra illustrates further to pacify Sheppard, "Well, let me put it to you like this. If you have no love for me. What would be the most likely thing for you to show me? Like a student under instructions, Sheppard gives the obvious answer, "My hate! My hate toward you!" Libra smiles, "You are again right but why didn't you just say not love? Based on her knowledge, Sheppard exclaims, "Love and hate just cannot prevail in the same space eventually one will give in. From what I have gathered you did say, the Gouddaaians were once a peaceful race, who lived in harmony with everything in nature. It tells me that those who came from the sky brought, chaos and havoc and destruction with them and that is the most of what we have in the world.

"The scale of life is just not balanced and where is all this negative energy going?" Libra goes into the depth that Sheppard maybe firm in her understanding, "It is being gathered and stored away and taken in large containers back to their homeland to be transformed and used to feed their great leaders." At times you can see gigantic canisters moving across the skies, compelled by gravitational force to its location. Overwhelmed by her sister's knowledge humbles Sheppard's disposition, "How do you know all of this? How is it possible that you know!"

Libra continues, placing her hand on Sheppard's hand, "Our ancestors long ago found out that the people who came from the sky built an upside-down pyramid beneath the surface of the earth in the Black-Forest and at the very bottom chamber is where they store this negative energy to, later on, be removed. This knowledge was long, long, ago handed down from the lamb of the high archives to our ancestors and that is why it is always forbidden for us to go there. The magnetic field of gravity at the very bottom of the chamber is at zero." Like a riddle or game, the pieces fall in place for Sheppard, "I now understand. We are by bloodline mixed with the others from the sky and the crave for power within us, is like not eating."-

Time has passed, much has been explained that may not have been shared before. The aches of them sitting too long takes its toll, standing up gingerly, slowly they begin to walk together. "Father once told me, you are the seed of wisdom. Tell me, are your abilities that of the pure race of Gouddaaians? Libra smiles wishing it so too, "Maybe, but still, how would I truly know? We are what we are, but this course is definitely not for the swift" Sheppard stops her from finishing, "No, no don't answer! Let me, But for those who withstand to the end." Libra, acquiescence only to say, she couldn't say it any better. Graciously Sheppard thanks her, "You have filled a cup that was once empty and now that it has been filled and the void is no more. Thank you! And though I may still be eager to know more, I am still in need of your guidance."

The King's Adviser approaches, Libra, must be returned to the hall of thrones, and Sheppard satisfied, back to her chambers. Weary, Libra said much in the scheme of things that has Sheppard drained, laying her head down to rest there she falls into a deep sleep. In her dreams she digests all of what Libra, has taught her, she envisions herself in a robe of binding chains, walking out from the sea of death. For each step she takes, a piece of the binding chains falls from her body back into the sea. She yearns to look behind at the pursuing black mist soon to engulf her, but instead of ignoring it, she keeps moving toward the seashore until she finally makes it. The binding chains that held her have all fallen back into the black sea of death. She finds herself alone, naked on the seashore. Grieved, looking back and all the darkness behind her is light. Radiating light touches her changing the molecular components in her body to sand. She watches her body structure changing into a pillar of sand. She awakens out from her dream with sand on her hand.

Gouddaa Rides Toward the Black Forest

Gouddaa rides at high speed toward the Black Forest. He and his white stallion are in full dress, armed with the incantation of white magic to do battle with the Black Widow, and her many warlords of death. Over hills, mountains, valleys, and Saxon streak he crosses, before finally arriving at the great open plains. The great plains must be crossed to reach the Black Forest. His fire-breathing white stallion moves on the wind and he is riding against time. Finally arriving at the outer limits of the Black Forest, where he brings the white stallion to a trot and then to a walk.

The journey has been long, he draws in a few deep breaths before moving on. It is the calm before the storm but he is ready, prepared without fright nor fear, concern for his wife Laurrennius is foremost in his mind. The mighty King and his brave stallion cross over and into the Black Forest. His arrival triggers an alarm as such that even the Black Crows scream out unto the Black Widow, alarming her and all the others to prepare themselves, for war is upon them.

From dark and hidden places, they come out to do battle with the mighty King Gouddaa, they battle him from all four sides. The fury of battle is immediate. Jumping out from the tall trees to the ground to fight, from behind hidden stones they appear injecting themselves into the storm. From beneath the under pillars of the under Earth lurking they come to do death with the mighty King Gouddaa. From his white silver-plated stallion, he battles them all, killing them by the thousands of thousands. Armed with the mighty holy crystals he is shield with the incantations of invincible powers. There is nothing they do can harm or stop him. A bright light glows outward all around him, and anyone who is touched or caught within its bright ray dies. There in the middle of his headpiece is a crystal that channels out his thoughts, but death does not stop them. Numberless they continue to press on him in battle, from the east they come with rods of iron from the west with boulders and mallets of large stones, from the north with spears and daggers, from the south with many unknown crafts of weapons. Still, they are no match for the mighty King Gouddaa. Charging at him by the thousands and as many as they came, so did many fall into their deaths.

For long ago they were told and promised by the Black Widow, eternal life and power, shall be given in abundance in exchange for the one who can bring forth Gouddaa's head on a platter before her. Their reward is to be granted a seat at the table of glory and power above all others. This they all believe, it is in her driven promise and power to bestow such a grant of eternal reward. This keeps them loyal to her. The battle counts its toll upon them, still, they refuse to give in to defeat. Vented, Gouddaa's white stallion comes to a halt, thousand upon thousand, numbering several one-hundred-thousand lay dead out across the floor of the Black Forest.

Ominous gray clouds roll across the skies, flashing lightning whipping winds stirring the air. With sudden alarm, Gouddaa's blazing white stallion mounts itself into the air turning, towards the powerful presence entering into the midst. As the white stallion's front feet hit the earth, standing there before him in the ray of his absorbing light is none other than the Black Widow, her rod of power in hand. Up to the sky, she raises her Rod, causing the battle to stop. Like the sands on the seashore, the Black Widow looks around at the carnage of bodies littered dead and dying. Incensed by the loss, laying out across the Black-Forest, she cries out to the mighty King Gouddaa. to stop the killing of her people. Her eyes burning embers, filled with hate and fury like that of fire. To the mighty King, she cries out, "You! You! Look at what you have done to my children! Look what you alone have done! But I know why you have come."

To her, the mighty King Gouddaa said, "Then let no more of your people die." A seething tempest, the Black Widow spews her malice, "What is it that you want?! And what are you willing to exchange for it all? It is you! Who had turned my disciple the Black Scarlet, against me and made her one of your own. She did not bring your blood back to me. Instead, she chose you over me and now, you have come for my help. (Cackling) Look around you great Gouddaa! Is the life of the one you love worth more than the hundred and more thousands laying out dead all around you! Tell me great king of death! Have they ever done anything against you? Have they? Your hate is against me not them." She rants.

Possessed in the spirit of the incantation that surrounds him, his eyes turn into a deep green color as he speaks from his white stallion. "My hate is not against them but them forever being born." Formidable, she moves in even closer, she can withstand his light. The faith of followers, witness the wonder of how great her power is matched superior above that of the immortalize King Gouddaa. Cloaked by incantations bestowed upon her, whenever she speaks, her eyes turn black as grave blood.

To him, she said. "Who gave you the right to determine, who should be born?" Gouddaa does not relent his position, "Why don't you ask yourself that question and while you are at it! Ask who gives you the rights to allow all of them, laying dead before you to have lived?" This pricks her anger. There is an abyss which separates them, resolved she is content to know the light and the dark can never coexist, they will be forever opposing sides. Spittle spews in the snarled twists of her conversation, slobbing wet she licks her lips, "As I have said! I do know why you have come. Her life must be important to you! Is that not why you seek out your own enemy help."

The course for Gouddaa was always leading to this point, he knows that now. "I come not only for her life but also to settle our difference. Further obliging him. She mocks, "Then please continue, Mighty Gouddaa, of the Arawaks and the Caribs." He is the King, dignity is his armor, integrity is the blood of his strength, sitting high the baring of his confidence conveys the sentiments of his quest. "Should you give me the cure to awake her. I shall hand over the crystals."

Upon hearing his words her head tilts slightly in unbelief, "That's not enough! You once stole some herbs out from my garden and in the process, you also killed three of the guardians of the garden. How then will you pay for their lives and all the countless lives around you mighty Gouddaa?" Looking at her with those deep green eyes of incantation, he asks, "Can you be trusted to keep your words, Old Widow?" She snorts disliking, his choice of words, "The worry and the old test of time do show on your face. But my words are only as good as yours, great King." He understands her meaning. "What else is it, that you want of me? Awake her first and I shall remain." With a taste for revenge in her mouth, "Can you be trusted to keep your words Old Father?" From behind glowing green eyes, she sees the smothering blaze of his eyes, he said, "Your assurance are my words."

With eyes pinned on each other, it's a stand-off. Stepping back into the outer circumference of his bright light alongside the others, the Black Widow, takes from her clothing another holy crystal. To one of her young subjects, she hands the crystal. "Take this and give it to him! Think not of the light but of me who is with you!" The young subject takes it, afraid to step into the bright ray light, her body betrays her with buckling knees. With each step in apprehension, she focuses her eyes on Gouddaa's deep green ones. All around him, the thousands upon thousands of dead souls and spirits, portend a warning, waving out to her, go back, out away from the light. Petrified, she is too afraid to move, in her head, she is made to come back by the incantation of the Black-Widow. The Widow reassured her, "Little one. You have been chosen for an undaunted task and there is no room to be afraid! Come and I will show you." With guile of a caressing touch, down her arm, the Black Widow gently removes the crystal out of her hand. Kissing the young subject on the back of her head, she trusts a dagger from the back into her heart. Bewildered the young woman falls to the earth dead.

The crystal is passed on. Next in line, none dare tremble. Into the light, the successor who took her place steps forward without fear and up to the mighty King Gouddaa. He views the crystal through his green vision there's no mistaking its authenticity. In his possession is an identical one. Living up to his undaunted words in exchange for the awaking of his wife Laurrenius he gives the servant two crystals, one at a time, in exchange for the one she holds. The young subject returns, handing two holy crystals over to the Black Widow. She and Gouddaa are both satisfied the mark has been met.

The holy crystals are a formula of much power and now they in the hands of the Black Widow. Gouddaa is surprised she and the young subject are still standing after handling the crystals. He knows combined they are poisonous. Rearing on hind legs the blazing white stallion turns around. Gouddaa's previous observations are confirmed as the young subject falls dead to the earth before The Black Widow, frightening the others.

The way is made clear for the mighty King Gouddaa to ride off. Over the boundaries he crossed through the open plains, he rides with urgency on the wind, back to the Kingdom. The Black Forest is an oasis concealed in a vast desert territory with open and harsh plains surrounding all four sides. It's a place of the void, no one dares to come. The surrounding magnetic fields are known to distort and disorientate one's mind in a very short time. Many who enter succumb to the atmospheric depreciation's, but not Gouddaaians, and those of the White Lambs, it is for this reason, the Black Widow fears them all. Those who have entered the dead- zone discover there is no exit, no escape.

Sheppard Walks Among the Leagues and Bronze

Sheppard awakens from a deep sleep sometime later. Into the halls of statues, she strolls, among the great league of warrior statues, and others ready awaiting to be mounted. Coming to terms with all of what she has been through she wonders among the greatest warriors ever lived in search of solace. Walking, admiring, touching them, strength from elite images of the past and present warriors comforts her. This is a new wing, coming upon a league of bronze statues their masterful creations have warmth stone lacks. Gracefully she trails among them, it seems as if they are gazing back, studying her. Coming face to face with a bronze copy of her warlord sister Leoha, triggers flashbacks of that brutal moment that left her badly injured.

Venerable of that moment evokes suppressed pain, frightened she is afraid. In her mind, haunted, she hears the statues taunt her. The bronze statues reverberate "If you think honey is sweet, revenge is sweeter." "If you think honey is sweet, revenge is sweeter." In many different languages, and dialects they resound, in the silence. She runs out from the hall hounded by the chanting echoes, into the hallway, breathless from breaking away she stops, coming to a calm. The many leagues of voices has stopped. In its place, two voices are in the debated conversation up ahead of her. Curious, who could they be? to know who they could be, gravitating towards the direction of the sounds she moves in closer to further hear the conversation.

In the distance she sees them, concealing herself behind one of the massive pillars she listens.

The unbeatable General Nemmissis is giving orders to his second in command, "Send out a raven with a message to the soldiers in the far North, at first light they are to cross over the boundaries in the Black Forest and search without being seen for the Warlord Princess Leoha. Bring her back to the Kingdom at all cost, and at once." Back pressed the pillar, Sheppard smiles, wistful thoughts and possibilities just favored her chances for revenge against her Warlord sister, Leoha. The brutal beating, she endured by her hand was vicious and renting in more ways than just physical damage. In that very moment of reflection Sheppard, formulates a plot of retaliation, revenge against her Warlord sister, is imminent. Despite of all of what her sister Libra, had taught her, turmoil emotions of abuse are a constant torment, it is easier to disregard Libra than to take the high road of acceptance. Leoha must pay!

Going back to her chamber - Sheppard puts a plan together, first, she has to meet with a long, overdue friend. Sneaking into the camp after asking a few questions to some of the other guards in the strangest way, she is told where her friend is to be found. She finds him as said on his station. Dressed like everyone else, she doesn't look the part and no one takes notice of her because she does her best not to be recognized. Wanting to surprise him, she sneaks up behind him Without the others hearing, she whispers out his name, "Roobbye, Robbye, Robbye. . ."

The strange voice makes him turn to see who is whispering. He is surprised at the sight of a scruffy and skinny looking soldier, who has no rights to be in any squad, let alone in a uniform calling to him. The quizzical look expressed upon Roobbye's face forces Sheppard to take notice of herself. Looking around at the others in uniform, she tries more to stand upright before anyone else could notice. Her head and shoulder pieces are too big and heavy for her to remain balanced. Some of her underpads which make her look big are now falling, quickly she adjusts them back in place. To the odd, skinny looking little soldier, Robbye asks, "Who are you? What are you?" Keeping her voice low, makes him wonder. What's in Gouddaa's name is going on? Again Sheppard whispers out to him, "It's me. . . Roobbye,

Sheppard! Now you stop that and come here!" Surprised by her new look, he responds "Princess! You should not be here. What are you doing here? And why are you dressed like a soldier? I know you're not here because you now want to marry me. So what is it this time? You and I always get into trouble when together and it is always my butt on the line."

Sheppard hasn't spoken with Roobbye for some time, if she is going to be successful in coercing his support, their past relationship will be paramount in securing her objectives. With a look of endearment, pleading with coy allure she plies her feminine wiles. He has no defense to withstand the ploys of her request. She knows it works every time. Sweetly Sheppard encompasses the past of their exchanges, "Are you saying, you're not please to see me?" Straight away Roobbye reminds her, "Well. . . It has been a while, you know." She won't deny it, "Now that you know that. What are you waiting on?" Looking to her, resolved so honestly, he submits, "What choice do I have? You are a Princess and my wish is still yours to demand. You know, am always pleased to see you. But that doesn't explain. Why are you dressed like a soldier? You could at least make the uniform fit better. You do have a problem with the head and shoulder piece, you know?" His tirade of questions reassures her, knowing, he must eventually give in, she gives him a dazzling smile, "I figured! It would be easier this way to see you. It doesn't draw any attention. Now, do you believe me?" On that note, he sighs, "Princess, how could I not believe you."

Playing on his emotions, Sheppard goads him as she had in the past, "So, are you still the best archer?" Pausing for a split instance, suspicion dissipates to the vanity of his self-worth. Being so sure of himself, he proudly boasts, "Graduated, top of the class! How is that? And how is that strange raven of yours? Is that bird still trying to killing people? Sheppard laughs, defending her bird, "If you are talking about Silk! He is no killer! He may be strange at times but he moves only on my orders. Something you have never learn to do! But you know! Now that you mentioned it. I think that the bird can even read my mind."

Not wanting any of the other soldiers passing to take notice of her, Roobbye suggests "Come, let's go into my tent. Though you dressed like a soldier! You don't really act like one and I just wouldn't want others to start a talk." Moving away, walking side by side each has a wily smile upon their face. Sheppard inquires deeper, "What kind of talks are you talking about?" To make her understand better he explains, "Talks, like being in favor of one soldier over another. Better still a soldier like you." With a look of concern, she asks, "Does this means you have other women coming here, to see you?" Roobbye has had feelings for Sheppard for a long time, but duty demanded adherence to proper decorum, a man has needs, and the Princess can never be his. Looking to spare her feelings, there's no good way to say it, "Yes, you're right."

What did she expect, mulling in silence, she says nothing until they reach the door of his tent? There's a contemplative air about her. He wonders what she's really thinking. Getting her to talk, he coaxes her response by commenting on her clothing. Even in disguise, he knows her vanity, if he gives her a distasteful face, it will get her. He looks begrudgingly at her uniform so that it doesn't go unnoticed by her. Sheppard immediately catches the look, puzzled, "What, what are you looking at?" As they enter his tent, he teases her, "If there are other women like you say! I hope they are better dressed than you." The playful banter is reminiscent of older times. It's cozy, grabbing his hand more because she needs to touch him, the ordeal with Leoha has left a scar of dependency. Roobyee was always uncomfortable whenever she crossed the lines of propriety, at the beginning of this plan she knew this had a chance to get intense. To make him relaxed, she takes hold of his hand, "Okay Roobbye, I was only joking and am sorry." Her touch enchants him.

At the in-side of his tent, they get comfortable at his small table. On a more serious note, he begins to tell her about how much he's missed her and their long friendship. Roobyee knows more is going on with Sheppard than she says, easier to play along, one thing about Sheppard, things were anything but boring. Deceptively, she in return tells Roobbye, it was much too long ago and that she is more interested in his now well being. Oh, how he loves this woman, even when she's in deep over her head she's beautiful even if she is crafty. Of course, he buys it, as all men in love with beautiful and intricate women do. The two longtime friends, eat and drink talking for hours.

Sheppard tells Roobbye, about the wager she and her sister Libra, had made to settle a small matter of difference. Whosoever gets up first in the morning and shoots down the North raven at the first sound of the morning bell, wins. Roobbye, having to drink much of the wine no longer cared about, who was releasing the morning raven or why? In his condition, it didn't matter that Sheppard had fabricated the story to suit a private agenda. Only that he is the best archer in his rank. All through the night, she and Roobbye, stay awake, until the darkness brings forth the morning light.

The two friends make their way to the raven's location and even though the wine was having its way with him, Roobbye is still able to shoot the fast-moving raven out from the early morning sky. With a single arrow, the raven falls dead to the earth. Roobbye exults triumphantly. Having seen many dead and living in his time he knows enough to know, the raven Sheppard had asked him to shoot down was no more than a message-carrying courier. Roobbye doesn't have to be sober to see when Sheppard pulled the message out from behind its wing before asking him to bury it. Something is odd, he'll wait … it's only a matter of time before she trips up again. He gets the feeling she has again tricked him.

Sheppard has not only tricked Roobbye, but set in motion an action to endanger not only the life of her Warlord sister Leoha but that of her beloved brother, Dicious. The army at the outer limits of the Black Forest awaiting orders to help them would get none. The army was scheduled to enter the Black Forest one hour after to assist Leoha and Dicious, in eradicating the evil ones. The needed help never comes. Blinded by her revenge Sheppard doesn't register the harm she will cause Dicious whom she loves. After Roobbye, finishes the so-called urgent matter for Sheppard, he returns to camp. He needs to sleep before his next shift.

Sheppard is back in her chambers where she reads the dead ravin note, only to weep for her mistake. The order she intercepted was also scheduled to assist her beloved brother, Dicious. To pacify herself she burns the note down to ashes while revising another plan to leave the Kingdom under the cover of darkness. Should there be any question asked, about the missing raven, she would be in the clear and the focus would be elsewhere. With the help of her close confidants, she again disguises herself and can pass as one of the kitchen cleaners. Once the way is cleared, her contacts hide her again in one of the large outgoing garbage baskets. With their help she able to make it to the outside. Through a secret passage in the thick walls, they pass her through. Now dressed like a food laborer she again is helped through the forest without anyone ever knowing she is Princess Sheppard. Beyond the forest, beyond the hills, mountains, rivers, and over the Saxon streak in through the valleys she stays alert. Thereby the river of Uttula, she comes to a stop.

Sheppard On Her Own

For the first time in her life, Sheppard finds herself alone and her eyes behold a way of life among commoners she had never seen or experienced before. Her will is strong, continuing to move on she finds herself disgusted with looking like a boy, and the advantages make it easier to ask directions. She makes it to the other town, there some of the commoners find her behavior somewhat odd for a boy. Others looking at her just keep their opinions to themselves, but most talk with their eyes. With further instructions, she makes it into the next town. To make her situation better, she covers up her face. Covering her face only exasperates the situation because face covering is not a custom among the locals. Resigned to her fate, she finds out parading around like a street boy is not an easy task. Her journey has been long and arduous, she is tired and at times her tiredness makes her regret ever leaving the Kingdom. On the side of the road, she finds a comfortable rock to sit on, there she begins to regret what she has done.

A lady on a horse cart with two little children on the back comes along the dusty road. The family stops offering her a ride into the next town, which she is most grateful to have. Finally, she makes it into the small town of Nindavva. There she is given directions by the locals on how to get to the house of Lady Urobeha. After toiling the streets for some time, she again becomes frustrated by the lack of results. Again finding a comfortable spot on the side of the road there she begins to eat and drink the last of her food.

The Undaunted King Gouddaa of the Arawaks and Caribs

Out from elsewhere comes a ragged looking small child with hands out wanting some of her rationings. To makes matters worst she has to turn herself away from him to enjoy the rest of her remaining rations. The quiet causes her to turn, maybe he left now she won't have to offer the little beggar some of the little she had left. But to her surprise, he is still their hands extended. He didn't get the message, instead, he crouches down taking a seat on the ground against her back. Now sitting back to back with the little beggar, she ponders the situation. At a loss with him, she turns and shares the last of her rationing with him. This makes the little beggar so happy, she has made a friend. Her new little friend rambles where and how to find the house of Lady Urobeha. Using the little beggar directions, she makes it to the front door.

Composing herself Sheppard better fixes herself before knocking. From within a voice out loud, shouts! Inside an old man yells to be left alone. "Go away! Go away! leave us alone! We have nothing more to give you!" The low pitched voice is not Urobeha. She senses she ought to leave, she feels the atmosphere is charging up to get ugly, but it's too late. The door swings open, standing on the threshold holding a broom above his head is a little man ready to swing. By the looks of things, he means business, his face drawn and angry, attacks ready to bash whoever seeks to enter. The old man mumbles out loud raging, "I'll kill you all! You." Sheppard slowly steps back, looking at which way to run. Again the old man accuses her, "You come because of them? I'll kill you! No, no nothing more." Feebly he steps forward wavering erratically, he swings his broom missing her by far each time. Sheppard not knowing what to do, runs for it, leaving her things behind. When she gets to the corner of the house, looking back she finds the old man is still in hot pursuit. Pressing, she runs to the back yard and into a dirty shallow water pond she stops. So does the old man, not wanting to enter the dirty pond. Sitting beside the pond laughing is the old man's daughter. She can't believe her eyes - her father is chasing after a young boy in the pond with that old broom of his. Laughing hysterically, she finally takes notice of the skinny looking boy in the dirty pool wading back in forth to avoid her papa. Out loud to her father she yells, "Father stop! I don't think he is one of them! He is so skinny! I think he may just want food but we don't have anymore. Leave him and I'll send him away."

Sheppard is out of breath, puffing, out the corner of her eye bent over prostrate, gasping she looks at who is talking. She knows that voice, with a ragged breath, Sheppard screams out to her, "Urobeha, help. . ., help me." Urobeha does not recognize the voice at first, looking closer she focuses on how the boy knows her name. Standing up, through squinting eyes she tries to recognize the face but can't because the face is dirty and covered. To the boy in the pond, Urobeha asks, "Do I know of you?" Stunned for a moment Sheppard realizes it's because of her head-covering Urobeha can not recognize her. Quickly removing her headpiece to reveal her face and long black hair. Urobeha instantly recognizes it is Sheppard. She runs immediately into the pond of dirty water to save Sheppard from her angry father. The girls hug and kiss each other. Urobeha's father upon seeing this is stalled in question, the shrieks and prancing around of joy brings him to calm.

Out from the back door of the house come Urobeha's mother in search of her husband. Approaching him she wants to know, who is in that dirty pool, alongside her daughter. Winded he could say nothing, repeating only that, he will get them the next time. Mother knows her husband has bad eyesight. "Husband, that is your daughter and her friend you are referring to." Again he says nothing, realizing his bad eyesight just caused him to make another erroneous decision. Mother shakes her head in awe marveling in the joy on her daughter's face - something she had not seen in some time. To her daughter she cries out, "Urobeha, It's high time, you two get out from that dirty pond and into some dry clothing, now come on in."

Taking her husband by the hand, together they, one by one enter through the back door. Into the small living room of the house, they eventually gather. Sheppard remembering her bag on the outside turns to look at Urobeha, "Urobeha! my bag is still on the outside, just beside the front door." Urobeha's mother, then tells Sheppard she found it resting on the outside, and reaching down beside the front room chair she hands the small bag over to her. Sheppard, "Thank you! Thank you!"

Urobeha's father with his bad eyesight focuses his attention on the boy's long black hair, to his daughter he calls, "Urobeha? Urobeha answers, "Yes, father?!" The father goes on to say, "Who is this boy with such long black hair and unique colored skin. I may not see well but there is a brightness about him. He must not be from around here." To Sheppard, the mother asks, "Please excuse my husband, his sight is nowhere near, what it use to be." Sheppard looks at the mother, empathizing with the burden she has to bear. In few words to the mother, Sheppard responds, "I understand."

Urobeha's mother lovingly looks at her daughter to explain who is her friend? Urobeha, says nothing, her silence raises her mother to voice the question out loud. To her daughter she again insisting this time, "Well Urobeha, does your friend have a name? Even with a dirty face, her color shows. Where is she from? She's not! She's not in any kind of trouble I hope." Both girls look at each other, Sheppard head and eye movement tells Urobeha not to give her secret away. Urobeha understands the meaning of not wanting to betray her friend's confidence. Papa is tired of confrontations from the outside, outright he states, "We have already enough of that, Trouble! And we can't afford another mouth to feed."

To her mother and father, Urobeha confides Sheppard's name but doesn't elaborate on who she is. "Her name is Sheppard! An old friend from elsewhere and don't worry too much, about her eating. Whatever amount I eat, half is for her but please don't make me send her away, because I will leave with her." Astonished, Urobeha's father wants to understand his daughter's stand for her friend to stay. The peril of the times and his failing eyesight makes it fearful to provide let alone protect his family. He's not young anymore, the situation grows direr daily. While knowing, his daughter's mind is made up, there is no way he or her mother could ever change her thick and stubborn way of reasonable thinking for these desperate times.

It's because of the love they both have for their daughters, they submit to accommodate her request, Papa reminds her, "Your, room is pretty small. Are you saying, where you sleep, she also sleep?" Urobeha lowers her gaze in respect, "Not in so many words, father." Sheppard doesn't want to be a burden to any of them. "Please! If it's a problem. I don't mind sleeping on the outside." Upon hearing

Sheppard's words Urobeha, parents recognize there is a mutual bond between their daughter and this woman. Just how much their daughter cares for the outsider is obvious. They hold their tongue to say nothing more about it. Urobeha mother, looking to her daughter and at Sheppard, "Well Sheppard, welcome! And I think it's high time, you two go upstairs and clean yourselves up."

Up the stairway, they make their way to the small upper room. Urobeha, father looks to his wife, "Where did she say that boy---aaa girl is from?" Mother smiles correcting him. "Husband! She's a girl, dressed like a boy." Again he asks, "And she wants to sleep outside? These young people, I don't understand them anymore." The mother replies, "Husband! What makes you think, she really wants to sleep on the outside? It sounds incredible to him." "No wife! I don't. The danger outside is many and it tells me, she is truly not from around here." Speculations on Sheppard's origin brings many questions, mother comments to Papa, "Are you thinking, she is with those mountaineers! Robbing and killing our own people. Your thinking she's one of them! She hasn't not one bruise on her skin and that I have seen." Papa is resolved, "I was never drawing any conclusion. I was only saying. . ." Of course they will continue to discuss this through the evening. Although the times were difficult, receiving company in these parts was rare.

After the girls had bathed and dressed, Urobeha looks at Sheppard's unique clothing, in this settlement, it's sure to stand out. "You better let me give you some things more local to wear. It's just for the time being and I'll hide those for you. You must fit in, even if you can't, you could look it." Sheppard smiles out to her and agrees. After a change of clothing, they both returned to the downstairs.

On the small dining table is little bread and water. The family graces the table and finishes the bread. Sitting around the table in talks, Sheppard finds out Urobeha, has a little sister named, Cllay. Visiting with her grandmother she will soon return home in a few days. While the talks go on, the long journey begins to weigh on Sheppard's tired eyes. The girls excuse themselves returning to the upstairs room. There Urobeha, tells Sheppard, about the robbers now living in the mountains, how they come down at will to rob and pillage the villagers of food and clothing. Eventually, their young love ones also began to disappear.

There are two pallets in the room, one belonging to Urobeha's little Sister, Cllay. Sheppard's tired eyes can stay open no longer, moving over to the small bed, she finds it very comfortable. Resting her tired head down on the small pillow, minutes later Sheppard is fast asleep. Urobeha, calls it a night, the Princess is in her house.

In Sheppard's dreams, she envisions a white horse with a rider moving up the mountain, as much as she tries to see the rider's face, she could not. High above the rider in the sky is a white raven. Out from the sky, the raven spirals plummeting to the earth. Sheppard awakens drenched in sweat, the memory of the dream shakes her, she is consumed in fever. With the help of Urobeha and her mother, she is given medicine and falls back asleep. Much later her eyes open, she is on a much higher bed in the same room. Over here, a small child sits watching her. To the little girl, watching so attentively Sheppard says, "So why are you looking down over me like that?" Quickly pulling her face away, the child's toothless grin sparks in delight that she is now awake.

"Where did you get that skin from? When I first came in, you were glowing. Are you some kind of angel?" The little girl inquires, inquisitive to know all about the strange skin woman resting in her room. For a minute Sheppard's eyes hurt to open, roaming the room slowly, she didn't remember ever getting up now on another bed in the same room. To the little imp watching her, she has a good idea who she is, Cllay. Smiling weakly Sheppard said, "Are you an Angel?" Wide-eyed the little girl perks up in response, quickly shaking her head she says, "Angels, don't look like me." Sheppard's eyes are still painful, she shuts them temporarily, saying to the little watcher, "So, have you see Angels before?" Drawing back, she contemplates what the lady laying on the bed is saying. Cllay gets up suddenly and walks over to the chair across the room and she takes a seat. The child's sudden distance and quiet considerations leave Sheppard not really knowing what to make of the little girl's actions. Maybe if she takes the initiative to take the lead, she might start her talking once again. "Hey, You must be little Cllay?" Sheppard winces from the discomfort she feels, it wasn't that long ago that she was recovering in the healing chamber.

Cllay cocks her head to one side, smiling with her lips pursed together hiding her missing teeth. Breaking her silence, "My sister has spoken much about you so I know why you are in my bed. She said, you are tired like the old people, who need rest so I can't talk too much to you. She also said I must give you water and there is your water above your head." From her seat, she points out at the water mug resting just above the bedhead. The little girl is sweet and yet so different. Sitting up, Sheppard tells her. "Well, am saying… I am now awake and it is ok for you to speak. Why don't you come, a little closer? Sit by me." With a wide smile, the little girl drags her stool beside Sheppard's bed.

Exuberant she introduces herself to Sheppard, the little watcher is exactly where she wants to be. "Yes! My name is Cllay, and I am Urobeha's sister, and we have just again been robbed by the men from the mountains. My sister hates the men in our town. I forget what she calls them because they do nothing about it. They just let the men from the mountains keep robbing us all. Oh, I remember now what she calls them, cowards, yes cowards. Now, what is coward, do you know?" It hard not to like the little watcher, she's not only intelligent and clever but very entertaining, Sheppard chooses her words carefully answering Cllay, "Well I think! Who and whatever coward is, according to your sister is in this village. We all lack courage at times and a lot of us make it up by having a little more courage in other ways."

Cllay tried putting it all together but could not. To Sheppard she said. "Ok! So. . . aaa coward is someone without courage." Sheppard responds, "Well! It's really someone who has not yet turned on their courage button. Happily, Cllay said, "Now I understand. So what is your name?" "I thought you would never ask! My name is Sheppard. Cllay mulls over, "Sheppard is a beautiful name. My dad said, he ran you away because he thought you were another of those robbers. And why were you dressed like a boy? Is that also what you call coward?" Sheppard smiles at her, "I bet! Your parents didn't say that one." It's a bonding moment between the little watcher and the Princess. Sheppard doesn't have many opportunities to relate to small children. She hasn't had much to smile about in a while, embracing the occasion. Sheppard looks at little Cllay. Such uniqueness, and brilliance she finds much favor in the little girl. Once again Sheppard explains. "As for me being dressed like a boy, that's a long, long story."

Cllay rolls her eyes, just when she thought Sheppard was not like the other older folk. Cllay interjects "Are you saying! You wish not to talk anymore?" She starts to give her usual vague answer but the astute eyes staring at her accusingly force her to concede, "No! No! I don't mean it like that. When will your sister be back?" Crossing her arms over her small chest, Cllay speculatively answers, "I don't know. My mother told me, they raised your bed because of the dry mildew on the floor so I have to sleep in their room until you leave. It's been two days now, actually, three so when are you leaving because I would like you to stay. I like you! You remind me of my other sister Meiha. I never really met her but my mother said she is beautiful as you. She left us before I was born. Mother said she is working in a faraway kingdom, somewhere in the north."

Sheppard recounts Cllay's information on the number of days she had been out with much concern. To little Cllay Sheppard asked, "Then how long was I...? Before Sheppard could finish, Little Cllay said, "Today will be your third day and that is why your body is so weak. You need to eat. There is only bread on the table mother said. Mother also say bread is good because it will keep you alive and mothers know best. Sheppard shakes her head in agreement, mothers do know best. Agreeing with Cllay, "I think she's right. It will keep us alive."

Sheppard bathes and robed herself, Cllay stays with her. After finishing her ablutions together, they move to the downstairs table, where bread is set out for them to eat. Cllay reaches the table first taking her seat. She is a proper little hostess, breaking the bread together - they eat it with fruits and dried nuts.

Soon after Sheppard finishes the last of her drinking water, Urobeha's mother, and father come rushing in through the front door. Taking their usual seats out in the small sitting area oblivious to her presence their faces are drawn in the discomfort of thoughts each is burdened by. From the table Sheppard walks over, their stoic expressions forebode something harsh and unpleasant has occurred.

To Urobeha's mother, Sheppard asks, "Mother? What is so wrong? And where is Urobeha?" Mother sits silent and despondent, this causes Sheppard to look at Cllay for answers. Cllay reaffirms the fears of her parents, "It's been three days and nights, and sister has yet to return. Mother and father are afraid that her faith has already been sealed by the robbers staying in the mountains."

With that said, Sheppard looks back at Urobeha's mother for confirmation. "Mother, no. no. . . that cannot be. Where is she? Where did she go?" Urobeha's mother feels a deep concern, which Sheppard has for her daughter, standing up looking into Sheppard's eyes she consoles with a calm face, "Young one, this is none of your affairs." Weary and tired Sheppard has only just awakened to the dread she and her husband have prayed would bypass them. Watching Urobeha's mother breaks Sheppard's heart, here is a woman of strength despite of the odds. Unknown to Sheppard, she starts to glow before Urobeha's mother. The glory of her royal bearing righteously manifests. If mother knew who Sheppard really was she'd have no fear. Her friend is in trouble - it will not be easy. "Mother, I am here only because of her. Where is she?" Sheppard reiterates to Urobeha's mother and father, the extent of her concern for their daughter.

To mother, Sheppard reminds her, "Mother, you fed me when I was hungry. You draped me with your own garment when I was sick. I am not only grateful but also thankful." Sheppard drops to her knees before Urobeha's mother. Astounded, never having seen such a strange custom and behavior mother helps Sheppard back up on her feet. This latest news has Sheppard in arms, pained to know her closest confidant in her weakened state of unconsciousness has been absconding. To have searched so long to find her, to have her there only to be ripped away does hurt to Sheppard.

Strange, because of Sheppard, emotional hurt. Urobeha's mother begins to see a glow forming around Sheppard's aura, which makes even her husband stand tall to his feet. Urobeha's, mother breaking down, cries, "We tried, but we could not stop her. She went in search of our lost goods and a peaceful solution, to stop further damages to us and the village." Sheppard again turns to Cllay who is still sitting, watching from her seat at the dining table. Cllay confirms everything allaying the course of events, "About four months ago, A group of men, I think they are called warriors because of their size." Suddenly with constricting anger, Urobeha's father cuts in, "They are not warriors! that they are not! They are only robbers and thieves and killers, who feed on the weak. They have robbed this village over and again and taking at will.

"At first it was the food and vegetables, then we notice one or two of our own were missing and now more and more of our young women are being taken by those idiots, just like my daughter is missing because the village people are all too afraid. It's not that we can't fight, people don't want to fight. I have been fooling myself for some time now. The truth is! We do not know how to fight and the people don't want to fight. We have always lived a peaceful life. It was handed down to us that way from our forefathers but now all the other surrounding town people call us cowards and cowards we may truly be, by the standard of my daughter. She could not even find two brave men to go up the mountains with her. We are not brave enough! That is why we couldn't even take her half the way up the mountain. We all got scared and we left her and ran back down the mountain. There is no shame in being cowards, the shame is in others who notice it." Sheppard hears the integrity of his words of courage and defeat.

These peaceful natives need a champion to herald their plight against the invading marauders. For a fragment of an instance, Sheppard wishes her warlord sister Leoha was here, but this one on her, it's her friend. "If you don't mind me asking, who runs this town? Who are those in charge?" Father not wanting Cllay to further embarrass the town people answered, "Please try and understand us! This town is run by peaceful people in peaceful positions in this peaceful place at the bottom of the mountain. And though my sight may not be as good as yours. I estimate, there are about three hundred of them and they require many provisions to sustain them and the only things which are of value to them are in this village and that is why! We don't want you to go outside." Nodding her head, she accesses a possible strategy, "From your words. I gathered there are no authorities here, only peaceful people, in a peaceful position, in this peaceful place, which is no longer peaceful." Happily, the father complies, "Now you get the picture little one. You got the picture." Hands raised, looking up, consumed in grief he cries out, "My daughter, my daughter, my daughter. Why do you have to be the one to sacrifice yourself. Why you?" Sheppard not knowing what to do looks at his wife for help. Mother gently consoling guides her husband back down to his seat. Little Cllay walks up to Sheppard giving her a cup of water to hand over to father. Taking little sips, he becomes calm again. Sheppard looks at little Cllay, sitting back at the table nodding to her no words of gratitude is needed. Cllay, as young as she is, is wiser than her years. Wishing there was more she could do, this feels worst than the beating Leoha put on her. Hopeless and helpless, Sheppard caught in the void of emotions, everything begins to spiral again, choking her, closing in on her. In denial shaking her head Sheppard runs back up the stairs into Urobeha's room, on the bed she falls in tears.

Not soon after, Urobeha's, mother enters the room, stifling her own tears. Her pain can't be more than what Urobeha's mother is feeling right now. This brings Sheppard to her feet, together they embrace wiping away many tears. To Urobeha's mother, Sheppard reflects. "She is out there all alone, and I feel so helpless because of things I have done in the past. I feel so confused about it all," Sheppard cries. They are both suspended in the same hurt of pain, crying under the weight of imagined possible afflictions their loved one may be enduring. With growing words of encouragement, they comfort each other. Out of respect to Sheppard, Urobeha's, mother said, "Whatever those things are which you did, they must have brought you here for some reason. We all have dark spirits behind our clothing and to live a better life, we must at some point face up to the things we have done don't you think?" The way she speaks reminds Sheppard of what she did to her warlord warrior sister Leoha.

Sober memories only serve to personify the present circumstances, Sheppard reminisces, "Your words remind me of my sister. She usually talks to me that way. But still, Urobeha is out there and up against so many. Please, make me understand. Why would she do such a thing? Why would she? For what it is worth Urobeha's, mother tries to justify Urobeha's actions. "Just maybe, It's for the same reason you did what you had to do. My daughter somehow never liked this village, nor the villagers. And for whatever her reasons are! I may never know. She calls them all cowards despite their so call positions and their peaceful way of life. But our peaceful ways are what set us aside from all the other surrounding villages. I think in some strange way, they all admire us because we can live in peace with each other despite our small differences and they cannot. Lately, the town has seen its fair share of strangers and they bring with them their violent culture. My husband doesn't see so well, but his little courage makes up for his loss, and as for that group of killers in the mountains. There are about four hundred of them." The number of warriors in the mountain is formidable, giving even more cause for concern. Urobeha's, life stands in jeopardy if she is still alive. Sheppard utters, "Four hundred."

Urobeha's mother pleads with Sheppard. "Yes! That is why you must! You must keep safe and do not stay out after dark. You have the most beautiful skin - I have ever seen on a person. Who are you?" Sheppard does not recognize her skin to be that different from any others, "Just one, who is born different and am also working on your question." As Urobeha's, mother turns to leave Sheppard says, "Thank you! And it's not so much my safety which I am concerned about. But that of your daughter. You see, mother. It tells me, her courage alone out weights the four hundred and those in this village."

Sheppard's words are direct and appeal deeply to Urobeha's mother's troubled heart. Mother turns back to Sheppard, "My daughter has always believed, we are all born special and for a special purpose we are all here. And it grieves me deeply and you will have to forgive me for my abstract words because it is the only way. I could have peace within my heart so that I can justify my daughter's stupendous ways of thinking. I too want to know. Why, would she do something like that. How could she value herself to go up alone against four hundred strong warriors? They will kill her or stretch her to no return and that I cannot live with."

Granted a first-hand view of a mother's unfailing and unflinching love for her child, the mother walks away leaving Sheppard to weep on her own.

Absence of the King

In the absence of the mighty King Gouddaa, his daughter Libra sits on the throne. The royal adviser walks in to present a local matter before the King. The King looks on indicating to him, go on, "Adviser you may continue." The royal adviser announces, "My King, on the outside are two parties left. Would you like to address them at a later time?" The King looks him down, and says, "That won't be necessary. Please do send in another." While the adviser turns to leave, to him the King calls out. "Adviser stop." He stops, anticipating the matter of concern. Before turning to the King, he fixes himself. The King calls out to him, "Adviser." Bowing his head out of respect the King goes on to say, "For future matters such as these, I am entrusting you and the second minister to gather a committee of four and any matter which the committee is unable to deal with, shall be presented to the first ministers of the throne and should the first minister fall short, the matter then shall be referred to the throne." The adviser affirms, "I shall have it all written up by evening." More surprising to him, the King said, "That is unacceptable. Please get to it after you finish here." The adviser understanding his duties, "It shall be dealt with as ordered." Leaving quickly he returns with a young lady, who wants the King to hear her case.

Before the adviser takes his position, he leans into the young lady and whispers in her ear, "You have better choose your words carefully before the King." He continues, the young lady is not up to the task of speaking directly to the King. The adviser's words bring no comfort to her at all. From the throne, the King looks down at the frail-looking young lady standing in her midst. The condition of her clothing tells the story she is not from around here. Thinking about it, her eyes resemble that of another the King once knew, the King makes no mention of it. When the young lady realizes she is all alone and surrounded by so many guards, she begins to panic, breathing heavily. She tries to contain herself, her knees shaking gives her away. The King lets her know, "You may begin young lady."

Frozen in panic, losing her courage only her tears answer the King. The King seeing her mishap, say nothing. The young lady tries again to compose herself but her feelings of unworthiness make her choke for a second time. She stands lost for words. To better assist the young lady, the King orders she be taken out at once and placed into one of the holding rooms. The young lady does not understand the King's instructions - she thinks her death has been ordered for wasting the King's time. Quickly looking to escape, again panicking she runs toward the exit. Stopped by the spears of the guards to her throat, she passes out to the floor. The young lady is carried out and placed into one of the holding rooms beside the courtyard. A short time later, she awakes in a room reserved for royalty, filled with eats and treats like she has never seen before. With all she could ever need at her fingertips, she digs in having her fill until she could eat no more.

After the young lady had been taken away, the last person was bought in late. The soldier had to explain why he was where he should not be according to in house protocol. Standing on the commoner's line Roobbyye knew this was the fastest route to seeing the King. The young soldier had not really broken the in house protocol. He finds favor with the Adviser in the clever way he handles his business. The soldier is then allowed in to see the King. After looking over the young soldier standing fully dressed in his uniform the King said, "Young soldier. Your Armour fits you well." The young soldier is pleased, "Thank you my King, but it's me Roobbye, Sheppard's friend."

Attentive now the King looks at him. He is the Roobbye, she remembered and to him, the King asks, "Roobbye, approach." When Roobbye, reaches the last step to the top where only the King sits, he is abruptly stopped by four of the throne's hidden elite guards, weapons at his throat. The speed with which the elite guards execute their impeccable and flawless duties makes the King's throne irreproachable. To the elite bodyguards of the throne. The King consents, "Let him pass!" And as quickly as they appeared they are gone. The King sees the discomfort on Roobbye, face. To Roobbye, the King said, "Roobbye, please be at ease and come with me." She removes her crown and leads the way into one of the many hidden chambers under the throne. Roobbye follows stunned by the amassed artworks on the chamber walls.

As a youngster, he remembers visiting the King's chambers, before his father passed away he was one of the King's top advisers. But he didn't recall ever seeing or entering such chambers as these before. The marble walls are embedded with streaks of gold, silver, emeralds, and pearls. It's impressive, that for a minute Roobbye, loses the focus of his artistic eye, and love for beauty captivates him. The King is amused by Roobbye's reaction not many who are allowed to view the display of artistic opulence aren't left enthralled by its brilliance, clearing her throat he composes himself sheepishly smiling at his gawking. Another stunning blow awakens him as he looks at the woman of bearing standing before him.

Roobbye can't believe how much Sheppard and the King look-alike, sisters unmistakable with slight differences. He remembers her, he wonders if she recalls who he is? "My pardon! Without your crown, you now look more like the Libra I remembered, and thanks for seeing me without proper protocol." The King gives him a twisted smile, "And that was brilliant of you to have gotten in line with the outside commoners." Lowering his head a little embarrassed he smiles weakly, "Well. . . am really sorry about that, but the protocol can be slow at times." Libra looks him over summarizing auditing her reports in her head about his service performance, "Roobbye! You have grown and I have heard the top of your class. Gladly Roobbye takes advantage of the opening, "Yes, aaaa, that and Sheppard is why I am here."

The King's curiosity is piqued, what has her sister done now? In a demurely fashion Libra confides to Roobbye, "She has not been seen for quite some time now. I think it must be because of her recovery, she is staying away." Right away Roobbye elaborates the concerns of

The Undaunted King Gouddaa of the Arawaks and Caribs

his obligation. "No, no. It's not that at all, and am afraid where ever she is, she may need help. The report about a raven not showing up in the north is my fault. Sheppard came to me about a wager made between her and yourself. At first, I thought nothing of it, but as time passed a soldier must be at ease."

Libra mediates for a moment on the report Roobbye brings to her. The surprising news about Sheppard's fib fills in the blanks in a report long sent in by the unbeatable general Nemmissis. How dare she, the King is not pleased with Sheppard's actions but is appeased, that Roobbye, has come forward to clear up the abnormalities stated earlier as to why the army failed to respond. Relieved, and concerned Libra puts on the crown of duty to find her. "Roobbye! Thanks for bringing this to my attention. She is a princess so I rather not this news gets out. Please say no more about it. I shall release the four falcon and her raven into the sky, and I will have her found, where ever she is. And when she is found and return, you are to come back and see me. Your further duties shall soon be beside her."

Libra sees Roobbye out, before going on to visit the young lady who earlier stood before the throne. There are four guards on the outside of the young ladies holding quarters. Upon her arrival, she dismisses the guards from their duties. On the door, she knocks. The voice from within the chamber gives her permission to enter. "Please enter." Libra enters. By the look of things on the eating table, the young lady had had her fill and is now restored in strength and courage. Libra walks up to the young lady and is greeted by a bright smile of gratitude. The King looks at the young lady, "I hope our accommodations have made you more relaxed."

The young lady takes a closer look at Libra. She looks like the lady from the throne. "Yes, they have. Are you also the lady from the throne?" Libra, smiles with an acknowledging nod, "Yes! I am." Surprised by it all the young lady exuberantly stands at attention to be in the presence of the King. "You are also the King?" A woman King is an appointment Libra holds dearly, "At least, until my father returns" The King, Libra lets the young girl absorb and take it all in. Her head and eyes, begin to roam around equating the marvelous accommodations with the King standing before her. This lady lives in all this splendor, all this was hers, it was all hers. Her focus of attention comes back to Libra and she can't help but comment, "It's so beautiful in here and I feel so much at peace with myself but this is only a dream. When will I awake?"

As the King, Libra has seen so many destitute citizens from outside of the Kingdom come for an aide or seeking asylum, her compassion empathizes with each of the prevailing conditions from her words, Libra gathers the young lady is heavy laden with an issue of complaint. To focus her on why she came. Libra said, "I have seen from the report! You go by two names. Which one would you have me use? The one or ark." The young lady has never imagined such accommodations existed she can't help looking around at the good manner of things in the chamber. Again she loses her focus and Libra has to call back her attention.

With humble innocence, the young lady is elated by the comfort of grace the King shows her. To Libra, she desperately appeals, "No, no one has ever shown me so much respect. Why do you care?" Libra wants to make the young lady better understand. "Judging from your clothing, you are not from around here and it is only proper to show persons like yourself good manner but right now I need you to stay focus." The young lady nods her head in affirmation and goes on to explain, "My brother said. I am only to ask you to look deeper into my name and you will understand. I am not the message only the messenger." From within her waist cloth the young lady withdraws a paper. Libra examines the young girl's message and her names. It makes her heart drop one beat and she takes the seat in front of the young girl to better comfort herself. For her message had taken Libra back to a time and place, she had over and again tried to erase its memories from her mind but could not. The secret behind the message is truly worthy of her time and she takes in that deep breath of fresh air before gathering her thoughts.

To the young lady, Libra said, "Your message comes as a surprise, and the messenger is an even greater surprise. Thank you! The ark one! Well! I don't wish to ask, how is he because it is for that reason you have come and now I do understand the resembling I earlier saw in you." Libra, slowly rises from her seat, and to the young lady King Libra, asks, "Who exactly are you?" Absorbed in past thoughts, Libra slowly begins to walk about in the room to better situate her mind.

Up to the young lady, she walks, knowing she has more pressing matters pending that will need her attention. She wants to finish this expediently, but matters of the heart are always given first prudence over one's mind, it's never simple.

The King reminds the young lady, "You are a woman as I am. The only difference between us is where I am and where you come from. Your duties have brought you here, and my duty is here. What I am saying is we are both laborers but is your labor any different from mine. Please go back and tell him from the day I told him never to return. It was for my own good and since then. I have never left him out of my dreams, he has long won my heart from the first time I first saw him but he would never be able to touch my flesh, ever again. The message is in the labor." Libra tries to hold back burning tears, the wet of her glossy eyes shimmers. The resurface of touching moments can not be barred, as much as she tries to hold back her feeling, she can not hold back her heart. The young lady realizes her message has opened an old wound, the King's heart is damaged as a result.

In lowness of remorse, she drops to her knees before Libra, earnest in all honesty she apologizes, "I am so, so, sorry about this. I had no idea you still love him as much as he still loves you. Where I am from, we hear much about the wisdom in the house of Gouddaa. And after meeting you, I do now understand, why the ark-one still love you so. Rejection is sometimes hard and painful and can become even harder, and more difficult when you're the one being rejected. He explained that although you both love each other divisions bind you both to principles. We of the ark-one, the family have lived being rejected by so many others and only because of our last name, we are treated like animals, and rejects, only because of something others did before us. They curse us! Are we not like others? Do we not have needs and desires? I am so tired of being treated, like being less than nothing."

"My grandparents still live in what remains of a Kingdom, once surrounded by four gigantic walls in the middle of a no man's land. I still don't understand, why and what keeps the surrounding grounds and the large apple tree so green throughout the many cycles of the moon. And though there are some remaining guards, thanks to my brother the ark-one. For his contribution, was just enough to keep us and a few others alive. If not looters would have killed my grandparents long ago. So now, you know the ark-one story, and thank you."

Later Libra, helps the young lady back to her feet, she reconsiders a moment, she has always known the ark-one story but not painted in such detail. Still, for the ark-one, his rejection and her loss remain the same. As the King, Libra bestows favor, by granting the young lady privilege to know her name. "My name is Libra and it was good to have meet you." The young lady is relieved and pacified by the King's gentle manner, meekly she thanks her again, "Thank you for being the King you are! And I hope, that I can make the ark-one understand things the way you do."

Urgent matters of the throne serve to align the objectives and focus of crown duties. Libra, concludes, "Come with me, so we can make provision for your return. I don't have much more time, due to other pressing matters so please come quickly." Quickly they moved to the throne room. There Libra summons one of her father, Grand-Varese.

The Grand-Varese, although old in years is young in spirit. Having been out from active duty for some time he is always ready and prepared to be called back into service. As ordered he shows up before the throne, ready and prepared for war. His metal suit no longer fits him and his sword and spear have grown heavy. The King looks out at him standing in his armor brave and bold. Standing like glory days of old like a once-mighty soldier, the young lady looks at him and his looks make her smile. The uniform has aged the looks outdated have long been forgotten. The ancient habiliment is strange to the day, the King takes great notice, detached in observation the King declaims, "Grand-Varese!"

It feels good to be back in the station of authority after being away on hiatus. Straight away snapping to attention, the Grand-Varese salutes reporting to duty. For an instant, the King is puzzled by his antics, "What is he doing? Who let him in the hall with all these. . ." To him, with patience, she again said, "That won't be necessary and neither are your weapons and shield." Removing them from his tired arms they drop hard to the marble floor, and the King says to herself, "What the? This idiot just broke the marble floor." CLANG! PING! And all his other hidden weapons he tosses out to the ground. The room stands still in silence, this is who the King called for?

With a firm stand, that could not last much longer, to the King he replies, "Ready for active duty my King!" The King realizes he has not changed with the times. She outright commands. "Soldier be at ease." At ease, he responds, "My King! I know you are only fore-filling your father's promise. And for this! I am so grateful to be able to serve the throne one last time, for I and your father have." The King thinks to herself, not only is he old but long-winded in explanation, Libra cuts in on his speech. "Grand-Varese!" He stops to hear the King speak as she puts things back in perspective. "Yes, I did say, I would be needing you again. And the records show before you became Grand-Varese, under my father's rule you were." Proud of his long years of achievements in service he forgets the King is speaking and he cuts it on her talks declaring, "I was gatekeeper for all food supplies!"

King Libra reiterates with urgency to the Grand-Varese, "The Storage Gates must be open once again."

He Knows What That Means

He knows what that means. Libra hands a royal pass to him and presents the young lady, along with his orders. At first sight of seeing her a rejuvenating awareness reminiscent of his earlier days of vitality creeps back into his life. Gently he takes the hand of the young lady and off they go.

The royal pass is a symbol of absolute power and authority it allows him to do everything his way. He gives the orders to have things ready in swift time. High in the pride of his strength, he demonstrates to the younger soldiers he still has what it takes. He reserves one of the fast moving chariot wagons for him and the young lady. Preforming every duty as ordered, all is in readiness to go. He gives the order to move out and they leave the Kingdom behind them. The chariot wagons travel with an abundance of food, wine, drinks, clothing, precious stones, monies, and gold.

The young lady is so very pleased, spontaneously she reaches over and hugs and kisses him on his cheeks over and again. Her exuberance is overwhelming for allowing him to be generous toward her needs. For a minute he forgets he is also one of the wagon drivers. He has been alone for some time and her kisses bring back memories of a long and forgotten time. Never the lest he is pleased to be sitting close to such a beautiful young woman as she is, and she doesn't mind his ripened old age.

His talks with her, is of love as she accepts his mischievous remarks. The many gifts have made her forget about her brother, the ark-one, who still sits in a small tavern waiting for her to return.

Across mountain, hills and valleys through Saxon streaks they travel, while she points the way home. The journey is long and arduous, her acceptance of him, has drawn her closer to him. In such a short time, the two have become good friends. He understands youth is no longer on his side so what ever else he must do, must be done now. Her joy makes him feel alive in such ways that he becomes blessed by the great God Penis. His manhood grows long and strong towards her.

The few large bumps in the road forces him to keep his eyes focused on the road ahead, and he looses the urge. In charge he could and at any time order one of the younger drivers to take his place so that he is able to relax with his prize. His pride won't let him relinquish his position, he wants to prove to the other young drivers, age is nothing but a number. Dismissing the notion, the fast moving wagons are moving at high speed. The young lady is enjoying the thrill of the high speed ride. At times he finds the fast moving six stallions a bit much to handle, but he refuses to let the young lady see his weakness.

For a price he offers the sweet young lady a job to stay with him in the Kingdom. Without first consulting her grand parent she agrees. Her life has always been nothing but endless insults of abuse, hardship, and disappointments from others. His offer is a God send. The sweet opportunity makes her think about a future and she offers him an ultimatum, never to tell or mention her last name again. He must come and collect her from her grand parent home on the next cycle of the wind if their plans are to be fruitful. He agrees. She tells him of her grandfather's dictations, he may look well, but his predisposition to always control everyone is a plague to the lives of all those around him.

Her grandfather would never agree to her ever leaving, she warns not to cross him. The under valley where she is from is held hostage to a tyrannical order of ancient rules ages lost. Her grandfather is controller of the overwhelming force maintaining its ordinances. There are fireballs set with explosion to contain and deflect any who dare venture there uninvited along the perimeters. Even more dangerous are the domes set in the under pillars of the earth filled with even more power to destroy the entire area. They have seen the evidence of those who tried to leave and those who tried to enter, their bodies or what remained isn't even enough for the vultures. It's best she leaves without him ever knowing, the chariot wagon will give her coverage and safe access in and out.

The fast moving chariots enter into the quiet desolate valley, in the middle of no mans land. The Grand Varese follows her every instruction to her home, while the other wagons follow in a straight line behind. It's sometime after; the sun is not high in the sky anymore, they finally arrive in front of a large metal gate. The wagons come to a halt one behind another. She closes her eyes, deeply exhaling, she opens her eyes to see a mirrored reflection of her own. He is watching her with the same satisfaction. They both smiled to each other as to say, (we finally made it). His happy smile is like no other and with happy speed she jumps from the wagon to the ground into the large fortress she makes her way, leaving behind the Grand Varese.

Calling out to her grandfather, she finds him sitting in his study. Her joy barely concealed is explained while hugging him. Assuaged in the exuberance of her joy, he wants to know what is it all about. Hugging him, the good news about food and wealth in abundance at the front gate brightens even his composure. Together they run to welcome the royal givers. Emerging the grand father is surprised to see his remaining guards are already assisting with the off loading. Its been a while since the grandfather has beheld so many great soldiers in one place, its most impressive. While the second in command approaches, his grand daughter runs toward the front wagon, where she left the Grand-Varese sitting.

Making her way up on to the wagon, she wants to be first, to present the Grand-Varese from the far north to her grandfather. So strange, drawing nearer to him, his smile is as she left it on his face. His smile frozen, his body is stiff, open eyes do not see her but the veil of death appears to have parted for him. She waves her hand before his eyes. He is still as ice, it startles her back and so sadly, she calls out for help. The second in command, who is now nearby leaps up onto her wagon and upon examining the situation, he gives the orders to quickly and urgently bring in the on board physician.

The physician examines the Grand-Varese confirming him dead. The young girl, so sadden by her greatest lost, faints out. She is caught by one of the other soldiers before hitting the ground. Her grandfather ask she be taken in and left to rest. The dead body of the Grand-Varese is removed and lock away to be returned to the Kingdom. The battalion schedule was set to return in a day's time but because of the untimely death of the Grand-Varese orders are soon to be given. After the platoon had off load everything, the second in command makes the announcement they will no longer make camp but return back to the Kingdom at once.

They move out, the grandfather, and his few soldiers seeing them off, wave their good bye's. The platoon is long gone when the young lady awakens in her room sadly consigned to her faith. Pulling herself up from the pallet soul weary she rises to sits down in front of the room mirror. Taking up the task to comb out her hair, in the reflection of her thoughts she recollects leaving her brother behind. There comes a sudden knock to her door, slowly she comes out of it. She knows the knock to be that of her Grand-Father, "Do come in Grand -father." He enters with a proud smile to his face. To her he said, "We can now live but where is your brother? Where is he? Was he not with you?" It is rather late in the morning, she knowing the ways of her grandfather. Making up a lie, cloaking aspects of the circumstances she weaves the tale because in the excitement of it all, she had emotionally become consumed and had forgotten her elder brother. He should still now be waiting for her on the out side of the tavern.

Go back with the young lady in care of the Grand-Varese, Libra gives the orders. Release the four falcons of death into the upper skies, to seek and find the whereabouts of Sheppard. By means of sight and scent, the four royal falcons of death, take flight to the sky. To cover the lower altitudes, she goes into Sheppard's room ordering out all the staff. Opening one of the chamber windows and she walks across the floor to where Sheppard keeps the one called Silk. From its cage she removes the dark covering and opens the cage. Upon Silk head she places her hand over the bird's eyes, when she finishes speaking to the raven, she set it free. Out through the opened window the raven takes flight into the sky, in search of its owner. Before the four royal falcons of death had taken to the sky, they had to smell Sheppard's clothing but not the raven, her scent is always with Silk.

Circling the high skies with their lightning sharp vision the four falcons, have long seen Silk from the time he had exited the window. Making itself know, Silk screams out to the four royal falcons, high above him. On the upper wind's the royal birds takes flight, reaching their final heights on the wind the four royal falcons direct themselves out and into the four corners of the earth. Stretching themselves out and across the land with lightning speed, Silk remains at a lower atmosphere. After miles and miles of traveling, Silk is first to pick-up the Princess's scent. Silk screams out to the four falcons letting them know of the position. On fast moving trade winds, the sonic of his screams echo out reaching the four royal falcons. From the four corners of the earth they answer him changing directions. The royal falcons cries are heard not only by Silk but the Kingdom and far beyond the ends of the trade winds. With lighting speed, the four royal falcons take position back across the sky, bending time and space to reach Silk, they are not alone.

Fortune Favors King Gouddaa

Fortune has it, the undaunted, Gouddaa, has long returned into the Kingdom. On Laurrennius' forehead, he places the crystal which he received from the Black Widow, immobilizing the poison. From her long, long slumber the poison is absorbed into the crystal turning it black, and she awakens. From her forehead he removes the crystal and quietly places it into his garments away from her. Her eyes first behold his blazing image, then his face comes into focus. The elation of peace on his face tells her, it's finally over. She is pleased to look upon her husband's face once again. He is the guardian and protector of the gateway back into the world of the living.

She reaches out to him, enfolding her tightly, he embraces her in his arms treasuring the fragile moment. With the help of his strength, she is made to sit up. To him, she cries "Husband! I have been asleep, for far too long!" Quoting the poetry of life, caressing her face. Dream not thy sleepless dreams any longer but bring into the light thy visions. Eager to see all that it is, "Help me up and let me have a look on the outside." She said. Ever so gently, helping her out from the bed and across to the window, it's early morning and the sun has just lightened the horizon. Before returning to the bed she watches the sunrise from where he has placed her.

Returning to her bed feebly on her weaken limbs, to her husband, she said, "Husband! It was as if, I was in a deep dream and I saw you standing. One foot on land and the other in the sea. Tell me! What is the meaning of such strange omen?" Looking at her he shares his vision, "Laurrenius! I too have seen a dream. Where I stood one foot on land and the other in the sea. The land represents the dust beneath my feet and the many, who had died beneath my feet in the Black Forest and when I looked up into the heavens. I became afraid for the sky was where the sea should be and the sea where the sky should be. And I look down at my feet at the remaining water, time as we knew it was no more." Laurrenius upon hearing his words begins to cry for the lost souls, and so sadly said to him, "Gouddaa, It frightens me so. Does it mean that drastic changes are soon upon us? Have I been awakening only to witness this unfortunate moment? Why the loss of so many lives, why?" Pulling her in, he embraces her even closer to his heart and said. "Thus it is written in the heavens. But be not afraid my love for I shall always be with thee even unto the end of the earth. My love for you shall always remain for not even the thunder in the heavens can roll away from my heart of love from thee."

Laurrennius, after hearing his true words, clutches him even closer to her bosom. While in her tears of sorrow she is still able to understand there is always the sweet, before the bitter. Just like the calm before the storm. Now Laurrennius had never kept secrets from her husband but for one. She was present and hidden in the forbidden halls at the death of the Black Scarlet. She remembers clearly each of his spoken words to her on that day and she kept the hurt and pain locked away in her heart, never again to be revealed. And from that time on, Gouddaa gave Laurrennius a time she would always remember. For he stayed with her and he enjoyed her and loved her and he embraced her as if she was his last breath of fresh air. And it comes to pass, that one stormy evening dark clouds moved in across the land. While he stared out through the chamber windows, at the many raindrops falling from the heavens, the mighty thunder began to rumble across the Earth and over the sky.

In the throws of the lightning flashes Gouddaa, recalls his promise to the Black Widow, in the forest. His mind is deep in thoughts when Laurrennius calls out to him, but he does not hear her. It's not until she calls out a third time that her voice brings him back to her bedside. "Gouddaa! What is it that troubles you so? I feel you must leave once again. Many moons ago you told me. The one person who has the power to reverse the deep sleep is the Black Widow of the forest. How is it that you now have it?" Before she could finish, Gouddaa explains, "My love. There is still so much to be known. Yes, I did it! But only to protect that life which is so dear to me. I once told you, my love, there are no secrets in this life, only unopened gateways. I was wrong about the Black Scarlet. I did not kill her. She saved my life to become the sacrificial lamb of life and she is now buried, among the great pillars of the ancestors. High above the pillars of her tomb is written." The child of hope and though she saved me, by piercing her skin with the black poison of death. She would have still died from the white poisoned dust of time. She could not have lived. You see, on her last dying breath, she asked that I save her child, hidden away in the dark cave of treasures."

Laurrennius is stunned to hear that news, "Gouddaa, surely someone else must know about the child. How would a child know how to protect it's self in the deep and dark cave of treasures and live? That's just not possible." To better appease the thoughts of her mind, he said. "It seems that besides the Black Scarlet mighty weapon. She had another secret weapon, the unseen cloak of death. I believe, she must have stolen it from the Black Widow to cover and protect the child. It's the only way the child could have survived in the deep and dark cave of treasure. Questioning him further, she, asked, "And is that child now here?"

The litany of questions weighs on him, he does not want to further trouble her with such talks. He wants to spear her of not ever knowing the truth. "Yes Laurrennius, and as one is born innocent. One innocent does deserves his or her life. For time reveals not the secrets of today but reserves and preserve its secret for tomorrow. After I had buried the Black Scarlet. I went in search of the child but I could not find the child. By some strange turn of events, the child found me. She came out from behind her cloaked robe and she found me. I wanted to leave her behind but my heart could not because her mother saved my life and begged for my forgiveness, she asked, that I will be her father like her sister Aries. Her mighty weapon was removed and taken from her tomb by Leoha. Now I am only afraid the blade and its powers may have already begun to consume her" Therein Laurrennius, begins to weep for her warrior warlord daughter Leoha.

Sheppard Revised a Plan to Go Up the Mountain

Sheppard has revised a plan to go up into the mountains to find Urobeha and bring her safely back. She is much unaware of the danger lying ahead or the risk that comes with it. The group of lawless warriors, in the mountain love women above all wealth, but their folly is, none of it is worth anything on an empty stomach. This is why they so often ravished the town of its food supply. Sheppard is cleaver, she honestly believes, she can out-think a bunch of empty-headed warriors. With a little courage of her own, she puts together a strategy that will save Urobeha and have her back home before any of the warriors can realize she is gone.

Over the next few days, while everyone in the house sleeps she will leave under the cover of darkness to gather and put in place all she may need for the journey. Stealing a horse from far away she makes it back before the others awaken. Another evening passes, it's soon time for her to make her last move. Little Cllay, having taken over her sister's empty bed begins to tell her new stepsister about one of her sister's best kept secrets. She love's Sheppard. "Long before the warriors in the mountains. My sister would at times take me with her up there and showed me a strange looking table, make out of some kind of shiny stone. You see, that was her hiding place before they came. She would often spend much time feeling and admiring the worm surface of the strange-looking table. If I remember right, she called it an altar used long ago by a group of people called the

"Wemits" for sacrificing virgins to the great God Penis. She also said because she is no longer a virgin, the table is not for her kind and I don't understand some of the things she says!" Little Cllay, continues while Sheppard sits listening. It isn't long after some time had passed, the little girl's eyes become heavy, and she yarns. Minutes later little Cllay is out cold and asleep.

It is early morning before sunrise, Sheppard is set and ready to put her plan into action. The stolen white horse she took the day before from one of the far-away barn-yards is hiding away for when she was ready. Looking over Cllay for the last time, she robed herself. Everything she needs is packed to go. Quietly she makes her way down the stairs. She must pass Urobeha's mother and father's bedroom door. They always leave their bedroom door cracked, in the event Cllay is not able to sleep.

Peeping through the cracked door, she watches Urobeha's father swat the air. He is a little bothered by the flies and mosquitoes, it's still not enough to awake him. Urobeha's mother is sleeping deeply, after a long day of work and worry, sleep is an escape. Tiptoeing past their bedroom and to the outside, she goes. Disappearing away from the house and onto the side street, she makes her way out. Into a nearby abandoned shack, there she takes another change of clothing. Running into the nearby high bushes she retrieves the white horse she stole. It's early morning and it's pitch blackout. She feels so alone, knowing there is no turning back for her now.

Up into the mountain, she rides, at times her mind tells her to go back, but she ignores it and continues on her way. The full black cape makes her appear as if only a bright head rides the white horse. The mountain pathway is narrow but wide enough for a moving wagon. From behind her, she hears the growls of a lurking mountain lion searching for his next prey. Not wanting to become his meal, she picks up speed until the sound fades in the background. Up and up into the mountain she rides before coming to a slow. Ahead through the tall trees, she sees light again slowing her horse to a trot. Getting closer, that which appeared as light are two large bonfires burning on either side of a large gated entrance.

Nearing the camp, she pulls the lace from her long black cape exposing her all-white sheer silk clothing. The black cape drops on the hip of the white horse before finally falling to the earth. A luminous white light moving through the darkness, she is watched. Hid high in a tree, a lookout sends a silent alarm to alert the other warriors. The horse of light moves at a slow pace into the camp. Silently they await her. Moving deep into their camp she passes the two bond fires at the entrance moving up ahead until she could go no further. As she comes to a stop, they gather from all around.

The cover of darkness makes it almost impossible for her to see them clearly but they can all see her. From the whites of their eyes, she can tell they are many. Still astride on horseback, she remembers little Cllay's words about the stone altar. In such darkness, she can see nothing but that which is in front of her. The warriors surrounding her sniff at her sweet scent, ready for a thirst of her flesh. Like angry wild animals in heat, not far in the distance, she hears a muffled scream. She knows the voice so attentively she begins to purvey the surroundings. Looking around, this causes the warriors watching her become more aggressive. The echoed voice is that of Urobeha, but it is too dark to see anything. Up above night clouds move to allow the moon to shed some light. Now able to see, she quickly glimpses the woman spread out on a stone table like the one Cllay, had described.

Upon the altar, warriors take positions, ravishing Urobeha's bound body. Her hands and feet are chained to four upright pillars which holds up the big structure in place. The warriors filled with lust possess, punishing her body before the great God Penis. Once more the clouds hide away the moonlight. Fired torches are being lit all around the camp. She can see them more clearly now. There is another burst of moonlight through the dark thick clouds and Sheppard's attention goes back to the lady on the altar. From one of the stone pillars shreds of Urobeha's clothing hang. The thought of so many warriors abusing Urobeha like raw meat because of the disregarded and mangled bodies of broken women horrifies Sheppard. She quickly snaps back, a warrior throws a stone hitting her directly on the forehead, it cracks her skin, causing her to slightly bleed. Scoffs of laughter and jeers taunt that she bleeds so she must be human. She is aware of the warrior code because her sister Leoha, show no weakness, they will never see her cry. Keep it together, you are a Gourddian she reassures herself.

Now the warrior, who had injured the beautiful merchandise, suffers blows as a consequence. His comrades bombard him with blows, questioning his stupidity. In defense he exclaims, she is much too bright for his eyes to see. Like a moth to the flame, he feels urges to out her light. Savagely breaking free he parries in the brawl growling he howls his desire to consume her for himself. This makes them laugh out at his foolish retort, at the top of their voices. The others tell him he should think about getting a new pair of eyes and the beating stops.

When Sheppard, first glimpsed Urobeha's on the altar. Urobeha also observed the illumination of what appeared to be a bright light coming towards her. Hope stirs in her bosom for the first time since she embarked upon the peril of this quest. Desperate to be saved, she never thought she could withstand the torments these men have subjected her to for this long. If this true light hadn't arrived when it had, her fate was sealed, she too would have been disregarded broken to the side like so many of her friends and neighbors she recognized. In her mind through groans and the scream from pounding wounds leaving her numb, she pleas, reaching out to the bright light. From the light, disoriented, the abuse, barely conscious she holds on, through the haze she hears a sweet voice calling to her, "Hold on, help is on the way." She is much too weak to answer. Her tired hand and body give in as she falls unconscious in and out beneath the pressing bodies using her. One by one sometimes two and three they spill on and pump in her. The hope of saving Urobeha, before it's too late is marginal given the surrounding warriors.

Sheppard cries out to the camp of warriors. "I am here only, to see who leads you. Where is your leader?" They say nothing but look to each other before turning their attention back to her beautiful image. Another of the warriors in the pressing crowd cries out to the others, "Is she what an angel look's like?" His dumb remark draws another warrior to pock him across the face. Others laugh out at him. Jumping down from nearby tall trees a warrior distinguishes himself causing all the others to come to a halt. This must be their leader or one in charge. He walks up to her sitting on the white horse. Circling the beast twice to get an even closer and better look at her desirous body, her clothing he comes to a stop in front of the beast. Looking up at her sensing no fear from her. With a direct tongue, he orders her, "Get down!" Turning and walking away he leaves her to oblige his request.

Urobeha's, life is at stake. Sheppard dismounts not without a little help from a few of the warriors who cannot wait to touch her skin. Gently pushing Sheppard forward, the one awaiting her, licks his lips taking in a mouth full of her luscious looks. Her bright nature will bring many rewards - he finds this a favorable development. He has a job to do and the others are awaiting his instructions. They stand face to face for some time until he has had his fill of lusting over her. The warrior from the trees lets Sheppard know she is a subject in question, "I have long been watching you! And your eyes, have told me much about you. We are not into sacrificing beautiful women like you. I must say, you do have courage Bright Skin, and you are truly a specimen to be admired. But your faith Bright Skin shall be likewise to the one you seek, laying out on that far away table! You see Bright Skin, your eyes have long told me, you are here for your friend so you need not say much more. Now, let me tell you something more about us. We seek only richness and above all women for pleasure." Sheppard scoffs giving him a sarcastic smile.

He orders the men to tie her hands and throw the rope over the nearby tree limb. With the morning sun rising, the gore of the previous night occupation is revealed in decay and filth. Unlike the dungeon chains of Leoha that once held her captive, the irony does not escape her of the dire circumstances she has now landed in. She is not afraid of them but she is concern about what they can do because of the brawn of their outer and inner strengths. Taking care, not wanting to further bruise the Bright-Skin, they pull her by the rope to a shady spot under the tall tree. They hoist the long rope over the tree limb, Sheppard does not resist. Not wanting to be further injured she doesn't put up a fight yet. When the rope is pulled, her hands glide up into the air, they secure the rope.

The warriors are all waiting with demented glee, they want to hear her scream out for mercy like the ones before her. Even more, each of them wants to have her. The one from the tree wants her whipped and tamed for her insolence so that she will remember who's in charge. Attached to his hip is a whip, and he is an expert killer with it. Sheppard's eye rivets to the whip wary of the lengths coil. She'd rather not have to taste the cut of that tail. Slowly he glides the whip through his closed hand and on examining its tightness, it fails his test. He orders one of the warriors to take it and wet it all the while looking directly into Sheppard's eyes. With a snarling curl of his twisted lips, the whip returns now flowing to his liking. The sing of the whip slicing through the air cracks Sheppard's resistance defense. The salivating lust of the warriors shines in their eyes. They know she must be broken first, made to scream so that they can relish enjoying her screams on the altar.

Well, this isn't turning out as she thought, Sheppard realizes she's in trouble. She promised they wouldn't see her cry through flowing tears of water, she utters not a sound. When Sheppard feels the first lash hit made on the ground, she screams out loud. The warriors laugh at her false bravado - snide remarks lewdly jeer her forever entering their domain. Their insults only serve to charge her courage making her stronger. When the second lash hits her across the back, she tries to be strong. Its burning heat lights into her, it's the third lash, which strangely causes her to scream out at a pitch so high, it disturbs the eardrum of the mighty Warrior Golattus in his tent.

The supreme Warrior is in his tent trying to shave with a dull knife. The disturbance makes him scratch himself and he wants to know what in the hell is going on with his men on the outside. Quickly washing his face Golattus dries it with an old towel. In concern throwing the towel to one side, he crosses the room making his way to the small tent window, quickly looking at what is really going on. Apart from the altar and the brightness of what he can assess through the many heads, it makes him take a second look.

To be exact and correct on what his eyes are seeing, he blinks rapidly. He can't help notice the woman with such brightness and agreeable skin, this is a treasure that can captivate any man. Wanting to see more of her he doesn't understand why and what a beauty of such would be doing in his territory. To the outside, he makes his way and the Gong is sound letting every warrior know Golattus, is in their midst. The pathway opens to him, and the great Warrior Golattus, comes to a stop in front of the bright-skinned woman. He takes a few steps across to the one holding the whip, his second in command. To his second he quietly states, "You should not damage such a beauty." Reprimanded the second in command, confesses, "I understand Golattus, but I was just softening her up a little before the feast."

Golattus turns to walk over to Sheppard, grasping the hem of her garment he wretches open the sheer white top exposing her sweet flesh for all to see. The crowd shouts in revelry, they love it. Her sweet taunt suckling breast brings them all to a stunned gasp and panting breath. Her beautiful bright cherry-colored nipples mesmerize them, mouths salivate to taste her. The great Golattus hands roam touching and squeezing the mounds of exquisite flesh. Pulling away, he sees how one could easily get lost in this woman. Having his fill examining what could be valuable merchandise, he steps back to his second in command. "Who is this one with such bright skin? And why is she here?" The second in command pauses not really knowing, why. "I don't know. I was about to question her before you came. She came in on that white horse." Golattus earlier noticed it on his way out from his tent. Exceptional horse flesh is always good.

The second in command has never seen anyone like Sheppard. "Tell me Grottus. If she came alone, then it must be for some reason. I have never before seen one like her. Is the other one dead as yet?" The second in command in whispered tones replies. "No! Some of the others are still working on her. She is of strong, strong nature and like every other, she too will soon pass out." Grottus looks at Sheppard for several minutes. "I think it's best to finish her off and clean down the Alter!"

His every word is heard by Sheppard - she must do something before something else goes wrong. She is not ready but she must now make a move for Urobeha's sake. Hot waves of pain from the lashing throbs with each twitch she makes, it's now or never, Sheppard cries out to Golattus, standing alongside the second in command. "Please, please. I came to see you about collecting the girl and if wealth is what you desire, just you tell me the price and I'll pay." That note strikes a cord getting Golattus attention. It takes wealth and resources to sustain the four hundred warriors he houses. He and his men are presently searching for the lost mountain of solid gold. A source said it was once owned by the late notorious old king cole. Golattus turns back to his second in command. "I believe her bindings are too tight. It may be best, you loosen them up, just a little."

The second in command heed. Golattus with a wave of his hand, causes the warriors to fall back. Sheppard awaits the next move but it is she who cries out again. Instead of her binds being loosened, Grottus tightens them even more. Again her high pitched scream echoes into Golattus, eardrum, he watches the laughter of his men growing excited because of her scream. Golattus raises out his right hand and all comes to a quiet. Turning directly to face Sheppard, "Bright skin! Now that's you have made a sound. I prefer to hear before discussing business, please aaa do continue." Before she could utter a word, the second in command slaps her twice across the face reminding her of his ruthlessness, she gets the picture. Defiant, Sheppard gives Grottus, the second in command a searing look. Grottus signals to two warriors. Into Golattus's tent, they run returning with his mountain throne. They set it down a way off, in front of the Bright-Skin, and there, Golattus takes his seat. Grottus orders Sheppard. "Now speak."

With rancor looking at him, retribution lives in Sheppard's eyes, spitting blood out her bruised mouth to the side. Sheppard says nothing but turns her attention back to Golattus, sitting most comfortably on the mountain throne. Before she could utter a word, Golattus issues a declaration. "Bright skin! If I order your death now! Do you think, aaa we would aaa still get hold of that so call wealth of yours? There it is, sensing another opportunity to get Golattus, full attention, Sheppard takes hold, baiting has caused some nibbling. "You may not get that so-called wealth but you would gain the pleasure of enjoying a Bright – Skin." The confidence this Bright-Skin show makes him pause taking reserve. Her response evokes his anger even more. He can see why she gets under Grottus skin. Something is leading him to think, she is not only toiling with his emotions but plotting for time.

A warrior's emotion is not one of their strongest attributes. Abruptly he stops mentally chortling but still, he keeps his calm, to find out more about her so-called wealth in abundance. Golattus is a giant of a man, one of great strength and prowls for battle. With a firing right hand, he commanders over four hundred warrior men. His speech impediment of stuttering does little to defray his influence but is attributed as a unique quality of his character. Abrasive, his callous and coy expression, propagates him with loftily temperamental airs. He is a warrior of victory, one who has never lost. One on fifty he takes them all on in the battle, his vicious brutality is renown throughout the region. Mothers tell stories to their children, this band of men permeates fear where ever they tread. Shrewd, cunning, and clever in tactics of battle and war, he has never missed his target.

The second in command Grottus is rumored to be even viler than he. This common bond and his forceful acts garner Golattus respect. With all the warriors focus on Sheppards red cherry colored nipples, they are aroused by the sight. It causes some to run across and join the line to mount Urobeha again who still is spread upon the altar. Urobeha is still being punished under the great God Penis, others dear not touch Sheppard before Golattus gives the order.

Deep down hidden in Golattus, is a feeling for the Bright-Skin. Bind by the circumstances, things are too far in motion. Sitting he abides to watch and wait for the beautiful Bright-Skin to soon break. No tears, her courage surprises him, she refuses to show further weakness for them to enjoy. "Bright skin! I do aaa enjoy seeing you, and I and my men would love to see more of you." Golattus's words please his warriors. "Now Bright Skin! Killing you is not the answer to your wealth! So! aaa, so I must ask! Where is aaaa this so call wealth of yours and what are you asking in exchange? After all, you did come here alone and without an army. Are you another who aaa wants that we leave the town people alone?"

With an assured plea she looks to him, and "Yes! And you shall never see me again." Golattus smiles at the supplication of her averment. "Bright skin! If I don't see you again! Then we would have no wealth. I want nothing more than to see you again. There must be more to you than meets the eyes. You, aaa you come here alone, knowing there is no way out. Now you tell me Bright- Skin! Are you truly after the half-dead?" Sheppard knows Urobeha and her life is in danger, she needs to move quickly. "Just the girl on the

The Undaunted King Gouddaa of the Arawaks and Caribs

altar for the wealth you seek. And could you please, please stop them from further punishing her?" Golattus wipes his tongue over his lips. "Only you alone can decide that, now!" Golattus looks at his second in command, who at all times has one eye always on him. "Cut her down." Grottus is not pleased but does as ordered. Cutting away all the bindings, Sheppard is pleased to finally drop her hands rubbing her wrist where the ropes held her. The grimace smearing Grottus is frightening the hidden dagger exposed sticking into her throat draws a drop of blood. Sheppard remains very still this demon is in control. In smothering fury, he then rips away all of her remaining garments until she is naked in front of all the warriors. Under the condemnation of this exposure of this low Sheppard feels she can not, a naked and defiled princess ever return to the Kingdom. How can she gain back honor and integrity from all this?

The warriors gaze upon the unobstructed beauty standing before the altar. Grottus then goes and takes his position standing beside Golattus's throne. Golattus and Grottus know there is no place for the Bright-Skin, to run. Naked the warriors erupt in frenzy at the sight of all her Bright Skin bare. Sadly, Sheppard shakes her head from side to side, looking over the madness before her. Please don't defile me she thinks to herself. A breeze blows in her ear causing her to shake out her long black hair that covers her nipples. The warriors say nothing having even more of her to admire looking further down her thighs. They have never seen before a lustrous body like hers. Frozen they can't avert their vision from the sight.

Golattus is charmed, gathering his thoughts, where could one of her nature have come from, and without an army. She is willing and ready to die for the half-dead woman upon the altar. He wants to know why and who exactly is this Bright-Skinned one? He orders some of the men to go quickly check the perimeters again for anything moving. They come back with nothing amiss. The morning light is on the earth, seeing is not so difficult now. The altar is now in her vision, far above and behind Golattus, sitting on his mountain throne. The men show no sign of heeding her request. The desire to emasculate and kill those who are still punishing Urobeha's helpless body is tangible only in thought. Sheppard's eyes fill with tears, Golattus knows why and still she utters not a cry. "Bright Skin, you aaa want to give me endless wealth for a half-dead! Now is your chance!"

Without further words to him, Sheppard removes the silver chain around her neck pulling it until it breaks free. Off the chain she takes the metallic ring tossing it to Golattus, Grottus intercedes catching it in mid-air. Looking directly into her eyes, he hands the ring over to Golattus. Golattus examines the ring, finding it to be authentic. How ironic this girl holds a missing piece to what they seek. Turning to his third in command and he gives a signal. Watchful Sheppard notes the reactions of the warrior men before her. The third in command does not move Sheppard waits for Golattus, to make the next move.

"Bright skin! The tombs of Old King Cole open with two metallic rings." Sheppard is surprised to see Golattus, possess knowledge of the metallic rings. He is even more surprised when she pulls out the second metallic ring from her finger and tosses it out to him. Fast-moving Grottus catches the next ring with displayed flare he kindly passes it on to Golattus. Examining the rings and he finds them both genuine. To validate this finding he quickly calls for an authority. Without moving them from his hand, the artificer concurs with the finds authenticity. Golattus stands up with definite assurance. Here in his possession are these rings, the two keys that will open the tomb of Old King Cole.

Golattus leans into his third in command with instruction before addressing her, he, in turn, runs off in the direction of the altar. Sheppard sighs a breath of relief, but she and Urobeha, are still not out from danger. "Bright-Skin! I have long, long been searching for the keys to that tomb of Old King Cole. But I would have never thought, they would be hidden on one such as you. This is a mighty joyful day." Golattus right-hand holds a tight grip on the rings, holding them so tightly for a minute, he can feel nothing in the grip of his hand. Shaking his head, for generations he has searched for these rings that are now in his possession. The search is finally over, he doesn't even ask Sheppard, where did she obtain the rings?

Sheppard knows she and Uorebha are not out of the woods yet, Gollatus could still renege on the exchange. He returns his attention to her with a satisfied smile. "Bright-Skin! A half-dead for endless wealth! Well, Bright- Skin! I aaa gave the orders as agreed but my men are not all finished with your friend. I would have like to do more for both of you but you aaa caught me at a bad time. She is free to go but I'am afraid she cannot move. Her courage is as great as yours and I have already agreed to her demands, me and my men would ride out at the setting of the next moon. She came without wealth or richness, only to sacrifice her body to us! The four hundred warriors and we do with her as pleased! The great God Penis showed her no mercy but like I have said! My men are not all finished and neither is you!"

Golattus's admiration for the Bright-Skin doesn't allow him to set her free. To not lose face among his men and keep the rules of engagement, he must do what is necessary. And to the Bright Skin, he again said. "Bright-Skin! Now that I have the rings. I have no more use for you." Sheppard knew she took a chance, that these brute of men would not show honor to the terms. Without fright nor fear for her life. The blood drains from her face, she's numb from it all. Without uttering a word out to Golattus, for him to hear, deeply saddened Sheppard's countenance is deflated. "I know." Grottus has been watching her intently, reading her lips he leaps into the air out at her. On landing, he smacks her hard across the face and she falls to the ground with a thud.

Golattus leaps from his throne into the air to stop Grottus, from further damaging the Bright-Skin. Not understanding what prompted Grottus's excessive act, he places his left hand on his friend's right shoulder. Restrained, Grottus stands down. Turning he looks over his shoulder at Golattus, behind him. Golattus puts the question to him, "What bothers you further old friend?" Grottus's guts tell him Sheppard is not right, "Just a hunch, about this one, just a hunch." Golattus respects Grottus apprehension because he also sensed disparities from the onset of Sheppard's appearance. Still holding the rings tightly, it doesn't matter now. "We now have it all." Golattus turns, looking down at Bright-Skin laying out on the ground. "The Great God Penis, has truly favored you!" Out loud and to his warriors Golattus cries, "Now take the Bright-Skin to the altar and do with her as please."

Barbarians, reprobate of respect. Sheppard cries for herself, no facade of emotions show. Rallied up, the warriors take her raised high above their heads. They all, want to touch her for luck and many do while passing her from one to another. They are primed to taste and probe her flesh. Another sacrifice is readied to be presented to the great God Penis. There is no way she can escape. Her brightness is first displayed for all to see and still, she utters not a word. She is carried away to be blessed on the altar, like a gift for the great God Penis. Golattus and Grottus look on, at such a beautiful specimen of nature, taken away to be serviced. They go towards the altar, pensive Grottus still doesn't like it, "Don't you find it strange, she utters not a word." Golattus reserved affirms, "I find everything about that one most strange" They leave it at that wanting it to rest, but a nagging still lingers.

Golattus does not read lips, he did not hear Sheppard, last words. (I know), Grottus does read lips and he did understand the cognition of what Sheppard's words meant. It is for that reason he slapped and pushed her to the ground. She makes him uncomfortable. Her words trigger danger to him. While they take her away towards the altar, The warriors all shout out over and again. ("All hail, Golattus, another for the altar.") ("All hail, Golattus, another for the altar.") ("All hail, Golattus, another for the altar.") ("All hail, Golattus, another for the altar.") Standing together looking out at the action. Grottus reminds Golattus, "What will you have us do with the half-dead?" Golattus looks to him, "We keep our word. The keys are in my hand and we have more than we would ever need. The tomb of Old King Cole is a mountain of gold."

Speculatively thinking Grottus, looks to Golattus and said. "How can we be certain, the treasure of Old-King Cole is still there? After all, she had possession of the keys and for all I may know, she may have already had it all removed out elsewhere and there is something about her that just doesn't add up. Golattus acknowledges." It would take many lifetimes to remove a mountain of gold! We must move fast! The sooner the better! We have already been in these parts too long and that's not good. I will be in my tent." Golattus walks away and his throne taken back in his tent.

After the warriors unchained the half-dead from the altar, they quickly push her to one side. She falls dead weight to the ground alongside the other bodies. They must make way for the Bright-Skin, and they do not want her bright liquid mixing with the unclean liquid of the half-dead. Cleaning down the altar to receive the fresh meat, they fight to get first in line. Order is restored and soon after the line gets longer. Golattus has only a chance to make seven steps ahead of him before stopping, he realizes something is not right. With speed, he turns back to Grottus, who is watching him and he too gets the feeling from seeing distress on Golattus face something is not right.

In that battle tone of voice known to Grottus, Golattus cries out to him. "Bring her back! Bring her back at one. Get her back here at once!" He orders Grottus! Never in his life has he spoken more clearly. Thinking quickly Grottus looks around for the gong master to sound the alarm but he too is with the action. So Grottus picks up a large stone and with all his might, tosses it at the big gong. He hits the target center on, and the gong echoes out across the mountain warning all to return with the Bright-Skin, at once. With the prize still high above their heads, they turn back toward the front. Grottus, urgently moves beside Golattus, standing and watching the procession return. Out of concern for his friend and leader, he looks at Golattus, for an explanation. Golattus orders, "Have her dressed and bring her to me at once!" He then continues to walk to his tent, leaving Grottus puzzled.

The warriors approach with the untouched prize still high above their heads. They are ordered by Grottus, to put her down and they do. Grottus is still staggered and as much as he tries to put Golattus's sudden change of mind together, the more mystified he remains. The warriors stand not at ease because their pleasures have been interrupted and the prize called away. They want answers, but Grottus has none to relax them. Outraged, a rude jester throws out that he and Golattus, want the Bright-Skin for themselves. Temperaments escalate, a few just refused to wait, the younger warriors turn on each other. Ignorant to their lust, they do not realize it's because of the Bright-Skin, they want blood. Grottus contains the situation, giving orders to his closest subjects. Immediately blood and death become the reward of the dissident and peace is restored. Grottus orders garments and Sheppard is clothing before being taken before the mighty Warrior Golattus.

Sheppard is bought in. From inside his tent on the mountain throne, Golattus stands up. "You have to handle things out there as I would." With a slight incline of his head, Grottus steps back to the guarded entrance. The warriors on the outside are still disgruntled with the long wait of doing nothing. Murmurs spread throughout the minions among themselves, once again swiftly it is brought back under control by Golattus third in command. Another falls dead as an example, because of it. Most of the warriors have been with Golattus and Grottus for some time. Then there are the newcomers who at times challenge the old rule, and like always, they pay with their lives. The others know the retraction is not of Golattus's nature. With their loyalty to him intact, his legion of warriors brings the others to calm by making those out of line to see. Constrained in their own will, the want of the Bright-Skin is so bad it burns from within, they must remain patient until Golattus gives further orders.

When Sheppard was first brought in to Golattus, he sat large and in charge on his mountain throne. The way he now stands, she is relieved to know his decisions could only be vital to her cause. "Bright skin! The advantages and disadvantages of being a leader is knowing the difference between winning and losing. I have the strength but you have the power. You came here alone and it aaa tells me, whoever sent you do not value your life and I believe, you don't value your own life. How much time do I have left?" It's his time to feel the pressure. To make him punish himself, Sheppard places Golattus in the same position, he had placed her.

With roles reversing, Sheppard reverberates, "That all depends on you!" This wench is setting them up, he could have doomed them all if they had continued. He's beginning to get a full picture. "Is your demand likewise?" She repeats what she started earlier, "And you would never see me again. That along with your fastest chariot." He asks, "Where am I to meet you?" Trying to be strong, her limbs are weak from being stretched and her back still throbs from the lashing." At the top of Black Beard Hill, in four hawks (four hours). Grottus guarding the door becomes even more confused. He thought

Golattus called her back to use her for collateral in the event the tomb of Old King Cole is found to be empty. If he had his way, he would not spare her life.

One of the young archers comes running, made to first stop at the door by Grottus. Before proceeding up the front the young archer makes his way but his attention is distracted by the Bright-Skins, aura. He is brought back by Golattus, a thunderous voice. "Archer! What is so urgent, it cannot wait?" The brave young archer turns his focus to Golattus. "Warrior Golattus! There is one strange-looking raven, hovering over us in the skies, and high above it is four falcons. Three of the falcons have long left the area. We have never before seen such strange things. What would you have us now do?" Immediately in a pressing tone, Golattus yells, "Go quickly and tell the others to shoot them from the sky at once! Now make haste!" In urgency, the young warrior leaves, but not before taking a last look at the Bright-Skin.

Golattus attention returns to the Bright-Skin. "You can move much faster without the extra weight of the half-dead." His remark incites Sheppard but she keeps calm. She thinks only about Urobeha's life and how soon it could be lost. Urobeha has lost a full amount of blood and body liquid and still, she fights for her life on the ground under the altar. Sheppard realizes it's now or never. She pressures Golattus to make his move. "I do not mind dying do you?" Golattus, understands her meaning, he orders Grottus to go and fetch the half-dead along with his fastest chariot wagon and put them to the front gates at once. She and the half-dead are to be granted safe passage out from the camp. Golatus steps outside for a moment, after handing orders down he returns to the inside. Later he is told by another warrior all is set and ready to go.

Though Grottus does not comprehend the motives of Golattus decision concerning the Bright-Skin and the half-dead, he obeys his orders. Having returned back to the tent, he recalls the Bright Skin words to Golattus. ("I don't mind dying do you?") He has been with Golattus long enough to know the signs of when one's own life hangs in the balance of time. With prudence, drastic measures are first taken. When Sheppard had first heard the words from the young archer, about a strange-looking raven and four falcons flying high above the camp her heart becomes thrilled. Two of the sentinels sent to find Sheppard remain behind circling high in the sky. She knows it could only be the works of the Kingdom from the throne.

A sense of relief washes over Sheppard, it's a comfort knowing Silk, has found her. It brings silent tears to her eyes as she shields her emotions away from Golattus and Grottus. Awaiting further orders Grottus indicates to Golattus, all is prepared. Sheppard, has noticed subtle changes in Golattus movements and even more in his words, not forgetting his attitude. Displaying compassion, for they are now more gentle. He seems remorseful. Never the lest she loathes him and all his warriors for what they did to Urobeha and her. They made her become someone she never thought she could be. Her demands have all been met, with Golattus issuing Grottus, a second order. It is his task to escort the Bright-Skin out to the front gate - where the chariot wagon with the half-dead is set to go.

As Grottus leads the way Sheppard tries not to look up in the sky at silk, she doesn't want Silk to give her away. Grottus noticed the screaming bird but he hadn't made the connection to Sheppard so he keeps moving ahead. Passing the shooting archers Grottus is disturbed by the bird's cries, "Shut that bird up!" Referring to Silk, continually they shoot up into the sky at the hoovering birds. Reaching the front gate, Sheppard's eyes automatically takes to the sky. At the same time, Grottus happens to turn around. The raven and the high flying royal falcons are flying at a height the archer's arrows can not reach. Useless the arrows fall back down to the earth. Sheppard knows for as long as she remains there, so would Silk. She doesn't want Silk screaming to give her away. Grottus has a hunch, the birds and the Bright-Skin, may be associated but it's a suspicion. Even if he was willing to pry further, the precedence Gollatus has embarked on defers him. Following orders, he leaves it alone.

Sheppard hobbles across to the six-horse wagon, on the inside floor lies the half-dead Urobeha balled up in one corner naked. For the last time with the malice of hate in her eyes, she turns to glare at Grottus gruesome tactic. Grottus smirks, taunting Sheppard's fortune, "I could use a pair of eyes like those to add to my collection." Holding out the eyeball chain around his neck he shows it to her. Repulsed Sheppard turns her eyes away. Golattus, has given his fastest chariot, and his best driver. In four hawks the Bright-Skin must meet her obligations to him at Black Beard Hill, as scheduled on time. Sheppard mounts the fast-moving chariot wagon with Urobeha's body on the inside. Allowed to now leave she and the half-dead are granted safe passage.

Down the mountain, the chariot wagon descends, gradually picking up speed. Urobeha is still bleeding outward from her encounter with the mountain warriors. Sheppard looks over to Urobeha who's trying to give her comfort, but the state of Urobeha seems so useless. Never the less she has come too far to give up on her now. Urobeha's body is cold with shivers, and her skin balmy. To help warm her, Sheppard tries to create friction by rubbing Urobeha's skin. It feels like all her efforts are useless, deflated she doesn't know what else to do. From outside she hears Silk, calling out for her. The chariot wagon reaches the bottom of the mountain.

The driver needs to know which direction to take, he pushes his head through the draped entrance to ask. The sight inside the wagon, even covered in grime does little to diminish the exposed beauty. There may yet be a chance to sample the wares of these women. At the first opportunity, he will have his way with them and none will be the wiser. The lust in his eyes favors Sheppard and the naked. The leer of his intentions is visible and licking lips could be nothing less than good. First chance he will jump her. Sheppard knows she could have a problem with this driver by the looks he's casting them. The disdain she feels displays candidly on her face for him to see. She glares back at him with hate-filled eyes. It tells him she won't go down without a fight - with pause, he swallows his breath.

With the wagon still rolling forward, the driver rapidly asks, "If you don't mind! I am require directions here." Returning his focus to the roadway he flicks the horse reins. Sheppard lays back Urobeha's head and shoulders on the floor of the wagon as gently as she can. Moving to the front and she pokes her head out. Up in the sky, she sees Silk, screaming in flight above chasing the moving wagon chariot. She points the way to the driver, "Go behind the town and go north but follow the raven in the sky. And the next time you look at me like that or my friend! I'll take your eyes out from your head." She pulls her head back to the inside.

Her abrasive retort riles the driver to rage, spitefully he pushes the horses to run faster making the ride hard and dangerous. She and Urobeha are tossed to one side of the fast-moving wagon chariot. Sheppard screams out to slow down but the slighted driver only laughs out at her. Silk hears Sheppard scream of being in danger, coming down from on high he whips past scratching the driver's face with his razor-sharp talons. Touching his face from the high assault, the sight of his blood causes him to slow down. Silk takes back to the upper skies while Sheppard steadies herself checking Urobeha. The driver realizes, it is she who is in control of the birds. If the Bright-Skin, persuaded one such as Golattus, to let her and the half-dead go, he discerns its best he does not underestimate her weakness. This could cost him his life.

His face torn, bleeding the open wounds attract flying insects. Their bites add to torment him, slap and waving his hand to be rid of the pestilence over and again. The blowing breeze clots the flowing blood on his face, comfort is elusive, his face burns like fire. Watchfully studying the sky for any other signs of attack, the driver continues to follow the strange looking bird in the sky.

After seeing Sheppard and the half-dead off Grottus mediation remains unsettled. Why did Golattus reverse his decision concerning the Bright-Skin and the half-dead girl from the altar? Now the men have nothing to entertain or occupy their time. He walks back to Golattus tent to ask why but one of the archers is there. Taking a position at the door he waits until the archer is finished with Golattus.

The young archer reports to Golattus. "Because of the great heights, all attempts failed to shoot down the birds. One is following with the wagon and only one falcon now remains high in the sky." The young archer's information to Golattus, confirms Grottus hunch about the Bright-Skin and the birds being connected, but to what extent he does not know. Golattus is caught off guard and stumbles. Reaching out quickly to steady himself he grabs hold of one of the tent poles for balance. It's imperative to conceal his weak state from the young archer, "Young warrior! Did you see me stumble?" Bewildered by the question, the young archer does not comprehend Golattus, full meaning. To the great leader, he said. "I see you are not well Golattus. I shall take my leave." Golattus disregards his concern, "There is no need for that and I am well" For a suspended moment the young archer is lost. Golattus notices that Grottus, is still standing at the tent door. Golattus gives the young archer a task that he may be excused to attend to whatever Grottus has to say. "You know. . . I could use something to eat sweet. What about you?"

Grottus reading between the lines gets the message, but not the young archer. To Golattus, the young and puzzled archer said. "Would you like me to bring back some eats, great warrior?" From behind Grottus, walks up to the young archer. Golattus, comments to the young archer leaning forward-searching his face, "Young archer there is something in your eyes?" The young archer not knowing any better raises his right hand to wipe his eyes. Behind him Grottus grabs him thrusting him straight through the under pit of his arm and he falls dead. Grottus, then calls in two to clean up and remove the body.

Without an audience Grottus wants answers about Golattus reversed decision. With attention to Golattus, Grottus notices his pallor is void of color. Something is wrong. The right hand in which Golattus had received the two rings is now bleeding, a single drop of blood is noticed. It doesn't seem crucial he attests this may be due to Golattus holding the rings too tightly. Reaffirmed, Golattus establishes the pride of his actions to his first commander, "You must never show any weakness before them. Now let me see the palms of your right hand." Grottus, extends out his right hand open to Golattus. "You have also handled the rings but you feel not its effects. It is only now that I understand. You handled them one by one so did the examiner. But together with my error, I have discovered they are poison and most dangerous. This I couldn't have known. My hands are numb and my feet are as heavy as iron. I don't think I can last much longer but say nothing, not a word about this until my return from Black Beard Hill. This is an unknown kind of poison the cure must be with her. Should I not make it back, you must find her and kill her where ever she is. You must take care of the men. It is your time to now lead. I have little less than three hours so I must leave as soon as I gather what's necessary."

The turn of events is sudden, Grottus, realizes the danger ahead for his friend. "Why don't you let me ride with you? The men can handle things here until we return. That wench and her tricks have to answer for what they have done." He knew this was too easy to believe, the keys to Old King Cole treasures obviously held secrets that only those who are privileged understand. With labored breathing, Golattus confirms, "That would be the usual plan, but we are not dealing with anyone. It just occurred to me, we may be up against something else. I ordered a tracker to follow behind the chariot so we can find her, where ever she goes and it may be best to move all the men out earlier. Like you once said. It's just a hunch."

News Comes to King Libra

The news comes to Libra, on the throne through her first adviser. The screams of other falcons below indicate one is on its way back. Libra gives orders to open the window above the throne so that the falcon can return unobstructed to take its place beside the throne. Soon after from high above, a falcon enters the great hall coming to perch, as trained on a white-covered post beside the throne. The King places her right hand upon the falcons head and eyes. To the falcon, she speaks., "Show me! Tell me! What is in your heart and mind?" Closing her eyes pictures of terrain opens to her, she envisions all of what the falcon has seen, heard, and experienced. Opening her eyes, finished, she removes her hand from over the falcon's eyes. Into the falcon's face, she blows her breath. "Now go and return to the sky until the others return." Up into the air, the falcon rises flying out through the window above the throne and back into the upper sky. The window high above the throne is ordered closed. The king's adviser is summoned and she gives a second-order. "Release the four other falcons into the sky to accompany the others," and it is done.

Into the sky, their destination is to the top of the mountain, where Golattus and his men are. The screams of the four released falcons carry on the upper winds and into the sonic ears of others miles, and miles away. The others know, they are on their way, Silk also picks up the signal. King Libra issues the third order, release her father's black-army of death. An army of ten thousand shield warriors, armed with weapons dipped in the incantation of white magic is concealed from the enemy not to be seen until the appropriate time.

The falcons travel at high speed on the winds. Together with the ten thousand, they move out as one unit. A second battalion follows with the preserved order to collect the royal Princess Sheppard, and see her back safely to the Kingdom.

Led by the four falcons flying ahead in the distance the black-army of death marches forward armed with brutal force. The falcons spread themselves miles upon miles in front of each other. Altogether, eight falcons lead the way for the ten thousand to battle. Unknown to Golattus and Grottus, neither, nor his men have ever before seen such a formidable mass of soldiers gathered before.

The chariot carrying Sheppard has been moving at high speed for some time, with Silk leading the way. Urobeha's body shows no signs of movement. The loss of blood has eased but she still has lost a lot of her body mass. The warriors in the mountain stretched her to her last breath. Urobeha begins to convulse violently, Sheppard barely manages to hold her down and relax her. She needs urgent medical attention. Her chances of making it is slim but Sheppard isn't giving up on her. With a sudden jolt of the chariot one of its wheel's roles over a big rock in the road. This raises Urobeha, body into the air, she comes down slammed on the wagon's floor. The smash jars Urobeha conscious, there is movement from her hand and legs. Sheppard is pleased, it gives her hope to know all will be well. She takes Urobeha's hand, briskly rubbing them to warm her. Afraid its still not going to be enough to keep her nakedness warm. Frustrated they are so close, Sheppard begins to weep at the situation, defiant struggling she refuses to let Urobeha, die. The only thing to warm her friend requires she sacrifice removing all of her garments. Covering Urobeha's naked body with her own clothing she receives no comfort from her own nakedness. Asking for forgiveness, weeping she embraces Urobeha. "I am so sorry. I am so so sorry. What have I done to deserve this? Father, please help me, Father please help me..."

Crying out over and again, the fast-moving chariot passes over mountains, hills, valleys, through Saxon streak, and behind many of the nearby towns before finally arriving at the great open plains. Silk again calls out to Sheppard. Naked Sheppard remains silent. She must stay put to avoid any other mishaps. She will not give cause, allowing the driver to be exposed to her nakedness and lose control of the fast-moving wagon chariot damning them all to death. The wagon chariot continues moving at high-speed racing across the great open plains.

Far ahead in the distance, a nasty looking dust cloud forges towards them. Having been in the worst situations, the driver is experienced, privy to many dangerous runs before. He cannot outrun this one, charging forward is his best option. Roaring out loud he goes, ready to challenge the dust storm. The sound of rolling thunder moves towards them, but the weather is good. Sheppard too hears the sound, getting louder. She can't determine which direction the thunder is coming from as it gets louder. Then it comes to her, the thunder is coming from the under pillars of the earth. Without warning to the driver, Silk swoops down from the sky with lightning speed taking the chariot driver two eyes out from his head, and returns to the skies.

The driver shrieks screaming inaudibly. The only thing Sheppard hears is the rambling thunder growing closer. The driver screaming out in vicious pain soon thereafter his upper body falls through to the inside of the wagon dead. Silk is still screaming out for Sheppard's attention. There is a black arrow protruding through the dead man's chest. The arrowhead declares it's a kingdom arrow. The man's eyes are missing and his ghastly image makes Sheppard gag. Operative she takes an advantage of the situation, quickly taking the man's upper garment off, she clothes herself. The black-arrow is a sign she is found and the thunder is the many riders from the Kingdom coming to her aid.

The wagon rolls on out of control less the driver. Sheppard relaxes a bit, only the moving wagon is a threat. The wagon chariot continues moving at high speed, she must stop it. Taking hold of the dead man she pushes him back up to his sitting position. Jostling with the wagons rumbling, his body wavers falling from the chariot bouncing and rolling to the earth in dust clouds. Drawing a deep breath, a few attempts later, she manages to slip into the driver seat. The flaying of reins flapping in the wind makes it hard to grab the reins. Having the reins in hand, she tries to bring the firing stallions to a stop. They are too strong she cannot. Out of control, the fast-moving wagon chariot enters into the white mist. Her strength fails, she needs much more help.

Silk is flying above horizontal to the fast-moving wagon chariot engulfed by the white mist, she does not see him. In a clear spot of the white mist at the top of her voice, she screams out to Silk. "Silk, help me. Silk, help me. Help meeeee!!!" Diving from the sky the raven comes down with lightning speed hoovering meters in front and above the head of the two leading stallions. Silk screeches out to them, hovering in reverse flying backward. Silk screams bring the firing six Stallions to a trot before finally coming to a full stop. The white mist surrounds her and Silk takes off back to the upper sky.

Gasping from tiredness and exhaustion Sheppard sits. She tries to look out and around but it's difficult to see anything with the thick white mist. The rumbling is moving a distance away from her, the echoes of many are fading. The white mist casts a ghostly silhouette image of the many riders passing against the sunrise. The worst of it has passed and the deep rumbling moves away like the wind.

Quietly the white mist dissipates evaporating before her, allowing her to better see what's near. Swiftly the last falcon passes over her. Silk screams out, letting them know his position. To assure Sheppard is protected, Silk descends through the lingering mist landing on her right shoulder. In the mist, she still sees the ghostly shadows caused by the sun's rays reflecting off the remaining platoon. Cloaked in the incantation of Libra, the ghost army has long passed on both sides of Sheppard. The falcons, sharp eyes have long left her.

The black army is one unit made up of three divisions. Together they make up a town of people, all experts in their craft they move only on the King's orders. Restless Sheppard jumps to the ground seeking to have a closer look at things around. Down from the wagon chariot not far away, she discovers the dead body of another with a black arrow protruding through his heart. It is the body of the tracker Golattus had sent to follow behind her.

Silk screams out taking a flight to the sky alerting everyone the princess is here. She is surprised to see so many of them. The mist has settled, looking up she finds herself encircled by royal guards on horseback. She knows they are there to protect her from the high-velocity speed of the passing ghost army. She cries out to them. "Please, Please hurry. I don't want her to die." A unit of the Kingdom warriors disburses themselves rapidly in and around the chariot wagon. Another six women guards enter along with two of Sheppard's chamber keepers. She is elated to see them as they are pleased to see her. Her garments and disheveled appearance does not diminish the show of respect due to her station and status as a princess. Cordially the chamber keepers greet her, "Welcome back, Princess."

They present her clothing which she accepts not. Instead preoccupied with concern she runs over to see how the physicians are doing with Urobeha's body in the wagon. After oiling Urobeha's body with healing ointments reserved only for royalty, the physicians order she be taken from the wagon chariot and placed elsewhere. To the four physicians, Sheppard inquires, "Please, Please, tell me one of the healing chambers is with you." The eldest physician confirms, "Yes princess, though she is badly injured, she will recover for we have brought back others close to death doors" Relieved, his words give her the encouragement her heart so badly needed. "Elder, thank you for your assurance."

The badly injured body of Urobeha's is taken and moved out. Placed into one of the onboard healing chambers, two female guards approach Sheppard. One of them notifies her, "Princess! Your coach is prepared with previsions and the necessities needed changing." It's not that Sheppard does hear what they say, the priority of meeting her obligation to Urobeha and her family is foremost in her heart. "I shall stay with her until we reach the Kingdom." Both royal guards concede. "As you wish, princess!"

With the guards turning away, Sheppard hurries across to where they took Urobeha. Entering in, she sees another group of physicians who are working on her. Into the healing chamber, Urobeha is encased to promote the wellness of a quick recovery. Once they are finished with Urobeha they leave, but not before seeing to the Princess's injuries. A female royal guard from the outside enters to notify the Princess of their logistics, "Princess, we will be moving out now!" To her, Sheppard asks, "Tell me, soldier! Who ordered my return? And what orders were given to my father's black-army? The female royal guard reports, "Your safe return was ordered by the throne. As for the black-army, they are to lay waste the whole mountain top before dawn."

Astounded, for a minute Sheppard speculates how is it possible her sister Libra could have that level authorization of clearance. She has always believed, the black-army of death could only be accessed and activated by her father Gouddaa and no one else. This confirms to her just how powerful her sister Libra has become. Should her father or Libra ever find out what she has done it could mean grievous consequences or even drastic punishments? She could be stripped of her title if the King deemed it necessary. To the guard, she simply said. "Thank you!" The guard notices the troubled pinched look on the Princess's face, to give her ease she feels compelled to share with the Princess more of what she knows. Before leaving her she offers, "Princess! That is called orders through the eyes of the Falcons."

Mulling over this new, Sheppard gets the picture. They encircled her with Urobeha's body, closing in, until such time they would arrive back in the Kingdom. Alone with Urobeha, the jerk of the wagon tells her, they are moving out. Glancing at Uroebeha. it looks like she's resting peacefully for once. Slumping down beside her chamber Sheppard can't help but be disgusted by the odd fit clothing of the wagon driver stained with blood.

Rising she walks into the storeroom over to the chest on board. As she thought, it is filled with an array of clothing, but nothing looks appropriate, or are to her fitting. Never the less, they are clean. The bath is ready so is the basin and water jug rest on a table beside it, it's a sight of pure euphoria. She can now take a long and needed bath. If she scrubs hard enough she may be even able to wash away the filth from her body. With each trickle of water cleansing her body, remnant bruises remind her, the shame and defilement linger. Oiling and clothed she returns over into the holding room to Urobeha.

There before the healing chamber, she collapses to her knees overwhelmed in grief from it all. Never in a million cycles would Sheppard have thought the price of friendship could be so high. Running from one thing into another, it probably would have fared better if she had just remained home. Then again Urobeha's fate would have been sealed for sure. She and Urobeha have suffered through much and the reality of things begins to reconcile with her. The only comfort she gets is in the release of her own tears. Deep down she knows there could be no possible explanation for her behavior. She better have a plausible story together before they arrive back in the Kingdom. The fact that she even needs one reflects badly on her choices as a princess. This saddens her even more.

The black-army of death rides on at ghost speed under the incantation of Libra. Transforming the mist rises to cloak the traveling platoon. The metamorphosis of the spell weaves them into the charging ghost entity the world has only heard whispers of in children's stories. They pass on through many of the small side towns. Their horse breed is tireless, showing no signs of slowing down, the earth feels the rumbles beneath their thundering huffs.

In town, the local people are held transfixed by the dark and dangerous appearance of the black-army. Many run for cover, others close their doors hiding away with their children. With hurry, many strive to bring in their livestock, whoever isn't busy trying to preserve what little value they have, is paralyzed in fear's grip. This causes some to pray for a quick death. The sentries in the air, have provided a road map. Flying high ahead they follow the other front falcons led by a sonic echo. Arriving at the location, the black army extracts spreading and dividing themselves into four groups each being lead by a falcon around the mountain.

The rumble is so great, that it is heard at the very top by many of the warriors. The black-army ride commences up the mountain from all four sides, the sunset conceals the falcons from sight. Warriors in the mountain watch the falling stones, rocks, and boulders coming down the mountain peak. The rumble is great enough to move them out from their places and shakes the very foundation on which they stand.

The instant Golattus received the second ring, combined, they released a hidden chamber of poison into his system rendering him almost useless. The poison can not be seen by the naked eye. It can kill a man in less than four hours. It's only because Golattus is a large man in mass and honed with great strength the poison takes longer to spread. It is expected he will be dead in a little more than five hours should he not receive the antidote Sheppard has. The poison can only be detected by the royal falcons and Silk who have been trained by Sheppard in the event the poison is ever released. The poison combined with Sheppard's essence becomes a beacon enabling the birds to find her quickly.

It doesn't take much for Grottus, to convince Golattus to let him tag along. In his weakened condition, it is declining more rapidly than anticipated. Just as they are about to vacate the camp, the mountain rumble grows louder to exploding evidence breaking loose. Looking to one another, no one realizes the sound bellow is being caused by a swift and moving black army. Riding information they will soon be in a position to lay waste to the whole mountain top.

Shrewd observation allows Grottus to draw a conclusion, but none touch the truths of retribution they will soon face. "It sounds as if the mountain is coming down." Sweating profusely looking up at the surrounding trees, Golattus gut prompts him to act, "I to have a feeling about this. Tell the men, they are to saddle up at once." Grottus, gives the orders knowing it will take the men some time to gather up their belongings. The short notice starts an irregular movement of panic among the men. Bustling movements of camp warriors loading up to leave, jars, setting in motion large boulders moving out from their places. Startled and spooked, runaway horses clip Golattus, stallion hard trying to get away. Jostled in his weakened state he falls to the earth with a thud. Stumbling unsteady, barely holding onto the flanks of the horseback up to his feet he mounts the horse once again.

The black-army of death is upon them, everyone begins to scatter for protection, looking for avenues of escape, to find none. In the confusion, many warriors don't even get a chance to pull their weapons, before being beheaded. The speed and agility of the black-army could never be imagined or comprehended. Unseated once more, Golattus finds himself back on the ground wobbling he trips over the headless body of his second in command, Grottus. Golattus high octave screams shrills of seeing fire from above.

The order was clear, only one will be spared. The black-army of death lays waste the whole of the mountain top. Everyone of Golattus men are cut down, killed, but not him. He is saved as ordered by the throne for punishment. There will be no prolonged suffering for the mountain warriors, Only a sting to darkness. Having concluded their orders, on the wind the black-army of death rides back to the Kingdom. With his hands tied behind his back, Golattus is strapped to the horse. In the wake of events, the black-army leaves behind the second division of the platoon, to clean and make compensation to the townspeople until relieved.

The Royal Convoy

The convoy has long made its way back into the Kingdom with Sheppard. She orders Urobeha's body to be removed and placed into her own healing chamber. In all the commotion and shambles of confusion, she manages to sneak past the guards and some of the advisers. Without being seen she makes it to her room breathing hard, only to be questioned by her two youngest chamber keepers, Vertt and Triaa. With scrutiny they bombard her wanting to know all about what they call a princess adventure. Exhausted she is tired and would only like to have a real royal bath and rest.

Memories of filthy hands pawing, covering her body, and touching her in intimate ways resurface. The walls around her begin to close and the avid chatter is making her physically ill. Holding her hands to her head, she orders the two to be quiet. They ignore her, that doesn't work, so she orders them to leave at once. Dumb they seize from speaking and stare at her. It is settled, so she thinks as they walk away. A sudden knock on her room door causes her to draw a quiet breath. The royal message is very deliberate in its request. She reads it twice before dismissing the guard. Vertt and Triaa are never far when she's home, they probably are listening at the very door they exited. Quickly she calls back Vertt and Triaa to help bathe and dress her and they do. This visit with The King has to be everything if she was going to get away with what she had done.

She must commend Vertt and Triaa if she pulls this off, she's never looked so good. Arriving before the throne, even the King takes notice. She stands fully adorned in all her regalia, her beauty is immaculate and radiant. From the throne, the King stands up. To the King's surprise, Sheppard drops to her knees before the throne, something she has never before done in her life.

The King waves out her hand and the hall is made clear. From the throne, the King dismisses her sister's embellished antics. "There's no need for that little sister. You have already passed that so please, end of the show!" From the tone of the King's voice, Sheppard knows she has much to answer for. Her fate may already be sealed. Burdened with ailing thoughts for what she did, Sheppard's conscience gets the best of her. Pure nervousness hits her before the King could utter her next word. Sheppard cries out for mercy. "Please, please, allow me to speak." Libra gives the remaining guards around and above the throne further instruction, "Guards above and below seal the hall."

Right away the great doors of the room are closed and sealed. The elite guards disappear until the King's privacy is concluded. The throne has very specific rules and orders. By rules of the throne, should there ever be a leak when orders of importance are given, the elites' guards are responsible for rectifying the situation by any means necessary. They must take out their duties without bias or discrimination. With swift justice, no one but the King has the privilege to know. Sheppard's countenance tells her guilt, humbly she relays the crux of her experiences, "I have never felt so humiliated and dirty. I am so, so sorry for what I have done. I had to give up my rings in exchange for life and I also promised the antidote will be delivered at Black Beard Hill. I believe I can exchange the antidote back for my rings. I really wish none of this would have happened, and I really don't wish to face him again."

Libra is the acting King until Gouddaa returns, she makes it her business to know everything that is of importance to the Kingdom. Thanks to Roobbye, she knows more about Sheppards case than she thinks, this will work to her advantage. The state of Sheppard has her a little concerned. Libra appeals to Sheppard, "And if you rise now from your knees! You will never have to!" Her thudding heart regulates to normal. Sheppard, assailed with gratitude is delighted, being granted the opportunity pleases her. Fumbling to stand on her feet she gladly complies with the King's rule.

Abased as a result of rising to the occasion, Sheppard feels the weight and degradation she has been feeling leave her she is lighter than before the ordeal began. The King removes her crown and she rests it in its holding place beside the throne. Turning to her little sister Sheppard, Libra pats her hand for Sheppard to sit beside her. Joining her sister, the King, Sheppard's movements are open and fragile. This puts her at ease as Libra continues speaking. "You no longer have to! His report is here." The King shows out the report to Sheppard should she need to read it. Dropping it back on the tray board by the mighty throne. Sheppard does not fully understand what her sister' is trying to say. "I, I, don't fully understand?" Satisfied with the outcome of her orders, King Libra has every right to be confident. With intent, Libra looks deep into Sheppard's eyes. "Your adversary is already here! He is being held deep within the black dungeons,"

The tightness in her chest dissipates. The four hawks (four hours) for her to meet with Golattus, was up some time ago. With barely constrained venom her fury returns "Why is he not dead? Why is he?" Libra smiles at the nativity of her sister's passion, death is an easy escape. Letting one live under the judgment of their actions allows them an opportunity to redeem themselves. Any good leader is governed by these principles this is just another reason why Father appointed her King. If he left it to Sheppard, Libra shutters at the thought of how she would run the affairs of the Kingdom. Not even Sahara with her prideful disposition could run kingdom affairs objectively. That too would end disastrously. Sheppard could be so petty at times and spiteful. "I gave the orders only to save the one in command. He can do you no more harm. He can only remember seeing fire falling from the skies. Please go and prepare yourself. Swift justice must now be applied by your hand only. You must Remember a swift death, is much too pleasant for one such as he." The logic of the King's comprehension impresses Sheppard. The King has garnered her respect. "I shall remember your every word when the sentence is given."

Bright Skin Face Her Adversary

Listening to the King gives Sheppard room to pause in her actions. She thinks about what the King has said about her never having to face her adversary, it is forgiveness for her behavior. With the tensions dissolved Sheppard figures it's best to get moving, away from the King's presence before something else comes up. Turning to walk away, the King stops her. Dread again pushes the rushing blood of anticipation, just when she thought she was free. "Now follow me!" Commands Libra. From the throne, the King pulls a cord opening all the doors. The guards and superior guards fall back into their respected positions. Into one of the hidden chambers, she and Sheppard enter to further discuss Golattus's future. Sheppard listens attentively to Libra's instructions and then she is allowed to leave. It feels like she's in the clear, just some unfinished business with Golatttus remains. Let see what the barbarian says now that the table has turned.

After departing the throne room, Sheppard walks across to where Urobeha's body is at rest. Her friend is still sedated in the healing chamber; the numbness of events hasn't worn off yet. The keeper on duty gives her the privacy needed. While she stands gazing upon Urobeha's body, she takes notice of her friend's healing process, and it's much better than before. Urobeha is now out of the danger zone but she still has ways to go. The memories roll in flashes in her mind. Sheppard remembers the courage and defeats she and Urobeha bore through in their encounter with the warriors. It gives her strength to now face Golattus, for the last time.

Closure has never been so hard to obtain, her anger needs no encouragement, heat emanates from her touch. Therein does blood lust shade her vision, walking away from the healing chambers. Across the courtyard, with determined strides, Sheppard makes her way. Silk is in the sky and his sharp vision sees her every move. Sheppard knows he's there not even having to look. To let her know of his presence, Silk screams out to her. Out in the open garden, where the grass is green and the flowers fill the air with their sweet fragrance, unblemished colors guide the way to the black dungeons. Sheppard outstretches her arm and Silk descends, comes down he rests on her right shoulder. Rubbing her face against his feathers she thanks him for their safe return. With a cooing breath, Sheppard blows over Silk. The bird immediately relaxes.

The royal black-dungeon guards run to meet Sheppard as she approaches, they escort her into the black-dungeon. The dungeons are as old as its walls are massive. Formidable in structure the pillars are humongous, there is no equal. In the library archives of the Kingdom, it is written in the book of pillars that this massive dungeon was once designed and built by spirits called into existence under the control of King Aggaddaa. With holy emblems shrouded with power the dungeon became.

Silk takes to the air as Sheppard steps deeper into the lower dungeons, following to where Golattus is being imprisoned. The lower dungeons are a place reserved for the most vicious and heinous of men like Golattus. The powerful Golattus, now separated from his warriors, is helpless. Captivity is not a foreign condition with which he is not familiar. Shackled in chains, Golattus roars defiantly, straining against the bondage of his restraints. He fights like maniac berserk to break free. The steel holding him has been forged to resist any force.

From the dungeon gates, she observes him chained to the wall. Just like he had Urobeha bound to the altar now his hands and feet suffer identical circumstances. The dungeon gatekeeper and the punisher greet the Princess. The guards dismissed are allowed to leave. The Princess has only to look at the gatekeeper for him to know his role. Massive iron gates open before the Princess and the punisher. They enter leaving the gatekeeper behind and up to

Golattus they walk. Loud grinding sounds from the opening gate, awakens Golattus. The confines of his imprisonment bring to his mind the comforts he has forsaken, badly needing to sleep, slumber is elusive here.

Silk has made his own way in through the high above cross iron bars, coming to rest high above Golattus head. Golattus has been badly beaten, bruised, and injured, he finds it hard to focus. The Punisher throws boiling hot water into his face. The scalding water shocks him pealing his skin like melting wax, he screams. His scream gives her a thrill. As Golattus, catches himself the pains from his face blurs his vision. His vocals still work as does his will to inflict harm. Threatening the punisher, "Big one. . . Better still. . . I'll kill you!" The punisher is not troubled having heard the maledictions of many before.

Through his blurred vision Golattus, blinking rapidly he sees what appears to look like yellow, blue, and black cloth moving towards him. He is transfixed to see the most magnificent and beautiful glow on a person he'd ever seen since the Bright-Skin. The Bright-Skin every waking moment he thinks about her and the men he has lost. Still, in the shadows of the confines, Sheppard does not reveal all of herself yet. The silhouette of Sheppard's magnificent beauty causes Golattus to cry out, "Where?! Where do you people come from, and why me? What do you want from me? Just leave me." Barely able to hold up his head it hangs down in exhaust. The punisher throws a bucket of ice-cold water to make Golattus, fully aware of the Princess's presence. Gurgling and sputtering for breath the water suffocates him momentarily. Before the punisher could add further injury throwing a third bucket of hot water onto Golattus, he is made to stop by orders of the Princess.

The light in the dungeon is low, from his dungeon walls, Golattus looks down at the radiant Princess. "Who are you?" Sheppard taunts the great leader, "Why don't you take a closer look." Out from the inky darkness, she walks up even closer to him. The voice he remembers parts the veil of his sight. It is her, the tormentor of his body and soul. Most surprised, it is the Bright-Skin. "Bright skin! Bright- Skin! I... aaa knew, it was more to you than meets the eyes, but a princess living among peasants. I could not have imagined! A Princess you are from the far north! Uncharted territory for me and my men. Now I see and understand who you are Bright-Skin. A royal from the house of Gouddaa. And as you are a royal. I am still a warrior and as you already know! A warrior who isn't ready to die. Just that you know! I aa. . . was already stripped of your rings by your people and they say that my men are all dead! Is it true?! I already received the antidote and is being punished. So you can say, we are even now. You aaa. . . see Bright Skin. I have chosen a warrior path and if you Bright-Skin expect me to beg for my life before you, a mere woman, that won't happen." With his ranting Sheppard turns to the punisher, the Princess inflicts treatment of her own. "Tighten up his chains a little."

In pain. Golattus cries out again. With menace to the punisher, Golattus, verbally accosts him. "The aa big one is not a man. I aaa would like to have my way with him one on one and I'll kill him." Ominous and void of emotion the punisher, walks up to Golattus's face, "Go ahead! We are both in the position, we are." Golattus lunges, reaching out to grab him. In desperate pride, he forgets the chains holding him. He struggles frantically just to fail. He may not be able to touch him with his fist but the saliva of his mouth will serve adequately the purpose of insult.

Many prisoners have made the mistake of doing what Golattus has done. A diabolical glee smiles with the darkness, not unlike his second in command Grottus, the punishers takes great satisfaction breaking the defiant and reprobate scourge of the earth. Golattus is whipped into the submission of blackness. He can hardly move, the moans and groans alone tell Sheppard he lives. When the Princess sees Golattus can take no more, she puts an end to it.

To the punisher, she orders, "Stand down." The punisher withdraws to inspect Golattus's lack of response, he discovers that he's unconscious. Looking to the Princess relentless she adamant, "Awake him again!" Through the haze of pain Golattus quirks, he does not want to receive another hot and cold bath like fire. "No need! Is that the best you could do, big one?" In the gore of his situation, Golattus's spirit is not completely broken only humbled. His head falls back down. Silk, Sheppard's protector rests high on the ledge, looking down out over everything. The squawking bird flits back and forth between the bars of the window to window. From time to time Golattus would look up, trying to locate the strange-looking bird. The tight neck brace restricts his movements against the wall, each time he tries, he fails to fall short.

The Princess looking directly at Golattus, says to the Punisher, "I need a minute with him alone, Take the Keeper out with you and wait for me out at the front door. Further orders will be given when am through." At first, the punisher is hesitant about leaving the Princess alone with such a powerful adversary. She assures him of her safety with Silk. He walks out taking the gatekeeper with him. The massive outer dungeon door is made to close and lock. She, Silk, and Golattus are now alone.

Silk takes flight to the air, hoovering himself high above Golattus, head. The little bit of light on the inside comes from the outside through a diamond which bends the rays of light from high above. The air flows down an open shaft through a small space on high enough only for one like Silk to use. From the light of the spectrum, it is just enough for them to see each other clearly. Golattus makes no excuses for his behavior as a warrior seeing, she is now alone. To her, he said. "I know you want me dead, but why this way?" Princess Sheppard does not confirm his statement, "I am not here to kill you. I only want that which you have stolen from me." Perplex with pain, he knows not of what she speaks about. "Bright Skin! You aaa have me at a loss. Haven't we both lost enough?" Trying to reason with her. Cool and composed the Princess reminds Gollatus of the crimes he has committed. "Did you think that! When you ordered my friend to the altar, to be brutally stripped of her women hood. You have taken my dignity, and all I want is my dignity back. Is that too much to ask? And like I have said. You will never see me again."

Blabbering, his folly of excuses only serves to infuriate Sheppard more. He continues, "She came of her own free will and I only agreed with her terms. Would you believe me! When I say! I would have rather set you free but sometimes as a ruler one's hand is tired because of the rules! No one knows rules better than one like yourself! If I had a way of giving you back your dignity now would be a good time but I still don't aaa understand?" Nothing he can say will pacify her,

"Then as the man you are! Look at me! Pierce your eyes upon me again. And like I have said! You will never see me again."

Gollatus scoffs at the wounds of her pride, confronting her. "Look at me! Look at me! Bright Skin! I have nothing more to give. You people have destroyed me and my men! What can I give to have saved them?" Sheppard confirms the demise of his men ever so calmly. "Yes! Your men are all dead but at least you will have the last feast and I will have the last say and my stolen dignity back." Unexpectedly what happens next would be Gollatus's ultimate downfall. With intent and determined vengeance, in front of his eyes, the Princess disrobes herself of every piece of her clothing until she is naked. Naked visions and fantasies of her bright naked body haunt him of his passions denied. The desire to have her for himself makes him forget the pain he has suffered be imprisoned. His body can't hide its attraction, the bulge in the midregion beneath his robe has expanded the great God Penis possesses him, showing out its strength. In a breath for mercy, the great Warrior Golattus cries because the pain inside is more unbearable than that without release. "Bright aaaaaaaa Skin! What areeeeee you doing to me.? Screaming back at him, she looks at him straight in his eyes. Laughing without control, demented she dances around him clapping like one possessed making no sense. Yelling out at the top of her lungs, "Thank you! Thank you! Silkkkkk."

Golattus manages to look up, his last sight of one of silver wings descending upon him and razor-sharp talons. With strike force, Silk takes Golattius, two eyes out from his head, and flies to the outside to feed. Golattus is hit with racking and excruciating pain, his cry shrills out from pain unimaginable. The echoes of his continual screams, loud, thunderous cries, are heard throughout the dungeon walls even by those at the far entrance. On the outside, the guards look at each with approval. Whatever method of torture the Princess has applied, not even the punisher has been able to get that kind of reaction.

In the throes of his pain, Princess Sheppard robes herself regaining back her honor. She walks out and away from Golattus's dungeon. Using the hidden lever, the massive doors are once again made open. Running to meet the Princess is the gatekeeper and the punisher. They are eager and curious to know what Golattus, thunderous screams are all about. They run in to see him. The answer is clear, Golattus gouged out eyes answers their questions. Golattus finally understands the Bright-Skin, last and final words to him "And you shall never see me again." Golattus falls out from the pain. The keeper and the punisher look at her. It is there she recalls, the King's last words to her. "A quick death is much too good for one such as he." To compound the infliction done to Golattus. to the punisher, the Princess adds. "Now drive large spikes through his hands and feet and put chains into them to bind him forever."

During the process of Golattus's gruesome punishment, he cries out for mercy, but mercy has long left him alone. His pain becomes so great, that the all-powerful Golattus, faints over and again from his afflictions. For the first time in all his battles, he is broken and want's to die, not even death favors him. They whip him to further submission and shame for his past deeds. After the Princess could stomach no more, she walks away across to those in charge showing her pass to leave. Within minutes after she is gone, orders from the throne come down for Golattus. The judgment of his sentence has been passed.

Sheppard Returns to the Main Hall

Sheppard returns to the main hall, to stand before the King. Sitting upon Gouddaa's throne, King Libra inquires, to her, "I take it! swift justice has been served of course." Sheppard sighs somberly from all the dealings of Gollatus, "Yes, but still, somehow my soul is still so sad." Before Sheppard arrived, the King had just ordered a glass of wine to be brought in. Seeing Sheppard's fallen disposition, she discerns she may need it more. "A bit of wine may do you some good!" The King hands the glass of wine over to her. Walking up to the throne she receives the wine. On taking it, innate thoughts trouble her. She begins to wonder if the wine is poisoned. If she drinks it and its poisoned that would be the end of her. It reminds her of the poison she placed in her brother Dicious's drink. Unlike him, she is not immune. The King sees her hesitant behavior. "The wine is not poisoned! You can drink it! If I wanted you dead, there would have been no reason for me to save you."

Mollified to hear Libra assuages her concerns, there is no longer apprehension to hinder her from enjoying the wine. She drinks most of the wine before passing it back over to the King. "Please forgive me. It's just that the wine reminds me of something. I wish not to remember and thanks to you." The King looks on at her, "Is there anything else?" Weary Sheppard declines. "Nothing more, that may be of interest to you at this time! So I will take my leave."

The Undaunted King Gouddaa of the Arawaks and Caribs

The Kings, intense gaze waits for what Sheppard isn't ready to divulge. The scrutiny with which the King watches her makes Sheppard uncomfortable. She should remove herself expeditiously from the King's presence, not to be reprimanded for the part she played in actions committed. Excusing herself stepping away, again to her surprise the King stops her, she is not finished as Sheppard feared. "Sheppard!" This is what she was afraid of, she turns back to the King wishing her circumstances were different. The King. "I need you to come with me!"

Removing her royal Junkanoo crown, the King walks away from the massive throne down to Sheppard. Following her lead, Sheppard is shown toward an exclusive and private chamber beneath the throne. As they enter, the massive door is closed. Nervous Sheppard wonders what's in store for her behavior, it appears it has not gone unnoticed. King Libra recognizes that Sheppard needs containment. Her lack of confidence to confide in her leaves her no choice. "You must know why I asked you here!" Sheppard stands doubtful, it's best she remains quiet until the King has had her say. "I have appointed you a body-guard." This unexpected news throws her. Sheppard gasps for air stuttering for the first time in her life. "May I aaa know the name?" King Libra has great faith in the man she is assigning to Sheppard, his past credits confirm he is best suited to handle her affairs. "Roobbye!" Trying not to sweat, though she is surprised, a blush spreads over her face. "Thank you! And I do prefer. . . May I have a seat?" From what King Libra has observed of Sheppard, she is in no condition to watch herself. It's for her own good. Whimsical is the King's response, "Please do! Do take your time."

Sheppard takes a seat knowing the ramification of her actions, thinking to herself Roobbye, must have opened his big mouth. "I don't understand." King Libra's patience is limited, she doesn't want to implicate Sheppard by any means. Sheppard must by her own speech implicate herself, admit or submit to her own dishonesty. "If you are asking why? This is not the time. For a soldier to live with himself, he must first be at ease." In remission, Sheppard knows her secret is now out. Only one person could have caused this, to herself. "Roobbye! I'll kill you." King Libra becomes abrupt and short deliberating to Sheppard. "So, when were you going to tell me?"

The heavens know, it's now or never. Sheppard envisions in her mind, Roobbye, with a spear down his throat for talking too much. This is one time she would rather stand before her father, than her sister Libra. Thinking to herself, stranger things have happened in the presence of the King. The hope is that Libra will show her some form of leniency. Instead, standing up from her seat rather than submit to her sister Libra the King, Sheppard is still muddled when she replies, "I think! I need to walk a little." Pacing from side to side across the great chamber, gathering her thoughts, she must choose her words most carefully. Contemplating her reactions, Libra looks at Sheppard burying herself deeper in her own lies. It makes her, think, what a strong will her little sister has.

Sheppard does not know what else to say or do at the present. The compiled fabrication of lies begins to cloud her ability to further think straight. It shows on her face. Sheppard falls to her knees before the King again. "What will you do with me? Will I be stripped of my title? Will I be imprisoned, exiled, put to death?" From her knees, she looks up at her sister. Libra mercifully looks down on her. "I didn't say that! You did." When Sheppard realizes she has implicated her own self, she falls out cold to the ground. Libra shakes her head incredulous at the course of events before her. What are the odds of one falling out because of their own lies? The chamber physicians are called in to wake her. With a little help, she is made to sit again and the chamber is again made clear. The guards have not been summoned to take her away, so she knows there must be more.

When she comes to, the King is still waiting, her fate has not yet been sealed. The time of reckoning has finally arrived, to clear things up Sheppard stands and walks across to her sister. Most disappointed with her behavior Libra awaits a sound explanation. Mild in her most humble words she seeks to defer the judgment she believes will be imposed. "Sister! I know what I did was wrong but I was so angry at the time. Am I to be punished? And if so may my punishment be only by the hand of my brother Dicious, or by my father?" Libra can't believe her ears, discordant with Sheppard's mental acclivity, "You have placed countless lives in danger! You may forgive yourself! And you may even convince your brother Dicious, of your forgiveness but if this gets out! Your warlord sister may not forgive you! You have been running for some time now and look where it gets you, into more trouble, and right back where you started. Is that your fate?"

Sheppard still does not comprehend or fully understand the dangers her actions have provoked. Ignorantly, pleading she moves one step closer to her sister the King. Although she is naive, she does not drop her guard and effort to contain everything is with the King. "Will you help me? I too will rather this not get out. Will you help me to keep it a secret?" It is exasperating dealing with Sheppard, "The secret is not on you! I am placed in an awkward situation here! I have already given you my word, but only as long as I can." Like a petulant child, Sheppard reiterates Leoha's offense against her. "You know! She nearly outright killed me so why do I have to be so forgiving?" Libra feels like she has accomplished nothing, to make the Princess better understand the stakes and needs of the many, which shall always outweigh the state of one.

To simplify things, Libra provides an analogy, "Tell me, Sheppard! Do you think this is all about you only? No, it's not! I am saying! I don't want to have a preference between you and her. Like father said, there cannot be an inner war, and though she did hurt you. It doesn't mean that she doesn't care or love you. She did it because she loves you and you must never forget, that your sweet life is given because of the sacrifice she and your beloved brother Dicious, and all of those called by the duty of the throne have made. Since her last battle with the Black Scarlet and the Black Widow, she is not the same. Something portentous must have happened, but she is not telling. It is she who has desecrated the upper tomb of the child of hope and removed the sacred blade. She has now become so obsessed with that blade. Can you understand? that what happened between you two was an act of her being frightened by father's orders to kill the widow and her minions. I guess what am saying is, your differences can be fixed and worked out, but what you did, endangered all of the Kingdom. You could imagine if she and Dicious had died. It would have been only because of one lie! You lie!"

The contrite emotions she had dismissed earlier return, aptly chastised by Libra, she stands dissolved in her beliefs. "It has always been my understanding, that Father sealed that tomb with an incantation and it can only be broken by himself, so how is it she can break into it?" Libra points back to what was said, "As you have said. You and I are apart of him." This does not compute right away for a moment Sheppard seems puzzled by her sister's words. Libra gives her a minute to gather her thoughts and Sheppard remembers, "Mother once told me. I will become telepathic in due time. Maybe that's why am not getting it." The association of the relations Libra wants to convey has missed its mark again to Sheppard. "I won't say that! We are all apart of father genetic makeup and that is why Leoha, was able to remove the blade."

Sheppard finally gets it, "Now I understand. Any one of us could have removed the blade because we are all apart of father's genetic makeup and what would be her gain by having it?" The King smiles out as she points out the obvious to Sheppard. "To be the best at it." She had never thought of it before, "Is that possible?" Libra, turns from her, having said all she thinks. It's time to move on, she is curious to hear what developments have taken place. "Only if one believes it, tell me, did you sentence Golattus, to death?" She had forgotten all about him until Libra asked, "No, If I did that, I would be no better than he. Libra is satisfied and gives her a silent smile. "Wise choice."

The significance and magnitude of her actions are far-reaching and have affected many. The gratitude of being spared has endeared her sister Libra the King to her in a new light. "I am again at your mercy, and I am in debt to you, but it is a must I ask. Did she question you about me?" Suddenly there is a knock on the chamber door that calls a close to the conversation. Libra turns toward the door. "You may enter." It is the King's first adviser, reminding her of a pending engagement, awaiting her. Walking toward the open door she stops, looks at Sheppard, and said "Remember, lies are like the raindrops." Not understanding the connotation Sheppard expresses she is puzzled. Then Libra said. "They never fall on one rooftop." Sheppard could only gasp for breaths of fresh air. Libra takes her leave of absence while Sheppard soon after makes her own way out.

On the First Cycle of the Wind

On the first cycle of the wind, the Black Widow does not kill Leoha, but instead, poisons her to never be able to love again. On her way out from the Black Forest, she accidentally walks into the pathway of the equinox of death, the Black-Scarlet. Without warning, she attacks the Black Scarlet with all she has left, but it is not enough to save her from the horrible defeat at her hand. Besides begging for her life, she finds herself on her knees asking Black Scarlet for answers. She is shown mercy and given the intimate secret of how to heal her illness and she is told, who is the fifth element, the rightful death guardian of her Father's throne is. Black Scarlet looks down on the wounded Warrior on her knees and said. "Now you must save yourself, just like I must save myself."

With the Black Scarlet turning to walk away, the badly injured Warlord Warrior and Princess from the house of Gouddaa, cries out after her, "Scarlet! Don't you dare walk away from me! Scarlet! I will kill youuuu!" She falls to the earth. A short time later Leoha regains enough strength to get back up on her feet and she looks around. Struggling to regain her balance the poison in her system has weakened her. She sets out and begins to walk back towards the border. Scheduled to meet with a Platoon of soldiers there to collect her. It is their duty to dispose of everything, should her life be in danger. In the time of her greatest need, when she arrives at the checkpoint, not one solder is at the scheduled position. There has to be a reason why she has been abandoned.

She makes it out on her own only to discover, there is a large storm brewing ahead. There is no way she can pass through or outrun it. Altering her course not to return home she takes the Black Scarlets advice and goes after the cure. The healing chambers of the Kingdom are not capable of rectifying this malady. Though it's not easy, she locates the cure. After doing what is necessary for her survival, the Warlord Warrior Princess returns home.

Leoha Enters the Main Hall

Into the main hall, she enters but the colossal doors to the throne room are closed. With brute strength she pushes the gigantic doors open, allowing herself entry only to find the soldiers spears at her throat. Slowly reaching into her garment and pulling out her royal seal all normalcy returns, and she is allowed to pass. Walking towards the great throne, her eyes are welcomed by the new King high and mighty upon her fathers' throne. Showing the Warlord Princess, the highest of respect, the King rises to the occasion and greets her. "I know your journey has been long. Welcome back home. Somehow I knew, you would make it, despite of the odds." The King claps her hand twice and the sixty-six guards from around and above the throne come out to welcome the Warlord Princess home. To the Warrior and Warlord Princess their voices raised in unison, in one tongue, they all say, "Welcome back, Warlord Princess!" She accepts their kindness before they disappear back into formation.

Surprised to see so many changes made in her absence in the grand hall it brings to mind one question. "Libra! Where is father?" The King removes her royal crown placing it beside the throne. It's good to see Leoha has endured the trials she is sure to have experience on her quest to destroy the Black Widow and Black Scarlet. "Guards, dismiss yourselves." They exit as ordered. Now that they are gone the King, Libra expands on what has transpired in Leoha's absence. "He is no longer here and much has changed since you were gone." The evidence she sees about her declares that. "Why are you on his throne and where is everyone else?" Leoha is direct in her inquiry and the King honors her request. "Though it is much too late for those questions. Why don't you first rest and we shall talk later? There have been some minor changes, but you should not look so surprised. I warned you not to leave, but you wouldn't listen."

Since Leoha's return, news of her relatives has come to her. "The news about my two aunts. Is it true?" King Libra is surprised someone has informed her so quickly, "How did you know?" Leoha doesn't disguise the sarcasm in her tone. "I came in through the seventh gate and as you already know, the guards do talk. "Yes, the guards do talk too much, and Libra will deal with that later. Not wanting to further challenge her sister on the issue of the guards at the seventh gate she answers her first question. "Both are in a safe haven! Where I had promised them, they would be."

The Warlord Princess falls to her knees before the massive throne. This surprises the King. "Sister please help me. I have killed many innocent, just to return home. Now I seek only vengeance upon the Black Scarlet." Returning to her upright standing position. King Libra looks at Leoha, "Please don't expect me to have mercy or compassion on you. Like I have said before! You are a Princess and do have choices! Live by blood die by blood. It is the only code, warriors like yourself understand."

It was her decision long ago to learn and be trained in the art of war. Looking up at her sister Libra who in her absence is now King, she finds her condescending remarks degrade and insult her craft. With respect for the throne, she asserts. "You sit on Father's throne high and mighty. I know you despise what I am but don't you blame me! I did not want to be a killer! Father made me the executioner I am, so don't you dear pass judgment on me, sister!" Even before this, Libra and Leoha shared strained relations. "Father only allowed you to be trained, not because he wanted, but because you pushed him too. It is you alone, who have accepted the missions, and you alone take out your orders. Please dear sister doesn't expect much from me. Killers like you are not born killers. People are taught how to kill and as for me being high and mighty. Should you ever so desire to have the throne! You have just to rise to the occasion and demand it and I shall freely give it! What is it, that you want from me?"

Time is short and Leoha realizes debating with Libra is defeating the purpose of her visit. "I want you to help me! And no I cannot take the throne. I just cannot accept that. I am what I am! please tell me! You tell me where is my brother Dicious?" I thought you would never ask! The contentions between them do not detract from the fact, King Libra is relieved to see Leoha. Everyone now is accounted for that matters. "He was badly injured by the Black Scarlet and had to be placed into the healing chambers and he has already made a full recovery. Please, before you decide to leave again. Come and see me, there is something important you must know! As for your aunts. Unforunately, you had to hear it that way." Leoha will not give Libra the satisfaction of the last word. "Let me remind you, sister! They are also your family and I don't think, that's this kind of secret could remain hidden. Please don't blame the guards at the seventh gate. It is I who asked to be brought up to date." With that said Leoha, turns and strides out the hall.

It Feels Good to be Home

It feels like she's been away forever, into her chamber she enters. Finally, she can let down her guard. Tired and exhausted, after taking a long and needed bath, she nourishes herself with food and wine. Tumbling onto her bed for a quick rest before moving again, that long and needed relaxation comforts her. She fall's deep, deep into sleep. In her dream, she envisions how she had made it out from the Black Forest alone without any help. Not even one of the royal guards was there to deliver her.

The journey ahead was long and she is crossing the great open plains by foot. In front of her, a storm is brewing and she is badly injured. Knowing the great open plains well enough she moves to the outer lands to cut much of her journey. The conditions along the way are dry and harsh. Baron and void of signs of food or the lush green foliage of plant life. To sustain herself, she takes the last of her herbal food.

In this region cannibals roam, nomads drifting from place to place in this barren wasteland. She knows they are there, they started to follow her sometime back. Circling her like a pack of wolves they will close in and attack. They need to feed, many pilgrims who have ventured to cross have fallen victim to their bands. Right now she is the only food insight and they want her.

The storm is raging towards them as they reveal themselves to her. She cannot outrun them nor the fury of the storm. The rolling storm encases, surging around Leoha. She feels no pain, it feeds her strength, as each vagrant steps towards her, she cuts them down killing them all.

The storm whirls, whipping over the slain men lying dead littered around her. They will now be meat for the scavengers of the plains. She must keep moving, there is a town far in front of her and she must make it or die. With the storm high front wind in her face, she struggles to see ahead. The strong winds now upon her brings the rain, lighting, and thunder. The angry rain beats against her injured body causing her steps to fall from time to time. It's her warrior training and instincts that preserve her to keep on moving. Each labored step brings her closer to the town until finally, she is there.

The townspeople it seems have already locked and barricaded themselves in from the angry storm. She tries knocking on doors and windows but no one answers or lets her in. There's something she finds to be most strange about this town and its people. Even as she arrived something didn't feel right. The only thing to do is to keep moving. The winds are strengthening, facing high winds she is carried around like a leaf wafting on a breeze.

She keeps close to the house sides inching along. Squinting against the blurring winds, from the corner of her eye across the road there is a large metal barrel. It's the only shelter she can use from the storm. She must get to it. It isn't easy but she makes it across to the other side. The wind and rain have now become her fiercest adversaries. Reaching the large metal barrel, it is filled with rainwater. In her condition, with what strength she has left, she pushes hard against the barrel until finally it overturns and emptied itself. Turning it up-right she crawls under for safety. From inside the large drum enveloped in darkness, with her dagger she pierces breeding holes just enough to allow fresh air in from the outside while she waits it out.

The rumbling howls of the wind rush through the town making eerie sounds. The brunt of the storm is now weighing down upon her and the town. Feeling its effect, loose flying debris, boards, and rooftops rip away like paper. The rapid succession of objects hitting the metal barrel reminds Leoha how fortunate she is. It could very well have been her out there with no cover. With no time to relax the wind reminds her how easily it can rip her security from her. For a minute, it seems she had lost control of the large barrel but she manages to hold it down from flying away.

Then suddenly there's a lull in the wind's blow. The storm calms, listening, the stillness tells her they have just entered the center of its peace. In the repose of any storm, there is a space that suspends the winds from entering. It is in this, where it's quiet for a time, she will be able to have a short rest. It starts again, with whipping burst slicing the air, the wind force increases. Groans and slamming boards loosened slap in the wind. When the howls resume Leoha braces herself for the second half. The storm batters the town like a death stroke and then as quickly as it came, it's over and gone.

Unknown to Leoha

Unknown to Leoha, she does not know, the small town in which she has entered is being over-run by a group of four men known as the four Sadistic Bastards. They are looking to make a name for themselves by any means necessary. Deserters of the legion army in their wake have left a trail of destruction. Taking over the whole town, their brutal tactics have put everyone in fear. Many of the locals have barricaded themselves in as much from the storm but also because of them. This town and its people face the ravishment of tormentors. In search of a haven from the storm, it's only by chance they came upon this remote town. Walking into the town bar hall they decide it's a good place to hold up.

The four Sadistic Bastarda begin their reign of terror first by killing the madam who resisting, refused to sign over the bar to them. There is no hesitation as one of the bastards takes out his sword and runs her through. Stunned, the owner is dead before she is allowed to reconsider the option. The original madam planned to leave ownership in the event should anything happen to her, the daughter is next ink in.

Her daughter is mortified, by the sudden demise of her parent in front of her and the bar patrons. The four Sadistic Bastards continue making their threats to the young daughter. She too refuses them ownership and each time she denies them another patron in the bar is killed until only eight persons remain. Many of those lying dead tried to help the young and beautiful lady but their efforts were in vain.

One of the Sadistic Bastards sets about teaching the young lady an everlasting lesson. Slapping her over and again repeatedly, held by the roots of her hair she is grabbed up off the floor many times. To appease them she finally consents, the carnage around convinces her to comply. Little did she know no matter what she was prepared to give or not, it would make no difference to these men. One by one, each of the men presses perverted pleasures, penetrating usages of her body? For fun, they enjoy her together dividing her parts. The last survivors can only watch aghast, helpless to do anything. For not submitting to their demands, she pays the ultimate price before being killed.

The storm has gone, tired from being closed in the four Sadistic Bastards begin pulling away the wooden barriers holding the doors closed. Together they make their way out to the open road to look at what remains of the town spoils. Minutes after smashing through the tavern door, Leoha, tosses the large barrel over her, up into the air. It comes down simultaneously crashing to the earth.

The crash calls attention. Reaching the open street four Sadistic Bastards run towards the sound. Noticing the over-turned barrel they look down at the ground. There in the dirt, imprints of footprints lead behind one of the side buildings. The print size and impressions are that of a wounded, and they follow. One of the four Sadistic Bastards is a tracker, by his calculations, all indications say it's a woman and that woman is walking hard on one foot. In no time they find her, limping she struggles to move along. The afflictions of pain ripples through Leoha's body, curse the Black Widow. Without turning Leoha senses danger coming towards her. Four on one they approach her and she stops.

The eldest of the four Sadistic Bastards, speaks first. "Warrior, you look not so well. Come with us and we will help you." Leoha has been a warrior long enough to know predictors when she meets them. She refuses his help. The youngest of the four Sadistic Bastards smiling sweetly insists. "Lady, come with us. We can help you. Would you like that?" The manner of their clothing does little to diminish her tensions. She looks at him so well dressed as he stands there. "If you come here to help me. You wouldn't have come with so many weapons don't you think?"

Many innocents have been fooled by the first impression of meeting them. Right away trying to conceal their weapons behind their clothing they realize, but it's much too late. The four Sadistic Bastards look to each other she has seen through their ploy. She is no fool. The youngest bastard interjects explaining. "The weapons are only for protection. Do you need our help or not?" With a sneer of disgust, Leoha lays down her law putting it to him straight. "The kind of help, you and your friends offer could only get all of you killed." Leoha turns to walk away, she has issued her ultimatum it would be in their best interest to leave her alone. Reaching for her weapon the youngest bastard is cut and pays with his own blood. The fight begins and Leoha finds she is much too weak to fight at peak performance. The poison put into her body by the Black Widow is strong, it is making it difficult for her to control her vital body points and their movements.

The townspeople watch from the confines of hiding places but none dare come out to aid her. In the midst of the fighting, the third Sadistic Bastard, shouts out. "Stop, stop, stop, the fight!" Pulling away from the brothers back off. "The third Sadistic Bastard, as if nothing had happened tries to sway Leoha's attention, "You're not from around here, are you? And there is no need for us to further injure each other! We only want to help you!" From her expression, they gather she will never freely surrender to their help. The second bastard, consoles. "You see lady! my brothers like weapons but I don't. I believe in being civil."

Secretly his eye movement to the others tells them to attack her. Collectively the fight resumes. A trained and skilled assassin, Leoha battles them quickly to the ground without killing not one. Putting away her weapon her vision wavers, her focus blurs her head feels like it's spinning, spiraling she falls to the earth. Getting up, they believe her fall is a result of one of their strikes injuring her. The four Sadistic Bastards can't account for why she put the blade back in the holder. Never the less, the opportunity of victory is what counts. Together they jump the injured warrior beating her unconscious body stomping, and kicking her.

From hiding places, the townspeople still watch but can do nothing for fear of death. The Bastards do not want to lose face. Two of them drag her by the hand-tying her up against the old oak tree. With their whips they add to her injuries, making her pay. This is done for the town's benefit that no one else gets any ideas to resist them. The townspeople get the picture. This is a strong message, they lose her bloodied body, it collapses, falling to the earth.

Lost to the darkness, Leoha did not kill any of them because she was too weak. Thinking about the odds against her, if she had killed one, she wouldn't have been able to get them all. Eventually in her condition, one of them would have killed her. Even if she sent out a distress call by removing the top of her blade. They would never have arrived in time because of the direction of the storm, she is on her own.

Two of the town citizens run out from their hiding place, no longer able to stand the brutal and unjust cruelty against the stranger. They die bravely. Matters are only going to worsen, the bastards deliberate, beginning to believe she is a hired hand paid to dispose of them. Who is this woman of exceptional skill? Troubled and paranoid, anxiety builds to pressure them. Compounded frustrations lead them to the insanity of mad thinking. They know they have not broken the hope of the town yet. The two dead bodies of courage lie in the street is a testimony to their strength. The townspeople need a lesson in a respectful manner.

She still breathes, bruised, torn, and lacerated, the bastards are amazed by Leoha's endurance and ability to withstand their punishments. Others have died under less duress. Maybe this will teach her, stripping her of her lower garments, one by one they waste themselves in her, defiling her body. After they are finished and pleased, two of the Sadistic Bastards want more, so much more. Things definitely were not turning out like the last town. The bastard she earlier injured, walks up to her face getting low gripping her hair he picks up her lifeless head and spits into her face.

A foul smell close to her jars her senses to consciousness as the slime of spit hits her face. In a lifeless tone somewhere from the recesses of her pain, she utters, "Even. . . if you kill me. . . I'll come back. and kill you all." Before Leoha passes out. there is a slim chance they may kill her. To protect herself, mentally she tunes down her body's vital organs, rendering her own body close to death's door. All appearances will indicate that she is dead. The youngest bastard is astounded to hear her talk and drops her head back to the ground. The blue hue of her lips says she's dead. To be sure, he walks on and across her back and most of her lifeless limbs. Raising her arm to the air, letting go it falls lifeless. Placing his finger under her nose, there is no breath, he pronounces her dead. The others have seen enough death to know she is no more. Two of them laugh, another conquest defeated.

The third bastard wants to know more about her and where she came from. To satisfy himself, he quickly searches her dead body but finds nothing. Picking up her weapon, he finds he is unable to remove the blade from its holder. Showing it over to the others, neither can they. They agree, (the blade is stuck) throwing it back to the ground, it's good for nothing if it can't be used. It falls beside her lifeless corpse. Walking away, discussing her. Her tightness was a delight after so many saloon women. They all agree, she could have caused any man to be tamed by love.

Leoha Meets Arrius, Bleaha, and Trottus

    Hiding and watching are three very good friends. Arrius a serious man in his fifty's, Trottus who can be unpredictable at times is forty-seven years old, and the beautiful Bieaha thinks unlike most women open-minded. They are close, and at times, much more to each other. Sitting in hiding they wait for the chance to help the Warrior. All but one of the three never loses faith that the Warrior still lives. The three Sadistic Bastards are not in sight. The three friends engaging the opportunity, run to her body just before the Warrior brings herself back into the world of the living. Her eyes open briefly to a startled trio and then closes as her breathing restores to normalcy. Gathering the ripped material Bieaha modestly covers her exposed extremities. It's a good thing she brought something she could use. Clothing her with what they have, the true question is when and where could she have come from?

    Slowly her body moves, flexing fingers curl to a fist grip. The others are elated she still lives, together they hurry to lift her to a more secure area. Out of reach from the four Sadistic Bastards, they look over her for injuries. There is none, not one broken bone and they wonder how could such a thing be possible? Her odd face color is what they don't understand. Mulling over the questions about her condition, they end up with more questions. It is determined by the oldest of the three friends that she is suffering from poison. But from what? He can not tell and neither can they. They all agreed, she requires urgent medicine and the medicine house has just been destroyed by the storm. The medicine house is located in the same direction the four Sadistic Bastards went. Following them is not an option, they all refuse to go that way. Justified, by the actions of the Sadistic Bastards, they agree it's too risky.

Most of the town doctors live in the same direction as the medicine house. They agree if they are to help the Warrior they need to think hard about another way. Exploring other avenues, they do. With careful planning, they make a decision, to take the Warrior to the only place left. The green bush doctor Exuma. He is more than familiar and better equipped than the town conventional doctors to deal with symptoms like what the Warrior has. Trottus suddenly gets a crazy notion and he disagrees. He is afraid of the bush doctor Exuma he deals in voodoo and black magic.

A few harsh words from Bleaha, whom he would die for, calls him a blue belly coward. Mustering up his strength he finds the courage to agree, as long as he stays on the outside. They agreed, Trottus loves Bleaha and would do almost anything for her love. She loves him but she has other ideas about what love truly is. He doesn't know, because of his stubbornness he is blind to her true affections. Most times Arrius plays the intercessor between the two. Watching the two of them he thinks likewise what Trottus can't see. Bleaha, thanks Trottus, for his bravery and he finds her flattery sweet. For her to say such encouraging words, he feels motivated and leaves to return.

Minutes later Trottus returns with extra help and when the way is cleared, they load her body on the back of the small donkey cart. Off they all go. Many of the town's buildings have fallen in from the wind forces. The horseshoe den is no longer standing where it was. The town has been hit hard by the storm and while they move along, the evidence of the shattered serves as a distraction all around. To be safe from being seen, they leave the town from a hidden direction, unknown to the four Sadistic Bastards.

Traveling Distance Away

Traveling a distance away they arrive at a small green bushy area with few tall trees. No one remembers the way and they find themselves lost. Arrius, who is the eldest and most knowledgeable directs his friends and the donkey to a small side road. It would seem they are back on track but the road just keeps winding. Ahead of them, a man sits by the roadside.

From his expression, they are all pleased to see each other and the donkey cart is made to stop beside him. The man places his hand out, meaning he is no more than a roadside beggar. Bleaha and Trottus jump down to the ground in front of the beggar. Trottus, who works hard for his own money tells the beggar his mind and that fortune was not going to shine on him today. Trottus can't remember his last job being it so long ago. He was thinking of going to another town and taking Bleaha with him before these dastardly men showed up. The storm didn't help, maybe now there will be work to clean and fix things. As long as these marauders remain no one will be able to work. That is if they don't kill everyone first.

The old beggar looks at him, strangely he questions him, "But you do work! Don't you?" Impatient to see the old beggars point Trottus replies, "Yes!" The old beggar continues smartly. "Mr. If you are working and you can't find a coin. Maybe you shouldn't be working." This makes Bleaha laugh out at the top of her voice. She and Arrius can't help but watch the exchange between Trottus and the beggar. With a straight face, Trottus turns to her embarrassed, "What's so funny?" Not seeing any humor in the situation, especially since this old man has him looking stupid. It's all in harmless fun Bleaha chides, "I think he knows what makes you click." Trottus, who at times believes he knows it all, say nothing more. Arrius, still on the cart with the injured Warrior, watching. He is impressed, himself he applauds the old beggar's wisdom "Good lesson learned," keeping it to himself.

So entrenched in their conversation, it seems like the main reason for them being here has escaped. Arrious calls out to Bleaha and Trottus, and their heads only turn to him as to say, what?! He reminds them both with serious urgency, "Will, you two stop fooling around and get on with it! I have a sick one here!" Bleaha pulls out a copper coin and hands it over to the beggar. He kindly thanks her, hearing Arrious talk of a sick one it is he who tells her the directions in which to follow.

While Bleaha and Trottus mount the donkey cart, still in a mood and displeased is Trottus. Looking at Bleaha with a frown, contentiously he asks, "Why did you give him a coin?" Taken aback, she looks at him searching his face not certain of his seriousness, "That was good! He deserves it! He makes me laugh, something you should try once in a while?" Just to have the last say exasperated Trottus, toots, "You women, always think men are fools because they care. Womennnnn!!!" While the cart moves away, the old beggar waves good-bye. Bleaha reminds hiding her smirk behind a stoic face. "Maybe you should remember what the beggar said." Trottus head snaps to look at her expression to see if she was making fun of him again. Not liking her gesture, he only growls under his breath and turns his focus and attention back to the impatient Arrius.

From the look on Arrius face, he is more than ready to say something about their behavior. "Do you all now have it together!!" Before he could finish. They both cried out. "Yes!!!" Referring to the directions, they move along while Arrius focuses on the injured Warrior's condition, who at times shows little movement. Bleaha and Trottus leave off working on the direction of their relationship and put themselves to concentrate on the road ahead. They have already gotten lost, and once is enough.

Finally Arriving at the Location

Finally arriving at the location, in the middle of nowhere. Tall green trees and bush all surround a wooden structure. The walkway inn is guarded by high and tangling brushes, making it much too narrow for the cart. They now must move on foot. To the ground from the cart Bleaha and Arrius jump down, but Trottus does not follow. The wooden structure looks like a house but it is more like a fortress with a small porch and few windows on both sides. Through slightly open windows strange noises and chanting spills to the outside. Bleaha and Arrius, stand waiting for Trottus, to come down and join them. They will need a helping hand moving the Warrior. He can feel their eyes piercing him from his seat, this journey, everything they going through, for someone they don't know. He watched like everyone this woman took those men down. What if she's worst than them. Any excuse at this point is a good one, looking up the pathway with dread he turns to them both with a faraway look in his eyes. "Well! Don't look at me! I agreed not to go any further and am not! So I will wait here until you all are finished."

They both say nothing further to him but walk back to the donkey cart. Together Bleaha and Arrius, try to move her body but the dead's weight is much too heavy for Arrius and Bleaha to lift on their own. They look at each other and Arrious shrugs his head in Trottus direction. Up to the front of the cart, Bleaha goes, and Trottus is still sitting, posing like there is nothing more to do with his legs crossed. This woman has no idea what she's putting him through, no... no. . . don't look at her he tells himself. Ignoring his inner voice, Trottus looks down at Bleaha. It's just as he thought, from her sorrowful expression it tells him he's in for it, again. Pleading, Bleaha tries to get Trottus to concede, "Trottius, she calls?!"

Not wanting to look in her face, he looks elsewhere, folding his arms in front of him. "What now?" Sighing, there's no way around this, Bleaha has to convince Trottus to help, this woman's life depends on it. She can't let him do this to her, not now, this might be the one. . . a ticket out of here. She is humble when she asked, "Do you think, I would allow you to die here alone?" He can't help but turned and look her in the eyes. "What is that suppose to mean?" Sometimes Trottus doesn't see the inevitable and it has to be explained plainly. "If we do die here, we die together." These words seriously take to his heart and his full attention comes to her mercy. Now that she has his full attention, "Please, please give Arrius a hand. She is much too heavy for me to carry and I shall bring her blade."

From his seat, Trottus slides down to the ground in front of her. For one intense moment, he looks into her eyes deeply as she into his and time stretches. Together in silence, they walk to the back of the cart. Arrius looks to Bleaha, and says nothing further. Together Arrius and Trottus take hold of the Warrior by her two hands and places them over their shoulders to maneuver her out of the cart. Bleaha follows behind with Leoha's blade in hand.

The front porch is minutes away, to distract Trottus she encourages him. Walking closer behind him, the bush surrounding them is intimidating, the spider's web is a canopy over their heads. Together they make it onto the front porch. There Bleaha looks at Trottus and he is shaking from the knees like a leaf. He is so afraid of the great medicine doctor Exuma. To calm him, Bleaha places her left hand onto his other shoulder, the look he gives tells her, it's a bad time so she simply removes it. Without warning to either of them, Trottus lets go of the Warrior and runs back to the cart, leaving Arrius to best deal with the unbalanced weight alone.

Wavering from the unbalance, Arrius tries to hold her up by himself. All he can do is make sure she doesn't land hard. She is the size of the amazon women who are tall in statues. There Arrius lays the Warrior's body out and Bleaha is nowhere in his sight. Looking around for her, she can only be nearby, he looks once more at the

Warrior moving over to the front porch corner. Peering around the side of the house, Bleaha is standing on an old bucket. What could she be looking at, peeping in through one of the side windows?

Bleaha is transfixed with curiosity by the chanting sounds emanating from within, this is a great opportunity to see the bush doctor called Exuma at work. On the inside, there is a man other than Exuma on his knees in a circle of fire. On the floor are strange like drawings. Exuma continues to circle the shirtless man's body while rubbing him with a strange green tree branch she has never seen before. Chanting in an ancient language Bleaha has never heard, Exuma's voice resounds through the air. Croaking sounds like a frog and billy goats neigh. Around the man, he goes bending and stretching. His body contorts in the subtlest of ways not normal for a human being. Exuma chants.

"Obeah, Obeah, Obeah, Obeah in me."

"I drink the water from the fiery sea,"

"I'm Exuma I'm the Obeah man."

Bleaha is intrigued, it must be some kind of love ritual. The man in the circle has turned to the witch doctor for aide. The woman he loves won't see him. He has asked for a spell and potion of favor to cleanse away the dark spirits that have to alienate her affections. Many in his village visit the witch doctor for cures and aphrodisiacs. Sometimes the possessed are bought in for him to exercise the tormenting spirits.

"Obeah, Obeah, Obeah, Obeah in me."

"I drink the water from the fiery sea."

"if you got a woman and she ain't happy"

"come see me for camalamae,"

"Take that camalame and you make her some tea"

"and she will love you all the time,"

"Take some flower and you make some pap"

"that will give you, strength in your back"

"I'm Exuma, I'm the obeah man,"

"na, na, na, na, a na, na, na, na, na,"

"na, na, na, na, a – na, na, na, na, a."

The chanting comes to an end, Bleaha jumps down from the bucket. Running toward the front porch she almost runs over Arruis bumping into him. Smiling coyly, she is pleased to see Arrius even his frown of disapproval doesn't dismay her. They turn towards walking back to the Warrior. On the porch bending down beside the Warrior, Bleaha searches the perimeter around for Trottus. He has long gone. Exuma's front door is open to receive them. From the interior a crocked and strange voice beacons, calling out to them to come in. "Come, come in ye black sheep from de town."

Together Bleaha, and Arrius, struggle, pulling the Warrior's body to the inside. The voice in authority commands them, "Bring she into me!" Arrius and Bleaha drag Leoha through the fortress door entrance. Bleaha and Arrius's eyes survey the inner sanctuary of the witch doctor. Tools and evidence of his trade display on shelves and walls. Containers and jars hold various herbs and bones.

Exuma walks up to them. His face is white, covered in what looks like ghost powder, piercing blood-red eyes stare at both Bleaha and Arrius. This is why Trottus ran, the witch doctor standing before them is an imposing figure. Power radiates from him lighting the very air surrounding them. It gives them chills. Frightened and wide-eyed, both Bleaha, and Arrius keep their attention on him at all times. His red eyes rest on Bleaha, "You! Peeping uman, together you sit over dea." Bleaha gaze falls away from his, embarrassed. Bleaha and Arrius move, getting the picture, he points out at the spot for sitting. She was careful not to make a sound, how could he have known she was peeping? Nervous and frightened, she dears not utter a word. To her, Exuma again singles her out. "Uman no speak here. You, he, sit over dea."

Arrius too is silent, leave it to the women to make things awkward. Shaking his head, you'd have to be a man to understand the witch doctor's position. Sometimes women don't know their place, as his good friend Trottus would have agreed if he was here. Trottus would probably be furious with Bleaha for intruding on the man's privacy, it's a good thing he caught her. Bleaha doesn't even think she has done anything wrong. She perceives, he must have something against women.

Both she and Arrius have trouble understanding Exuma broken language but they comprehend his meanings. With hand gestures Exuma paints a picture, both concentrate closely trying to understand the signs of his finger movements. He points out the way to them once again for the last time. Across the room, they make their way to a thatched bundle of horse hay to sit and watch. The Warriors body has been placed in the middle of a circle on the floor. Bleaha and Arrius look at each other, neither of them remembers putting her there. The great witch doctor Exuma spews on the outer circle of the floor, fire encircles he and the Warrior.

The great Exuma is a largely built man with bulging muscles and sculptured sinews. He wears no shirt on his painted body. His large muscles ripple, flexing with his every movement those large hands appear very capable of crushing a man to death. In this age, reproductive organs are worshiped and highly prized possessions, the loincloth does little to contain all of what he has. Exuma is exceptionally endowed. Bleaha's eyes gravitate to his nether regions, she can't help but notice. She can say nothing to Arrius of her innate contemplatives. Siting transfixed awed, she drinks in Exuma's every move and twitch. Bleaha thinks he has an interesting big sack.

In a circle of fire, Exuma sprinkles powder over the Warrior's face. Taking from his lower garment a strange mirrored object he uses it to examine the Warrior. Arrius, nor Bleaha, have never seen such a device or practis before, and attentively they watch. He then pours over the Warrior's face some sort of purple liquid and right away it begins to react. Her earlier skin tone was dark, the liquid draws absorbing the poison out from her skin. The purple powder turns black stunning Bleaha and Arrius. Without warning, Exuma leaps from the circle across to Bleaha and Arrius. Still sitting in their given positions Exuma lands right in front of Bleaha's face.

A blush rises to Bleaha cheeks, raising her hand to rub her eyebrow, through slits of her fingers she shields her eyes from the egregious sight standing in front of her. She has already been called out for peeking, she'd be mortified if he exposes the object of her observation. Turning her head to the side, she feels bad they came there to help this woman and all she can think about is how big this man's balls are. Uncertain how to show and regain his respect and redeem herself, she composes to contain her hands to her lap, removing them from her face. The corpulent size of his egg sac is bound in white linen, slowly her jaw drops, her eyes stare with an exclamation. Not knowing what to make of this in front of her eyes, pulling her eyes away she is meek and soft when she speaks, "Thank you." Swallowing the lump in her throat.

Arrius has never met a man gifted as Exuma, not knowing what to make of him, he sits in disbelief. To both of them, Exuma explains, "She is in circle, have poison in the body, kind poison me no-no. But I can give her something so she can go." Both Arrius, and Bleaha, can do nothing more than nod their heads. Backing away, the witch doctor leaps into the air returning over to the Warrior. Gently lifting her head, he pours into her mouth something unknown to drink. He looks back at Bleaha he is enjoying making her feel uncomfortable. Because of who and how he looks, Exuma is a man used to woman worship. Exuma has intentionally targeted this woman, the teasing he hopes will cure and spare her the folly of future actions. Like any, to Arrius looking on, he is most concerned about Exuma's methods, Bleah brought this on herself.

Exuma lets them know, "Now she rest and soon she go." He walks over to light four candlesticks on the floor and again begins to chant. This time he brushes Leoha with many different kinds of tree branches lit and burning. The smell permeates the air most disturbingly. Just like before with the man, around her body he begins to move turning himself in many different ways. Uncoiling, slithering like a snake he moves around her body. Bleaha and Arrius are sitting a distance away thankful not to be assailed by the smell of the burning bush.

The window beside them allows fresh air into the room. Exuma resumes chanting bring it to a close.

"Obeah, obeah, obeah, obeah in me."
"I drink the water from the fiery sea."
"I'm Exuma I'm the obeah man,"
"Exuma was my name when I lived in the stars"
"Exuma is a planet that once lit mars."
"I've got the voice of many in my throat,"
"The teeth of a frog and a tail of a goat,"
"I'm Exuma I'm the obeah man,"
"na, na, na, na, a na, na, na, na,"
"a, na, na, na, na, a na, na, na, na, – a,"

At the end of the palmist verse the Warrior's, eyes flutter open. Alert, immediately Leoha instincts kick in. With her eyes, she observes all and detects everything within her peripheral vision. She even detects Exuma who now stands ways off from her. Bleaha and Arrius's eyes widen, elated to see her breathe without laboring. The flames on the ground around her spontaneously extinguish, leaving only the four candlesticks burning. From her laid out position in the charcoal circle, she leaps into the air revived. Coming down to stand among the embers of the dying flames without looking at them, she calls out, "Bleaha! Arrius!"

Bleaha and Arrius are astounded, shocked by her recovery, but even more, so that she can identify calling them for who they are by name. Looking to each other, the Warrior goes on to say. "I remember everything." With an adoring smile, Bleaha is pleased to see the Warrior finally back on her feet. Stepping out from the circle, Leoha crosses the floor to where Arrius, and Bleaha, are sitting. Hastily they both hurry to their feet while gazing upon the statuette figure of the Warrior Warlord.

Bleaha removes Leoha weapon off her shoulder and hands it over to her, noticing the color change when touched by the Warrior's hand. "I think this belongs to you." Leoha smiles happy to see it, retrieving it also by the belt strap, she places it over her shoulder. There isn't a mark on her, Bleaha and Arrius are amazed. "I thank you both for what you have done for me." While both stand in awe speechless, she turns her head to the witch doctor Exuma standing over at the opposite side of the room. Without any words, she bows her head down to him once and in response so does he. Bleaha eager with anticipation looks at the impressive Warrior with renewed interest, now restored in health. Before anyone could ask, Bleaha puts a question to Leoha's future plans. "Warrior. Where will you go from here? "Her strength has never felt so sure. With a resolve like a flint Leoha does not hesitate to respond, "To War. . ."

This was almost perfect, Bleaha, wishes she didn't understand her intent. Reaching for the top of her head from her hair Leoha, pulls out two carefully hidden gold shaped marble balls. Calling out to the witch doctor, "Exuma," she tosses one of the gold balls over to him. Catching it in the palm of his hand, placing it to his mouth, he examines the golden marble with his teeth. To Bleaha and Arrius surprise, the other she hands over to Bleaha, "I am entrusting you to take care of the needs of your friend here and the one you called coward."

Somehow in her unconscious state, the Warrior heard everything. Surprised by what the Warrior said. Bleaha acknowledges her private spoken sentiments. "You really heard me when I said that?" Even though Leoha doesn't have much affection for her sister Sheppard, there's something about Bleaha she finds similar and endearing. "Think nothing much of it." Arrius can't believe his eyes, especially in these times of famine the value of such a rich treasure is transforming. In all his years, he has taught himself not to live or reach beyond his means. This unexpected boon brings uncompromising relief. This surprise and all of what it could mean make him and Bleaha look at each other. Each can tell what the other is thinking, with this kind of wealth the town's problems are solved. The only problem is getting rid of those four who are terrorizing the town.

The witch doctor, Exuma walks over and presents a change of clothing to the warrior. She kindly accepts them putting them on over her garments. This will make it easier for her to fit in with the local town folk. She thanks Exuma, bowing once more and he also reciprocates in kind. Arrius smiles admirably to himself watching the warrior's dignified clothing fit so well. Leoha is ready to finish her mission, she has missed a lot of time she must make up for. With her obligations compensated more than adequately for their care of her, she must leave. "I bid you all, farewell." In gratitude of respect Leoha, turns to Exuma, and with her head slightly bowed to say goodbye. He nods his sentiments in kind. Walking away from all, Leoha turns toward the door, it opens.

Nudging Arrius with her elbow in his side to do something this may be their only chance to stop her from leaving. Bleaha, really does push too much, his hands are tied. What more does Bleaha want? When you are a Warlord Warrior there are rules and codes of conduct one must follow. Because Arrius, understands some of the obligations associated with the Warrior's code he leaves it alone.

Bleaha is hard-headed and stubborn at times, not knowing when to give up. She again takes charge of matters. Shouting out it takes all her courage to approach Leoha. "Warrior, please wait up!" Leoha turns, stopping in the doorway. Bleaha, runs up to her. "The least we can do is give you a ride back into the town." With penetrating attentions, Leoha gives Bleaha the best advice she can. "Your chances are best here."

How could she make the Warrior comprehend what is the heart of her matters? If she can persuade Trottus to bring them to the witch doctor, this Warlord can't be that bad. "We are in this together!" Leoha does not deny or refute the logic of her appeal. Without further words, the Warrior continues to the outside, with Bleaha following behind. When Arrius realizes he is alone with the great witch-doctor Exuma, quickly he runs to catch them up. Walking together, the change feels different as they head for the pathway to meet Trottus.

Tied to a tree, the donkey cart is there, but Trottus is nowhere in sight, only the Warrior notices him standing ways off. To Bleaha, and Arrius. The Warrior presses, "Let's not waste any more time." Trottus, having gotten tired of waiting in the sun, secured the donkey cart within a short distance under a cool tree. There he sat waiting when he spotted the Warrior, and Arrius coming towards him. Hurriedly getting up, he grabs its strap pulling the donkey cart to meet them.

All along the pathway back to the cart, flashes of past stories in the town about the witch doctor makes Bleaha question the truths after her experience with him. It seems unfair that he has been defamed and ostracized as a result of his practices to help people. Then it comes to her, deep down she knows its the right thing to do, it would only take a moment. Bleaha, leaves off, encouraging Arrius, to go along with the Warrior. Making an excuse, she left something behind on the inside of Exuma's fortress. She will catch them up and she runs back. Arrius and the Warrior continue.

With an abundance of smiles, Trottus, greets the Warrior pulling Arrius aside with a deep look of concern on his face. In a whisper of urgency, "I was wondering, what is taking so long! That Exuma man! I hear he is a fast healer, and. . . I wish I could have a body like that one." Trottus points to the Warrior, admiringly, referring to the strong physical body structure, before looking around for Bleaha. His distress is obvious, to put Trottus at ease, Arrius, tries to appease him, "She left something behind and will catch up." Too late he should have rephrased that differently, Trottus fixation with Bleaha is border line obsession if you asked him. Trottus reacts, of course with outrage that Arrius could be so irresponsibly. "And you left her with that mad Exuma?" Leoha looks on observing the exchange with some amusement.

Pushing Arrius to the side, Trottus forgets his fear of the witch doctor, in face of losing Bleaha. He can't lose her, living wouldn't be the same without her. So what if she hasn't seen him for what he is, one day. . . maybe. He runs toward Exuma, the fortress door.

On the inside, Bleaha and Exuma are in conversation. To Exuma. Bleaha is in process of making amends to the great witch-doctor, "I have always thought the worst of you, just like many of the town people but that will all change. We were wrong for voting against your practices. We became afraid of not understanding. People are often afraid of what they don't understand but I have seen and understand now and thanks for helping us." Before him, all Exuma the witch doctor sees, is a naive woman who is too stubborn for her own good. In that voice like a frog and a billy goat, Exuma does nothing to entertain her, "Uman go!" He will waste no more time with her. he points the way out. Exuma never has to say it twice, Bleaha wastes no time in getting out from there.

In her haste to get away, she runs straight into Trottus. The bursting force of Bleaha rushing into his arms is an unexpected pleasure he has only has dreamed about, it stuns him for a moment. . . Then she speaks looking up at him still holding her. Reluctantly, he lets his arms fall away from her so she won't feel threatened by his true feelings. "You sure have a lot of courage when I don't need you." In a dis-favorable tone, "What else am I suppose to do! Just leave you with that mad Exuma!" Rattled. Walking back toward the others, Trottus lags sullenly behind. Glaring back, Bleaha firers at him her disbelief, gesturing for Trottus to hurry up. Her agitation and dissatisfaction is more than enough to push him. "Your leap of courage always amazes me." Leaning into her ear, "You could call it a leap of faith."

The Silence Between Them Is Thick

By the time Bleaha and Trottus reached the others, the silence between them is thick. Arrius is tired of being the intercessor between them, to lighten the air, "I gather, you two are in a good mood." Arrius's sarcastic remark is ignored as Bleaha exclaims her frustrations about Trottus. "He makes me so angry at times." Trottus, isn't one to back down or take last, not holding back his words he informs Arrius, "She says some of the most hurting things at times." Their behavior can be so embarrassing at times. "Look you two! We have enough trouble back in town! Don't let our mutual friends see this side of us. We need her if we are to try and take back the town." Together and at once Bleaha and Trottus turn to Arrius. both besiege him, "Tell him that!" "Tell her that!."

Bleaha and Trottus soberly do understand what's at stake. The two moving expeditiously, gather themselves onto the back cart. The Warrior is waiting and off they go. The atmosphere is strained in the presence of a guest. Each is contrite for reasons of their own, in looking to warm the chill of communication, even a casual comment can become a painful word of grievance between friends with strong opinions. There is no easy way to interject the balm needed to amend, hurts as Arrius finds himself looking for an out. "Do we always have to go at the same speed, can't you get that beast to go any faster?"

Trottus is still upset with Bleaha, he casts a looks at her with an under-eye. In respect for the warrior, Trottus invites Arrius to take over "The driver seat is open!" Arrrius does not miss the sarcasm, Trottus knows he cares not to have anything to do with this beast. His concern is only for the warrior and not Trotus who at times can be very facetious. Usually, in most donkey carts, the driver seat is in the middle of the cart. Trottous the genius decides it's best that his driver's seat be to one side. His reason being, he can better see everything that happens on the inside. Most donkeys don't need much prodding when guiding them. Trottus donkey is the exception, he always seems to have the upper hand on him. Trottus has never dictated or trained his donkey. His jackass is quite comfortable moving at his own pace, even stopping on occasion to explore the path vegetation available.

Looking to avoid Arrius, and Bleaha questions that may cause him to lose his temper. Like a child, he pouts, not liking people talk about his donkey, especially when they don't have one. Looking back to the warrior, Trottus ignores Arrius. "Warrior, are you well enough now?" Leoha response is pensive, "I don't know if I'll ever be well enough again." Bleaha studies the warrior's countenance as she speaks. Sitting calmly, Arrius is intrigued to know more, he is hopeful this may be the prime opportunity to inquire. "You know Warrior, we don't even know your name?" Bleaha looks at the warrior in agreement. Trottus's eye is on the road ahead but he is also listening. "You can call me Leoha."

Arrius, being the knowledgeable one, more out loud than to himself recites what he has been told. "That is a name from the far north, Arawak's land, and Gouddaaian Kingdom." Never has he had the pleasure of meeting anyone from that remote side of the world, not once does he take his eyes off her. Leoha partially smiles reminiscing at the thought of home being mentioned. It's a fresh reminder of who she is and where she comes from. "You are well informed." This excites Bleaha, she is a person from the north. Out loud Bleaha can't help but add in. "So Leoha, from the far north. What are the chances of us ever meeting you again? And am sorry about what they did to you." In one sentence the Warrior answers Bleaha on two points. "So am I and so are they."

None of them grasp her meaning but Trouttus, "No, no, not them. People like them don't regret anything. They should pay with their lives for what they did to you. How did you recover so fast?" Shaking her head, Bleaha is blunt, and she concurs with her own assessment. "You're not normal! I can tell you now! That blade you carry, when you touched it the color change. I tried but could never pull it out. How is that?" Trottus adds he noticed it too but not the color change, "Neither did the killers," Bleaha added and goes on to say. "I saw them you know. I had a feeling it's of value but if one can't remove it. It is of no value! I think that's why they left it behind like they left you." Bleaha glares at Trottus insensitivity, with an under-eye that says be more gentle with your words. He returns her look, as to say she's a warrior, she can take it. Unfortunately, Arrius doesn't stop her plied questions but he too wants to know more. Then again to the Warrior Bleaha, becomes more excited, "So what is the secret?"

As a Warlord Warrior, this is the first time she has had to interact with locals this closely. Leoha does her best to explain without divulging too much. "It's no secret! Maybe It's just your mind, then again it may be the hand which holds the blade and that's no secret, only an advantage." Considering all of what they watched happen to the Warrior Warlord, her remarkable recovery under the witch doctor's administrations and healing abilities are a marvel to Arrius. Being a thinking man he asks her the obvious, "Warrior Leoha if you are from the far north. Just why are you so far away from home and all alone." It's for the best, they remain ignorant about her Princess status. "Just a traveler from the far north doing the King's bidding" "Maybe she is the assignment sent her to help us Trottus," anxiously adds, "So, were you send out to kill those four Sadistic Bastards, who have taken over our town?" Bleaha reiterates.

The day the Black Widow cursed her became the bane of her existence. "No! And you don't have to worry much about them anymore." The cryptic response the Warlord offers them is puzzling. None of them fully understand, why she said what she said. Retaliation burns in Bleaha heart to see those Sadistic Bastards pay for all they have done. She can't contain her outrage, "After what they did to you. How could you say. . ." Arrius knows how his friend can get, he cuts in on Bleaha's speech. "I think her plans were set before we left Exuma's place." Bleaha is still at a loss, it's Leoha who clarifies. "I did not mean it like that! I won't forget it, nor will I forgive for what they did to me. I go now only to collect their heads and as for where I go next. The House of Zebb, in the next town, to find the cure." The witch-doctor has given her a reprieve, but she still must locate the cure. After all they have been through, Trottus feels confident she has a plan that will work to get rid of the four Sadistic Bastards. "Warrior, you must have a good plan to go up against four to one." Although the men have good fighting skills, they are still no match for Leoha who has destroyed many. "I will have to."

To make Arrius better understand her meaning Trottus doesn't hide his delight. "It means she must have a good plan. Too many of our people are already dead because of them. Maybe by the time we get back, the whole town may be dead." Trottus, words are brash putting it bluntly makes Bleaha, speak up. "Do your words have to be so rude?" Apologetically she turns to the warrior to explain. "Warrior, we small-town people do things the only way we know-how. When we first heard the news of them coming, the town people all agreed to stand together against them and things were going good until they killed off the first four wealthy businessmen, they stood up against them and one by one the four Sadistic Bastards, took away the courage by force and it frightened the others. Their brutal methods have broken many of the town people's bodies but not our spirit. Others ran from there post not realizing they were already dead and divided they picked us apart. It is only now I can better see, we were never any match for them and very much unprepared because we have compassion but they don't. I may not be of much, much use against them but whatever help I can offer, please take advantage of it, because it is all I have to give to help you."

Looking to each other Arrius and Trottus, are accustomed to Bleaha antics and liberal notions. Arrius laughs to himself the expression on his friend Trottus's face, says he wants to put a gag on Bleaha's mouth. Trottus may not like her talkative nature, but he still listens to her words. Thinking it through, her courage touches his heart and causes him to feel guilty about not giving a helping hand. To Trottus, surprise, Arrius, looks to the Warrior with great emotion he confesses, "She is my best friend. My faith too is now in your hand." The truth of Arrius sentiments touches Bleaha.

Trottus looks at them both rolling his eyes, now Bleaha, has him talking mad. It might be best that he reminds them both, that they are not heroes. Just as he is about to say it, they both look at him in a peculiar and isolating way. Trottus blusters at them. "What! Am no hero! Noooo way am falling for this! You all did this to me before! No, no, don't look at me! I prefer running!" Bleaha loves Trottus but he can be so trying at times and this is one of them. "Run! Run to what?! Why don't you start running now?!" Trottus chimes on defiantly, "Run for my life." Sitting by, the warrior smiles inward at the disposition of Trottus stand. Arrius proceeds to rationalize with Trottus. "We all want to run because it's the easiest thing to do. She may need our help. Are you with us?"

Trottus, stubbornly looks away, saying nothing. Not wanting to lose face with the Warrior, Bleaha thinks of a way to make Trottus, feel guilty. "What about all the talk about us dying together Trottus, is it all lies?" Again Trottus said nothing. Thinking, why does she have to be so persistent? Getting no response from Trottus, she looks to the Warrior, "Don't pay much attention to him, he knows what to do when my life is in danger and we have agreed to die together. Have we not, Trottus?!" To avoid confrontation with Bleaha, indifferent he only shakes his head, as to say, yes. Coming up to a bend in the road he recognizes, he alerts everyone. "This is the last turn before the town."

Impatient to return to her affairs, she lets them know. "I need to get out here. Just find out where they are holding up and stand out front in the middle of the road and no harm shall come to you." Trottus sees failure with the Warrior's ideas. "If you don't mind me asking. What are the guarantees of us not being killed while standing out in the middle of the street?" Reassuring him, "As I have said! No harm shall come to you!" It's Arrius who defines the prospects of her intentions to help Trottus, better understand her meaning. "I think it means, she will be watching." Still bent on the possibility of dying, Trottus, after analyzing the odds of them all dying in the middle of the road before she gets there challenges the foundations of Arrius's confidence. "We will reach the town long before her. What's the guarantee?" There is no filter on Trottus's mouth.

The time for talking is over. Before Trottus, can pull the donkey cart to the side and stop, the Warrior leaps out. From the cart and into the air she is gone, leaving them all stunned in her wake by her sudden actions. Wide-eyed Trottus, looks at Arrius, "If she can fly like that. I don't think, she needs us." Arrius, nor Bleaha, comment and he is abandoned to his beliefs, with ambivalence he continues staring the cart forward toward the town.

In the Absence of the Four Sadistic Bastards

In their absence, the four Sadistic Bastards have continued to reap havoc on the small-town people. That is until they all started feeling uncomfortable and ill. This does not stop the killing immediately. It isn't until they had become fatigued, too ill to remain upon their feet that things change. They gather in a room with many, calling for the small town doctors to find a cure or die. Desperate to live they do their best to accommodate the wiles of the evil men holding the town hostage. The first two doctors have already been killed. The others dare not confront the four Sadistic Bastards. They can't be helped. The small-town doctors have never before seen a sickness this grievous. It attacks, melting body tissues, and flesh at once. Gathered together and struggling to find a solution to an impossible situation they meander for time.

Time has passed, and the doctors again gather to explore alternative options. Nothing that they have prescribed thus far has worked. The complexity of the disease has them baffled, and even with time each knows the fruitlessness of the situation. One of the doctors convinces the others to believe their best chance is to kill them all while they are weak. In his weak state, the youngest Bastard getting up from his bed in search of help stumbles upon the conspiracy by chance. The plan to do away with using lethal injections is foiled and another four doctors are killed.

With new measures put in place, whenever a doctor needs medicine from the Medicine House, the Bastards only allow one to go. On this occasion something goes wrong, two of the doctors have a disagreement causing both their lives to be forfeit. The last doctor sent out returning late, he too is killed. The last remaining two doctors realize they are the only two left. Stepping forward one of the doctors comes clean about what he knows of the illness to the Bastards. Consumed with fright, pressure forces him to tell the Bastards the truth. To determine the rightful cause of the fast killing virus, he will need the town chemist.

The chemist, a dear friend, works from out of his home. Allowed to leave, he goes to fetch him. Should he return without the chemist, or not at all, they will kill his whole family? The doctor finds his friend home with his wife and daughter. He explains the situation to his friend, the chemist. The chemist is incensed, grabbing hold of him by his shirt for implicating him. He has endangered his whole family. A fight ensues, it begins by slapping the doctor around the room and escalates brutally.

The chemist's wife tries to intervene by holding her husband but in his fury, he is too strong and all her efforts fail. The doctor tries to thwart his blows fighting back, but the old coot is just too strong. He is punished to the utmost. Across tables and chairs the two old friends battle, again the wife tries stopping the damage being done to her home. She grabs and pulling on her husband to stop. For the first time, her involvement is met with his anger. Before her eyes she watches the man she's come to know transform into a savage crying out at her, "I had this for you a long time now. Don't think I don't know about him!" The chemist unleashes a beating on his wife like never before.

Even though the doctor is bloody and injured, he still finds the strength to help the chemist's wife from being beaten to death. Together they both assail the chemist, but the old man is strengthened in his rage and refuses to go down. Each of them takes a fair share of beating before it finally stops.

Their daughter stands shocked by her parent's behavior. She has never seen them act in such a way. She is confused about whose side must she take. The daughter runs to constrain her mother, but the angry mother is upset with her husband's duplicity. She has long regretted those moments of weakness. He back then was so involved in his work that he barely noticed her. She was lonely. The fact that he knew for years, for him to only now punish her makes her wroth. Turning on her daughter with a daring slap across the face, it's a warning to stay out of her business. The daughter tumbles over two side tables landing on the ground. Getting up, she tries again to stop her mother The venom that her mother spews at her, mortifies her. "Am not your mother but your daddy just don't know."

Confounded by the news, it liberates the young woman, now that she no longer needs to respect her as her mother. Before the woman she's come to know as the mother could slap her a second time, the angry daughter draws back her hand. Slapping the woman back, stunned, the mother stumbles backward into her husband catching his third breath. Together they both fall to the ground. The doctor uses this opportunity to break away. What is he going to do now, crawling away? The young girl, runs outside the house, disappointed by it all.

Bruised, battered, and bloody, they struggle to their feet, each forlorn and haunted. They stare at each other wondering why? The chemist is the first to speak. "We! We have a lot to talk about when I return." Desperation flickers in his wife's eyes, he will get himself killed. She wants to reach out to him but exposing her pain stills her. Looking to his old friend, "I'll get my things!" To himself, the chemist admits defeat because should he have killed his friend, that would not make him any better than the four Sadistic Bastards. Staggering across the broken house he collects his work bag. Grabbing it up, looking at his long time friend. "Let's go!" Together the two old friends trudge towards the front door of the house.

Wringing her hands she can't help but cry out, "Husband!" She may not have been faithful in her marriage, but she loves him. He stops, the cords of her appeal softens him, slowly, he turns to her. Her concerns have no validity anymore. "What about our. . ." Before she could say daughter. He snorts at the shallow woman who is his wife. "Am not really her father you tell her that." He and his old friend continued to the outside.

Along the way, the chemist notices his daughter. Sad and crying against one of the old homes. She may not be the bone of his bone, but she is the child of his heart. Searching his face, despair registers in her eyes. In its depths, she looks to him for help and answers. He stops, softly, "Go home, daughter! I will explain everything later." And off she runs.

Sadly, She Runs Away

Sadly, she runs away from him, leaving him and his friend to continue. It doesn't take long to arrive at their destination. They are allowed entry into the four Sadistic Bastard's hideout. The four Sadistic Bastards slap them around for wasted time and then they are put to work. It takes metal to impress the four Sadistic Bastards. Finding favor with the doctor, they know it would have taken some convincing to bring the chemist back. The bloody garments they wear provides a telling story.

The symptoms of their illness have increased and time is against them. Into working to produce a cure, the old doctor and the chemist give the Bastards the good news. Believing they have isolated a solution, the chemist must have one more toxin locked in a safe at his house to be absolute in their assessment. The safe can only be opened by himself. No one other than himself can access it due to the nature and collection of toxins stored for research. There is a specific toxin connected to the combination lock that will kill anyone instantly who touches it. The old chemist shows them compositions of his work based on precise calculations. Itemized charts determine how long an orgasm can live and die. Released on the merit of his skills, they believe him. Mollified by the verdict of his prognosis, the four Sadistic Bastards decide to hold the doctor friend as collateral.

On the journey home, he is numb from all he has undertaken. The cure, evil men, unfaithful friends, his wife, ... his daughter, life in general, everything about this situation is surreal. Making it home standing at the threshold, he reminds himself, inside is his family. Walking into the broken house, all is mostly restored to its original state. Everything has been made presentable for his return. His wife and daughter turn at his approach pleased to see him again and alive. The daughter runs to embrace him while the wife hesitantly looks on despondent of amends. He looks at her, stretching out the other arm his hand opens for her. Even bruised, she is his beautiful wife. Desperate to rectify her position, tears of shame welds in her eyes, her steps are fragile, uncertain, he had never hit her before. She trembles going into the crock of his arm.

Embracing them both tightly, "You all are the only thing I have left and I refuse to let those idiots take it away from me. Can you forgive me? I was angry with Levvi, for involving me and putting my family at risk and it turned out, I am the only risk. I was angry because you never told me the truth but the truth is in oneself, am only happy to be here with you, all and that is all that truly matters." He feels the grip of his daughter tighten as he speaks. The sob of released tears racks her frame, "Daddy! Will you be leaving again?" Now that he is home, in the presence of his family, touching them, holding them, the decision is clear. "No! They will have to come here for me now and they will never be able to. Whatever is damaging them is far beyond my understanding but what I do know is their bodies and bones will soon turn to gel, rendering them stiff. As for the amount of time they have left before death, I just can't say. Should I return to them, they agreed I will have ownership of this town, but I know better."

Back at the four Sadistic Bastards hideout, other doctors have come to volunteer their assistance in search of a cure. Instead, some find death waiting. Time is passing and the chemist has not yet returned and this concerns the Bastards. The doctor implores, trying to convince them his friend will return. In front of an audience, he tells the others about the chemist's pursuit to find the cure. He is ultimately killed for recommending the error of his information. This makes the remaining few others realize, they have all foolishly walked into the lion's den and there is no way out.

The Bastards grow weaker with each passing moment, most of their agility is now gone. When they realized the chemist wasn't going to return, they decide its best to secure their well being before the remaining doctors turn on them. It's an impossible situation. The remaining doctors in the far corner talk over what things the Bastards do know about their illness. They are all somewhat afraid.

At the Chemist's Home

At the chemist's home, orchestrated events continue unfolding. Something is happening on the backside of his house. He and his family run toward the back window in hope of seeing, what the noise is all about. From their position, they see a hoard of people coming down the street. It is the Warrior, making her way through the town with others following behind. The town's old windmill is still standing, turning from the storm, on ahead the roads are quiet and vacant. She feels eyes watching her from all their hidden places.

Many of the townpeople do not know her and have never seen her before. They all do agree on one thing, she walks without fear, and with vengeance in her steps, they know why. Many of them recognize her as the stranger who was raped, whipped, and left for dead by the four Sadistic Bastards. She survived, this gives the people hope that brighter and better days are soon to come. The numbers behind her continually grow with each of her steps. Out into the open street. they wed, paces behind her until finally, she reaches the last turn in the crossroad. Up ahead is the landmark, Trottus, Arrius, and Bleaha are in position. The glow of joy on their faces reveal they are more than pleased to see her and the massive crowd following.

Before Bleaha, Arrius, and Trottus arrive back in the town, they tell Trottus about the gold marble ball. He too is a very wealthy man. All this is due to the Warrior, despite of his negative thoughts about standing at the landmark in the middle of the road changes. His eyes become glossy wet, the life he has always wanted to show Bleaha is within his grasp, a better life, now he has a chance. They show him the golden ball, he agrees to stand side by side with them, as long as he remains behind them, agreed.

While en route they visit friends and family asking for the whereabouts of the four Sadistic Bastards. They deduce from conversations, all they had to do is go and wait. That's just what they do. Seeing Bleaha, Arrius, and Trottus, standing in the middle of the road, some of the town people gesture at them to find a hiding place. Others watch baffled, some want to know, "Why are those three fools standing in the middle of the road waiting to be killed?" When the Warrior approaches Bleaha, Arrius, and Trottus, then the crowd gets the picture. Everyone falls silent and Bleaha, Arrius, and Trottus breathe lighter feeling a sense of relief. The confidence of the town people strengthens, encouraging a receptivity of empowerment. Others are still coming out to joining the crowd. Trottus, Arrius, and Bleaha are pleased to see the town spirit revive and again lifted because of the Warrior.

The Warrior greets Bleaha, Arrius, and Trottus, with a head nod which embodies her earlier sentiments of assurance. "Like I have said no harm shall come to you." They understand her meaning now without a doubt they trust her with their lives. Bleaha's smile radiates, "You were right." looking at the Warrior. Silently the crowd gathers around the noble heroes standing guard in the middle of the road. For the first time Bleaha, Trottus, and Arrius feel the bud of purposes bloom. They have become the reason life quality will soon become enhanced in their town.

Out the corner of his eye Trottus, catches a whimsical expression on Bleaha's face and it's not directed at him. Following her glaze, the trail leads to the object of everyone's curiosity, the Warrior. Looking at the woman Warlord concern registers and he is confounded by the passionate display for the Warrior. He dismisses the fear on the grounds, she is only too happy to see the Warrior back up on her feet. At the front door of the four Sadistic Bastards hideout, she walks. Cautious these are still very dangerous and capable men the last time he saw them. Trottus gives a hand signal to two of his friends in the crowd to watch Bleaha. Shifting they adjust unbeknownst to her getting closer around Bleaha.

On the front wooden porch, the Warrior steps up, alert to any coming danger. Silently she pushes against the front door, but it's jammed close. With a firm push, her silent impact is deep to the door. Latches rip out from their position and the door falls swinging open. With speed, she enters leaving the door to swing back close and this causes an alarm to those standing on the outside.

Inside the stench of death and chemicals saturate the confines. The four Sadistic Bastards are all sitting in a row gasping for a breath, that is fleeting. They have seized trying to move at all after killing the last doctors. Resigned in the face of their deaths, only time keeps them alive. The air is thick with decaying stench, it suffocates them. Fresh air is but a length away yet it's as if it's a mile. When time is finished death will begin, fresh air will never come.

The toxic air does not affect the Warrior, immune because of the poison already placed in her virginity by the Black Widow. For anyone else, death is imminent. The four Sadistic Bastards have long killed the remaining doctors and have agreed with each other to just sit and wait. Trying to reserve strength until such a time more of their comrades can arrive. The Bastards are very ill, they can't move, the pallor of their distorted faces is further disarranged by melting skin and rotting flesh, but they are not dead yet. The Warrior vividly remembers the words of the Black Scarlet. "Now you can look at your newfound gift as your last blessing or realize, you have been touched by the Black Widow herself" Looking carefully out at them before approaching, they do not even know she is there and their condition speaks out to her. The urgency of reaching the cure is immediate so she must hurry and get to the House of Zebb before it is too late. The Bastards now recognize someone is with them, they try to get her attention not realizing who she is or caring how she got in. The state of their bodies prompts her to give them a quick death. But a quick death is much too pleasant for these men. Sheathing her weapon, she hides it away.

On the outside the crowd grows uneasy, speculating about the Warrior's fate. Her life being in jeopardy, some assume the Warrior had been pulled to the inside by the four Sadistic Bastard, only to be raped and debased a second time. Others quip delusional remarks, forcing Beleaha's emotions to get the best of her. Verbally she begins to argue, it's not so and that she is still alive. Bleaha can take no more of the debating crowd rages, she makes to run toward the front door only to be stopped and held by Trottus two friends. Returning to a rational calm she knows the two men, sadly she turns to Trottus, they let go at his insistence and she remains still. Trottus shouts out, he may seem unmanly in many choices he makes, not when it comes to Bleaha. "I don't want you to die in there! And it's for your own good."

The Warrior is still on the inside, and death has not yet claimed the Bastards. Sitting close to each other, they speak out to the Warrior about their much-hidden wealth. They are in no position to bargain but they do so anyway. Should she agree to help them, they can make her rich far beyond her means. She agrees, they are desperate to live. Rasping to talk, The Bastards reveal everything to her of the location and their hidden wealth. One goes on to tell her about the map hidden in the handle of their third blade. Leoha finds it just where he said.

With her back turned to them, two of the Bastards catch a glimpse of her weapon. Horror swells, frantic they try to warn the others she is the Warrior they had raped and left for dead. Too weak the illness debilitates even the utterance of many words. Two of them rationalize they have been fooled by her. Their fears raise to sound an alarm to the others. Leoha's Warrior instinct warns her of the pending danger and with precision accuracy, she extracts her blade with one ghost stroke, their necks are severed swiftly. They are still pleading for forgiveness, even after the blade had returned to its case. They are already dead before she replies, never to hear, "You have all been forgiven."

The light of life in each of their Sadistic eyes is extinguished permanently, their heads remain attached to their dismembered bodies. Leoha goes through into other rooms, searching on an off chance someone still lives. The discarded bodies of those murdered, lie motionless, and bloated in many cases. Quickly she gathers cloth and clothing. She throws them all onto the laps of each of the four dead Sadistic Bastards. By their long black hair, she gathers each of their heads in the grip of her left hand. Pulling her weapon again she places her blade under one of the four Sadistic Bastards blades laying out on the side table. Up into the air, the blade goes, coming down in the lap of the last young Bastard who had spit in her face leaving her for dead. Using her weapon, she strikes the blade in his lap. A spark flash, ignites the vapor of deadly gases, in static the fire lifts, crackling explosions burst into devouring flames climbing higher. The flames churn, spreading over-consuming everything within its pathway.

Bleaha notices the smoke first and then bellows and plumes of smoke expand upward to the sky. It can't be after everything that this is how it ends. Why isn't she coming out from the structure? The fire brings with it a heat of anxiety, it makes her frantic and even more concerned about the talks of the Warrior's life being in grave danger. Her struggles with Trottus friends call his attention. "Bleaha! What is it with you and that Warrior?!" Shrugging his friend's hands off, "Please let me go. She needs my help." Again Trottus forbids Bleaha to go, not wanting her to lose her life foolishly. To get away, Bleaha knows she must bate him if she's to be successful. Out from her pocket, she pulls the golden ball tossing it into the air over to Trottus. It's a distraction, before he could catch it, she twists free of his friends running towards the front porch. Trottus recognizes the ploy too late to reach Bleaha.

The crowd looking on watches as the front door falls open to the flames stopping Bleaha in her tracts. Out from the burning structure, the Warrior emerges leaving it ablaze and burning behind her. The crowd is pleased to see hanging from her left hand, the four decapitated heads of the four Sadistic Bastards. The lonely wooden structure is now engulfed by flames and Bleaha steps back away from the heat.

The town people scream out in elated joy. Gathering around Bleaha, Arrius, and Trottus from the ground they pick them up and acknowledge their three heroes. They rejoice, throwing them up in the air over and again. The calls for a great celebration resounds. Out from nearby homes, wine, drinks, and food pour out in abundance for their heroes. The people give many thanks to Bleaha, Arrius, and Trottus, for bringing the Warrior back and saving the town. It's finally over, for the second time Arrius, Trottus, and Bleaha feel celebrated like they belong. Forthcoming plans to rebuild the town is mentioned, measures discuss putting in place protections for the town and its people from other scourges and plaguing matters.

United in one cause, the elders have come to agree, under oath of law, the warrior, who saved the town shall be given a permanent residence by the state, for all times before the next cycle of the wind. The old mayor of the town has stepped down and given room to the new town mayor, Arrius, who has gladly accepted the position. Special consideration is given to Trottus, and they appoint him chairman and civil head of town donations. Whereas Bleaha noble heart and altruist disposition is most aptly rewarded in establishing banking and loan expansion for town exchange and markets.

In Motion of It All

In the motion of it all, patting her pocket where the golden ball once was, she smiles at the surreal harvest reaped in the occurrence of the dark tempest storm and its malady of evil men. With time passing, Bleaha realizes the Warrior is no longer there. She begins inquiring, asking about it, it's a little boy who points the direction to which way the Warrior's left. On the horizon, Trottus sees Bleaha's retreating figure running with speed in a direction he presumes is in search of the Warrior. He saw when the Warrior exited, he didn't bring it to Bleaha's attention intentionally. He was just glad for the reprieve of her discretion not calling attention to herself. Noting Bleaha in flight because of the Warrior's absence brings concern.

Glad to make his excuses, removing himself from the others Trottus rolls his eyes, the excessive yammering was starting to get on his nerve. The distance between him and Bleaha is too far for him to catch-up. He breaks off running towards his stable to fetch his donkey cart. Pleased to find all is still attached as he left it, jumping up onto the cart he takes up the donkey reins. With haste picking up the side whip he frays the donkey hind-quarters eager for speed. The donkey is worn, from its last tiring journey.

Trottus fails to remember that, losing whatever sanity he has in his all-consuming love for a woman who barely knows he exists in that manner. Chewing hungrily the donkey is oblivious to the urgency of Trottus's pursuit until Trottus lashes the whip twice. The beast sputters, taking off, Trottus is dragged some distance ahead before it comes to a stop. Sputtering in the dust he gets up still holding onto the reins. He forgot, earlier he unstrapped the donkey belts from the cart for the animal to feed. Brushing the dust from himself he shakes his head at the beast. With reproach of contempt the donkey, does not allow him near. He tries cajolery, wheedling and coaxing the donkey sweetly, it finally complies.

With the ass finally under his thumb, Trottus jumps onto its back but it will not move. Useless tries later, he dismounts thinking the beast is still spent from its last run. Increasingly, time becomes a pressing factor, he must hurry if he expects to catch Bleaha. He'll not lose her again, with steely determination Trottus runs off on foot to catch up to Bleaha before she makes a turn and loses him. When the donkey notices his master running away, he mindlessly follows in pursuit, running after Trottus.

The celebration is ongoing, Arrius is being sworn in as the new mayor of the town. Full joy fills the air and Arrius smiles contented, out from the corner of his eye he sees Trottus, fly past. Moving faster than the donkey trailing behind is braying loudly in protest. Confusion ensues as Arrius quickly looking around assesses that Bleaha and the Warrior are gone. He knows Trottus, with a groan, intuition gets him thinking, it can only be Bleaha who has him in this erratic state. What could it be now, agitated he shakes his head unconsciously exasperated. In a conundrum of emotions, his distraction doesn't go unnoticed. Those swearing him in wonder, what is with the new mayor? Inwardly they question the judgment of their choice, maybe he's not really suitable for the position. Having already sworn him in, the decision cannot be reversed.

Here we go again, in his heart he knows whatever is going on, they will need him at some point. As the new mayor, he calls for an urgent time out without providing a proper excuse. Jumping to action, to disengage himself, he blames his exit due to a loose bowel condition. He must excuse himself. Watching with scrutiny, prude officiates observe less than tactful but crass connotations of behavior precipitated by their new mayor. This is another shock to the new board of committee members. Many of the committee members mull questioning the mayor's loose bowel situation or is he losing his mind? Maybe he's not worthy of such an elevated post, they save reserving their opinions until they have more on which to deliberate.

Just as they are to leave it like that, the new town mayor drops everything and he too breaks off running down the open street. This is shocking behavior, one of the committee member's swoons. The old coot is brought back with smelling salt. Perturbed, the rest of the committee questions the closeness of the bathrooms and why is the new mayor still running down the street? Arrius disappears before their eyes. What is going on? they all ask one another. Looking around they all realized, the Warrior isn't among the counted. Arrius may have just been made mayor, but his friend needs him. The Town will have to get adjusted to the fact they cannot define his actions. The new mayor follows suit after the donkey knowing it will lead him to Trottus, Bleaha, and the Warrior.

Adrenalin of the chase explodes in pandemonium with Bleaha running after the Warrior, Trottus after her. Even the donkey, in character, is running witlessly behind his master. His master blindsided with tunnel vision, only the woman he loves matters. The idea that she is won't let the Warrior go bothers him, he wants her to act like that with him. With his heart, he is committed to making sure she not only knows that but becomes resolved to play her role in his life.

The bonds of their friendship have long been forged and established in the trials, of opposition, and oppression. Only by staying together have they weathered the currents of events that have befallen their Town. Arrius runs until his body can take it no more, stopping at the end of the town holding his side from cramps. Bent over gasping for breath, in the distance, his eyes keep watch following the dust trail left behind by the donkey as a marker. "Am getting too old for this." He tries to run a bit further, but the pain won't subside. His small Goombay legs trembling won't allow him to go any further. His shape is like that of a frog, all body-less legs but his love for it, something not many others can say. Looking around he gives up but then, there has to be another way. He looks around for help and shelter.

Standing in the middle of the road at the end of the town, it's a very hot day. All the moving around adds to his tiredness, very little wind blows just enough to rustle the little of his hair to one side. Disheveled, before he was dressed like the mayor but he doesn't look or feel the part anymore. His parched tongue is dry he could use a drink of water. Nearby there is a freshwater pond but his tired legs won't move. Panting for breath, his dry mouth makes it hard to swallow.

Chirps and buzz, croaking, crickets sing in the silence of the day, fluttering butterflies in their splendor of color enlighten the pathway. In the stillness of nature's movement sunlight filters through tree branches, Arrius calms in its serenity. He doesn't doubt that he will catch up to Bleaha and Trottus, it's just a matter of when. There is a sound moving toward him, he looks up and out. What appears to be an apparition in the distance, is a beautiful stallion running in motion. Heading straight towards him he can't be certain it's not a mirage. He wipes away the dust from his eyes. The stallion is pulling an enclosed coach. Unbeknownst to Arrius, the coach is carrying a newly married young bridal couple, well dressed in attire for the occasion.

The young newlyweds have traveled for miles without seeing a soul. The litany of changeable landscapes unfolding before they fade and blur with each horizon. It's in the distance they see Arrius lounging ahead in his crouched position. Pleased to finally see someone, to see anybody, they are eager to ask for directions. The young driver brings the bridal coach alongside the new mayor and stops. Leaning out to better greet the stranger, the young driver is pulled by his upper garment hoodwinked, to the ground as Arrius mounts up onto the coach. The mayor takes his seat beside a hysterically screaming bride. Her annoying screams cause Arrius to cover his eardrum, taking measures he normally wouldn't. For Arrius this act of fortune couldn't have come at a more appropriate time. With no time to waste, in face of a hysterical woman screaming in piercing octaves, Arrius gives her one bitch blow. The impact of the slap, muffles her instantly knocking her off balance. The commotion raises the birds in the trees to flight.

On the ground entangled in the folds of his wedding attire, seeing his stricken bride unbalanced and about to fall, the bridegroom is immediate in his reaction. Protectively reaching out, he rushes reaching out to aid her. Flustered by the screams, Arrius has just grabbed her. Gripping the dress elaborate collar, off-balance, flaying arms fling wildly threaten to topple them both over. To him the choice is clear, it's him or her, and he pushes her out from the coach. Into her husband's arms, together they hit the ground one on top of the other.

Arrius turns the coach round, out loud to the jostled bride and her husband Arrius throws back over his shoulder, "I am the mayor of this town." Before they can compose themselves, getting back up to their feet, and away he goes Scot-free. The young couple is left behind baffled. This incident is enough to damage any newlywed couple on their honeymoon experience. With a red welt swelling her cheek, the bride turns to her husband, "My mama said I'd have hard times with you!"

Looking to close the lost distance between he and Trottus jack ass, Arrius snaps the stallion's reins. The stallion performance is not as he should. The horse's pace and strut have him puzzled. Along the way he finds he can not control the moving coach. It's one problem after another with this horse. Arrius jumps down from the coach to examine the situation. What else can go wrong, he can't believe it, the stallion is a crossbreed, its beauty is only surface superficially. The beautiful stallion turns out to be more than 95% donkey and 5% percent stallion. The five percent accounts for its beauty. The Jackass only looks like a Stallion. In the wind, the beast has caught the scent of Trottus female donkey. Enticed, the hormones of Trottus's donkey in heat beacons him to mate.

Bleaha's Unawareness

Bleaha has been running for some time trying to catch up with the Warrior. Bleaha is unaware that Trottus is tracking her from behind and closing in fast. Like Bleaha, Trottus doesn't know his female donkey is following him. Their friend Arrius is not that far behind. The cross-breed stallion stamina has increased his pace to find Trottus's donkey. Which to Arrius delight gives him the speed he needs to catch them. Bleaha finally reaches a T junction, and the Warrior is still nowhere in sight. In confusion about which way to go, the road left and right is sandy because of the nearby beach. Straight ahead on a large rock is a fisherman pulling in his catch. Bleaha takes her time over the treacherous slippery boulders and walks over to reach him.

The fisherman has long observed her act of bravery over the slippery slope. and she asks. "Please, kind sir. I am looking for a friend. Have you seen her passing by?" The fisherman replies. "I have been here a while and I don't see nor hear everything." Bleaha knows time is not on her side, pleading out to him. "Please, kind sir. Where do you think most will go when passing this way?" Looking around urgently in every direction. The fisherman stops his work and looks at her. He can see her innocence. "Young lady, there is a good amount of sand on the road. Why don't you just look at the footprints but start by ruling your steps and mine out and what remains is what you may be looking for." Bleaha smiles at him for his clever deduction. "Oh! Why didn't I think of that? The old fisherman only smiles back, Bleaha, is so happy she can't stop thanking him profusely. "Oh!

Thank you. Thank you. kind sir. Thank you so much." Abandoning the old-man to his duties, she returns to the T junction. There in the sand, she finds just what she is looking for, the Warrior footprints. In the distance, she spots the object of her pursuit, off she runs to catch up with the Warrior.

The old fisherman has finished gathering his catch and is walking back out to the T junction where he sent Bleaha. There in the sand, he looks down at the map of prints lining the terrain. Gently he canvases the footprints left behind like a scout, something he often did before beginning his long journey back home. One can never be too safe, with marauders, and cutthroats roaming these parts. He remembers his love for reading footprints in the sand began a long time ago. Reminiscing the smiles fondly and he thinks back to the young lady he had given advice. His mind returns to Bleaha smiling to himself all indications suggest that she has found her answers.

Everyone seems to be in rush these days, coming at him another wayward traveler approaches with the same urgency. Here comes Trottus frantic, running towards the fisherman out of breath. Trottus reaches him with heavy breathing unable to speak. To him, the old fisherman instructs, "Try and take in one deep breath and hold it." Doing as he is told, Trottus collects himself, looking to the old fisherman. "Well, tell me sir. Have you happen to see a young lady dressed in some odd color clothing?" It obvious from the generated fervor of the day, the course of these two are related. To satisfy him, the old fisherman simply points out the way Bleaha went. Trottus thanks him kindly and keeps moving.

Following in succession soon thereafter, a braying donkey runs bucking pass, taking the same direction as the running man. Moments again pass and he looks up to see a stallion pulling a coach roll by. The gangling trot of the horse or at least what looks like a Stallion moves by, lead by a strange-looking man dressed in black. In the confusion of the rushing movements, it makes him giddy, he can't figure it all out. Scratching his head, he thinks maybe it's time he slows down on the drinking in his old age. Taking out from out of his pocket a bottle of amber liquid he tosses it away.

It's Hot

It's hot, the sun blisters heatwaves against the bleached white sands. Bleaha hasn't stopped running since starting to find the Warrior. She is fatigued, running across the thick white sand her leg muscles are ready to cramp. She can not fall now, her courage motivates her to continue. They're on a hill of sand ahead of her, she must cross it to get to the wide-open sea. It takes all she has to reach the top. Over the wide and open expansion of the beach, her eyes focus to find the Warrior making her way out to the sea. With the last of her strength Bleaha, cries out. "Leohaaaa, Leohaaaaaaah, help me."

So much has happened, the storm, the Sadistic Bastards, meeting with Exuma, destruction of the town, the dead, quarreling with Trottus. . . Her tired body collapses beneath her. Recognizing Bleaha's voice The Warrior turns to witness her crumbling to her knees on the hot sands. Her limp body tumbles, rolling down the hill. The last thing Leoha expected was to find Bleaha following her, leaping into the air at once she reaches Bleaha at the very bottom. Throwing down the four lifeless heads she attends to Bleaha, who shows signs of dehydration. The sun heat has blistered her skin and it's red and peeling from exposure. In the desert, under these conditions, all warriors know the importance of proper coverage in extreme conditions. Here by the ocean's side, many are deceived and often suffer harm due to the sun's rays. There is none better to help or comfort Bleaha, not to fall asleep.

Bending low, the Warrior braces Bleaha's head and back up against her leg. The caring manner in which she is lifted attests that she is in good hands. Resting Bleaha realizes she is finally with the Warrior again, gingerly, she opens her eyes. Shaded by the over bent shadow of the Warrior tenderly she speaks, "You could let me die you know." The Warrior is pleased to see she is still in good spirit and has a sense of humor. Little does Leoha know Bleaha is serious, the chills have set in with a fever. Trying to keep her awake more than anything the Warrior asks, "Are you hurt Bleaha? You must not fall asleep."

As a Warrior, she is familiar with her symptoms, she needs to keep Bleaha talking until her strength restores itself. Leoha speaks firmly to her, "You must not fall asleep, Bleaha." In a low and breathless tone Bleaha whispers meekly exclaiming with wonder. "If you ask, I won't. I finally found you." Welling tears shimmer and flows out and down her cheek sides. In her disabled condition, she knows the Warrior will never understand the meaning and again she goes quiet. They are churning undercurrents at work with Bleaha, Leoha can't quite grasp. The emotions so eagerly displayed run high and this concerns Leoha. "Stay with me Bleaha! Stay with me!" The gentle prodding of those said words brings even more tears to Bleaha.

Though the fixation of her fascination to be close to the Warrior she slowly revives. "I am so pleased that it's you. How could you just leave without saying goodbye? You see. I have grown so fond of you. There is a place here for you now, and I would so much like you to stay." The fact that Bleaha went to the trouble to find her at grave consequences to herself, speaks volumes to the Warrior. "And I would so much like that, but our worlds are so far apart and different, and I don't think I can." It's the rebuff of those words that cracks the revere of Bleaha's heart. Not wanting to hear anymore, she refrains her true intentions, turning away from the Warrior. Placing her hand over her aching heart, she rubs her chest, clutching tightly to her garment doesn't diminish the pain of rejection. Wistfully, she turns back to the Warrior. "You don't have to say anymore and even if you can't stay, just promise you will return."

With darting eyes Trottus searches the landscape being familiar with the area. The high hill of sand is before him, it's easier to go around and shorter to reach the shortcut that will bring him out to the open beach. Resurgences of memories as a boy playing with his brother through many short cuts calibrates the knowledge of his steps. He also is tired and exhausted but for Bleaha it's worth it. For Bleahas love he finds the strength to keep forging ahead, coming to the beach open all he can see ahead is sand and sea but no Bleaha. Slowly his strength ebbs away from the fatigue of disappointment.

The hill of sand which Bleaha crossed is now in his vision but he is still ways off. From his calculations, she has to be somewhere within his range. The brilliance of sunlight against the whitewashed sands blinds him temporarily. Desperate, with his right hand shielding his eyes from the sun's glare he scans looking carefully and intently out and around the bottom hill of sand. His eyes light on the Warrior's clothing and Bleaha on the ground. The sight causes his heart to race, anxious with the last of his strength, he takes great strides to get to her side.

The Warrior knows if Bleaha is here, her comrades are soon to follow. For Leoha, it's good to have met such a loving trio, it's rarity to see or even better to experience love unconditionally. It's without a doubt that Bleaha is very loved, but this fact seems to have evaded Bleaha's notice. The life of a Warlord takes many paths, but it is a solo quest of service she has committed herself to. To have friends is a novelty she can not afford. She will wait with her, help is sure and soon to come. The heads of the Sadistic Bastards rest nearby in the sand Bleaha, has not yet gained her strength but her courage is intact.

Being this close to the Warrior, she feels safe like she has never felt before. Breathing in deeply, even the sensation of her sweat is clean. Beneath lowered eyelashes, Bleaha eyes flutter open to view the contours of the Warrior unbeknownst to her. What she sees makes her longing increase, the Warrior's body muscles are granite in shape and form. More to herself Bleaha, again tries to persuade Leoha. "Warrior! If I could give back the wealth you gave. Would you allow me to follow?" It's a subtle innuendo, that Leoha does not comprehend. The true meaning behind Bleaha words does not register to Leoha. It is perhaps best that the Warrior does not understand, in the Kingdom where Leoha is from, proper relations is a paradigm in the Order of things.

She is a Warlord Warrior of the highest order, her course has yet to define the action yet she must take. Ever-increasing in her mediation is the Black Widow and that Scarlet. Her vendetta with the forces of darkness is a consuming interest, that will not be denied. It's amusing to find one so weak as Bleaha championing the choice of her walk, after being ridiculed for it so many times by her own siblings. Bleaha's admiration is touching, but naive. The cold hard truths of her life would make many cringe but this is her fate. Maybe if she gives her knowledge of this, it will deter the romanticism of her false impressions. "How could you follow, when you cannot even walk. Death has long been following me for some time now and am just trying to reach the next town."

Indicating more of herself, Bleaha expounds to further implicate herself insisting, "I know you need to find your cure and am willing to go with you. How else could I get better?" The Warrior takes a closer look at Bleaha, face. In the depths of her eyes dwells the frustrations of bondage and the cumbered restrictions of her society, Bleaha's tears translate in language to the Warrior. "Am so sorry but this is something I must do alone." This delay forces Leoha to reach for patience, it's almost absurd that she is wasting time with a wayfarer who won't let go.

Not wanting to further hear the Warrior's words of rejection, once again Bleaha buries her pain. If bait catches fish, she has failed miserably to prime the line, sadly, she utters in her distress, "I rather you leave me as I am. You see I don't control my heart." The petty expression of Bleaha eludes Leoha who is more concerned with getting back to war efforts. For her to do that, getting to the source of her healing is imperative at this point. If it wasn't for disposing of these heads she'd had concluded her business and returned to the fray of combat long ago. Because Bleaha, continues to push the issue, Leoha is a Warlord Warrior and coy deliberations do not move her. Her relationship with her sister Sheppard is the perfect example of that. She cuts her short. "I will."

It always worked with Trottus, why can't the Warrior see her reasoning. Maybe she has pushed too far, all indications stated lead Bleaha, to think the Warrior will leave her all alone. She quickly puts things back in perspective, speaking out, "No, no! I rather you do not leave," With a restrained hand on Leoha's arm, "I don't know if you understand... How much." With a silent plea in her eyes, "I... I love you, but..." If not for the shuffling pants of sound behind calling the Warrior's attention away, the message Bleaha labors to reveal would not be aborted. But all is lost in the surf of the waves rolling against the sands. Leoha looking around smiles at the loyalty and commitment of Bleaha's friend. Here comes Trottus, moving as fast as the sand allows. Stumbling over the thick white sand, drudging to reach her. Behind him, his donkey trails not so far behind. Closing in on them another donkey and coach ride. If she isn't mistaken the rider looks like her friend Arrius. The distractions of the riders and Trottus soon to arrive, erases whatever Bleaha proposed as a weakness to her condition.

It's important for Bleaha, to gain her strength, knowing the turbulent exchanges she has witnessed with the trio, may dampen the efforts of her recovery. Leoha says nothing to her about Trottus's rapid approach. Moments before Trottus reaches the Warrior, she touches her finger against Bleaha's vital body points on the far side of her neck rending her asleep never to finish the conversation. Trottus, arrives breathless, pained, burning from exertion, and gasping for air. Collapsing, worn and exhausted though he tries hard to look strong in front of the Warrior he fails, dropping to his knees.

Between breaths, trying to catch himself. This abnormal behavior of Bleaha has him concerned and he questions the Warrior. "Warrior, tell me. What... What, in the hell is going on with her, and you. I have never known her to be like this before." The Warrior gently rest Bleaha, head, and body back onto the sand. When she stands up so does Trottus, bent over he braces his hands on his knees, looking up at her heaving. She studies him tired and breathless. Small talk, rather than engage him in a vague conversation that gives no credence to the situation at hand. Now that help has arrived, she can continue her mission without obstructions. To him she simply said. "She has fainted and needs only rest. There is help on the way. Do take care and tell her goodbye."

Now that Bleaha friends have arrived, there is no more time for delay, she is set to turn away when Trottus calls her back. "Warrior, please wait." For the sincerity of his plea, she turns back to him. He

The Undaunted King Gouddaa of the Arawaks and Caribs

can't believe it, the commotion of yowls and neighs of his donkey has him momentarily stunned. This animal of his continues to prove its unpredictability, it's inconceivable, he followed him again. Looking around there is his donkey slowly trotting past him, stopping further down the beach to chew on seaweed.

In the distance kicking sand, something else is moving toward him He strains to recognize what, but doesn't know what to make of it. The priority of his focus returns to Bleaha, laying out on the sand unconscious. She needs to be moved, but first, he must have one last word with the Warrior. He is not immune to Bleaha's true affections, at least it's his belief with his care she will come round to see the truth. Trottus bares his heart to the Warrior, truthfully and honestly. "Warrior! Please don't think am stupid. I can see, you know! Since you came into our lives, she exits me. It is you she loves, isn't it? Please for my sake and hers, leave her, leave here, and don't ever return. I love her so much but with you around, there could be no me. How is it, that in such a short time of you being around, I lost it all and you took it all from me. I helped save your life and you rewarded us handsomely. If I give it back, would you stay away and never look back." The content of his words forces the Warrior to reset her considerations. The magnanimity of his fears she allays immediately. "The help you need is laying there before you but not in what I have said or given."

Trottus becomes an insignificant thought, in view of the ocean open before her, time to close this chapter. Stooping down the Warrior gathers the heads of her four prizes. The strange donkey coach approaching, Trottus can't help but look. It stops to turn around. Before he could reengage the Warrior, she leaps into the air in one bound. He watches her retreating figure disappear from sight down the long stretch of beach in leaps and bounds until she becomes a speck in the distance. In his mind, he bids her good riddance and good-bye, turning his attention back on the woman he so loves. Maybe now things can return to some resemblance of normalcy and she can finally embrace his feelings towards her. He tries to wake her but is unsuccessful. With all the remaining strength he has left, he picks Bleaha up off the sand and whistles out to his donkey to come.

The Difficulties

The difficulties he has incurred over the years since acquiring this donkey makes him want to put her down. She is so stubborn and obstinate, ignoring him, she trots past heading for the coach parked a distance away in the sand. The noonday sun is high in the sky above Trottus's head, the extra weight in his arms sinks his steps into the thick white sand. Yet straining he pushes on, his muscles burning with each step. His muscles lock, dropping to his knees with Bleaha, the sand grinds scraping the skin off his knees. Resting in the sand, he is disappointed with himself as a man. Right now, he a weakling who talks big, but can't even carry the woman he loves. The pressure of events he has faced recently makes Trottus questions himself. Previous pictures replay rolling in his mind, and his cowardly actions are magnified. He recalls vividly, the episode in town with the Bastards, on the path to Exuma the medicine man, displaying weakness to a woman, believing her to be his rival for his love's affections. His eyes become wet from frustrations and depression. In his arms is the only object of his desire, again he tries to awaken her but it's no use. Solemnly he cries out to Bleaha, "What is with you? What is it with you Bleaha?!" His head drops to her chest sobbing.

Rocking back and forth cradling Bleaha in his arms a shadow covers them from the sun's blazing light. He raises his head giving thanks to the clouds and its shade of glory only to find Arrius blocking the sunray standing over them. "Goddammit Arrius, it's you!" Appalled and slighted by the comment Trottus makes, Arrius responds with, sarcasm. "Are you expecting someone else?" Elation washes over him never in his life has he been happier to see Arrius. "Boy am I pleased to see you." He can't believe it, looking at his friend's concerned face and seeing his tears leaves him dumbfounded. He never once imagined Trottus feelings were so serious. "Trottus! Are those tears in your eyes?" He'd almost forgotten his state of mind before the shadow cover brought relief. Quickly wiping them away, hope restored and strengthened, "No! Must be from the dry sea wind. Just help me with her!" The joy he feels can not be diminished by the scowls and queries of his old friend. Trottus raises to his feet and he kisses Arrius, on his forehead while saying, "Thank you! Thank you! Thank you!"

Arrius, find his out of character friend behavior most strange but he lets it be. It's obvious Trottus is delusional from heat exposure and the exertion of his efforts to help Bleaha. Looking at Bleaha, she urgently needs to be taken out of the sun. With a little help, he and Arrius cross the thick sand, caring Bleaha. Into the back of the coach, they place her still sleeping body to recover. The two long time friends climb up onto the coach and take their seats. It's finally over, the Warrior has moved on much to his relief, his friend is by his side. More important the woman he loves has a reckoning coming soon, he'll give her the time she needs to heal, he knows it will take time. But time was theirs now to have and the future could never be better. Arrius begins to move out, Trottus will always be in debt to the Warrior, he wishes her swift speed to the next town, where she left to go to her next destination. Both Arrius and Trottus laugh out as the jackass, his jackass passes him.

Leading the way, Trottus jackass is now ahead of them. Sitting comfortably Trottus just begins to question Arius, when he interjects, "She's on heat you know, and this one is still chasing her. Don't ask where I got it. I will only be implicating you, should any question arrive." Must it always be something, Trottus shakes his head, "Did you steal it?!" The pun of his earlier declaration returns as Arrius echoes his earlier sentiment. "No! Must be from the dry sea wind." They both smiled at the omission of each other's lies.

For a minute, Trottus looks puzzled at his jack ass and the trot of the beautiful stallion pulling them. They walk identically, then it dawns on him. "Tell me! Is this one also one of them?" Arrius smiles, glad to see Trottus noticed the Stallions abnormal gait. "Only by actions! But don't you ever get tired of that ass humiliating you?" Defending his donkey's charms, Arrius is just jealous he doesn't have one so he makes a joke about his animal. Just like people to always have an opinion when they don't have. They give all the excuses about why they don't want one, but deep down they know they wish they had. "Actually, when she is well-rested, she's good, but am just waiting for the right moment to kill her. She really makes me wonder, why they are all called a jackass." Arrius, correct him laughing out, "That's why they are called jackasses." The laughter is contagious they laugh until tears come out of their eyes. It feels good to laugh again about mundane things not predicating on how to stay alive for a change.

After the laughter had settled, Arrius gives Trottus a slight nudge with his elbow, to his side. Trottus looks at him as to say. What now?! It feels so bizarre after all they had been through that now tides have shifted in their favor. No longer are they being pulled out to sea, but being pushes to wash upon sandy shores and golden opportunities only a touch away. "You. . . still have that thing right." Trottus quickly takes hold of his pocket, making sure the golden ball is still there and it is still there. Not that he didn't trust Bleaha, but she's a woman. The knowledge of her holding such an item could have only caused a problem with her safety. Feeling its roundness, he remembers his last words to the Warrior. "If I give it back, would you stay away and never look back." Confessing to Arrius, Trottus confides, "But I almost lost it." What hasn't Trottus told him if he almost lost it, thank the stars whatever happened he still had it. "What?!" Together the long journey back home begins and Trottus tells Arrius everything.

Miles away, the Warrior finally comes to a spot along the beach, where the sea meets the hills. Driven by the forces of the wind, the angry surf of the waves trash beating and ripping against the shores. It's here, that she trudges out into the deep waters to throw the four heads of her enemies into the deep. The lapping waters slap against the heads in her hands the deeper she goes until the water is chest high. Holding the heads high she dipping them down into the water, pulling them up and out into the air they spiral upward descending down far ahead in the distance. The rip currents snatch the bobbing orbs carrying them out further away. For a while, Leoha just wades in the waters watching as scavenger birds diving from the air take their fill.

With her arms spread out to her sides, she leans back into the water's bed, floating with the tide she drifts in the peace of the moment. Only the sound of warring birds mars the silence. The sea cleanses her mind, washing the filth from her body, soothing her soul. It's a shame it can't wash and erase the Black Widow's curse. Even the seas can't drown out the malice of her intentions. The Black Widow and Scarlet will pay. There no one to hear her roar to the skies. It late when she wades back to start her journey toward the town of Zebb. She stands alone on the beach Bleaha, Aarrius, and Trottus have long driven away. The Black Scarlet instructions recite repetitiously in the recesses of her thoughts, and she remembers everything.

Awaken Out from Her Dream

Awakened out from her dream, with haste she jumps to her feet knowing she has overslept. Out from her chambers, she runs to the front entrance. Swiftly pulling to the side, one of the last servant girls passing. The servant girl cries out surprised. "Aaaaaaaa. . ." Leoha does not know her own strength sometimes, grabbing the girl in a bruising grip. Before any others could become alarmed to hear her low screams. Leoha places her hand over the young girl's mouth to muffle her cry. To make the young girl understand not to make a noise, Leoha takes her own finger and places it up over her own lips. The servant girl is frightened but Leoha assures her, "Shhhhhhhhhhhh. I won't hurt you!" Slackening her grip slowly, the youngster becomes quiet.

Slowly Leoha removes her hand from over the young servants mouth still indicating for her to remain silent by pressing her index finger against her own lips. To the young servant girl. Leoha, questions the past state of her being, "Tell me!. . .How long. . . How long was I out?" It's a wonder, and her privilege to be face to face with the Warlord Princess. The servant relaxes seeing that the Princess is conscious again. In her presence The servant girl stands hostage, staring at her in awe. In a halting manner, she reports the findings she knows about her condition. "Princess! You have been running a high fever, for the past day. So the madam of the house deemed it necessary to call in the physician and she alone admitted your medicine, and it is good to see you are up and well again."

Her thoughts are blank at first, then Leoha remembers. If she's right her two aunts are being held in the dungeons. She thanks the young servant girl and returns back to her chambers. After bathing, and eating a sensible meal she dresses. On the arduous journeys of her travels, many hospices she has frequented only allow for the barest of necessities. For some, a straw pallet or enclosed barn was worth a king's ransom and palace. She walks out and across the courtyard over manicured lawns she makes her way. Into the open green gardens, it's there she takes the pathway across to the lower dungeons of the Kingdom.

The dungeon guards seeing the approaching Warlord Princess, run out to meet her. They welcome her, as they did with her sister Sheppard. On the inside she instructs the guards, be at ease, informing them of her task. Deep down they go, descending bellow, they guide her steps along the way, before handing her over to two of the dungeon elite guards. Their orders are from the throne to guard the dungeon cell of her two aunts, and they have been given strict rules concerning their care.

The place is dank and dark, walls glisten like coal under the torches burning light. There is no place for sunlight to enter as apart of the punishment for those who enter this forsaken place. Suddenly the eerie cast of a shadow bursts open, the last and final horrifying cry of the damned is released, emitting an echo across the dungeon. Leoha pauses concerned at the utterance. Halting, she reaches out to stop the guards in front of her. "Have you heard that?" The guards stop raising the torch looking back at her they wait to hear what disturbed the Princess. "I hear nothing much Princess, everything is at a calm here." The eldest of the two guards before looking to his comrade also confirms. "I hear nothing usual Princess." Mystified, but concerned by her words.

To their surprise, Leoha places her left palm onto the massive sidewall and confirms to them. "It was the last and final scream of a great warrior trapped within the fabric of these walls, but it's long gone now!" As she removes her hand, fear prickles down their spine. The Gourddians reaffirm their superiority when the extraordinary of their abilities manifest. It enough to spooks them. She goes on to question them about other confidential confined matters. "Who was it lately, severely punished here?!" The guards look to each other, how is that possible? The youngest guard confirms. "A warrior called Golattus, but he is no longer here." Wanting to know more she questions further, "Do you know where is he now." They can only report what they know, and they tell her, "That information did not privilege us. Shall we Princess?" He said with an open palm pointing the way. "Please do," and Leoha continues.

Now at the holding in the dungeon of her aunts, she is left with two other high-ranking guards. Security is tight. Removing the royal seal from her garment she presents it to the guards not wanting to face a confrontation. Stating it loud enough for them to register "Royal Seal!" They return the salutation, showing her the highest level of respect. The gates are made open and she is allowed to enter. She is then placed to stand in front of another closed gate, much larger than the first one. The eldest of the two high ranking guards apologizes for the inconvenience of restrictions ordered. "Sorry, Princess! But we cannot allow anyone on the inside. We were given special orders, so we cannot leave you alone with the prisoners. The ladies inside both claim to be innocent and held against their will. Please understand Warlord Princess! We have our orders!"

The regards of this news stun Leoha, "You know who I am! So is there a problem?" The old guard is weary in response, "I only wish there were Princess! But this is far above us." From deep inside of the dungeon, one of the two aunts hears her talking and recognizes her voice. The rustle, and scrapes of chains dragging, skitters across dungeon grounds. So happy they can't contain themselves, they both move from the back corner upfront to the iron bars. Ever so humbly, they fumble clutching and squeezing each other's hands. Crying out to each other, jolly to see her reach. "It is she! It is she! Yes! I know it is she. It is her voice! I know her voice." It is Crystal, Leohas my favorite aunt that cries out to her sister. "I always knew she would come for me. I told you so. I told you!"

From behind the iron bars, withered limbs frail, reaching out to her, calling her name. "Leoha! Leoha! Yes leoha, Leohaaa! It is you!" On seeing her two aunts deteriorated condition, she approaches the iron bars to their distorted frames and she cries, "Aunty, Aunty, am here. Am here." From through the massive iron bars, she allows them to touch her hand and skin. Suddenly overcome the walls of the past crumbles, time reverts and once again they are young. In her arms is a baby girl of favor, the expansion of space ebbs forwards, changing with each touch. The once baby girl transforms to reveal the Warrior Warlord Princess they've come to love and cherish. Squeezing and stroking as much as possible that the bar opening allows. In this act of solidification, the exposed passion of intimacies releases a balm of compassion. With their hands they anoint all over her body, gradually she pulls away drunken from their caresses. She was their favorite for she had always loved them despite of their indifferent ways.

Her favorite Aunt Crystal pleads for her. "Leoha, leoha, come back, let me feel the warmth of your face again child." Once again she steps forward and their touches lithe upon her becomes a source of joy, fulfillment, and warmth. The touch of her flesh soothes the darkest of moments they have endured. Leoha is silently appalled by their sunken dim eyes, uncaring skin, and poor clothing. The tangled and matted length of their uncombed long black hair makes them both appear like street vagabonds. There is no evidence of royalty. Examining them, "What is with your eyes and can you both see me?" It's her favorite aunt Crystal, who sadly divulges, "Listen my child! The King had us both exiled long ago and our status removed and with it, she removed us from her sight. I feel, the long and lonely darkness has humbled us and has long taken its toll on both our eyes. Could you please speak to the King on our behalf, to have us place just for a while into the sunray so that we may once again feel its radiant warmth upon our skin? You see it would so much better our condition." Leoha, after hearing her aunt Crystal's concerns turns to the guards and orders them, "Open it!"

The second high ranking guard was afraid of this. "Princess! Please do calm down and understand. We have our orders! The gates operate by the light coming in from high above and the little piece of diamond which bends the incoming light is in the hand of your sister the King. We can only suggest, you have words with her but there is nothing more we can say or do until further ordered by the throne." Leoha turns back to her aunts, still holding to the dungeon bars, she declares adamantly. "You have my word! This will only be for a short time longer." Leoha walks away, through the hollow of their tears, they remember once upon a time.

She departs determined to rectify her aunt's positions. Impatiently, it seems the distance out the holding is longer leaving than when she entered. Finally, through the last iron gate, the slam of iron reverberates chiming echoes against dungeon walls. Finally emerging on the outside, she is presented with a royal note by one of the guards. Right there she opened it and reads. She is to meet with her sister Libra, at the outer tomb of the ancestors, at the sixteenth hour. Looking up at the sun her deductions complies that she will reach the outer tombs ahead of time.

Leoha Gets a Surprise

To Leoha's surprise, the King is already there awaiting her when she arrives. Taking a few steps forward she maintains a discreet distance between herself and her sister. Unaware of why she has been summoned the discretion of her affairs has always been kept above board. The only outstanding event that may be questionable to account for is the beating she gave Sheppard.

The existing gulf between her and the King is due to the unjust treatment she has placed upon her two aunts. It's pivotal now that she practices caution even more careful with her choice of words. With a burdened sense of resentment toward her sister Libra, she detests the obnoxious arrogance of her disposition since she became king. Not that they weren't issued before. They just were not so pronounced. As a Warrior she has set bait many times before, it will be no different that Libra is now King. Leoha takes the first strike, "You are full of surprises." To her surprise Libra chides, "So are you! But it is only your warrior instincts. You are home now and you can let down your guard. Why the distance?!" so coyly she purrs.

For a minute, Leoha's eyes roam round the colossal layout of the newly built pillars and tombs of her great ancestors. Goading her for a reaction out of character, anything to put a dent in her armor. Slowly she moves forward a little more, a pawn to King. "I believe the crown has somehow changed you, sister." Libra, walks in even closer, king to the knight, and says "Please Leoha, let's not go there! And should you want to believe. I have changed! I haven't, but I have grown up!" Never one to shun a challenge, spoken or implied the Warlord Princess, takes a step even closer to her sister. The dark roads of her journeys have blessed Leoha with an aura of confidence in face of adversities. With leaving still a distance between them both Leoha broaches the terms of their understanding. "We once agreed, there would be no lies between us. Why did you lie about our aunts?"

How lively things are, the guile of Libra smile mocks of shock and drudgery. There is no explanation forthcoming or apology. Was she not explicit in her conveyance, to make things abundantly clear? Libra walks up even closer. Leoha knows better than to threaten the authority of the King. King Libra scoffs at Leoha's misplaced empathy. "Don't take my words out of context. I only said they are in a safe place." This only serves to incense the Warlord Princess, but she manages to hold her patience. Yet in a forceful rebuke, of not many words Leoha dares, "Do you call the dungeons a safe place."

Yes, that was her sentence for them, at the time it was most appropriate and deemed quite lenient considering their heinous offenses. For all the mighty Warrior Leoha is, this pardon she seeks makes her weak. Libra walks two paces from her before she responds with conviction and without remorse. "I call it being out of harm's way! And I don't want you to believe, they trust you. The ways of those two are dangerous and should be monitored closely at all times, but that is not why I asked you here." With her curiosity piqued, Leoha is intrigued to know more. "You mentioned in your note, you have something I ought to see before leaving. I think it must be here. Can we please get on with it? Now, what is it?" Conversant with Libra on any level has a tendency to turn debatable. Libra entreats, "It's a must! I ask, have you seen your brother Dicious, as yet?" This line of question is unusual, but Libra's duties as King require her jurisdictional review of territories and its citizens.

Dicious is their brother and his importance to the crown is far-reaching. If Libra could get on with what she has to say the sooner she can be on her way. "No! But am looking forward to it. Tell me, what does Dicious, have to do with my being here, because right now. I am numb and I really don't care about any of this around me. Like I always say and believe, the dead should remain with the dead I am in the world of the living. If you don't mind! And I can talk only for the living and not the dead." Libra, is dismayed by Leoha biting aggression "Your hostile behavior. Being the warrior you are, have made you cold. Do you care about anything any more? Let me ask you again. Do you care about me as your sister any more?" Why is this illustration necessary and still Libra has not established her point? Leoha walks up to her sister and looks her in the eyes. "You lost me. What is it, your asking?" Checkmate! King Libra is given no alternative but to share her concerns.

"I see you expect me to spell it out. I am asking you to stay. Not to leave again. I need you here. Can you do that?" This is a surprise, peering intently upon the carriage of Libra forbearance, Leoha, walks around her before coming to a stop. This is the bargaining tool she needs. "And I need you to understand, both my aunts may die if they stay much longer without sunlight. Can you do that?"

This time leverage is on Leoha's side, she forgets they are her aunts too. Libra gets the picture. Her sister is a warrior first, and the expectation of her demands are always met. Burning vats of oil, to her warlord sister. Libra reponses her stand. "Are you asking me, as your sister or as the King?" The King is surprised at what she hears next. "If I were asking my sister. I would not have to ask twice, so am asking you as. Although she is the king, what Leoha just expressed forces her conscience to accountability." Libra, interrupts stopping her from talking further, "Please just stop! It shall be done! Now there is something I need to know. And should you not want to further talk at this time. I can respect that. So, tell me! What did happen to you during your battle with the Black Widow?"

Even as children Libra was pushy. Leoha rolls her eyes upward across the sky. She herself is still trying to manage her temperament when it comes to the Black Widow and her cohorts. In a manner of composure Leoha shares what she can itemize on the course of places, people, and things she has encountered. "Truthfully! I wish not to speak about it. Please, say no more of it but I can say. It feels like I come from the cradle to the grave and the only thing I truly have left is my hate towards the Black Scarlet."

I had to kill all in the House of Zebb. I was the Warrior, without love and sex but the Black Widow changed all of that. The son of Zebb, may have lived a little longer, to share his last dying words with his family, if it had not been for me. I killed him and I watched him die. I guess the difference is, he did not deserve it. I did not want to kill his family but they attacked me first. Maybe one day, when am more comfortable with you. I will be able to fill in the degrading blanks. I have already sworn upon the House of Zebb, vengeance upon the Black Scarlet shall be mine alone."

They are sisters, regardless of the differences in their convictions or station in life. Libra, upon hearing her sister plead for unanimity, speaks. "So you're carrying around another secret, you wish not to further talk about. Is there anything else?" Leoha does not elaborate. "Yes! Don't we all carry secrets around at times? Am only asking, you not to push me. The army never arrived as scheduled, so I had no back-up. Can you explain why, sister?" The question takes Libra off guard immediately, she is reminded of her given word to her sister Sheppard. The statue of her father's word rings with alarm to reinforce the declaration of these spoken confidences. "There cannot be an inner war."

The deflection of the question detours the mark of inquiry from finding its failings. King Libra apologizes most eloquently on behalf of the obstructions that hindered the army's progress to retrieve Leoha with much fanfare. For the stability of the Kingdom to remain intact, the provided explanation had to suit the surrounding circumstances. "Am sorry but at the time, there was an incoming storm. A very large one that forced my hand. Sometimes the needs of the many to stay put, can outnumbers the one. After the storm had passed, they searched for you, but could not find you. I am still so sorry about this." The story King Libra conveys is sound and plausible to believe. Even Leoha nods her head agreeing "I too had to make a detour because of that storm. I understand."

Inwardly Libra breathes a sigh of relief and changes the topic. "Tell me, have you notice anything so different around here?" Leoha meditatively reflects, searching the area for missed observances she may have pasted. "Apart from the newly built high tomb! No." Nothing seems amiss or out of place. Insistent, Libra offers her a tidbit of insight, "Take a good look at it? Can you see what is written high above those Pillars?" The Warlord Princess looks again at what has captivated King Libra's attention, but she doesn't see anything untoward. "I already have. Child of hope but I know nothing of any child! And I hope you will try and bridge the gap between you and your aunts to a safe and peaceful family rest."

Libra laughs out, "Good luck with that! She was another of your sisters. I brought you here to pay your respect before leaving again." Leoha still doesn't understand the point Libra seeks to make. "Why is this so important to you? I have never met her before and she is my sister? I can only say how sorry I am for her loss and for not meeting her before her death. Did you know her?" Giving Leoha more line to catch her trail of thought King Libra does her best to explain the relations of this tomb. "I knew of her and met her once here in the Kingdom and the rest is easy to figure out." "What's so special about this tomb?" Again Leoha studies the columns for some sign that will answer beyond what she has been given. Finally, she asks Libra "So who was she?"

In retrospect, Libra does her best to prepare and buffer Leoha for the answer she drops." Aries sister." Strongly the warlord princess protests. "Aries sister! That can't be! You once told me Black-Scarlet, is Aries sister. So, who is in the tomb?" Even with additional clues, Leoha has no idea, but Libra is silent, waiting, and deep down she groans. Retracing, deducing the information garnered, the process of elimination still points in one direction. One she refuses to acknowledge. Speaking more to herself, Leoha asks knowingly. She just recently saw the Black Scarlet and was defeated by her, so it just cannot be her. That just cannot be. Leoha rages, "That's just not possible!"

She didn't want to be the person who informed Leoha her nemesis was beyond the wrath of her intentions. Being the king, it becomes her responsibility to states the obvious. "Like I have said. She is Aries sister and her name is written high above those pillars, child of hope. If I ask you now to forget about this, could you?" Without hesitation, the Warlord Princess, quips, "No! I can't!" Even though their relationship has been less than smooth lately, wroth in tension and opposition does not stay their bond in blood. Her sister will not obtain the prize of her heart's desire, to see her enemies vanquished by another hand. This consuming passion to destroy the Black Scarlet worries her as the King, she must tell her. "I thought so! And if I order you as King, then would you?"

Without fault, the Warlord Princess is fully prepared to commit treason against king, throne, and kingdom. "No! And should you try and stop me from leaving. I will fight my way out. I don't care how many sisters Aries may have. The Black Scarlet must die!" Gingerly Libra continues to ply her Warlord sister to understand what has occurred is out of her control. "As your sister. If you truly care about me. I would not have to ask twice." Stubbornly holding firm to her own convictions, the Warlord Princess refuses to accept her sister's words as truth. "Like you once said. We must all grow up and stand for something. If not, we may take anything. Everything around me feels like it's failing and I have nothing but hate and anger toward the Black-Scarlet." The King reminds Leoha, "That is because you are not giving yourself a chance to understand. Just do me a favor before you decide to leave again. Go and see your brother Dicious?"

Leoha is a Warlord Warrior and proud of her accomplishments, she concludes her session with The King. "As I have said am looking forward to it! I have a question?" Libra, obliges her, "Please." Being king requires that Libra display a certain amount of decorum. In this vein, she decides holding back, maybe its best advantage to leave things alone, there may be another opportunity later to talk. Leoha's question surprises her, "What do you know about the fifth element and who is he?" Again another question that requires finesse. Its good that King Libra's quick wit settles the matter amicably. "No more than you do. Why don't you ask your brother Cleattus? I would think, he is an expert in that field and should that not answer your question. I suggest you start by visiting the temple of the white lamb." The day truly has become one of the uncultivated surprises, Leoha is not moved to accept her invitation "Then I shall start there and good by"

With strong strides, Leoha turns and walks away. Watching her retreating figure depart, it's within her rights asking to order Leoha stopped, but who would it serve. She is the king now, and Libra knows the ways of her Warlord sister. She accepts that Leoha, would never comply with her wish to remain home. It's just like her to find something to cavil at every turn. This whole situation has placed her in a precarious position of entangled frustrations she does not like. Continually she reminds herself, like all Warlord Warriors, supremacy and independence are a part of the warrior code mantra.

Into the Throne Room

Into the throne room, King Libra returns with her superior bodyguards very much dissatisfied. Deep down she is relieved, the slight of Sheppard's affairs has not exposed the promise of her confidences. She is now entreated to adjoin matters as a consequence to improve relations with her aunts. It's a mundane task with which she must comply. Primarily due to her sense of obligation she issues the orders for her Adviser removing her two aunts from the dungeon. Contemplating where to stash them, King Libra mulls over her options short of having them put to a quiet death. Where can she place these two festering cretins that will also appease her Warlord sister, the Warrior Princess? If the transfer proves successful, maybe her actions will open better relations between her and Leoha.

Now, where can she put them that they can do the least amount of harm. Like a dawning light, she knows were, she'll send them. Sarraha is the best choice, why she didn't think of it before when she first had to face the wicked vices of these two debased old women. Maybe she will be fare better with them. By exiling them to her part of the Kingdom, she wouldn't have to deal with them. Only Leoha can't seem to see the truth about these women or she just ignores what they are capable of doing. It's a perfect solution, their care quality would be more than exceptional, Leoha would find no complaint.

The other sister Sarraha rules one-quarter of her father's mighty kingdom. In her instructions, the ordinances outlined stipulate clearly should they ever again set foot within the wall of her domain without her knowing first, they are to be executed on sight by orders of the King. Expeditiously. The King's orders are executed. The two aunts are most grateful, for the king has shown them her mercy. They are even more thankful to their niece Sarraha, for accepting them under such conditions. To have dotting and committed niece like Leoha, on their side, was a novelty of grand proportion.

The guards are given their instructions. It's very rare that a pardon comes from the Throne. The two women are removed from the prison. In each step, the hollow clang of chains rings against granite stone. The darkness of the dungeon confines lightens, the air becomes cool, and fresh ascending upward they climb. Their movements impeded by the shackles on their feet do little to contain the glee of tangible freedom close in their grasp. Grotesquely disfigured in appearance, emerging into the light they cringe to each other as the guards remove their chains. The prospects of freedom, new opportunities, and mischief await, aunt Crystal's curdling smile isn't observed. A small convoy escorts them out of the Kingdom. High from the recesses of her quarters, King Libra watches her aunt's convoy depart. They are her aunts too, but if she ever sees them again it would be too soon.

The aunts sit in comfort for the first time since their sentence was imposed because of perverted carnal appetites. The jostle of the carriage rides and the passing landscape is a blur to the old women. Cycles in the confines of darkness have deteriorated their sight. Sarraha is most hospitable, and willingly she receives them. Reports of their frail conditions were not exaggerated.

The carriage comes to stop outside of the gates of Darr. The Kingdom gates open allowing them access. The hobbled footsteps of the horse-drawn carriages enter in. The sentries allow entrance into the courtyard, the expansion of the palace stands before them. Even with their diminished sight capacity, the opulence of Sarraha's Kingdom is most formidable and impressive.

It's the splendor of this new realm that radiates glory. So, this is the other side of the Kingdom, Aunt Crystal marvels at her own regret of never visiting this site before now. From what is visible, King Sarraha's Kingdom is more than adequate to keep them in comfort. The trappings of the Kingdom's wealth and beauty are a striking contrast to their former dwelling place. Once again, with renewed resources, they can resume their habits and former practices, hopefully, this time without obstruction. Beautiful living accommodation is bestowed to each aunt at the opposite end of her domain.

They can take all the time needed to gather themselves. The deterioration of their condition compels Sarraha to give each woman, four might men to carry them around and serve them the necessary nutrients required to boost their mental and physical recovery. The impression Sarraha gives her aunts, makes them believe her rule is superior to that of her sister Libra. Libra is only an interim leader sitting in for the King and is nothing more until such a time her father Gouddaa returns. From time to time her two aunts flattered her, telling her many things. They couldn't believe life in her domain could be so sweet, they would have long humbled themselves if they had known. Maybe then they would not have had their titles stripped.

They pledge Sarraha never to let her down, making it known whatever they can do to assist her with getting Libra off the throne, they are ready to do so, but only on Gouddaa's return. As royalty of the Gouddaaian bloodline, they desire retribution against Libra for inflicting what they believe was an unfair judgment upon them. She alone welded the power, subjecting them to degraded lowliness. She used it, to bring them both down. When they were finished mumbling and complaining Sarraha, addressed both surprising them. "Let me suggest, you get rid of that kind of talk! Should that kind of talk ever get into the ear of others? It can only give Libra, a faster reason to bring me down and it's not like, I don't have enough problems, of my own." Suspended silence follows, after looking around Sarraha goes on to say adding. "But do keep that thought in mind! It could be useful someday and let me remind you both, any plot to kill the King is like talking with death. Just keep it quiet! Remember you two! We never had this conversation!" She leaves them to walk away.

There are many sisters, each differs in personality. The attributes of their strengths evolve with the passing of each season cycle. Sarraha's virtue of cleverness masks the coy slyness of a guileful will. Her nature is colored by ploy tricks - she never fails to use lies as a weapon. Smart, clever, and highly intelligent, she is most afraid of Libra. It's no secret Libra wants to dethrone her for that which had been given by her father Gouddaa, himself. Above all her other siblings, she alone stood for the post and was rightfully rewarded. Contrary to what her other siblings may think, she believes she is capable of running and ruling the whole of her father's Kingdom. With each passing cycle, Crystal and Cecyellet begin to forsake their retribution against Libra. Distractions and revelry of the Kingdom preoccupy their affections. The grace and protection provided by Sarraha's hospitality have given them new and viral pleasures to enjoy.

News of her aunt's pardon comes by means of a high courts official. Leoha is pleased that aunt Crystal and Cecyellet have been released. Her petition to the throne was successful, maybe Libra isn't so bad after all. Under the cover of darkness, they were extracted and placed under the rule of her sister Princess Sarraha, to spend the rest of their lives. The orator states that should they ever return without the King's written consent - they are to be executed on sight. This added exert could only hurt them if they disobey. They were far away and safe out of Libra way.

Before the next cycle of the wind is spent, Leoha secretly shows up before Sarraha's throne to discuss the well being of her two aunts. By reports and observation, she is satisfied with the short time Sarraha, has used to restore back to Crystal and Cecyellet, their royal status. Leoha doesn't let them see her, They look very pleased in their settings. Even though her two aunts are not pretty, the restoration of health revives a more youthful appearance. Their wealth and status make an immediate impression. Everyday adjusting more to kingdom life once again, they indulge themselves more and more. The starvation of prison life in the dungeons has left them famished. The liberty of rewarded freedom allows them to gorge themselves on many delights. Undercover, Leoha leaves returning to King Libra. She re-enters the Kingdom before anyone realizes she has been gone.

Afflictions and torments of the dungeon have passed. Deep in the confines of their minds chains remain. The long confinement of the dungeon has left them emotional and sexually deprived. Hostage to the light of darkness, sexual desires become a burning fever. Often left satiated, they cry out demanding the great deity of Penis bless them. All eight of the mighty men are sexually pushed to service them. The more they push them, the more outrageous their demands grow. After some time had passed, the pleasures of Saharra's aunts begin to show and take their toll on the massive bodes of the eight mighty men. The mighty men are not allowed to stop and breaks given are few. Unbeknownst to Sarraha or Leoha the aunts have regressed to their former ways.

Scorned by vicious intentions. Whenever the mighty men took a break, Crystal and Cecyellet strengthened the liquid potion in their drinks. This aphrodisiac was a trade they both learned on their travels to the east. Taken from a wild sweet plant each day, the liquid substance is secretly secreted into their food and drinks to further stimulate and enhance their sexual appetites. With passing time, the sexual strain on the mighty bodies becomes unbearable and visible to the many. Selfish, greed inspires the aunts to take drastic measures. The request for rest is denied, for the fortieth time their withered bodies faint under the straining demands.

With succubus tendencies, the aunts drain once massive and perfect sculptured bodies. Leaving the old, dry, and withered, the depletion of weight from form saps their strength and desire to further pleasure Crystal and Cecyellet. This is easily rectified when the aunts place more potion and lessen their food portion. Speculation and talks spread about the Kingdom of the eight mighty men withered state. Despite of their deteriorated conditions bravely all eight mighty men stand to perform their appointed task. When ordered to bring in Sudan chaise for the ladies to relax and lay out, although the men looked close to death, it does not account to them.

One early morning while moving along the streets and pathways around the town, behind whispering hands and stifled snorts they realize they are the objects of much amusement. Unsteady with stumbling movements, the eight mighty men are ordered to keep it steady. Aunt Crystal taps her fan against the chaise arm commanding their attention. As she goes by, usually Crystal and Cecyellet often flirt revealing naked legs and bared arms to most of the passing men.

Without care nor respect for Kingdom traditional customs between married women and men, their kisses and favor are reserved only for those after dark. Many indulge in their offered charms. This causes conflict among the wives and their husbands. The sisters gloat in satisfaction, loving it. News of Crystal and Cecyellet's behavior accidentally gains the ear of Sarraha. That same evening, when they returned home Crystal receives orders to meet Princess Sarraha at the gates of her home, she barely makes it in time. Sarraha is a shrewd thinker and at times uses such cunning most dangerously. Her words are subtle, smooth like honey but after the sweet taste fades the last bite hits like a bee, stinging and bitter in the end it swells.

With Crystal's arrival, they first greet each other, after small talk. Sarraha pulls aunt Crystal aside, "Come with me Aunty." The other attending servants remain behind as Sarraha leads the way to a private place in her garden never before seen by Crystal. The rose garden is like no other and its colors vibrant match well with Sarraha's garments. The overall picture causes Crystal to comment, "This is so beautiful and so are you." Sarraha smiles back at her. Reached the sitting grounds, aunt Crystal's eyes again dazzled by the beauty exclaims in awe, "Beautiful! Beautiful, so beautiful!" Sitting down Sarraha offers her a place beside her. "Aunty, please do have a seat."

They both take their seats, aunt Crystal still enthralled with the garden's landscape, has no notion why Sarraha may have called her. Sarraha confides her discoveries, "Aunty! There is much talk about you and Cecyellet, behavior concerning the eight mighty men I have given. Is it true, they are being deprived and starved of nourishment and have lost most of their body mass?" The impact of Sarraha questions, causes aunt Crystal to falter, being a seed of the serpent, she humbly succumbs to Sarrahas line of scrutiny. "It's all my fault and am so sorry. Yes! I have been punishing them and have deprived them of some of their meals but it was only because they became disobedient and the only way, I know how to discipline them, is to take away some of their rationings, or as you may say, privileges. I am sorry for making such a disturbance."

The compliance of aunt Crystal forthright response, admitting her falsehood makes Sarraha, reconsider. She gives her favorite aunt the benefit of the conversation. Leoha is not the only one who has a soft heart for the older lady. Gently she reminds her aunt, "Aunty! You are no longer in the dungeon. You are free and there is no need for such an incident. The feast of a friend is only cycle's away and I cannot have this kind of news lingering over my head. Do you understand? I don't need a reason for Libra to set foot in here. Please go back and take care of this." Pensively aunt Crystal stands up. "I promise." Sarraha, also stands, resting her right hand on her aunt's shoulder, caressing it gently," then we need not talk further on this matter. Come, let me see you out."

They walk together, no words are spoken. Back at her royal coach Sarraha provided, aunt Crystal leaves. Thinking all will be well Sarraha returns back to her throne. There is no further news of disruption. Things remain intact and quiet over the following cycle of the wind this pleases Sarraha. The peace of her kingdom is key to the ambitions and plans she has for her ascension to the Throne. Placated it radiates in her smile.

The Day of the Feast of Friends

The day of the feast of friends arrives and only Princess Sarraha, elite friends from all different nations are invited. princes, princesses, chiefs, assistant monarchs, viziers, iliads, and her most trustworthy. But never white lambs, lamb angels, kings, or queens. For such, privilege is reserved only for the King. Often this bothered Sarraha, making her envy her sister Libra even more.

Elites from various quarters and territories gather, converging around the colossal dining table enjoying, royal wine in conversation. An announcement is made and Princess Sarraha, enters the dining hall to greet and welcome, two hundred and seventy invitees. The servants all stand, and together they applaud her until such time, the Princess reaches her seat. Thanking her, the abundance of guests attending two hundred and seventy guests' leans in awaiting her lead. Her own wine is poured by her servant. She takes it up, waving it past her noise, she whiffs, to better examine its quality. Her gesture tells the participating audience, the Princess approves. Raising her wine for a toast, others join with raised mugs to drink with her. In front of all her Elite friends. "To all of you. I welcome you in the name of my father. Welcome once again to the House of Gouddaa. A toast to all my friends."

After drinking up they are seated in their prospective places according to the station, title, and rank. Sarraha gives her first adviser the signal to begin the feast. Massive doors open to the dining room and to everyone's marvel. Sarraha, royal Junkanoo dancers explode on the scene, all enter dancing to the rhythm of Junkanoo. Drums

The Undaunted King Gouddaa of the Arawaks and Caribs

and large elephant drums, flutes, bells, and cow- bells, keep the rhythm. With breathtaking costumes, depicting the Arawak and Carib culture, they enter. African bass drums beat magnifying the deep rhythm. Nova bright colors of joy and happiness parades circling the colossal table. No one is left untouched by the musical expression, even the elites move to rock in their seats. The vigor of booming drums, the high-pitched peal of bells reaches so deep, that it rumbles the under pillars of the earth, trembling the colossal table and every wine mug in hand.

They are followed by two hundred and seventy dinner servers, all dressed in white. On trays above their heads, the decadence of royal fanfare serves an array of succulent morsels, carved meats, and flavored sweet treats. Junkanoo dancers stay at a distance while the attendees eat. Deposits of treats are placed and spread out over the massive dining table. Baskets of bread and fruits are rest before them to sample. Diverse foods of a hundred different tastes and flavors are provided. Meat dishes are prepared in many ways appeasing even the most discerning pallet. All are furnished for the enjoyment of the elites.

In succession they are closely followed by two hundred of Sarraha's mighty men shining with beautiful bodies, this makes the elite group of women raise out of their seats. Eager to quench their personal thirst and desires, they watch bulging muscles flex for display. The rush proceeds on, followed next by three hundred virgin girls lining off in position. Posed, standing before the enormous table, draped in long black capes increased frenzy erupts in one breath as each virgin removes their covering. Revealed in colors of purple, blue, and red, sheer transparent costumes, the vision of beauty stuns every elite man attending. So many rare and perfectly formed women, the men don't know where to look first. Elite members of the party reach across the massive table, extending flashing hands. In lust, eyes grow wide for the want of virgin flesh. Never before have they witnessed such a collective sight of prime flesh in one Culture.

The novelty of possession, is quenched, a union with any of them is impossible because they are of the Kingdom. Sarraha, again signals her Adviser who motions to the Junkanoo Dancers, Three hundred virgins, and two hundred mighty men. All exit the massive dining hall, leaving behind only the servers for wine. Many of the elites closest to her, all thank Sarraha over and again for orchestrating such an affluent affair. The night moving on, encompassing the dining experience and pleasures of excellent food. After having their fill, and endless bags of wine, the remaining food and deserts are removed from sight. The room is cleared all the wine servers leave to ensure there is no leak in conversations discussed. With many conversing to pass time, the wine begins to take its toll. The consumed wine releases those visiting inhibitions. never before secrets reveal dark and hidden things. With longing they begin to lust at each other. In the happiness of their state, it causes them to laugh hysterically at jokes being made from each other.

Sitting ways off from Sarraha, is one of her most trustworthy Generals. He loves a good laugh and after swilling down a few more mugs of wine they ask him to tell just one more joke before the night ends. He has already used up all his jokes, but he manages to pull one last one out. In a preoccupied conversation with a Princess out of the east, the mention of her aunts turns her attention. He begins to tell the story about Princess Sarraha, two aunts, and how they have sexually weakened eight of the best mighty men in the Kingdom. This is not exactly what Sarraha wanted to hear. Actions revealed in the story, paint a different story from the one her aunt provided. What she wasn't told leaves her cold and furious. The General goes on to describe how two old ladies reduced eight powerful and vibrant men, to nothing more than reeds blowing in the wind.

It is the best joke of the night, roars of laughter, choking coughs sputter, they all laugh until tears flow down. The General elaborates for a stronger effect, he gives them much more and their laughter becomes a great roar. The laughter doesn't settle down but becomes infectious. The only one not laughing is Sarraha. The implications of the General joke, in truth reflects poorly on her ability to rule the Kingdom. The general along with everyone in the room is under the influence of wine. She will have the truth about her aunts and the eight mighty men. What else doesn't she know about them? To bring matters quickly to a close, quietly she calls over her Adviser. She orders immediately, to send a platoon for the eight mighty men she gave to her aunts. In a short time, robed at Sarraha's bequest the eight mighty men come in at once.

The hall of gathered elites listens avidly to the exploits undertaken by these old women with Sarraha most chosen. At present, all are still being entertained by the recap of the general's last joke. Saarraha is not amused, embarrassed, they are all still laughing when the colossal size doors reopen to admit what are the ghostly remains of what use to be Mighty Men. Reaffirmed in the sight of the men, The General harps on, "And there are your the Eight once Mighty Men, stumbling in position." Rapidly, Sarraha blinks at the sight of her men. From her seat, the Princess stands up in disbelief, the brunt of her General's joke releases more laughter. The sudden outburst startles the Princess causing her to stumble back into her seat. To make matters worst, the Mighty General stands up with loud cheer, "And there they areeeeee!"

If she wasn't looking at the face on she'd deny this? What her aunts have done to deplete the finest men of her Kingdom is unconscionable. To think she gave these men to her aunts in good faith. Again, the laughter from the elites becomes great at seeing the very men in discussion. Sarraha remorsefully leans forward in her royal chair in disbelief. Covering her mouth with her hand she closes her eyes to separate her from the howling laughter. She wonders, how is it possible eight mighty men could deteriorate to such a withered condition in such short time. The laughter is so great, two of the women of title fall out in their seats. The Princess waves to the adviser to have the men leave. Her adviser is always on top of things.

The physicians are called, running in they quickly attend to the two fainted women. They bring them to, and the room is cleared. The Princess sits incensed with what she has found. She mulls over if she should have the general executed for his insolence, but she may need him. She didn't need to give Libra, a faster reason to come and take over matters in the King's hand. Her greatest fear is to be denounced from her seat of rule. Looking at everything she has worked so hard to maintain, much of her success is attributed to the good general so she disregards the notion of executing him. From experience of observation, she knows one should never underestimate or forsake a good man. As for her two aunts, they certainly could both use a good wake-up call.

This embarrassment fills her with loathe, the need to desecrate her family obligations becomes very strong. The laughter from the elites becomes so great, that it echoes in her head to the upper ceiling. She desperately must think of a way to turn this disadvantage into a position of leverage. Signaling to her adviser, guards come running from behind the door with mighty spears. A guard taps twice on the marble floor, restoring order to the noisy hall. All laughing ceases and the Guard falls back in position. The crowd watches what next the Princess will do. The situation of her aunt's folly sobers Princess Sarraha, and she stands. She goes on to expound to her guest on where misconstrued motives can lead. "Let me just say! I did it, to show you all the outcome of intimate relations when left unattended and out of control. In the hands of others, there are those who can't control personal desires. You have all witnessed what sex is capable of doing to a person if left unchecked. What you have witnessed was done in a controlled space, for it is imperative that love and making love, should always be apart of a stable and securely monitored environment. Please, do remember this as a lesson passed down to you all, not only as friends but as leaders and future kings of your own nation and descendants."

All occupants in the room put their hands together, applauding her for her honesty, decency, and loyalty It takes courage to broach a controversial topic, many leaders would rather elect to leave buried in darkness. She knows when to quit, when finished they all thank her over and again for her open thinking and kind disposition. Excusing herself, "I have had my fill and please enjoy the rest of the evening." She departs to the cheers and applause of all as is accompanied by the counsel of her first adviser. The adviser leaves her Second and Third in command to oversee each elite guest's plans for returning to their country of origin.

When Sarraha and her adviser get clear of the festivities and its invitees it's the first adviser who knows her best. She looks to Sarraha, "Princess! What are your orders?" Dismayed by the conduct of her aunts she suppresses her fears. "First! Attend to the Eight men! See to it, they are taken to the Physicians right away! They are not to leave until they have fully recovered and before daybreak, throw those two aunts of mine into the dungeon and I will deal with them later."

Without a doubt, her sister King Libra was not incorrect when she placed them in the dungeon. It's easier now for Sarraha to disengages herself from the trappings of family knowing what she does. At her Warlord sister's insistence there were no hard feelings than to hinder assistance rendered to her beloved aunts. She remembers when her sister Leoha visited earlier on to provide a secure place for them. Just looking at her men weak, and frail, the dungeons of Darr should keep their aunts quite fine. It's what they deserve.

The adviser takes leave allowing Sarraha space to think. From the beginning she never much cared for taking in Sarraha, aunts, she'd heard rumors concerning them. Indirectly, there were signs that warned Sarraha not to allow them entry. If Libra put them away, it had to be a serious threat to the power of her rule. Weary to retire, she enters her chambers, angry and ashamed of what her aunts have done.

One by one, visitors depart taking with them memorable thoughts of Sarraha, and the great Kingdom. Just before daybreak, the adviser issues orders to sleep the chambers of both aunts. Cloaked in long black capes, unseen faces blend in twilight shadows of darkness moving swiftly. Elite palace guards go to the Chambers of Crystal, and Cecyellet. From outside they secrete sleeping toxins into the homes. The toxin vapor spreads throughout the chambers. Everyone on the inside is unconscious in a matter of seconds. Donning a hooded mask and breathing apparatus they enter before the poison air could subside. The orgy of naked bodies lies littered over floors. Among the naked, they extract both aunts wrapping them tightly in a black shrouded cloth.

Aunt Crystal and Cecyellet awaken much later within the dungeons of Darr. Imprisoned in its dark and creeping confines they are once more looking out from behind iron bars. Horrified to see where they are, insane screams fade becoming whimpers of regret. Calling out at the top of their voices for help no one other than the dungeon keepers can hear them. Help is no longer available and once again they are abandoned, no hope for rescue. The weights of chains attached to the walls anchor their movements, cutting into their flesh. Cast once again in darkened confines, it only a matter of time before their vision fails completely.

Early the Next Morning

Early the next morning. Leoha, catches up with her brother Dicious sitting besides one of the water fountains behind his chamber. The information King Libra shared, put him on defense. Although she has found some answers very little is known about who he really is. Sitting there alone, holding a cup of flavored herbal tea, he enjoys each sip. Leoha walks up to him, he is pleased to see her though he shows it not. With slanderous reports circulating, things cause Leoha to confront him. "You know brother. I have always expected lies from others! But you, no! Not you!" Dicious, had not seen his Warlord sister since their last order from the throne, bring back their heads, kill the Black Scarlet and the Black Widow. Her accusation bothers him slightly most times they work good as a team. Sensing a degree of uncertainty in her voice, he decides to leave it alone she will elaborate in her time. Dicious wet sarcasm greets her abrasive manners. "And it is good to see you too, again sister."

Her strides close the gap bringing him closer, as he stands to greet her, she slaps him across the face. Serenity of the moment is shattered, hot tea splashes over his hand. The slapping blow is an insult between warriors. Dicious recoils, standing, he is silent, to his sister's spontaneous act. He looks at her wondering what a surprise. Though the hit did not faze him he shrugs it off making an excuse for why? Still thinking it must be about something in his past, her repeated comment has him puzzled. "Why don't you spare me the talks and your lies, Dicious!" The vehemence of her attack is not reasonable Dicious is patient to await an explanation. "Though I am most pleased to see you sister. You have a strange way of showing it. But I must say! You do have me at a lost. What is it, that troubles and disturbs you so?"

It's Dicious steady poise that tones the hostility her irrational aggression. The frustration of seeing her brother alive after much of what they experienced winds her up. "I too am please to see you brother and am thankful we are both still alive. If it had not been for you reversing fathers' orders, may be both of us would have been killed in the forest. Your quick thinking allowed us only injuries. But you owe me much more than that! Much more! I have always stood by you. Tell me brother, who are you? And what secret do you carry? It's just that I find it a little ironic and most difficult to believe, my own enemy tells me, at a time when I was as close to death as I now am to you! That you are the fifth-element! The white lighting spear, and guardian of the king's throne! How is this possible! It cannot be a coincidence! Is it true?"

Such news could have only come from the lips of Black Scarlet before she died. Leoha words come as a surprise to him. This of course means she was still alive at the time she speared his sister life in exchange for him not killing her. As a child at the battle of the three warlords, she was the only child who had ever lived to see the power of the fifth element in action. A spear of white lightning, called out from the four elements of nature, is placed into the hand of he who guards the throne. The fifth element is a weapon developed by King Aggaddaa. Dipped in the incantation of pure white magic, it is handed down and given to each, second male born of the Gouddaaian's throne every ninety-nine seasoned cycles of each third eclipse of the moon. They are born to be the ultimate protector of the Gouddaaian's throne in times of war and need until death. This is the only secret Prince Dicious carries close in his bosom never to be reveled. If ever reveled by the word of his mouth, the incantation will be broken leaving him no more than a mere man, a straggler in the earth. The power and guardian of the throne would be lost forever.

Dicious listens to all that Leoha says spurning the report as inaccurate and false. "No! But what else did that witch tell you." Redoubling her efforts, she repeats with conviction what she's been told, "That the House of Gouddaa, will fall!" No matter what, his oath to the throne is binding, he can never reveal who he really is." And do you believe her? "The Warrior Princess isn't sure. "You don't have to turn my words around. This is not about what I believe, only what was said and who said it." Reluctant to divulge any thing that might give him away, Dicious can't help. "I would like to help, but like I have said. You do have me at a lost. So, I must ask again. Where from, did you received such news?" Without blinking Leoha retorts. "From the one I now seek to kill. The Black Scarlet."

She doesn't know, the Black Scarlet is dead, the very place dedicated to the child of hope is final her resting place. If Dicious doesn't help Leoha bring closure to her search, before beginning to seek another lost venture her pursuit will be in vain. "If, what you say is true. It would mean the Black Scarlet is still alive! As you already know! All who have ever seen this so call fifth element, are dead. Why then would she still be alive? If what she said is truth? To remain alive is why I choose not to go in search of this myth. And maybe, you should do the same. I too have heard much about this lighting white spear, and its radiant power. Maybe, just may be one day you and I could search out the truth. Would you like that?" She doesn't answer immediately, "Maybe! But the way I see it, she has no reason to have lied but you do. I was as good as dead at her knees but that won't change anything for what she did to me. I will seek her out and I will kill her. She will fall before my feet like all the others."

For all the advice Dicious imparts, Leoha is still adamant to do things her way, "I think, it would be best, if you now put that thought away. There is much we must now do here. You and I, have made it out alive and father is not here. That worry's me." She apologizes, "Sorry, but this time! I just can't." He tries again to make his Warlord Sister see the facts as he presents them and still she does not. It takes another long talk before he gets her to understand. "I know most warriors are head strong and your anger blinds you. Did you not see the tomb of the child of hope? She was not only your sister - she is Black Scarlet. In other words! You can call it quits. That is why Libra, asked that you now stay here so that together we can better focus on protecting the future of the Kingdom, until father returns.

Leoha, the Warlord Princess doesn't want to believe it, being most uncertain and disappointed with such news. In her uncertainly, she cries out, "No... no. . . no... that can't be! Deceive me not brother!" The pathetic look on Dicious face nods its true. Her anger gets the best of her, with raw power, she grabs hold of one of the nearby tables, smashing it against the water fountain. In the midst of the destruction, she pauses to vent her outrage. Dicious knows the nature of uncertainty does nothing but creates stress related anxieties. Short minutes later the guards come running in to access the situation, the loud crash jarred everyone's nerves. Dicious orders them to leave at once and they do.

So soon after Leoha, had crossed the grounds leading to the throne room, she meets a servant girl who kindly greets her. "Princess! The two cup of salt, which you have ordered have been removed from your room and emptied." Leoha, knowing connotation of the secret of her message, becomes most concern. In few words. "Where to?" The servant girl tells her what she knows. "Back down in the dungeons." The servant news is unexpected Leoha knows she must address this here and now. To the servant Leoha states quietly, "Thank you." And the girl walks away.

It angers her, with a swift slice of her blade in one stroke, she cuts through one of the large near by tree branches and it falls to the earth. With her blade still in hand, she enters the great hall of the king. Right away she is stopped by battle guards in formation. The King on the throne notices Leoha standoff opposing her battle guards. Something is wrong, it is her very own sister causing the disturbance. The King calls to the guards. "Guards stand down!" Leoha, is allowed to pass. Upon reaching the mighty throne, the King stands up concern with her sister's action. "Leoha! How dare you stand before your father throne with a drawn blade in hand. Have you gone mad?" The King's words only incite the Warlord Princess even more. For a minute she contemplates the importance of returning back to her sister Sarraha, before something else befalls her two aunts. Pointing out her blade at the King, the throne guards call to arms taking position to protect the King. Again, The King becomes agitated with the above throne guards, "Guards! I order you to stand down!" The throne guards back down but not that far. Indifferent to her sisters' issue with wrath King Libra doesn't mince words. "You know the in-house rules better than most. Should this ever happen again sister, you will not have my pardon so easily."

Collecting her sensibilities, out of respect for the King's words, to preserve her Princess status she puts away her blade. "King or not, sister! If you don't tell me. . . and now! Who lies in that tomb as my so call sister, so help me for I shall remove it from it's foundation and reduce it to ashes!" Leoha's warrior status does not intimidate Libra. As King after hearing her sister disturbing words she chooses not to further escalate the issue or Leoha urgent need for answers. "Sister! You just have to tone this down. Like I have said before. She is and was, Black Scarlet but that name is never again to be used within these walls, by orders of the King. Her name is written among the temple strolls, as the child of hope by no other than father himself! I am so sorry you had to hear the news this way!" The news further disappoints the Warlord Princess and her bitterness begins to show. To her sister the King she apologizes, "No, no sister. No, It is I who is sorry."

Pressed for time to reach her aunts the Warrior Princess must hurry. Bitterly she takes her leave out from the great hall of kings. After gathering her belongings, she goes into the stables, there having a word with the stallion keeper. The stallion keepers hands over to her a magnificent beast worthy of great speed and very much untamed. Walking up to the untamed stallion she stretches out her two hands and covers its deep black eyes to put the hyper stallion to an ease. Then taking hold of its mouth she pry's it opens and spits into its mouth down its throat. She then blows her breath into the beast nostril so that she and the stallion become one, and the beast is tamed. When the others saw what she had done, it shocks them. Over and again, they had tried to tame the fiery stallion without success.

Saddled up, she rides out leaving them speechless. The air is calm when she comes to a stop at the tomb of her ancestors but the wind sings a different kind of tune, as it whistles its way through the gigantic pillars. She descends from her stallion to the ground and walks up to the tomb of the child of hope. Placing herself between the two colossal pillars holding up the mighty structure, she begins to push against them to bring the enormous structure down. Undaunted by the difficulties she tries holding one of the great pillars and then she begins to push and pull on it. Slowly the pillar cracks and debris falls but still it will not fall. Brutally striking the massive pillar still it won't come down.

With a leap of faith, she lashes out one last time and the great tomb above splits in two. The Black Scarlet mighty weapon falls and is exposed. The gleaming metal is like none she's ever seen, its dark aura transfixes her attentions. Retrieving, the weapon from where it fell in hand it brings her to a calm. She can now believe the truth, which is told by Libra, and her brother Dicious. An empty void, now spreads over her and she feels cheated from her revenge upon the Black Scarlet. Looking at the superior and remarkable blade in her hand. she does nothing more than leap to her stallion and ride off, the great walls of the Kingdom hoover high in the sky. In route to the opposite end, she comes to a stop beside a hill connecting to the great wall. Over and into her sister Sarraha, domain she leaps and climbs. Secretly entering by means of her royal seal she is able to pass Sarraha's guards at will before ever being detected.

You Must Be Well Informed

Into the throne room she makes her way, her presence is noticed right away by Sarraha's adviser in conversation standing away from the door. The Adviser passes the news on to her second in command, who conveys it secretly to Sarraha. Right away Sarraha gives the orders to clear the hall at once leaving only the Warrior standing. To her Warlord Sister. Sarraha, targets her. "You must be well informed." The guards stand close by watching Leoha every move. "Impressive! The way they all moved. I see you are also well informed." Sarraha is exasperated, to see Leoha has reached so quickly. Walking down from her throne to meet her Warlord Sister, they stand almost face to face. "Am only here to talk." Sarraha chides, "So let's talk!" Making her last step down to the ground Sarraha has had enough of her Warlord Sister, and their aunties. "Who is in charge here, how is it you can sunder through my domain and am the last one to know?" Putting it bluntly Sarraha cuts through the chase to her sister Leoha. Each of them knows why she is there. she is stern when she suggests, "You should think about keeping them yourself!"

What kind of twisted suggestion is that, she knows that's impossible. What warrior could carry baggage on the missions she takes. "Please, don't joke like that." Sarraha, leads the way and her sister follows it's obvious her aunts have done something unpardonable again. She catches up, she's never seen Sarraha so agitated, what did they do now, she really doesn't want to know. Sarraha isn't joking when she turns to face her. "It's not a joke! I really think you should find a place of your own for those two. They make me look bad!

What else do you want me to say! What do you want and expect from me?!" It's hard not to sense the frustrations in Sarraha voice, Leoha feels guilty but she too is frustrated, "I only asked, you keep them safe! Why do you also think the dungeons is the safest place for them? They are your family also, you know."

Sarraha crosses her arms against her bosom and her lips slightly twist, "I wish you had told that to Libra, before she had them sent here, to me!" For Sarraha to mention Libra, images of them in the dungeon resurfaces and how they looked still pained her. Leoha, being most concerned about her aunts and how King Libra detained them, "Have Libra also attacked you?" Leoha touches a nerve that uncoils all Sarraha fears. "And my rule and everything else. Father said there cannot be an inner war. What do you gather from that?" The intricacies that composes the new King can not be fathomed. Sarraha shouldn't even try. "The same thing you do. One rule, but first things first."

Let me again remind you, they are also your aunts and family blood line. "Am only asking, you keep them safe until this blow over. They also brought you up! You need to understand, father is not here so he cannot defend them but just may be. If you can defend and protect them until his return, he may find more favor in you and your rule, than that of your sister Libra." For a minute, Sarraha, ponders the thought and decides to embrace the opportunity to take better care of her exiled aunts until such time father Gouddaa, returns. Maybe he will find better favor in her rule than that of her sister Libra, as Leoha suggests. "I have never looked at it from that point. This little sacrifice to bring that sister of mine down, is truly not much to ask and I do believe father would reward me handsomely in the end."

They come to a stop in the area, which the Warlord Princess often visited as children, nostalgia brings back, that relaxing free feeling of being a child. "Could we just stop here for a while. This area has always relaxed me." Looking around she to deeply breathes, and obliges her because she too remembered the times. The moment draws confessions from Leoha it's easier for her to confide to Sarraha than Libra. Maybe talking about it will help her to let the burden go.

In her mind she replays the events that lead to her cure. "You know! I never told anyone the Black Widow poisoned me and her disciple Black Scarlet, saved me. She told me how and where to find the cure and you would not believe, the cure lied in the loins of a dying man in the House of Zebb. I couldn't just show up and demand the cure. So, I waited until the way was cleared and night came, then I leaped up to his bedroom window and I entered. He was alone and after looking over him. I knew as much as his family, he was going to die, they just couldn't tell when but I knew he had not much time left."

He opened his eyes and found me there looking over him and he reached out his hand to me. With the whispers of death, his dying tongue spoke, "Please, Jullaha, give me a son to carry on my father's name, its all I could ask of you. It was foolish of me to have believed. I alone could have killed her." And he blacked out. I gathered, he must have been hallucinating. With time not on either of our side. I quickly hit his vital points and he again awake, then I hit all his vital sexual organs and he became sexually aroused. I disrobed him of his lower garment and I made love to him. While engaged in the act, he again looked at me. And he said out to me. "Thank you Jullaha."

I have never made love before. This wasn't love, but the means to an end. The act came naturally but this was the first time my mind felt as if it got separated from my body. I began to invasion seeing out there in the heavens, worlds upon worlds, out there in time and space. I could hear every thing around me and beneath me so clearly. I became one with the universe, I could even hear his family voices crying for his recovery, the approaching foot steps from the downstairs didn't move me until. . . the young lady, standing in the door way, dropped her bowl of water and start screaming out at me. "Stop it! Stop it! Who are you? How could you do this to my fiancee, you Puta!" By the time my mind did come clear to me, I turned to looked at the young man. I wasn't even conscious of my actions at this point too see what I was really doing. His face had turned blue and he looked so old and dried. I was still not fully cognizant, and was trying to get steady awareness but for a second I remained blank until the young lady in the door way screamed out again at me."

Dazed I looked at her as she ranted, "You killed him. You killed him. You killer."

Before I couldn't even move, the young girl ran up to me and she stabbed me in the upper chest. My Warrior instinct then kicked in and all my senses and reflexes came back. Rushing toward me were persons with knives, diggers, and weapons. I had to defend myself because there was no way I could have explain me, making love to their dead son. I killed them all and finished, dressed myself. Then I went downstairs and set fire to the house, leaving it to burn. On my way out, there is a young man watching only my injury stop me from chasing and killing him. I believe one day, he will come and seek me out. I've carried it ever since and it is my only secret. One day I must attune for what I've done I only ask that you keep it that way. This news is astounding to Sarraha, her sister confidence is a venerable place and she is sure there's more that she hasn't said.

With empathy Sarraha wants to comfort her with a touch but declines its too sensitive and she is a warlord. "Am so sorry. The sacrifice you have made is more than enough. I will see to it that they are better taken care of. I have been plagued with a situation here, maybe you can share some light?" With her attention piqued Leaha, studies her sister. "Should I not be of help. I should be able to point you in the right direction." Even more curious is Sarrahas response. "That is what I am afraid off. You pointing me in the right direction." Tilting her head to the side she leans in waiting, its obvious there's more, "Then why do you ask me knowing the outcome?"

Sarraha nods after thinking. Leoha is only offering to help, she sighs releasing her apprehensions. What better time to embrace and welcome the opportunity for counsel than now "Am sorry! Two of my closest matrons in the hierarchy have given birth on the same day. One of the boys was born with a strange birth defect, the growth is all over his body. The mother claims, its not her child but that born to the other. Hence my dilemma, the other woman says she lies. I want to help her and the other but I don't know how so I kept it a secret. Sister did you know at times having to rule makes one demented, sometimes I get the most destitute and morose feelings, I want to kill them both." Shaking herself Sarraha finds solace in the preservation to act, "But that's not the answer because I would also have to kill both children. There is no medicine and the physicians are all out of answers. What should I now do?"

The stalemate of this situation can only be resolved by a King, and she herself is not qualified to mediate judgments on such matters. She is a warrior, the code of the sword is absolute. Leoha pragmatically without emotions declares such diadems would best be shared with no other than. Never did she factor the malignity of their relations when she suggested, "You could start by asking Libra." With a sputtered apoplexy, Sarraha, turns to her. "Before I go to her for help! I'll kill them all!" Breathing hard at the thought of bending so low to Libra, makes her shutter in revulsion. "So now you understand why I am afraid of you pointing me in the right direction. You of all should know the hate between us."

Taken back a bit at Sarraha vehemence, raising her hands in defense she presses back "Yes! I do but your back is against the wall and you need her help. I too have my differences with her but she has never ever mentioned the word hate toward you, so should you fail. Its on your own head." Slightly shaken she feels immature, that answer bothers her but Sarraha still has confidence that Leoha will help her provide a solution "Then why don't you help me, like am helping you?" It's incredulous how could Saaraha disengage herself from the relations of family is beyond Leoha. Is she the only one with a strong sense of family obligation. "How could you Sarraha! They are also your family. Are you asking. . ." I. And before she could finish. Sarraha, cuts in "Yes! Am asking you to ask her." She can't believe it, "Please don't bargain this with me like this!" Just look at her the mighty proud warrior, sarcastic melodrama replaces earlier sentiments. How dare she put herself above her needs, when she selfishly impresses her own on her without any hesitation, the chill of Sarraha retraction surprises Leoha. "You should have said that to Libra, before requesting them here. Even you know! Its best you take them with you. Find a place outside!" Amazed at her disregard Leoha stares at her sister as if she is a stranger, "How could you go back on your words?"

Even now her sisters selfish pleads further infuriate her. "Yes! I gave you my words but I have a Kingdom to run, not baby sit those two aunts of yours!" Her heart starts to race, she can't believe it,

Sarraha won't help her anymore. The reality of now having to deal with her aunts is impossible, and Leoha, calms down. "I see we are at a stale mate here. You have now placed my back up against the wall. I'll meet you back in your Throne room in four horks (meaning four hours) I'll be back." The great Warlord Warrior turns and walk away. Sarraha looks on at her sister leaving knowing she is soon to return. Out loud to herself, she whispers, "Am so sorry about doing this to you, sister!" And the Warlord is gone.

On the way from Sarraha, Leoha makes a quick stop before continuing on. Her new stallion is swift and fast and with speed, she is able to cross the length of the Kingdom in half the time. She expects that she must make explanation to the King in order to get back out again. She strategizes thinking of a plan to distract the King from ordering her to be stopped by the superior guards of the throne for the destruction of the tomb of the child of hope. Entering the halls, the throne room it is bare. The suns regal glow begins its descent on the court's towers, she finds her sister not on the throne but in her own chambers about ready to walk out.

Surprised they both are, foremost to see the King in her quarters. And Leoha startled reaction to see her presence in her chamber makes the King think suspiciously, "What is she up to now?" Already alerted about the poor news about her petty actions. The King speaks with deliberate patience when she expresses, "I should have you locked away!" The King is even more surprised - to hear the brave Warlord her Warrior sister humbly appeal for her mercy. "Please, pardon my behavior earlier and I'll wait to be punished by father." Libra thinks, there goes another Sheppard, playing with kingdom rules for personal ambitions. This can't be the same sister who would fight before she rescinds her position. Livid King Libra marvels that she could be so immature and irresponsible. "You desecrated the tomb of the Black Scarlette and removed the blade and you expect me to do nothing?"

In submission Leoha, drops to her knees before her sister, she knows it was wrong but the paralyzing vortex of unexpressed emotions held her captive to commit baneful and pernicious actions. "Please, help me and should you want me to stay, I will." Crocked by her shocking change of behavior, calms the King's demeanor. The King orders her, "Get up!" From her knees she raises and again to her astonishment. The King relents "Please just leave, but the blade must stay behind." This is an amazing turn of events for Leoha never expected compassion but here it was and she was more than ready to accept it. "Then I will leave it at the throne, with whom ever you wish. But first I must get it."

What ever happened between their last visit has made a drastic change in her Warrior Warlord Sister. As Leoha is about to walk away. Libra comments, "That would do nicely." Excited that the charges that should have incurred have been dismissed, Leoha is stopped in thought and Sarrahas request comes to mind. "Sister!?" Libra, looks to her to continue, the question takes her aback when she asks, "Can you help me?"

Shrewd and cunning King Libra is astute when she considers whatever Leoha may need. "What is this all about?" Leoha uses the opportunity to address Sarrahas concerns as she requested without divulging too much. "One is dying of a grave sickness not known to us, can you be of help?" The symptoms are familiar to the King. Leoha is convinced, if she can cure the child, it should clear the situation between the matrons in Sarraha's kingdom. Once again, her sister the King Libra, lives up to the position her father gave her." How loyal are your words and is the sickness within the Kingdom walls? Leoha tells her all of what she knew that she could. "Yes." The King provides her with solid resources. "In the far south, there is a Forest called Cutterria, that lies between two great lakes, where the water flows blue on both sides. And in the center lies a tree called, the tree of Souls. There are only two left in the world and their fruits are like no other. You must get the fruit and boil it down to a tea and have them drink it. Instantly the disease is gone."

The Warlord Princess does not fully understand about the fruit so she asks Libra to elaborate. "What do you mean, like no other and why is it called the Tree of Souls?" King Libra describes the fruit. "It is because, the fruits grow in the form and shape of a woman." This is most unusual, as a warrior they are taught many things, but this was something she did not know. "Is that possible for a fruit to look like a woman?" King Libra smiles at her naivety. "Is this about, what you believe or what you want and need?" This knowledge was just what she needed. To make no further mistakes before her wise sister, she turns and walks away.

Back across the Kingdom she rides to the other side and she finds Sarraha, sitting high and mighty on her throne. Once again, the room is cleared and Leoha hands over the gift of knowledge to Sarraha, who is most pleased. Confiding her relief in pun, the Warlord Princess chides to her sister "I would rather this be the first and last time. You put my back against the wall." Relieved she too is satisfied at the out come she hoped but didn't expect Leoha to resolve the matter so quickly. "And I too wish. I would never have to say sorry to you again." Their deal now secures the Warlord Princess turns to leave, knowing her two aunts are now once again in favor. Straightaway Sarraha sends out two of her own along with trackers, on a journey to the south in search of the mysterious fruit and bring it back at once.

Ever Pursuant of the Truth

Ever pursuant for the truth Cleattius has been spending most of his life time investigating the fifth-element. A myth to most his journey has been long, arduous and painful. It has leads him to the temple of the white lamb, thousands and thousands of miles away from home. Restricted, it is off limits to most. Lead in his conviction, he follows the weapons path. It does exist because he has walked in the wake of its trail of destruction and death many times before. Unfortunately, it evades him, although always one step behind, he keeps pushing for answers. Plagued by haunting dreams that never goes away he is resolved to end this through confrontation.

He long discovered, the so-called fifth element has much to do with his father throne. He's close, but the closer he gets the further he must go. Should he not find his answers here at the temple of the white lamb it would mean starting again from the beginning. The idea of having to do that, is not of his nature. Canvasing the surrounding atmosphere with all its tall green trees, hills, valleys and mountains. The harmony of nature has painted its own canvas here, its a perfect place for one to forget about the world problems and live a peaceful life. In another time, in another place this may have had different meaning to him.

In the distance the temple looms. Slowly he descends from his horse to the ground, up ahead of him are two guardians, one posted on each side of a gigantic door. While moving forward his mind takes him back to a time when he was a child. He remembers the same gigantic entrance with his father Gouddaa, holding his hand.

He doesn't remember the inside, but does remember being told by his mother, that the gigantic structure was built by a race of giants. A sudden gush of wind blows in, the rustle of dry tree leaves whips up, and the thought of his focus returns.

To him both the Guardians, hail, "Greetings traveler." Looking to avoid confrontation, he pulls out his Royal Seal and shows it out to them. "Royal Seal! Please take me in to the one in charge, here?" Where there usually is acquiescence, the seal does not grant him access. To his surprise. One of the guardians, explains. "Please accept our most humble apologies but you cannot enter." With his admittance barred and his ministerial credits denied Cleattus being one of short patience, is mortified. Pompously sticking his chest forward, undignified that his royal status is being slighted. Right away he thinks, somebody needs to show me some respect. Maybe these men don't know who I am, let's see if I revise my manner it will give me the access I require. "I am not here to start a fight. Only to view some of your books on the fifth-element. Either you let me in or I enter by force. This in which I hold is a royal seal so please let me through."

The Second Guardian, officially addresses Cleattus. "Young Prince, from the House of Gouddaa. I am the second guardian, and my colleague here is number one. Though you posses a royal seal of supreme authority from the House of Gouddaa. That authority here is only for your King." If King Gouddaa was here there would be no need for him to here, presentation of the seal should have been sufficient to allow him in, this only slows him down further. He will not be denied, he only needs to see it, agitated tensions coil and twist, sweat perspiration glistens on his forehead. Angered Cleattus only respects the rule of brute force. "Oh yea! We will see about that!"

The two guardians are protectors of the keep. They are duty bound to death to guard and protect its content. In his irrationality state Cleattus draws his weapon, lunging an attack. Charging towards the doors he forges his steps unfruitful. Trained in the art of defense, the Guardians require no malleable weapons because their bodies have been honed to precision as Master defenders. This Cleattus discovers even with his weapon in hand he alone is no match for the Two Guardians. The whirl fury of thwarted blows and strikes take a hold on Cleattus, to escape injury, away from the massive doors he leaps. The two guardians square their grounds before the doors. Cleattus dares not look back, knowing the haste of his mistake, he leaps back on his stallion and he rides off in the wind disappointed with his actions.

The Still Dark Night

The still dark night is windy but quiet only distances away are many lite bond fires littered across the barren plains. Luminescent in the ink of night like a burning candle stick, robbers and killers congregate to devour. The Warlord Princess Leoha sits alone examining the Black Blade that fell from the upper tomb of Black Scarlet. Closely inspecting the craftsmanship of the weapon, she is most impressed. She has found the blade to be a superior weapon with many hidden attributes. It wields a power next to none shes seen. In the parry of practice exercises, from the moment Leoha lifted the handle of the blade it performed in synchronize harmony, effortless, as an extension of her movements and thoughts.

In the desert among the dunes there is no law, everyone is the law. Everyone consists of thieves and robbers waiting for the big kill. They are scourge of the desert, like rats that scurry the terrain searching of sustenance. The big kill for many marauders, is a score of slaughter, havoc and mayhem, derived from merchants of fortune, a caravan of gold and wealth. On this trek across the sands, many have meet untimely ends. Nomads, and sojourners alike traverse the desserts scorching heat, during seasons where other paths are impassable along the mountainous perimeters.

On occasion, there are some good souls, looking for a peaceful crossing but along the line there are the fools. Their dead bodies are left on the sand, stripped of their clothing and boots. The salvage is used by others to stay warm at nights. Out here, were the temperature can fall below zero it turns vicious. Crossing the sands many travels with armed escort, these hired men are usually Free Lancers. These bands of cutthroats, killers, rouges, and mercenaries are law breakers or slaves. On the desert sands many of these men will face the judgment of their errors instead of in some dank dungeon left to rot. Claimed by the sand and temperatures only the fittest can survive the journey.

As the scorpion on the sand, there is a stranger moving in toward her and his eyes is focused on her blade. Bold without introduction, he demands to have the blade or her life. He is not alone, and his death is witnessed by those eyes watching. Onto the ground his body slumps lifeless, this serves as a warning to all others who would dare. Death comes swiftly and fast to him. His last thought frames his last words 'What a fool I am'. Yet another is claimed by the sand. Talk spreads like wings about a Warrior traveling with a blade like no other. Whispers like embers spread hell fire on the wind and they are many out looking for her.

It's here in this world of parched beauty and folding sands, ever changing the course of her path finds illumination. For several nights there has been no fires lite. Barren before her the landscape stretches out void beneath cloudless skies, the moonlight cascades its glow. The nights without fire, makes it difficult for one to see each other but everyone knows each others position. The blade holds her captive, making her feel invincible. With a blade like this, no one can stop her. It doesn't matter how they come she's ready for anything. It is only a matter of time before they come for her. Just because the last man who tried was unsuccessful, that doesn't mean there won't be others who won't try.

The Warrior persona crackling with energy envelopes Leoha and she raises the sword defiantly for all around to see. A declaration to the sky engages the surrounding minions of vagrants. The invisible eyes are many as she shouts, "You want it? Come get it!" Her answer returns in her own echos. When they approach, it's subtle with craft of deception and trickery. They set traps for the Warlord Princess. The second man dispatched to kill her, meets an equally mortifying death as the first man. The net is set, and by means of hook and crook soon after she kills another and another. The nomads of the desert feeble attempts to eliminate her, gives reason and purpose to test the blades skill and metal. Studying the blade, she reminds herself this once was Black Scarlet own, and what a formidable weapon it is.

The sky sparse and wide seems endless betwixt the twinkling stars. The tranquility of the night is divided by the hoots of hyena's and braying camels in the distance. If all goes well this will be her last night sleeping in the desert. Seconds from sleep a sifting swoosh slides across the sands from various positions. In the valley of the dune banks, four men surfing the sands whip past her, forcing her rise. Alert the blade is ever close and warm in her hands.

The night does little to cover the mask of accosting jesters whisking by on sled boards. Slicing through the sands, only their mocking laughter tells her they are close. The prowls of their movements and quickness attests to their skills. These men are very good and they know how to maneuver. Toying with her they take swipes at her as they pass. The blade of one cut through the arm of her tunic, the sting only serves to increase her adrenal.

She slowly closes her eyes against the sounds surrounding her, reaching deeply within she finds her center. She is able to distinguish there are four of them. One by one the blade isolates them. The sun is rising, already the sands have partially covered the bodies of the men who attacked her night past. Walking through the sands of assassins, by the time she reaches the next town, she has killed thirteen men and eight women. From that time on, she becomes known as the black blade killer. For ever moving this is a warrior's creed and her path, to all her challengers and opponents she shows no mercy.

King Gouddaa
Black Army of Death

King Gouddaas black army of death, have long returned into the Kingdom. Not before leaving a formidable impression on the villagers. With provisions in abundance of thirty wagons accompanied by one hundred armed soldiers. Ready to assist Urobeha's people with their losses the wagons were filled with, foods, clothing, drink, water, shelters and much more. The elders of the town kindly accepted the goods. The undaunted task of distributing them is left to the elders. They are so happy and proud to have received such help.

At times some of the local people seemed frightened by the size and numbers of the Gouddaaian soldiers in their town. However, it isn't long before the women quickly come to terms of their own. They have never before seen such a battalion of strong men. Each soldier identical in physical attributes causes a stir the natives are not accustomed to seeing such viral and physically fit men in one band. Almost hypnotically some gravitate to them raising their hands to touch the flanks of their arms and chest. Seeing them others even ask to touch them to see if they are real. The local town women can't help swooning, and fantasizing what it would be like to have one of their massive strong bodies if only to pass the lonely nights.

Just as the villagers begin to relax with the one-hundred-man battalion, the word is given to move out. While they move out, some of the women cry out for the need of wanting a man. "Do come back again!" "No! don't go, its better here, I can show you." With lewd and raunchy manners some of the women make fools of themselves. The native village men hang their heads shaking it abjectly. Even after they had all moved out, joy and happiness remain in Urobeha's village. The storm has passed, and the threats removed. This peaceful people, will continue on in their lives of harmony.

Having returned to the Kingdom, Urobeha sister Meiha, has learned about her being placed into one of the royal healing chambers. A furor of hushed tones relays the Princess and her guest exploits throughout the Kingdom. This is how it came to her notice, in idol gossip of servants receiving the Princess's convoy. Straight away forsaking her duties she goes in search to find her. It becomes a matter of asking the right questions to the proper attendants. As favor would have it, she is allowed in to see her by a younger chamber keeper, who is in love with her.

The ties of her marriage is a binding one. The arrangement of her marriage was not one of her choosing but of convenience, forced to leave her village and family she now dutifully resides in the Kingdom with her husband. There is no real freedom here for her either, she is captive to her husband and forbidden from seeing others. If this is ever discovered by her husband what she is doing, it could have consequences. It wouldn't matter to him that she is her sister. She has come to learn to live with his controlling ways, at times she takes great solace in the similitude and isolation of her what is now her life.

On seeing her sister naked and bruised body, she thinks back to a time, when her sister said unpleasant words to many of the town folk. Ever so clearly, she hears her sister words reverberate to her. "I feel one day, I shall have to make a great sacrifice for this village, for the men are all cowards in this village!" There were many instances before the Mountain men appeared, that the weaknesses of their men performed inadequately.

Alone, here in the chamber with her Meiha, mind rewinds the news she heard about her sister brutal undertakings, stretched, and ravishment it's a miracle she still alive. If any of what happened in the mountain be true it's a marvel. Metaphorically speaking she has fulfilled the prophecy of her own words. Was this sacrifice, the big day her sister so often talked about, why must you always be a martyr for a cause, sister your restless issues give you no peace... tears swell, rolling drops Meiha cries out. "Make me to understand your logic sister for we as sisters never understood each other and its for this reason alone I left home. Why would you want to give yourself to a bunch of mountain men for nothing? Why would you want to do that you stupid girl?"

What did you hope to accomplish, Meiha, trying to rationalize her sister's behavior, the more puzzled she becomes. The chamber keeper who allowed her entry walks up letting her know the time is up. She must depart, the arriving courts high official was on his way. Living in the Kingdom many of its formalities were taught to her when she first arrived. Her husband only wanted her educated in the ways of court more that she didn't embarrass him than for her edification. She knows of the courts routine a report must be done. It is time she retired to her work, then to home.

On entering the compound, her ungrateful husband sits drinking at the dining table. The smell of alcohol is powerful entering the door it's serves as a lingering testimony of his presence. The penetration of his stare is familiar to her, this was his unpredictable state, any thing and nothing could trigger him off. Seeing her he demands his meal, she says nothing but passes him gently by. With a snap of his neck, he tilts his head to hear any response she may have before having to repeat, "My meal women! My meal." Her response not forthcoming prompts a reaction, in his mind he perceives she is ignoring him again. He expects his wife to be obedient to his demands, is that so hard to understand. Why must he always have to teach her submission to his will is her duty.

Sometimes Meiha wonders if something is wrong with her, when ever her husband becomes agitated with her, her mind multifariously wonders. He gets up heated from his chair, following her to the bedroom. With force he pushes her from behind and she falls face down onto the bed. Straddling her from behind, he pulls up the back slip of her smock exposing her bottom. The ragged scrap of his nails against her flesh, in her sadness she cries out to him not to force her again. She feels his thrust and because he won't stop, she again cries out. "Husband please, please don't do this?" But its too late. From her body the heat of the moment possesses him, he rips away all her garments, she answers futility back with spent tears.

In the recesses of her mind, her body separates from each pounding push into her. The climax of his release consumes him. Under the influence of a high percentage of alcohol it puts her husband down like a dead eagle. His full weight on her back makes it difficult for her to breathe. To better manage his weight, she rolls to one side from under him. Getting up she covers her husband's nakedness. Picking up what remains of her shredded garment she covers herself with piece of the bed's linen. In the privacy and lonely corner of another room she lets the darkness envelop her so that she can heal.

So often she is accused by him of being a worthless wife, one who cannot please him. No matter how much she tries to be the wife he wants the further apart they grow. In many ways she feels guilty having not bare him an heir.

With time, Leoha, has become obsessed, not only by the blackblade, but by death. Her name as the Black Blade Killer travels long and far throughout the desert and still, she does not stop killing. Her life has become a score of battles, killing, and challenges in the moment. Beside a water hole in the sand, she rests for a moment looking into the water. The reflection cast of an unknown image stare back at her. In a blink, she remembers her family and her life she leads as Princess back in the Kingdom. But even this is interrupted, cut short, another adversary falls with a single stroke of her blade. Death has summoned another in his folly of life to a sandy grave and she moves on.

In the far distance much ahead of her, there are persons crossing in the path, she has to stay low. Keeping out from sight, covering her hand over the stallion dark black eyes she commands the great beast to sit and lay down. They both do on the sand waiting it out until all around is cleared. She does not know nor recognize those passing is also from the Kingdom. These sojourners are many in escort with two others to the border before leaving them to continue on their journey. They are the chosen two Sarraha, appointed to go south in search of finding the Tree of Souls and bring back the fruit.

Urobeha, has fully recovered and is more than please to see Sheppard at her release from the healing chamber. Sheppard hands over to Urobeha clothing and she accepts not remembering why she is there. Her movements are sluggish Sheppard finds it to be a bit slow but with each step Urobeha takes she looks stronger. Dressing herself, she turns around and around reveling in the beauty of the Royal Garments. She stops to look at Sheppard. "I feel so different. I don't remember all of what had happened but I do remember you?" From her own experience, Sheppard does her best to take things slow with her until she's up to stand firmly physically and mentally. That part usually takes longer to heal. "You really don't remember?" Urobeha, tries to remember but can not. It bothers her that she can't remember anything other than who she is and who Sheppard is. "No. No. . . Would you like to remind me?"

To push her to regain her lost thoughts might do more harm than good. Once again smiling sweetly to her, thinking about the complications is utmost in her mind but she reassures her, "No, no, we don't need to go there now. Just you give it some time." The healing chambers effect each differently but it will all come back." She doesn't know anything, and the contentment of it makes Urobeha smile back at Sheppard. She couldn't be safer "I believe you! But where now shall we go?" After all, Urobeha has been through, its time for her to return home. It's a lot different now and in time maybe she will come to revive the lost thoughts without discomfort. "Well, lets start first by getting you back home." The restless feelings once plaguing her has rescinded, replacing the anxieties of frustrations with a contentment she can't explain. "I would like that. And I do miss mum and dad and my little sister Cllay."

Sheppard is relieved to see her memories still hold. Its best for now, not to awaken Urobeha mind from the slumber of events she's experienced. No further mention of it is discussed. She and Urobeha, dine, they talk throughout the night, until a sluggish haze chains both to slumbering sleep. Early the following morning Sheppard makes the arrangement for she and Urobeha, to return to her home town. With a little help from the throne, she and Urobeha, are set to leave the Kingdom. By orders of the throne, they are to be accompanied by the third division group of soldiers under the rule and leadership of none other than General Roobbye.

Appointed Sheppard's guardian after she and Urobeha, had return from their troubled encounters, with him rides a battalion of one hundred Gouddians and Arawak soldiers. The number of soldiers accommodating the long journey puts Sheppard and Urobeha mind at ease. Together they sit at ease in Sheppard's royal coach pleased with the accommodations. General Roobbye gives the orders to move out. Together both Sheppard, and Urobeha, find favor looking out through the royal coach window at the panoramic scenery floating by outdoors. Urobeha is most intrigued by the hundred-man battalion riding in rows of fifty on each side of the royal coach.

Unexpectedly one of the soldiers pulls up alongside the coach window. It is General Roobbye, Sheppard says nothing so he looks to Urobeha. Making small talk "You must be Lady Urobeha. Its good to meet you. You must hold tight we will be moving much faster." No response is necessary as Urobeha thanks him with smiles. The true object of his attention still portends disinterest. "You should not be angry with me. If our situation were in reversed. You would have done likewise." What is it about this woman that infuriates him, but when things are good its a radiant moment, he would give his life for. She is forever surprising him, like now. "So, we both have a lot to be thankful for. It made you a General and me a safe Princess. . . Thank you." The suspended air crackles with energy in the tension of each looking at the other. It's General Roobbye who stands down first. "Please hold on."

To the front General Roobbye rides, taking leadership, Sheppard and Urobeha sit back. The unspoken exchange between Sheppard and the General does not escape Urobeha. "Besides his uniform, who is he to you?" Urobeha turning her head to the scenic view outside passing without a mote of emotion Sheppard replies, "Another responsible for our safe return." Her tepid response inhibits any further comments from Urobeha, "Ohhhhhh."

Gradually the one hundred-man battalion and three coach like wagon move into high speed, passing hills, mountains, rivers, and valleys over Saxon streaks. Along the way Urobeha never misses a breath. She has never before seen the passing world from a moving

Coach window and this is a moment to cherish. The fast-moving battalion moves at wind speed.

The velocity stirs Urobeha, to have a flash back of her time being in the healing chamber. A jolt of the wagon snaps her out from it. At this moment she feels fine what if it changes later best to find out now. "Tell me Sheppard. How does that heal thing works? I have never heard about it." Sheppard head rolls back in thought, "Don't really know how or when. Now thinking about it. I have never even seen its blue prints. I can't even say when it was built. Something I must look into." The coach rolls on and Urobeha focus returns to the ever-changing landscape out side the window.

In her own thoughts Urobeha considers, being one who loves learning she never understood why the most privileged never take advantage of learning. Far be it from her to pass judgment, if she had the opportunities the Princess was born to, but she leaves it at that. With General Roobbye, and his one-hundred-man battalion are sent out not only to protect the Princess and Urobeha, but also the two forward wagons loaded with gold, and silver. Secretly they are to be presented to the leaders in Urobeha village. General Roobbye, again gives orders to pullback on the speed and covertly he allows two of his leading riders to break off from the pack. They are the ones responsible for reaching Urobeha's village and alerting the Elders of their coming.

Upon arriving to the village, the elders instruct them where they would like the wagons of gold and silver secured. The two riders are given strict orders and a map. In haste they speed back to General Roobbye, and present the map detailing directions. All General Roobbye, has to do now is follow the map. When they make the last turn towards the town General Roobbye, separates the two wagons of gold and silver. Fifty soldiers of his finest follow his every instruction to deliver the throne gifts. Its the elders who alerts the town of Urobeha return, something they have long prepared and waited on. The town closes up shops and businesses to attend the welcome prepared by the elders and town people for the sacrificial lamb responsible for saving the town. From many homes and dwelling places, they come out to join in the welcome. The streets line off with people just wanting to look at the procession. Many spectators, and neighbors seek to look upon Urobeha's face. Distant relations drop to their knees to give thanks for her safe return.

The name of Urobeha, becomes known far beyond that of the elders. To show their appreciation for what she had endured and suffered through, the elders erect a statue of her. They place it in the main town square for all passing to see. On the road they put down pebbles, flowers, green leaves and palms. When the royal coach enters the main road the people all applaud at the moving coach driven by the most beautiful stallions they have ever seen. Along the road side people begin to follow behind as it moves toward the great open square in the middle of the town.

The people were everywhere. Their joy is contagious, Urobeha and Sheppard wave out their hand to the people and the day expands for all. Finally, the royal coach reaches the middle town square with half its battalion and minutes later they are joined by those which had delivered the two wagons of Gold and Silver elsewhere. Joined as One Unit, the royal coach comes to a stop ways from the center of town. For the pride of the people Urobeha feels its best to walk her way in.

The door of the royal coach is made open and when the royal steps fall out to the ground in this defining moment they both look to each other for comfort. Together they reach out to each other, the trials of their friendship have fostered a sisterly bond. Into each bosom they hug one another as if its the last time. Outside the coach, collective bodies migrate to share in each others joy. Slowly they pull away from each other Urobeha has tears in her eyes and her cheeks are wet, Sheppards eyes are also misty. Dabbing her cheek dry Sheppard, says to her, "This is your day." It maybe her moment but she would never have arrived here if it had not been for Sheppard.

Taking in a deep breath, Urobeha, turns stepping out from the royal coach with Sheppard following. For a moment Urobeha eyes adjust to the suns glare after being in the confines of the coach. The view she is awarded allows her to see the massive crowd of people awaiting her, it stuns her. Sheppard takes hold of Urobeha's hand to better assist her, together they walk side by side down the royal steps and onto the ground. The applause of many brings tears again and across to the open square they make their way. Urobeha tries to be brave, she's shaking inside, her tears give her away.

The large banner waving in the breeze hanging high has her name written across it. On seeing it her knees buckle and she is helped up by Sheppard. Her mother, father and little sister Cllay are waiting alongside the Elders. The sight of her family strengthens her limbs, she and Sheppard run over to greet them. For the first time, she feels welcomed, this was home. She and Sheppard embrace her parents tightly. From the ground, she picks up little Cllay in her arms squeezing and kissing her over and again. In a breath she pauses to pass Cllay to Sheppards outreached arms. To Sheppard, the little Cllay bubbling in happiness reveals, "I did not know you are a Princess? I thought you are an Angel. Cllay sweet sentiments touches Sheppard heart in confidence she whispers into little Cllay ears. "You must keep my secret?" Little Cllay smiles out to her shaking her head yes, with one last squeeze she passes her back over to her parents.

The elders all extend welcome to Urobeha, and Sheppard back. Quietly one by one each of the elders thanks Sheppard for the wagons of gold and silver, all the foods, clothing, and everything else. Its little Cllay, who points out her hand and finger over and above the tall trees. This makes Sheppard and Urobeha look up at the great unveiling of Urobeha, full body statue. It stands towering over everything. On seeing the great image Urobeha stumbles backward, the elders give a short welcome and thank you speech to Urobeha, and Sheppard. They are the town heros. The crowd cheers out at them, the heart felt welcome is so overwhelming to Urobeha that her tears alone could never explain the feeling behind her heart. Urobeha drops to one knee before again being helped up by Sheppard and together they are led off by the elders to a private area.

The crowd follows, General Roobbye eyes is always on the Princess. The one-hundred-man battalion follows the crowd into a large open area. They all enter to an open banquet table prepared with the best of eats and fare sent by the Kingdom for all to enjoy. The elders offer Sheppard the honorable head seat which she concedes over to Urobeha. With pleasure she takes the next seat, followed by little Cllay, and the family. The hundred-man battalion secures the perimeter were the elders take their seats followed by the crowd.

Drinking and eating their fill the evening revelry passes well into night. The amount of wine consumed by Urobeha, and Sheppard animates them to speak out.

It's very late when most of the crowd has gone and so has Cllay, and her family. With all the wine drunk, having the girls a little tipsy they decide to walk it off, back home and they do. The walk home becomes one of amusement, and frolic. Finally arriving, into the upper room they go laughing and talking. That is until they find little Cllay asleep on Sheppard bed, they become quiet. Urobeha, has only to sit on her bed and her weary eyes immediately takes their rest. The wine has taken its toll and she is asleep. Sheppard tucks her in before moving over to the sleeping form of beautiful little Cllay. She kisses her too. This is her moment, surveying the room she preserves the concluding moment of this venture for prosperity. She knows the pain of saying goodbye is hard so she decides now is the best time to leave, now that the house is sleep.

Down the small stairway she makes her way. Urobeha, mother and father are awaiting her, the melancholy is fragile and bitter sweet. Sadly, she smiles out to them. In her smile is her promise fulfilled, stepping forward, she prefers not to talk. The thought of having to say good-bye to them is heart wrenching. She knows the royal coach will be waiting beyond the house front door. If she runs for it she can avoid this exchange but her heart stops her feet.

In reverence Urobeha, mother and father drop to their knees before her. Gracefully she shakes her head to them not to, in the poise of her charity she reaches out gentle to them "No, please don't kneel, get up!" With care she hurries to pick them up but to no avail.

Roobbye and the royal coach now await out side the front door to receive the Princess. The one-hundred-man battalion are all in line and waiting orders. With their hands on her Sheppard too drops to her knees with them to better make Urobeha parents understand her words. "Please, Please! I beg of you both. Please don't do this for it is I alone who should be kneeling before you." The elation in Urobeha, father eyes shines being the man restored of the house he looks to her. "Then let us all stand together." Holding of each other, by the hand, together they rise from their knees.

Emotions run high and it is difficult for any of them to speak out clearly. Urobeha's parents remember vividly when Sheppard first knelled before them, they hug each other sighing deeply, tears of joy flow. With a straggled voice Urobeha, father confides, "Even though, we found your behavior here most strange at time by our standard. We had long expected, you were more than meets the eyes but we never expected a Princess in our home. We may not have the space or the place here for a Princess such as you but we must let you know, here we do have a place for you as a daughter."

The reward of his words, is a force of pressure through the Princess's heart, crumbling overwrought she stumbles back. Touching her heart wishing it could all end their humble state of gratitude is too much. With few words, she looks at the front door itching to run but cannot. Mustering up all the courage she can, her heart cries out to them. "Then please, tell my little sister Cllay, when she awakes, and my sister, Urobeha, goodbye." With this last sentiment, she stumbled her way to the front door opening it with the last of her heart's strength. For one last time she stops to look back. They extend out their hands to receive her for the last time. She declines and speedily runs straight into the royal coach, leaving Urobeha parents washed in relief to weep on their own. The front door of the house is made closed by one of the two guards standing at the outside door.

General Roobbye gives the signal to mount and move out. He catches only a slight blur of the Princess crossing from the door into the royal coach. This lady love of his soul has been through much and if he can help it, maybe her future will be more secure with him watching. Her swift departure makes him realize how hard it is at times to say good-bye to our love ones. She's strong but soft when most expected. Resurgence of memories long past return, he once had to say good-bye to the Princess because he was not from Royal family.

From the inner confines of the coach, he hears her muffled whimpers. Her sobs bring with speed his concern, leaping from his horse onto the top stairs of the royal coach he gives the orders to move out and close in. Opening the door to her disheveled appearance at the sight of him she tries unsuccessfully to composes herself. Inside now with the Princess he finds her distraught in her tears, he knows he will always love this Princess. She reaches out to him, Roobbye, its in his arms she falls finding comfort. His tight embrace warms her and in her bosom, he reminisces in memories. The moving coach and streaming light flowing through the window sometimes, the shadows of the terrain lull them both. In a loving and graceful tone of voice she pleads to him "Roobbye, please help me. Hold me even tighter than ever."

The pleas of her request are General Roobbye longing desire. Obliging, he holds the Princess even tighter to his chest wishing the moment wouldn't end. In minutes her head falls to his shoulder and she is asleep. Gently reaching out to one side of the coach walls while trying not to disturb Sheppard, he pulls on a hidden rope and the comfort seat is made into a royal sleeping chamber. He picks her up resting her down tenderly on the bed. There she is allowed to sleep, and he is left to watch her in his regrets. He doubts if ever the time would come, he'll never get the chance to tell her that his heart belongs only to her. On the outside with wind the hundred man battalion rides holding no speed back to the Kingdom.

From Behind Leoha

From behind Leoha, the heat from the deserts winds brews a storm. The smell of rain hangs in the balance of the wind. Gale force winds are pushing in hard time to move to higher grounds or hurry to a safe haven before dark fall. In this region storms are prevalent through out the season tides. There is a place beyond the sandy plains not so far away she knows. Passing, many taking the same road to escape the incoming storm, its obvious some won't make it to the shelter in time. Riding hard, later she arrives at the only place within miles of sand and rocks. The place is ranked as a hell hole, inside filled with robbers, thieves, notable merchants of renown wealth, and killer's consort.

Pulling in reins, her marvelous stallion is taken to the back barn by a young keeper to be placed on lock down. With her notable blade hidden on her back under her clothing, she enters. Immediately, the eyes of predators observe and note her entrance. There aren't many fractions of bandits who respect the abilities of women mercenaries. In dankness of the smoky room, their primal lusts pant out reaching for her, grabbing their crotch they expose their genitals to her. Waving out at her lewd gestures and hoot beg for her attentions. Ever watchful she ignores them not and across the floor she walks to the bar.

Right away she is noticed by the bartender. Behind him another person stands whose face is obscured from her sight, only their back is visible. The bartender finishes serving ten shots to a man standing next to her. From the look on the mans face, hes had enough, but you can never tell a drinker that. The drinking man does not look like a trouble maker but in these parts one never knows. His withered face is a little beaten, and on the first guest, one would say he seems afraid. That fear too is expected in these parts.

The bartender inquiringly, looks to serve her, his facial expression accepts that she is not from around there. "Excuse me Warrior, May I be of help?" Leaning in that he can hear her better, "Just looking for a room for the night." Smartly perusing the room. "Isn't every one here." This causes those close to the bar to laugh out at the joke. Turning to the one in back of him the bartender resounds out. "Another looking for room! Madam!" The Madam of the house, who was on her way into the bar walks up to the one with his back turned to the customers. "Fix your self." A big smile spreads out to her and he fixes himself. Up to the bartender, she walks stiff faced. With arid disdain, "You don't have to scream out like that! You k now!" With mocked flair he turns his head to her and in her ear, he whispers. "We have another new one." She takes a quick look out across the bar at the newly arrived stranger. The one with his back turned looks to see what the madam is saying to the bartender.

He was hired to help the bartender like any good busybody he loves to get into people business. His eccentric looks bring light to dark minds as he struggles to find himself. He is called the great HeShe, and he lives up to his name. His voluminous smile is like no other and he twirls not just turns to have a look and listen in. Making no pretense of his actions he hears the madam lowered voice and to the bartender, "Just you keep it low. Trouble is what we don't need and I can see, its written all over her. Tell the others to stay away from her." Oww, this sounds interesting the great HeShe narrows to find the object of their discussion. The only striking figure he can identify is the amazon of a woman who has everyone watching her. The madam steps up to the bar counter to take a better look at the Warrior. To the Warrior, she directs her address, "We have no more rooms but if you choose to sleep here on the ground, that's ok too." Nearby in a corner lies just a person who has taken the offer, and she returns her attentions to the Warrior.

Princess Leoha the Warlord Warrior has meet many qualities of women on her journeys. This disparity of charity isn't smooth to her, the Warrior looks at her wondering what kind of woman could she be with such a stiff mouth and degrading attitude. Contriving that her rudeness could only be accounted because of means and the believed affluence of it. To the madam, the Warrior out right defends, "You think I cannot pay?" The madam cavalier attitude only further attests that her contentions where a feature of permanence in her character. "I really don't care if you can, like I have said! There are no more room." For Leoha the approaching storm allows room from further debate of options. "Then could you at least tell me. When one would be available. This is still a business. Isn't it?" The wit of the Warrior response raises the madam's hackles as the patrons closest all laugh out. Those who have felt the brand of the madam's manner finally see someone who can stand up to dictatorial proprietor. With a strait and stern face, the madam she is not flustered easy "Most likely but not to night."

Leoha does find it odd to be sparing with a woman who should by all dispositions be accommodating. Tactically the warrior of her training retracts her offense. The madam is an intriguing enigma this fresh attitude is displeasing to the Warrior. Being a Warlord Warrior means she is trained on various arts of war and combat which exist on four plains of consciousness, the physical, the mental, the physic and the verbal. As a person indoctrinated in this calling Leoha, decides not to let the madam off the hook.

Diplomatically she infers suggestively for another viable choice. "There must be something! Even if its a small space in your place, will do nicely." The Warrior words only further serve to insult the displeased madam. In retaliation at the noble Warrior, she take's a superior stand looking out at the Warrior. With resolved calm, the madam reaffirms her position. "That all depends on who's asking. I am also the owner of this place and believe me when I say! Your kind do have a way with words and, I would prefer you don't annoy me with your questions. Is there any thing else?" The madam is vicious without cause, it's her nature that's why she's a perfectly fit for this establishment.

Many of the drinkers standing at bay, know the signs good enough to say this will turn into a fight. Fighting is what the Madam does well she is not one bit intimidated by the Warrior. Not taking no for an answer Leoha is prepared for anything the Madam exclaims. Something about this Warrior is different, with intense study madam wonders if somehow, she can get the best of her. The Warriors is steadfast, the more they talk, the more it begins to make sense if she can pull it off. Little does this Warrior know, her persistence avails the madam with an opportunity long overdue.

Time to settle a score with her greatest enemy and close the game. A small smile sinister, reaches her eye twisting her retort to the Warrior, "I believe there may be something I can do for you!" She's tough, not wanting to take it any further Leoha promises her. "I will pay!" The madam's smile widens reassuringly, "But of course! You will have too! The room belongs to the big man in the far back of you. Take the key from him and the room is yours tonight."

The captive audience and bystanders who have been listening all along laugh out again, they know what's coming. Leoha turns to have a look at the man in the far corner and he is truly massive in size. It makes him not only easy to find but denotes also the company of goons standing and siting around him. The Warriors turned back to the madam, Leoha can't believe her eyes. "I see you tell a good joke." So this is how the bar is set, by the look on the madam's face she under estimates her in many ways. Smug and daring the madam states callously "That must be why everyone is laughing out at you And I hope, you're not waiting around for another room."

The Warrior looks around to mark those in her mind making a mental note of those who smirks at her. Erupting laughter quickly stops - some give space in fear of trouble. There is not much reasoning out here and most scores are settled by death. The people standing all around would like nothing more than a battle between the madam and the Warrior. Its in the air, most can smell the danger brewing. To ease the tensions, the madam looks to her. Verbal combat is one thing, a physical altercation on any level with an unknown adversary must first be finessed. "I'll call you. If any thing come's up." Most sweetly her smile seethes in wickedness.

The madam has had her peace, leaving her now to take hers. "Thanks for the nothing." Leoha throws back at her. Still cutting the madam can't help spewing, "If any one else dies before day break! I'll let you know. Until then, should you find the atmosphere in here not suitable to your liking. The outside is still waiting!" Sometimes the best defense is silence. Leoha says nothing further but watches the madam walks away. This woman has issues. It is known the madam has many connections to the outside and it is for this reason her business flourishes.

The man with ten shots on the bar counter is still standing and a man beside him is closely watching him. Two bodies on the floor have just been killed over nothing. Under the influences of strong drink many can't hold their liquor, both had no rooms. Insignificantly their dead bodies are cast out like dead rats. The wind has begun to howl, beating against the large wooden structure. Through small cracks in the walls wind streams whistling with the cracking sound of the large wooden beams rubbing against each other. Empathizing to the Warrior The drinking man offers to share his space. "Worrier. . . am only passing. . . through. We can share my room if its ok with you?" Finally, some compliance and Leoha looks at the drinking man. "Thanks! I may just have to take you up on that." She realizes then, he is not so drunk that he can not hold his drink. Confirming his room status to her he tries to introduce himself. "Warrior. . . or should I say strong lady."

The drinking man loses his balance stumbling into her, she is saved by her quick reflexes. She knows it is not a coincidence, only another idiot in back of him, trying to stir up trouble. If she's right the aggressor will expose himself and his intentions, there are many outstanding variables in the room that are suspicious to her. The aggressive brute cries out angry at the drinking man. "Heyyyy, just you watch your mouth! There are no women in here! Only harlots and if you say another more, I'll kill you!"

The sitting crowd is stirred up by a badly injured girl running across the floor towards the bar. This calls the Warrior attention. The sudden appearance of a fast dagger is launched into the young girls back. Her eyes strain at the impact force of the blade entering her flesh. Halted, her ability to further run fuels the crowd looking on as she struggles up to the Warrior and falls before her. To the Warrior, the young and beautiful dying lady gasps, "They raped me! Get out of here!" The Warrior tries to comfort her, but it too late. She slides down, dead, to the ground. Her untimely death makes the Warrior take heart after her own experience with the Sadistic Bastards. Thinking twice about innocence and dangerous encounters the Bartender cries out seared of emotion from having witnessing so many deaths. "Another dead to be taken outtttttt."

Summoned, the house cleans up team enters in with a strange carrier on which the dead are taken away. Further easing the tensions of the crowd the madam dismisses them and shouts for order to restore, "It's over, its over continue on as usual." The occurrences of death in the establishment is a daily matter. They all do, like nothing had ever happen. In the midst of it all, the madam walks up to the Warrior "I prefer your kind not stopping in! Death seems to always follow you people!" Princess Leoha can't believe the audacity of this woman, now she blames her presence for the death. It makes Leoha testy and the Madams abrasive manner is wearing her down. "Then I could only say It would be wise you stay away from me. You're really trying me aren't you?" The Madam has no shame or remorse looking at her, standing bold as she may. She quips, "I can do better than that." And walks away.

With her departure, it allows the Warrior to step back to the bar. To her the drinking man slurs, "I get the feeling she like you and you should have one also." Toasting to her again he throws back down both shots. There's much going on here at this bar that remains to be seen. Turning to her new friend she joins him. "I will prepare two specials. Don't drink the two last one, I'll handle them myself." The drinks have impaired his senses slightly, he doesn't have a clue, what she is talking about.

The death of the young woman will be avenged the Warrior saw the direction in which the fast moving digger came, that killed the young beauty. From across the room, laughing are a group of five, two standing, three sitting all at the table of the one call Big Nasty. She can see them all clearly within her Warrior vision. In the shirt of one standing, she glimpses the hidden dagger while Big Nasty is being served another drink. A digger with a signature handle, like the one that pierced through the dead girl's heart.

This is not a place for one to be alone or without protection. The young lady was obviously separated from her people, or stranded due to the high winded storm. She found her way here for shelter but like the changing weather on the outside here, inside has proven to equally vicious, dangerous and so cold. One must be vigilant on the alert for any danger. The frightening mistakes made like that of the beautiful young girl serves as an example, a rude awakening for others to heed. The storm churns on force and everything is battered up or locked down. No one is allowed to leave or enter due to the ripping winds and dipping temperatures. Those inside listen to commands of instructions, those who don't comply, die.

The drinking man, repeats his offers to show his room. "O, my room is the first one with the dog hanging, hanging on the door. I don't remember saying to him he can have my room, but he just told me. my room belongs to him, and I still have the keys." Referring to the man who had pushed him earlier into the Warrior. Seeking to intimidate him from further interacting with the Warrior because Big Nasty had signaled out to him to intervene. Everyone fears Big Nasty and his men. Big Nasty always gets his way. The Drinking man fumbling through his pockets showing out his room key to the Warrior.

Stepping up to the culprit accused, standing beside him she leans pressing a hidden dagger up against his heart. Low and silent words to him she whispers, "The next time you do that! I'll kill you!" Then the menace of her snarl smiles out to him, nervous, wide eyed he finds a way to return the smile. Leaving the frightened man, he looks nervously over at Big Nasty who is oblivious to the happenings. Retreating with haste to his next move he melts into the crowded room to escape her, she goes back on the opposite side of the Drinking man. When he realizes, she could have already given him a silent death, he silently moves away further down the bar. Returning to the Drinking man, "Like I was about to say before being rudely interrupted. I may have to take you up on that offer, if you don't mind. As for your friend lets hope he doesn't bother you again. Judging from your scars you two have already met."

The flooding memories from the battering episode is still a tender experience he'd sooner forget. "Don't remind me! Doesn't it show enough?" A sudden gust of wind racks the massive structure, flickering lights dim low, the straining recedes, like whips they surge coming back fully up. The Warrior has made her first move and to the Drinking man, she tries to turn his attentions. "Look! You need to take cover. Watch out for your friend down there. You need to watch him." Referring again to the man who had pushed him aside. Not exactly standing still the Drinking man rocks, "So you're calling it a night too?" Again she is over heard by some of the bystanders. Having drunk to his excess not knowing, what to further do he launches out straightly, "Yes, I'll have one with you. And he gives her one and himself two."

Why not, it isn't often that she gets an opportunity to indulge in libations, and under the extreme of the situation she releases her inhibitions. Like him, she throws backed the shot finding it a little hot to her taste and she sputters it away. The bruises to his face she reads like a map, clear enough to envision the direction in which each blow had hit him. Instinctively alert, behind her someone is walking up to her. Her heightened Warrior instinct warns her of pending danger. She turns to the stranger prepared for combat ready to un-sheath the blade of death.

In turning around, she is surprised, its another Warrior from the Kingdom and very impressive. Relieved to have an alliance from the Kingdom "Am not the enemy! Don't mean to startle you! But the man, who earlier moved away is also in league with Big Nasty. You aught to watch your back." His report only confirms her own observations. "Thank you." The Stranger from the Kingdom orders another drink and he leaves the bar. Leoha and the drinking man watch him as he makes his way up the stairs towards the rooms. For a minute, it makes the Warrior think upon the brave warrior's countenance. Reassuring the Warrior, the Drinking man interrupts her thought only to say, "Don't you worry about my drinking. It's only to lower the pain. and my asthma when it comes on." She says nothing.

The storm on the outside is at its worst and the harsh cold winds have the chilling digits to easily kill a person if not dressed properly. Radically temperatures decline, dropping drastically changing from sunny to below zero and pewter gray. During the end of the rainy seasons the sun can be ones of the greatest enemy if not prepared. Outside debris flies through the air smashing into the outer walls of the structure. At times, even the outdoors stables prove not safe for the animals. Some are lost to the tempest storms wrecking path.

The old building housing them was built strong with the ability to withstand divers' conditions. The structure is safe and sound, no one remembers who built it but it is now owned by the Madam of the house. By anyone's guest the place is such that is not generational passed but a product of the ravaged stealth of War ownership. This would explain why The Madam is so young and beautiful yet cold in her ways. In this hell hole her gentleness is obscured by her capacity to survive and thrive. The temperatures outside drop below zero for two hours billowing howls of gushing strong winds blow. And as suddenly as it began the heat again rises outside.

The temperature on the outside is unpredictable, there are no laws here. Because the structure lies on the border boundaries between two nations, each wants nothing to do with the compliance of the property. That is why this place is known as 'The in Between'.

The status of her Warrior garments attests to her skills. Leoha, the Warrior looks different and untouchable. There isn't one in the room that doesn't want to see what she can do. Everyone thought the Madam would have given them the show they desired earlier. Little do they know before they can make a move the deed is done.

The untouchable title is reserved only for the villain Big Nasty, and his five killers. Talk mummers about, Big Nasty, wanting the Warrior at his table and for that reason all others lay low. There is a price on Big Nasty and his men head and most of many insides, but here no one is bothered by it. Leoha has been a Warlord Warrior long enough to know sooner or later a fight will come to her. Upping the stakes, she decides to go to the fight. She had already established advantage, when the first gush of wind rocked the massive structure dimming the lights.

The blow aside one window took everyone's attention most wondered if the vibration from the roof would collapse killing them. All but not the Warrior, for she had passed this way many times before. No one sees, when she opens a secret part on her large hand bracelets to allow a small amount of ghost powder to fall into one of the Drinking men shot glasses on the bar counter.

When all had calmed and settled, to the Warrior petitions the Drinking man sigh for another drink. "Why don't we have another drink and may be, just may be. If you are still standing the next round is on me." Excited he loves the idea still under the scrutiny of persons standing by looking on. "What's the hell! We may all be dead by the time the storm ends." When he reaches for the back shot glass she had set aside, she taps him strongly on the hand. "Not that one! It's my third one?" Thinking nothing of it, he is happy to have a good drinking partner.

All around, bystanders' smirk, laughing out at him standing with the most amazing person, looking like a fool. "Oh." Is all he can say after drinking another shot. In the haze of the drink, he picks up another shot glass, together they throw back a full shot. He's never had so much fun and he loves it this time she didn't even cough. He shakes his head to her encouragingly as to say, you're getting better at it. Together they both rest down the emptied shot glasses upright on the bar counter.

Impatiently watching Big Nasty, and his men have long wanted the Warriors attention. Carefully he bides his time wanting to over step bully appearances. Big Nasty has a taste for different flesh, each man in his crew brings a unique skill sets to the table. As fate would have it, no prayer is needed, the object of their interest will shortly introduce herself unbeknownst to them. Plying the Drinking man with more shots, she shows him, "I think I almost have it right!" The Drinking man laughs out as she kindly massages her chest to help soothe the burning taste. Her back is against the dining and drinking crowd, having their own fun at the tables.

Once again, she is approached from behind, but unlike the last, his fowl attitude demands a show. Looking to make a name for himself so that Big Nasty, would allow him into the foal he's prepared to step up to the challenge if it will gain him acceptance. Ever alert, prepared, she turns around to see him. Before the man can utter his first words, he realizes her dagger is pressing deeply into his groin between his legs. Immobilized, he shutters not wanting to lose his manhood. On the tip of his toes, very much unbalanced the observing crowd with a view notices the stains of wet liquid spreading, running down his leg to the floor. He can't hear the laughter at him, the excessive and excruciating pain she applied to him makes him squeal. In a higher pitched voice of a girl for his manhood, he cries, "Please, Pleaseeeeee don't kill me. Please pleaseeee spare me!!!" All eyes are riveted to the Warriors actions. "Were you going to spare me?! Drop it!" She doesn't have to say it twice, the sound of cold steel hits the floor with a clang.

The Madam is on the floor in the far back when the matter at the bar is brought to her attention. Trouble is string up again at the bar. This time its her nephew. The Warrior is holding her nephew as she approaches, she can hear her say, "Because of your bravery, your cowardly behavior will cause you, a body part." The boy is a youngster, and he begins squealing like a pig stuck. Space is given, the Madam comes running in bringing things to a halt. To the Warrior, she directly appeals "Warrior! Please, hold it."

The bar quiets with attention on the Madam. It is the moment every one has been waiting to see. Which one of the two will die first? The young man who has the dagger between his Godly parts is still on his toes. The floor around him is now completely saturated with his own urine he huffs and puffs for his life not daring to lower his feet. The young man is the Madams own foolish nephew wanting to make a name for himself as a criminal in Big Nasty gang. Stubbornly he refuses to listen to his elders, ignoring their advice that nothing good ever come out bad choices.

This time the Madam believes he get's the point. None of Big Nasty men stand to help him. The Madam is a good fighter and she does not hesitate to uses it when provoked. She knows the Warrior could castrate the young man in less than one stroke so she must keep a calm head. To every one surprise, the Madam steps up to the young man. With stern venom she chastises him. "The next time you dirty my floor. I'll kill you my self." Walking in closer to the Warrior quietly she concedes, "You have already won! Please don't kill him! Just teach him a lesson!"

When she abruptly turns and walks away Leoha is incensed that the Madam continues to shows no filter for propriety. With that Leoha sends with force, kicking the young man away from her across the floor. His body slides straight beside his walking aunt. She stops and looking down on her troubled nephew, wobbling in pain he looks up to his aunt for a little help and sympathy but instead. She shows no emotion looking down at him, "That served you right! You fool!" He is mortified, and she continues on, the young man is helped up by two servers. The embarrassment of it all makes him walk to the back room.

Of all things, he is meet by the server girl he admires the most. What her aunt was void to give, the soft little words of encouragement he hears now from the server girl convinces him he is ready to turn over a new leaf. Some of the kitchen staff are still bristle with him because of the stupidity of the disturbance he caused earlier. They make him pay pummeling him with blows and whacks, again he is saved by the server. The Madam has returned back to the bar for a spilled drink causing problems on the floor by two idiots.

She isn't surprised to see the disturbance includes her favorite patron. Now standing between Leoha and the Drinking man. She orders another drink for her warrior friend sitting at her table. The Bartender prepares the drink. Cloaked intentions too can emanate harnessed energy and Leoha gets the feeling, Madam is not there only for the drinks. She doesn't have long to wait in a quiet tone only the Warrior hears the subtle threat. "Don't for a minute think am afraid of the likes of you! Try not to cause any more problems" she doesn't stop there, her words whisper, "Thanks for shedding no more blood." Once authentic sentiments now spoken, it pales to be recognized, Leoha is not moved, but ready for anything now that tone has changed. "I get the feeling this is far from over."

The Bartender serves the drinks to the Madame she asked for. She in turn while waiting, inspects the latest addition to her staff, the HeShe. Returning to attend to her duties on the floor, with so many of her loyal costumers it was important not to miss a thing. Offering a word of advice to the Warrior the Drinking man let her know, "Aaaa! Look Warrior, no one really messes with her, she knows her stuff, so just stay away from that one. I did say, we may all be dead before day break so just let's have another drink so that if we die, we won't feel any pain." The logic of his thinking feels no stress, she admires that. "Maybe it is high time we get some rest so I'll just say night to my friends before calling it quits."

Strangely being the thinking man he is, he looks at her muddled because she came in alone. What is she talking about, friends? Leoha then looks at the man who earlier changed his position was still standing and watching her every move. She does nothing but glare back at him with a cold stare, the man quickly focuses elsewhere. With eyes on him to the Drinking man, the Warrior again calls for more. "I think I can use another drink. What about you?" His type of talk. Oh, this couldn't get better, happily and rapidly he replies. "You don't have to ask, they are all right there before us, waiting for me, and he down's another with expression and its her turn, he loves it. From the bar counter she picks up, two more shots and he reaches for one. Strong drink does nothing much to a Gouddian, Leoha can drink all night and still not be intoxicated. "No, no! Am going to have a drink with my friends across the floor. You stay here and order two more and I'll be back soon."

Leoha signals to the Bartender to keep them coming, with a slight head movement that she will pay. He gets her meaning pouring out another two shots and adds them with the others. The Drinking man is even more pleased, he loves it so much he begins to counts his remaining shots over and again. When he finishes counting, he looks around for the Warrior, but she is gone.

Across the floor, he spots her walking directly over to Big Nasty table. Alarms ring off in his head, he gets the feeling its going to be very ugly and there is nothing he can do. The man who pushed him aside earlier with forebode returns beside him. He tries not to notice but the man makes himself known with a hard nudge to his ribs. It hurts, trying not to draw attention he muffles the Drinking man cry from being heard, warning him not to scream or die. Swallowing deeply the Drinking man says nothing. Taking one of the shots from him, "I'll have that drink! Now that your friend has abandon you! And when the chief finishes with your friend! I'll kill you too!"

With everyone's attention on the Warrior, the Drinking man is not so afraid anymore. "My friend will be back, soon, so have it your way." The man turns to look at the retreating figure of the Warrior. The Drinking man escapes the web of danger only because the man really doesn't want to take further chances on his own life. Taking up from the bar counter one full shot glass, he horsebacks it, with another. The last shot he pours out over the Drinking man head. He licks at the alcohol draining down his face, the adversaries hate is evident. "There is no place here for her kind. She sleeps on the floor like the others pigs." Right away the Drinking man gets his meaning.

The Madam is sitting on the open floor having a drink with the warrior Raackus, who is a friend. He has come again to declare his undying feelings. Secretly she gloats in the glory that she is the only woman he'll ever love and he wants to make her his wife. According to her, she will if he can fulfill her list of pending wishes. Long ago he agreed to help her refine her business affairs. A man of few words Raackus, is a very clever warrior in his own ranks and she likes him that way. He doesn't believe in taking chances and when striking his enemy, he always gets his target.

The place is filled with sitting guest all want to be served first. The kitchen is now depleted of food so the servers pour wine from the vats long ago set aside. The hands-on deck are few, however they are able to keep things under control. The warrior Raackus, is there to claim his prize and have the Madam as his wife. In the pursuit of a love match The Madame tries to make him understand, she is not the same woman he met cycles ago. His lack of success to kill Big-Nasty, in the last Eight Cycles of the Wind has exhausted her feelings. Raackus continues to ask her patience, "Eight Cycles ago! I had not the skills to kill him but now I do. Just you live up to your word!"

The desperation of his words and expressions conveys his frustrations. She will not submit to his demands until hers are meet under no circumstances. "You know Raackus, we need to talk further about this. He has been in my place for the past cycles of the wind and haven't payed a single cent to me. If I alone could have killed him, he would have already been dead. Everyone I paid to kill him are all dead and I know even if he does leave, he won't pay and he will return to do the same each time." The removal of someone like Big Nasty, is not simple, he is just waiting on the prime opportunity to strike, why can't she give him a little room to maneuver, "I am still waiting for the right moment, and it will be done, before the storm is over."

There he goes giving her excuses again, yes, she can't dispute he has had his uses in some of her ventures but his constant nagging irritates her. Getting up distracted the Madam inclines "Please excuse me. I'll be back! Just need to cool down some of the tension in here again." Out from her seat she can feel tensions building, smelling trouble in the air. So, it is the Warrior again, shes walking across the floor and strait toward Big Nasty table. Its important the Warrior doesn't interfere with what she and Raackus have planed. There's no pleasant course to finally doing away with Big Nasty.

She moves to try and stop the Warrior from making a deadly mistake that could ruin her plans. When it does happen, she doesn't want Big-Nasty, men to expect anything. She intends to keep it that way so she walks into the Warriors path. Just as they are about to collide, she slows her steps down, this doesn't come as a surprise to the Warrior. While in motion moving, she smiles out to the Warrior and ever so calmly, she warns her, "Please don't do it."

The dictated request of a shrilling harpy has no baring on Leoha having bested the most cunning of killers. The Warrior acknowledges the Madam somehow turning pass her with out spilling even a drip of alcohol from the two shot glasses. The levitation of evasive skill highly impresses the Madam and others in the room watching. Its a hint, that sheds insight, telling a story of the Warrior amazing skill and ability. With fluid movement, The Warrior pauses reversing one pace. To any looking on they would think the Warrior is succumbing to the drinks she consumed. In a moment of concealment, she and the Madam begin making turns around each other, in the Madams ear the Warrior silently whispers. "It is so silent in death."

The Madam doesn't contemplate her meaning and while they separate from each other. To her the Madam softly reminds, "We don't need any more problems in here. As you can see, we already have a lot of our own." While they turn around each other the crowd looks on anxiously wondering and waiting for a fight between the two to begin. Expectantly they wait, watching no one hears their exchange of words. Leoha doesn't mince words with the Madam, she is undeserving of such sensitivities. "All you have in here is trouble and I still need a room." Her words captivate the Madams quiet attention. As the Warrior turns to walk away The Madam lets her know, "Its your funeral."

Once again, the blood lust of the crowd is deferred, again disappointed not to see a fight between the two. The Madam and the Warrior look at each other and without uttering a word to the Madam. The Warrior through pursed lips lets her know, "No, it's his." Stunned she understands every word and intent it leaves her weak as she walks back to Raackus table. The focus shifts now on the Warrior and Big-Nasty table. Every one knows a fight must take place, except Big Nasty, and his men. They are just too busy in the carnal thoughts of their accomplishments.

The warrior Raackus is happy to see his Madam return to the table, even more the Madam again sits with news of alert. The pensive meditation on her face intrigues him to ask, "So what was that all about?" The Madam has yet to take her eyes off The Warrior sitting now with Big Nasty and his men. "I think she is about to ruin your plans." The dismay of her statement does little to ruffle him, being the careful warrior, he is. He looks at her, giving her courage, that all is not lost. "Even if she cannot beat him, she may some how injure him and that's good enough for me. And as for his goons. If she could get rid of even some of them. Its enough for me. Either way, we both get what we want." To satisfy herself. To him she said. "Accomplished."

He nods his head out to her in agreement, leaving them both sitting satisfied, waiting the out come. Big-Nasty and his men were just about ready to approach the Warrior by means of inviting her over for a pleasurable drink. With leisurely strides the Warrior Approaches Big Nasty table and with an acknowledged smile of respect to the big man she takes the open seat. Big Nasty instantly likes her forward thinking, ordering his men to make space. The men who work with Big Nasty are from many places far and near. It's a boon for him to accommodate the unique and most intriguing Warrior he has ever laid eyes upon.

His two captains remain seated, while two stand guard on each each side of him to ensure his back is covered. Big Nasty takes a quick look at his lookout man still standing at the bar, the signal he gets is good. Gently she places down the two full shot glasses in front of her and she say nothing. Waiting for the next move Big Nasty, looks at her and laughs out at her courage, so do his men and she smile back to him. Her introduction of conflict resonates well with him when she says. "The Madam is a friend of yours. I don't know what she has against strangers like me and may be even you but she said. I could stay with you because there are no more available rooms. What do you say?"

Big Nasty and his men all together laugh out to see what's a catch she is. So much like the dead girl the men anticipate how long before they can enjoy the wares being displayed. Looking at each man individually the Warrior goes on to say. "These are my last two drinks big man so you would have to get your own to join me. Am sorry about this but its all I have left to heat me. Big Nasty is charmed to comply "I can do much better than that." The blatant invitation was not suggested in innocence but as bait. She understands his every meaning to keep her warm and adds, "Then we must drink to that one." Again they all laugh out at her. Big Nasty notes the obvious, "I can see you are not from around here and I wouldn't say she's a friend of mine, but you can be. As for you staying with me. That can be worked out." They continue laugh out at her naivety, but he does not. He clears twice his throat and all the laughter stops. Gently she slides one of her full shot glasses over to Big Nasty, not spilling a drop.

This one is going to easy not like the other girl the men abused earlier. With the amber liquid before him she tells him to look at the gesture for what it is. "Look at it, as a peace offering." He likes her spunk and nods his head, in acceptance he agrees to house her in his room, "You have a place to stay!" Big Nasty plays up to his audience not wanting to lose face in front of the crowd. Out loud, with a smirk on his big face he admits "Warrior you sure have guts. I admire that in a fighter and specially in one like you." If the situation wasn't dire Leoha would be impressed, he is an easy mark. "Well thank you. They say that to much talk and not enough drinking is not good for the spirits. I have always wanted to know. Is it true?"

Just when the Warrior reaches for her glass, she is made to stop by one of the men sitting at the table. Without a word he switches the two shots glass around daring her to protest, he searches her face for any concealed deception. "Now according to our customs.

Its official." It wouldn't be the first time someone tried to poison Big Nasty. Leoha looks at him and with a smile, that pleases Big-Nasty, to the man sitting. She said. "I like that." So far, the woman has gained favor with him. Big Nasty, becomes even more pleased. Without further words, the Warrior throws back the shot, placing the empty glass upside down on the table before her. Many on lookers are waiting to see what the notorious Big Nasty will do next. The crowd becomes riotous, motivating him with their cheers and he enjoys the power of it.

The Madam is impatient sitting still speculation of the outcome is not easy to watch from a distance. Feeling the need to see more she abandons the warrior Raackus moving up closer to see. The crowd goads Big Nasty banging their mugs on the table tops. Over the hooting crowd, he chooses not to keep them wanting taking up the shot glass he swallows in one shot. Like the Warrior he too turns his shot glass upside down in front of him. The crowd cheers him on. After the crowd settles down, Big Nasty likes the Warrior for her kind gesture. And to her Big Nasty said. "Warrior! What is your name?"

The expression on her face is serene and she tells him, "Trace! "Her name is abstract to him, and he asks her to elaborate because he don't understand the meaning behind her name." Trace!? Trace of what? It's most unfortunate these men believe she is another they can use willfully, so she repeats giving him her full title. "Trace of Death." Every renown killer has a code name they are known by. Her name takes Big Nasty aback and he repeats, mumbling the name. "Ddd. . . death." Before he could enunciate the name a second time Big-Nasty head falls to the table. Headless his body folds over. The room explodes in confusion.

The Madam mouth drops open at the sight. From the looks of it The Warrior has just begun to unleash judgment. With her Warrior speed unleashed, she removes her hidden blade and dagger. Leaping from the table into the air over Big-Nasty dead body she slits open the necks of both men standing near him. The rapid flow of her movements lashes out with a whirl. While still in the air, she throws out her dagger at the informer standing at the bar killing him instantly through his heart. Up to the middle beam, using her two feet, pushing off, somersaulting back across his lifeless body back into her seat. It happens in a blur, so effortless was her motions that it causes the Madam to fall back in her chair. The two men standing, heads fall from their bodies to the ground. This leaves only the two men sitting, she warns, "You move! You die!" The two men are so afraid, they dear not move.

Many of the others standing by are terrified, rising from her seat she walks behind the men sitting on her right. Never before has anyone seen such prowls of ability because of fright, he cries out to the Warrior for mercy. "Please, please don't kill me." In a unison of chorus the other man sitting, cries out also, "Please lady, please don't kill us." To assure them of her mercy she promises them both "I will not kill you." This unexpected development of Big Nasty demise changes everything. The crowd now begins to dread the hand welding the sword and what her intentions towards them will hold.

The people of the room are not sad but pacified to know bad men have been removed. They deserved nothing less than death. Her good words allow them to breathe in a sigh of relief. She then steps around the headless bodies. With her foot she pushes Big Nasty worthless corpse out from the seat. The two men sitting can only stare at her witless. "Well, don't sit looking at me! Make your selves useful! Search him, and rest everything found on the table."

In urgent haste, they get to it. With one swift stroke she returns the blade to its encasement while taking her own seat. Big Nasty pockets reveals its secrets and everything found is placed before the Warrior. The Madam is pleased, Big Nasty is dead and for a minute joy shows on her face. When she realizes the crowd is watching her, she contains the glee she feels in the pretense of composure. The crowded room awaits the fate of the remaining two men standing next to her table. To them she demands "Yours too!" They hurry to emptying their pockets of all their earnings onto the table in front of her.

To be of some help to the Warrior, the Madam walks across to the dead man laying out beside the bar. His face is of a dark color, something she has never seen before and from his heart she pulls out the Warrior dagger, the on lookers are stunn With it behind her back she walks back across to the Warrior at the table. Raackus watches his lovers every move and so are many others. He knows her good enough to say she will kill the Warrior quietly with her own dagger. With in reach of the Warrior she stops. On high alert the Warrior tenses hearing the faintest of movement, the crowd is still watching and most are afraid of the skills she kills with.

To the two men standing awaiting their faith, The Warrior once again asks, "I will ask only once! Who killed the young girl? Who raped her?" Together they both stammer their response "Dadadada, The headless ones. Their cowering offenses her, "And what did you do? Their own guilt keeps them quiet, not wanting to implicate themselves. With a penetrating look at the first man again, frightened he opens his mouth revealing all the truth.

The other joins him dejected crying out despondently," We just had too. If not, we would have been killed. As part of their sentence in the heinous deed she orders them to, "Take out the dead bodies!." With help from the clean up crew the dead are removed like vermin and to her they returned. With the temperature on the outside is now zero below the two men don't dare think of running in such freezing temperatures. Out side one would only last few seconds and every one inside is there to wait it out. The Warrior takes from the loot on the table Big-Nasty room key. Calling to The Madam, the Warrior get her attention holding up Big-Nasty loot "Madam!?, I believe the rest belongs to you! Take it!" Walking up to the Warrior all the Madams problems have now been vanquished.

The Madam takes the hidden dagger from behind her back "I believe this belong to you." placing it on the table in front of the Warrior. Without warning, the sight of her blade in her hand prompts the Warrior to pull out her blade with speed and puts it up against the Madams throat causing it to bleed. Many are not troubled to see it happen, because of their past deadly encounters sooner or later the tide was bound to turn. Even though they work for a tyrant worker, doesn't mean they want her dead.

The sight of her blood causes a panic. One of the workers sounds out the alarm causing the others to rush out from the kitchen. Prepared with weapons to defend the Madam, capricious the situation is delicate, they cannot risk the Madams life. The treat to her life forces them to all step back in fear for the Madam. Her intended The warrior Raackus, takes position to kill the Warrior. In the confines of the close crowd, he refrains. Leoha quickly orders the Madam to, "Call for a cup of water or you will bleed and tell your people to stay back or I'll turn this place into a grave yard faster than death." This frightens everyone even the warrior Raackus. Everyone steps back having seen her skill. With her hand the Madam tells everyone to stay back the Warrior eases up on the blade at the Madams throat, nearby the server is given instructions by the Madam, "Do as she say."

The Madam begins to feel a little dizzy in her head, and she begins to wondered why does she feel like she dying fast. The server returns shoving her way through the crowd with the cup of water, all attention is on her. The Warrior leans close to the Madam, quietly she tells her, "I wish you hadn't touched that dagger." The dagger, a image of it in her hand flashes in her mind. The Madam get's a dreaded premonition, the dead man's odd color and the dagger protruding from his chest. It's too late and she figured it out. The dagger was laced with poison and the server rests down on the table the cup of water. Looking up at the Warrior with eyes full of tears, no one can ever say before this day that she has ever cried. To the Warrior the server pleads pushing the item at her. "Please don't kill her. Give me your word."

The servants heartfelt appeal and concern warms Leoha, the Madam doesn't deserve such fidelity. To please the young pleasant, she gives her word. I promise I won't kill her but the stakes may be your life in exchange." Uncertain of the Warrior's threat, the younger server slowly steps aside, from the look the Warrior gives her she dear not touches the Madam. On multiple occasions the warrior Raackus, tries to jump the Warrior from behind, but fails due to interference from the pressing crowd. His favorite server stands blocking the direction of his killing darts, so he waits for another chance.

Feeling a numbness moving up both her arms the Madam doesn't look well. The Warrior wants her to feel the sting of death that may curb the bitter nature of her mouth and attitude. It saddens the crowd to see one such as the Madam victim to a slow death. The Warrior removes the blade from the Madams throat and the young server nearby helps her to stand. With efficiency the Warrior acts placing the sharp side of the blade between her two fingers and with one downward movement she wiped the blade clean of the Madam blood into the cup with water. The blade is placed back up against the Madams throat. From her belt the Warrior pulls out a pill, while the Madam takes notice of her own frail hand color.

In an effort to keeping thing in perspective, the Warrior looks at the Madam dying. Out loud and for all to hear she exclaims with disgust her duty. "The reason why I don't kill you with my hand is because your skin is just too filthy for me to touch! Drink it or I'll sever your head where you stand!" The crowd of watchers are shocked as is the young and beautiful serving girl but not the ruthless killers. The friction between the two just could not be avoided. The Warrior gave her word not to kill the Madam. The young server becomes confused by all spoken accounts. The ultimatum the Warrior demands means the Madam will die by means of a poison pill and not by the Warrior own hand. Frantic she realizes her trust in the Warrior has no valid foundation, her emotions begin to suffocate her, moaning woefully she shakes her head in denial. "You! You promised!" She faints in disbelief having to be helped by another.

Very much poisoned, The Madam is dazed but coherent to everything. The crowd stands witness to skills and power most have never seen before. Without fear for her own life, the Madam feebly steps up against the table, picked up the cup of water mixed with her blood and the Warriors pill, she drinks it all down. The emptied cup drops from her hand to the ground as the beautiful server girl is rising from her swoon. Back upon her feet she is most surprised to see the Madam looking much better. So, the Warrior did keep her word. The Warrior beacons her to come nearer. "You!. . . Come closer!" Leoha has a task for the committed worker to perform on behalf of her Madam. The servant smile spreads out in humbled gratitude to the Warrior for keeping her word. Pointing to Raackus she sends her to him, "Go across there and tell that warrior. If he moves again be prepared to die."

In his break to attack the Warrior, he has been exposed, so Raackus gets the Warrior message very clear. The young server is ignorant not knowing his anger towards the Warrior. Before she can repeat the Warriors sentiment a sullen Raackus thinks to himself no one threatens him and gets away with it. To prove his point rather that loose face, he slaps the beautiful server mute, the strike is unexpected and she stumbles, to the floor. Helped back to her feet, disappointment shatters the impression she built around her preconceived notions of the warrior Raackus. The results of her best costumer's actions, causes her to run to the back.

All of the poison has now dissolved out from the Madams system and her skin color restores back to her original strength. She wishes to tell the Warrior thanks but instead, she reserves her silence. Raackus watching is outraged, when he focuses on her, she simply looks elsewhere. The Warrior looks to the Madam. "I believe this belongs to you." Indicating to the loot on the table. The Madam calls for her favorite server, now standing in back of her. Pressing the tray into her hands she directs her to, "Clean up the table!" The Madam is herself again, to all her other workers and guest she shouts "Everyone, just get back to work and you all continue doing what you were doing" Not realizing, her guest were all looking at her before. Things slowly falls back to normalcy.

Still there are many standing, waiting to hear the matter of the last two of Big Nasty's men. Quietly the Madam backs up to her favorite server and whispers. "You know where to put it. Make sure its safe and no one follows you." Only too happy to see her boss back to her old self again she smiles in agreement. Not trifling with a somber fortitude, the Madam stares at the Warrior. "You are serious about having your own room, aren't you? As for the cut and the blood! It must be paid back in full. The Madam punctuated response is perceived as a pundit. Pertaining to the gash opening on her neck. The Madam turns to walk away, there is much she must digest. To the last two men of Big Nasty still standing. Leoha isn't finished. "I have only one question. I suggest you get it right!"

Leoha has seen enough court matters before her King sisters to know how to determine the out come she now seeks. Pitiful, they both look to each other, before turning back to her. The room grows even more quiet to hear her deliberations with the men. "I believe you two are good men, just doing bad things." They both agree, the stealth of what she alone has ability to perform causes them to shake. Having done despicable wickedness, the bell tolls for their heads. Fear trades places and the men now have to face correction or judgment. Princess Leoha she goes on to say. "So, do you think a Warrior should keep their words?" The answers she seeks is of no consolation to the reversed positions they find themselves. Again, she compromises each of them standing dishonestly before her. The compliance of their consenting positions is temporary at best.

She goes on to allay their fears. "Then I' shall keep my word and I won't kill you." The two men breathe a breath a sigh of relief knowing she will spare their worthless life. "But!" The Warlord Warrior has had many dealing with desperate men, both faces sink to hear what else they will experience. "Your battle is no longer with me, but with the storm out there! Get out!" With the limited options she offers, it's more than what they gave others. They run away from her sight toward the exit door to find it blocked by many. The plague of the horrors they faced because of these men screams for retribution. The Door Keeper grabs hold of one stabbing him in the back whereas the other is beaten down with ripping force and stomped. Together the Door keepers take hold of them and toss each out into the freezing temperatures.

The door is again closed and locked. The others that remain inside get the message not to challenge the Warrior. Outside in freezing temperatures the two men can barely struggle disoriented from the savage beating they received. Forced to look for shelter elsewhere, leaning into gusting winds racked with pain, the biting temperatures decides their fate.

Big-Nasty was the first of his men to fall. The tail of a snake can not live long with out its head. He was not just a big and nasty looking man, but a man of ethics. Unfortunately, no one ever lived long enough to see that side on him. He and his men were wanted on both sides of the boarders which was why he stayed at the Inn Between. It was the only safe haven neutral for persons hiding away from the law.

Apart from the Madams outstanding beauty, is her ability to charm the best of fools, liars and many others. Some declarations paint illustration referring to her as a candle light burning in the dark, from behind the walls of doubt. Its not often that she gets to see that side of herself. On her way back to the bar Leoha passes Raackus close by. With her back to him, her eyes are vacant, speaking nothing. His pride is wounded he longs to launch his dart at her but by the Madam insists he leave her alone. He is made to stop. "What in hell are you doing Raackus! Trying to kill her back on! No, she saved me!" She maybe known for her harsh manners but when she answers a matter, she is just.

Yet still, Raackus remains disillusioned by the events of Big Nasty and his men. Having the Madams affairs put in order by a woman Warlord, and not himself, is demeaning him, it erases all of what he did do. For him there is no way to dispute the Warriors credits of accomplishment over his performance. "We should stick to the plan." For a minute The Madam ponders, what in hell is Raackus talking about? "Warning him to drop it." Its over and like me I suggest you stay away from her and move on. "The picture is broken and Rackuss is confused but he says nothing further to his love one. Nothing further is said, with Raackus taking his seat to further watch over his love one. The Drinking man is no longer at the bar. The only evidence left, is empty shot glasses and they are being removed.

The great HeShe is on duty alone relieving the Bartender who must be else where. With his voluminous grand smile, the great HeShe hands the Warrior her saddle bag she left earlier on the counter. "The Bartender stepped out, he asked that I hand this over to you." With out uttering a word the Warrior secures it. Just about to step away, the Bartender comes running in pushing the HeShe to the side. The HeShe rapidly huffs the displeasure at being handled inappropriately "You don't have to be so ruff." The Warrior stares at the HeShe with perplexity. The HeShe, in return crosses his eyes out at the Bartender and leaves it as that.

Not wanting to waste any more time the Bartender relates his concerns "You will have to excuse that one. Sorry am late but your friend fall-out and we had to carry him up to his room. Am pretty sure after what you did, the night will end smoothly. Go up the stairs and be careful as you enter Big Nasty's room. We have already lost one of our own going in there." The Warrior shows she is grateful by expression, "Thank you."

After her ordeal The Madam is back out on the floor moving around as she usually does. With one eye she watches the Warrior. Racckus calls to her, with a motion of her hand she lets him know she will be there soon. The Warrior is leaving the bar, the HeShe happily pulls the Bartender aside to gossip about the Warrior. "She is not only quick but strong and so cute, you know! I could use one like her. Why have you not introduced me? Why is a good question, why did the Madam see fit to hire a defected deity is beyond him?" Not every one is on your scheme. You know! You really need to decide, what side you are on, man or women. Remember you got this job because no one else is crazy enough to come out here and work! "In a high pitch and rasping shrilled tone the HeShe, with one hand on his side, a limp wrist and bent finger points randomly about." Does that mean we are all crazy? "The physical orientation of the HeShe pushes the Bartender to reveals his complications with him" You know! I really don't like talking to you. The boss said the place needs more flavor. Thanks to the great GODS there is only one like you here!" The Bartender walks away, having no more to say.

The Madam has again obstructed the Warrior way from getting up the stairs to her room. From where she now stands looking down at the brave Warrior. Instead of thanking the Warrior for saving her life, emotionless she tells the Warrior, "You have something which belongs to me!" The Warrior reflects trying to recall back on the loot given to the Madam and the room key. She looks up at the Madam standing so high and brave on the up step and she thinks to herself. What is with this women? "Could you please, just let me pass." The Madam has not mended her ways in light of what has happened the Warrior is still at fault in her books. "That was a nice trick you pulled back there! I owe you nothing because nothing out here comes free! So, don't think I have to cater to you for thanks!" Then so gently she goes on "Last door on the right. I suggest you watch your head going in." Allowing the Warrior to pass freely, up the stairs the Warrior make her way to the second floor. Everything downstairs has returned back to normal.

The hall way is dimly lit and candle lights burn low because of the storm. Continuing on until she reaches the Drinking man door with a carved-out dog hanging on the door. It makes her smile, it's just as the Drinking man said as she fondles the carved emblem. . . "Cute!" She keeps moving on until finally at the very end is Big Nasty's room. Pulling out the key from her garments placing it into the lock, it's a perfect fit. With one hand she opens the locked door standing aside out from harm's way. Pushing it open it's not surprising to see flying darts launching themselves into the cross wall. That would explain the establishment loosing one of their own and the HeShe being hired as the replacement.

The room inside is a bit dark with only one candle burning. She knows the risk of entering an unannounced room of a villain and thief like Big Nasty. Searching the rooms, she mobilizes all the traps in the room and she is safe. Being one of the Elites from the Kingdom she also is an expert in traps and killing without leaving a trace. Her knowledge and understanding goes far beyond commoners like Big Nasty. In the middle room is a table draped with a long red table cloth. It stands out some thing most unusual for a man's room. With her foot she kicks the table spinning over and in mid air pulls off the red cloth, the table lands face up. There is another red cloth attached to the bottom with a large bulge, something is in it. She removes it, knowing it could only be the reminder of Big Nasty's, loot. She takes it all out and into the other room where her saddle bag rest on the bed she opens it.

Tearing the red cloth into two parts, it divides evenly. Wrapping each separately and into her saddle bag she places them both. There is a sudden knock on the room door and from the tap, she can tell its the hand of a woman. With hurry she secures her saddle bag and she walks to the middle room. Turning the table back up right, she drapes it before answering the door. There is a second knock harder than before indicating someone urgently wants to get in. The door swings open it is the Madam making her own way in she closes the door behind her. The Warrior takes a seat is surprise to see the fast talking and enchanting Madam in her room.

The Madam smiles at her disbelief, "You don't have to look so surprise! Its only me! Its almost impossible to make the Madam understand, its not appropriate for one to come into other people's room at will. Exasperated, the Madam less than tactful manner is frustrating, "You may enter!" Ignoring proper decorum, instead of acknowledging the Warrior words, the fast-talking owner gets right down to business. "Have you found any thing of value in here? The dead man still owes me a lot of money! The people out there are all afraid of you but like I have said, am not. Further more! I can use a person like you. What do you think about my offer? Please take your time, while I search the room for your own safety."

The Madam begins to search the room, looking under everything that can be moved. The Warrior sits back waiting her to finish. Her Warrior training hears every movement the Madam makes. After finding nothing, the Madam takes notice of the saddle bag laying out across the bed. She doesn't dare's touch or look into it with out the Warrior permission. This time she's not as lucky as before and she comes back out to where the Warrior is still siting relaxed. The small talk is not in the Madams character, leaving Leoha ponder her motive. "So tell me Warrior. Where do one like you come from?" Leoha will play along, never taking her eyes off her she answers her, "The north!" Again looking around the Madam misses nothing, "And where were you heading?" This sudden change in her nature is interesting to Leoha. "Deep south! Tell me do you always ask so many question?"

Well, she really didn't expect the Warrior after their adverse confrontations to greet her with open arms. Especially after how badly she behaved. The Madam upon hearing the Warrior pinched remark, she states. "Its my place! Out here I must ask the questions! Its for your own good! If you don't like it, you can always fine a place out there with the storm!

From the interim of their meeting Leoha has experienced her consistent bites. "You do have a quick way with your words." Turning in no hurry the Madam has a quite a stunning smile when she does, and she does so now with her. "The room is cleared and safe. I hope you like it." Leoha has never met a woman of her baring ever. Since meeting her, the Madams behavior has been most hostile and strange in ways. The interaction with the Madam is proving to be an annoyance to Leoha. "Well! I did tell you, nothing is in here. So, what else do you have up your sleeve?" The Madam is truly a pearl for sunset among garbage. What does she really want, eventually she knows the Madam will expose the true cause for her change.

Leoha just hopes she can deal with whatever it is. The storm outside is starting to have appeal, even now the woman won't leave, still talking she tries to engage her conversation. "What interest would it be to you?" The Warrior shares her insight with her. "I think its your fast pace, which keeps you alive out here. Am afraid I may not fit in and as for the finding, like I said nothing at all."

The Madam has the heart of a mercenary, retrieving the personal items from the room left behind by the last occupant. "Then you won't mind. If I take a final search under that table?" To be respectful of the Madam and owner, the Warrior gives her permission to check freely. "It's your place so please, let me not stop you. Just keep your head up there may be more traps under there." The Madam remembers those words to be those of her own, very suddenly she loses the feeling to further search. "You nearly damn right killed me out there so don't think for a minute! I owe you. And even if you had killed me. My friends in low places would hunt you down and kill you! Still! Then so suddenly and so sweetly the Madam calms, and goes on to say. Still, that was some move you pulled out there. Never seen it before!" The Madam was very impressed, the Warrior looks to her, "I don't think you come here to start a fight? So. . ." The Madam agrees with her, "I too think not!"

Determined to cover all areas the Madam bends down and raises the red table cloth finding nothing, she let go of the table cloth and stands up right again. "All is clear and the the room is safe, but the color doesn't suit you!" Maybe the Madam too is turning over a new leaf, her nephew made the choice. So, what's to stop her The Madam doesn't leave without leaving a criticism. "Warrior! I hoped that quiet tongue of yours, would mean yes. With a strong body like yours around here. I wouldn't have so much to fear." Leoha right eyebrow rises in question she is not moved by the Madam pretense of warmth "Thanks for the offer but like I have said. I don't think I could fit in, your world." The Warrior denies her again. "Well, that's my lost, but if your ever in these parts again, please stop in and there's no finders' keepers here!"

The Madam walks toward the room door having done her inspection, she makes her way out leaving the room door open. Rising up behind her exit, the Warrior closes it behind her. Another fight breaks out downstairs, but that too is short lived. The Madam, leaves her authority approval with her favorite server until she returns. Whenever the Madam she goes out her favorite server always takes charge along with another who helps her out in tight conditions. The Madam strides back onto the floor. Raackus, seeking to gain her attention, again he is put to wait and off the floor the Madam goes.

Within the large confines of the wooden structure are many hidden doors and corridors which are known only to the Madam and few of her oldest staff. The Madam enters her living quarters in the basement to have a quick change of clothing and off she goes again. In the quarters that is now hers the Warrior has just enough time to bathe and change before another knock comes to her door. The knock is like that of the first but tempered with more patience, she is not fully dressed. Believing it to be another room attendant she calls for them, "Enter!"

Coming out to see who has entered her room Leoha is once again surprised. Standing before her in the wee hours of the mourning dressed to impress is none other than The Madam. Even though she is tired, the Madam is stunning. Her looks have changed, her make-up is flawless, and her clothing is that of an elegant lady. Who is this new creature, this can't be the same screw she first meet? She enters gracefully, closing the door behind her. Fanning her face with only her hand and fingers, Madam walks in pass the Warrior into the open room. The Warrior follows. Leoha ponders what is troubling the Madams to come back at this time looking like this. Is this continual display of attention for her benefit? Or is it something else? "If its payment your after! I'll pay downstairs."

Even though the bleak weather of the surging storm holds them hostage, Leoha doesn't know what to make of this visit yet again. The Madam speaks first. "Don't you feel a bit hot in here?" Looking around the space without thinking, it actually was very cold in here. The Warrior utters, "My! you are full of surprises. The temperature is not that bad but how could I be of further help to you?" With no urgency, the Madam begins pacing back and forward. She suddenly pauses, looking over to the Warrior, "Why don't you start by opening your eyes! I just came to ask would you be in need of a wake-up call in the morning. The Warrior is almost stunned by the Madam behavior, it is almost daylight, she can't make it out. And the Madam goes on "And you don't need to pay for the room! Its on the house. Earlier, I forget to say thanks to you. I figure now would be a good time." The Warrior begins to think to herself. What's the deal, with this lady again? For a quick moment her mind flashed back to Bleaha's attitude, nothing more than a failure to her. The Warrior dispensing with formalities does not want to further the Madam in conversation but she adds, "It's already morning and your welcome. The storm has already passed and the remaining wind is not that bad. I need an early start so I'll make my way to leave soon."

The Warrior had long noticed the Madam eyes burning her body and to discourage matters she needs to covers up more of her skin. Even now her strong body stature and immaculate figure makes the Madam pat away the heat from around her neck. She tries to look away, but her eyes still long out to the Warrior. The Madam clears her throat over and again for a simple relief. Leoha takes this moment, "Excuse me a minute." Into the bedroom she enters, over her clothing, she throws on something less revealing and comes back out. Seeing her dressed state,the Madam comments, "I too would rather you not catch a cold." Mystified the Warrior is baffled by the unpredictability of the Madams behavior. "You know, I don't get you."

Quickly focusing her eyes else where, and in a blink of passion. The Madam teases her, "Are you always this tight? Arching her eyebrow, that note gets the Warrior full attention. To the pretty Madam in conflicts of emotion the Warrior erects a barrier of principle" You know, I don't like speaking with you. . . my my! You do have a way with words." The Madam stands still, while looking so pretty she elaborates for her feelings to be returned, "Well! If you put it that way! In stead of being so strong. You should open your heart a little more. All am asking is for you to lead me and I'll follow, in your heart forever. . . but lead me not into any more temptations. Deliver me from evil and al stay with you forever." The Madam catches herself and realized, she let her guard down to quick, she stands at attention looking pretty. There is no place for flesh weakness in Leoha disposition she reiterates without a doubt, "Like I have said before." The Madam retort cuts in on the Warrior talk and bluntly, she repeats the Warrior words back out at her. "You won't fit in. Is that all you can say? Do you ever stop long enough to care?"

Guilty of not following love like so many other, who allows love to leave them by the way side, Leoha refuses to answer the Madams question. The Madam does not seem able to accept the folly of her feelings not being returned. "You don't even know my name? And why would you want to give up all of this to follow me?" Her conversation to the point is as sharp as a measure, could she have been rehearsing this? and she continues her persuasion to convince her? "Out here! One can live longer with out a name! And as for me giving up. If it is that good! Why don't you just stay?" Forth right Leoha interrupts the Madam speech. "No, I can't." For a minute the Madam is left speechless and after thoroughly gathering her thoughts, she tries again to make the Warrior understand her feelings toward her. "Then could you?" Again, Leoha cut's her off. "No, I couldn't!"

She stops, uncertain how to proceed, by what to say next. The awkward moment leaves both looking to each other. Extracting herself, calmly and gently the Madam said. "I think I have already said too much. May be its time I leave. I wish you were not so blind. Even a blind man could see love better than you!" All this time the hostility of the Madam was a facade, to hide the contradiction of her true feelings. And her tears speak out the rest. In all fairness to the Madam, the Warrior acknowledges her honesty and sincerity, which cannot be questioned.

There are but two involved here and its not about one having total dominance over the other. The rules outside the Kingdom variate on so many levels of social interactions. In the Kingdom such relations with like kind are forbidden. So, in all fairness and frankness toward the Madams feelings. Her creed as a Warlord Warrior, has attracted this woman intimacies. Whereas in the past some women did want her companion but what the Madam desires is not a friend or mentor-ship. Leoha realizing one such as she needs not the further hurt and pain. She tries to be honest to her about the true implications such an affair could bring. "Listen! You have a life ahead of you, live it. I am not like you and I could never be like you. Death is what follows me and that's not much of a life for anyone. I could only hope one day you would understand the meaning. The only guarantee I can give you, should I ever be passing this way again. It will be certain I stop in."

From the downstairs they hear the commotion of what sounds like a brawl. The Madam knows her attention is needed, instead of leaving she chooses to pretend by smiling out to the serious Warrior, as if she hears nothing, this is her last time to make an impression, not wishing to break the moment. The noise from downstairs only gets louder. The Madam can no longer avoid hearing the escalating situation downstairs, with a flounce of her skirt, "I think its time duty calls and thanks for your honesty." In the stalemate of stalling because the Warrior said nothing further, the Madam looks to her. "Then would you rather I wait." Even the stubborn determination of the Madam pursuit for affection is hostile and Leoha reminds her, "You should start by keeping this place in tact." Another crash downstairs, the Madam winces livid at the distraction, she knows the Warrior is right. "Dammit! I'll kill some body down there!"

Regretful, after realizing her poor choice of words, she looks sheepishly at the Warrior still there standing. With a weak and surly good smile, she denies herself "I didn't hear that." While the Madam walks toward the door, the Warrior smiles to herself. Cracking open the room door she looks back at the Warrior with a pleading pout and sultry bedroom eyes. Easing out the door she closes it firmly behind her. In the dim lite corridor leaning against the closed door her eyes closed, she sighs. Gathering her breath, on her first step away from the door she accidentally runs straight into two of her servers from the downstairs.

Startled and surprised by each other. The Madam gushes crying out. "What are you two doing?" The servants were originally trying to find her, and when they had located her, the conversation through the door kept them silent. With out warning, to ether of them, she slaps them both across the face? "God dammit! What are you two doing up here? You want to be killed?" The slap does little to deflect the surprise of seeing the Madams transformed look.

The sight of the Madam adorned, mesmerizes them, they don't feel the pain. "Madam, you look so, so different! Are you getting married? Is there a party?" The server girl agrees with him, "You do look so nice Madam. We come searching because we didn't know, what room your in. Its a good thing I did noticed you coming up. I only had to guess the Warrior room. You have been acting so strange since she came and they are breaking the place up downstairs so you see we had to, we need you? Without reservation, the Madam dignifies herself "You watch your mouth! I can be lady like too, you know!" The servant girl sympathizes with her and smiles, its the server boy who believes the Madam is guilty for hiding her true feelings.

"But she's right. You have been acting so strangely lately. I believe it have something to do with that strange aaaaaa Warrior, yes Warrior." The Madams eyes narrow steely at his reference to the Warrior "You always seems to know it all! Did that damn Drinking man pay up the rest of his bill?" Her question puts him on the spot, "Well! Three of us carried him to his room. He said something about being robbed by a fourth person. We don't know any thing about it and he said, you should bill it to his Warrior friend." The Madam having told the Warrior her charges were covered wasn't going to put the expense of an ingrate drunk to her attention. She maybe crass and difficult, but she is fair.

"God dammit! Just my luck! not another one! Take his horse to cover the cost! The kitchen could use some fresh meat." Flinching back from the scrutiny of her disappointment he adds, "He had an early start and I believe he's long gone. He was in a rush." This is the side of the business that often deflated her at times. There's always some wayward drifter thinking he could run out, and not pay his expense. The hearing of another sob story, she sheds off her beautiful head and blouse pieces shoving them into the hand of the boy server. "You keep it! Mr know it all." Looking at both of them, they have yet to move. Must she tell them everything. "Dammit! Let's go!"

Down the long hall way, they follow her, and on passing the room door where the Drinking man stayed, looking at the dog hanging on the door with its mouth open. The carving is obnoxious, growling out orders to the boy server, "Remind me to change that one It reminds me of you." The serving girl stifles a giggle at his expense. He gives her a sharp and disapproving glare, together they keep moving and while passing the door he kicks it. The carved emblem falls to the ground. Personally, he always thought he was handsome.

The Madam discards her beautiful long skirt and wipes away the rouge and make up. The server boy quickly snatches it after she disregards it throwing it to one side of the hall. Under the elaborate designed garments is her working clothes. Descending the stairs, she twists her hair back into a conservative knot at the nap of her neck. The mad look returns cold and granite. At the bar she enters to assess what the problem was now. The servants separate leaving her to return to their duties. Right away, the Madam is appraised of the Trouble Makers and the source of their controversy by the Bartender.

The Madam takes command, "Go quickly into the kitchen! Tell every one I need their help and come quickly." Off he goes off with she turning around to view the Trouble Makers. From across into the bar, she leaps into the air to action. The fight is many to stop, splintered tables, broken glass, smashed chairs, damaged is the whole place. The kitchen staff runs in from all sides they know the usual armed drill. All around they take up positions and one by one quietly, they neutralize each Trouble Maker with an arsenal of hidden pots, pans, and other kitchen utensils.

The Trouble Makers are effectively knocked out cold they fall to the ground. Even the Table Servers engage with their empty food trays like a puzzle unfolding execute the plan to keep things in order quietly bringing things back under control. The Chief Trouble Makers and their Second in Command are left standing from both sides. The Madam demands payment for her losses broken chairs, table, vases, plates, ripped curtains and much more. The perpetrators refuse to pay claiming their clumsy server missed his step and run into the other table of firing men looking to start a fight. Unaware they did not see when the opposite table tripped the server causing him to miss his step hence the chain reaction. Now things between the group leaders only comes to a talk because of the long Cycle of the Wind they both have known the Madam. The Second in Command refuses to see things like wise and blames the other.

Down the stairs she makes her way, the Warrior is fully dressed and across the floor to the bar. Littered bodies are strewn about leaving room only those standing at the bar to see the Warrior. The staff around the bar give her thumbs up, confident they all smile out to her for arriving just in time. She takes her saddle bag from her shoulder places it down on the bar counter. In no hurry then she turns around to better assess the trouble on the floor. The Warrior takes full notice of the Madams transformation back to her old self. Turning back to the Bartender over to him she tosses the room key, he catches it with a smile out to her. To thank her for all she did, he offers up a morning drink on the house. She accepts with kindness and gratitude, one milky shot, a full breath later she turns the shot glass upside down on the counter. Her smile out to the Bartender says thanks.

    The Warrior scanning stands alert to everything around her especially that of the Madam voice. Its piercing shrill bounces off the walls across the establishments floor, it's no conversation but a scream match for both chief perpetrators to pay up. Defiantly, they stubbornly refuse denying the Madam satisfaction. The Bartender walks to the far side of the bar and there he hangs the key on the key board before returning to position. The commotion from the bar calls the HeShe's attentions. Then speeding in from the far back is the HeShe, up to the Bartender counter. Alongside the Bartender he makes space.

    Just the sight of her amazon stature heats his loins, and other regional parts. With a bright face smile, and an elaborate flare the HeShe beacons with a crock of finger, "Warrior! The man with the dog hanging on his room door said, he needed an early start, so he left before the others could follow, and he also said you will take care of the balance on his bill. Are you ready?" The Warrior looks into the HeShe, eyes. The sight of a hermaphrodite in this unusual haven was just the type of establishment someone like him would cultivate. Just from the pupil dilation this HeShe was definitely more He than She, the deity. Leoha knows just how to handle such personalities. "I would think one like you have balanced out many things here. I don't even like your eyebrows."

    Astonished the HeShe gasps in outrage touching the eyebrows, and the bartender silently smirks hiding his smile. The HeShe instinctively gathers themselves, composing and dignified he caresses the beauty spot. He likes her even more from their perspective they detect no hidden guile or malice in the statement. The Warrior does care, this intrigues him even more, counting it affection, its just her way of showing it. To be certain of the Warrior true feeling toward, the HeShe. To the Warrior, they softly whisper. "You don't like me very much I see. Am I really that bad of a person? With a wry twist of her lips Leoha penetrating glare holds him captive. "No! But you're not good as one, neither." He didn't ask to be born this way, people have cruelly abused him because of it. Yes, this Warrior is a soldier of morals and integrity that judges fairly and without prejudice. This does prove the Warriors merit for care. With a silent smile, out to the Warrior. "Thank you for caring so much."

It's unique yet distinctively simple when she responds. "You're welcome." The Warrior turns to the action on the floor and she remembers the faces of the two leaders back in the desert and their men during one of her spying on both camps. They are the very ones, who had sent out the challenge to have her killed but instead she was victorious. It is time to bring about a quick resolution to the Madam problems, and hers.

Out loud to the perpetrators, the Warrior projects. "You all will pay or die." Every head turns toward the bar, they were all present when she killed Big Nasty, and all his men. Others dread, remembering her even more as the desert killer. Raackus stands looming beside the doorway, disappearing through the side door in fear of loosing his own life. At the moment her focus isn't on him, now is the best to get away. With equal measure of speed, the Warrior leaps into the air over the heads of the crowd coming down beside the imposing figure of The Madam herself.

The perpetrators immediately decline from feuding any further with the Madam. The ominous declaration of the Warrior leaves no choice other than death. Leoha looks down indicating to the empty table, they get the message. Out from their pockets they pull out everything and on the side table they lay out their moneys. Returning to position, the Madam is most please because the Warrior just made her job so much easier. The staff all grin out their teeth to see such bold men frightened out their wits by a woman. The kitchen staff retreats back to the kitchen, things under control, proud to recognize how good of a team they truly are. The treasures of the lost and taken

The Undaunted King Gouddaa of the Arawaks and Caribs

pour out on the table. When the Madam see the amount of loot, her eyes gloss over. To both sides, the Madam said. "Ohhhh! You guys are loaded! Let me get your change."

No one is happy, with smiles of hate toward her and so nicely they favor her with kind tolerance. "Please do, please do, please do and do take your time. Yes, take your time." Before the Madam could touch one bill, the Warrior reaches for her blade with speed, killing both leaders and their Second in Command in one stroke. she drops the others like flies, killing them all. It comes as a surprise to some, they deserve to be killed for all the wrong they have done. Putting away the blade, the Warrior walks in close to the Madam, and whispers. The Madam is entranced with each step the Warrior makes towards her. At the whisper of her breath at her ear, she closes her eyes from the thrill. "Its all in your hand now." If only the Warrior would put herself in her arms, swallowing hard.

Mentally shaking herself out of it, once again the Madam calls out to the server girl, who is just behind her. She come's out with tray in hand. The Madam points to the table, the server has never seen such a display of wealth before, and what a mess it is. "Get rid of this mess on the table!" She starts by wiping it from the table onto her tray. The Madam sunders up to the server girl and in the ear she tells her. "Take this bunch to my room! You know the spot! The safe under the floor. You know where the keys are. Make sure its locked back and watch those behind you!"

Looking around, there are many eyes watching. Looking at both dead leaders laying out on the ground. To the dead men, The Madam cries out "I guess you lot won't be needing that change any more." Studying the room occupants, the Warrior is also impressed with the offering amassed. "Now I see. Most of your guest are travelers with much wealth." The Madam is resourceful in command, resilient, she doesn't stop and Leoha is not surprised, covertly from beneath lowered lashes "You and I can settle up later! That is, if you choose to stay."

Already looking else were, the Madams comment is overlooked and the Warrior calls over another server. "Go and open that door and tell the Warrior to come out." On the other side of the door he hears her summons and on his own volition he walks out, everyone gives space. The dead are quickly taken out. The storm has long passed. Consumed, his own fears do nothing to diminish his thoughts of the Madam. Raackus wants to know if the woman he loves is still with him or not. If he is to regroup his loses, he needs her to disable the Warrior and his dart will do the rest. To his disbelief, the Madam walks to the opposite side of the room with no eye contact, this is his heart wrenching answer.

This confrontation between Leoha and the warrior Racckus was inevitable. "You want to see if a dart is faster than a blade. Now is your chance! If you don't know death! You will never see it passing." He has been exposed, somehow the Warrior saw him launch the dart earlier. There's no hiding, to stay alive Racckus unbuckles all his straps and his darts fall to the ground. One of Leohas eyes narrows at his omission, "And the one in your sleeve." He drops that too. The tension has dissipated and the crowd knows it all over. Things return back to what is normal.

The Madam and the Warrior are moving from different directions toward the bar and on approaching each other. The Madam extends in a whisper to the Warrior. "Thank you. My name is Kyddo." The Warrior is impressed, "Leoha!" In passing Leoha bids her good-bye. "Well, Kyddo, you take care." In one sway of motion they both continue their separate way. There's no more she can do to persuade her to stay, its bitter sweet, and the Madam sighs as its back to business as usual, and no more Racckus to contend with.

Seeing the Warrior coming back toward the bar, the HeShe quickly hides behind the Bartender. The HeShe, peeps out from behind him. Approaching the Bartender, the Warrior said. "I'll now have that last one for the road." With pleasure he pours out the Warrior last and final drink. From behind the Bartender the HeShe, shows his face. There's still the matter of an unpaid bill left by her drinking comrade. The Madam is never keen on customers who don't pay their lodging, nobody wants to be the one who tells her another has departed with out paying, her wrath was bound to be exceptional. "What about the bill?" Leoha smiles looking steadily at the HeShe. "That now belongs to Kyddo. You can take it up with her." Stunned, the HeShe look at the Bartender. "She knows the Madam name."

Oh my so the Warrior and the Madam were on first names, how wonderful. With gleeful giggles, "So how is my eye brows now?" The Warrior takes a quick look for mercy sake, not wanting to further the conversation. "Good! Just the way you like them." It's obvious from the arched contours of the eyebrows, that pain staking effort was made to make them appear perfectly sculpted. Excited for joy of acceptance, to the Bartender, the happy HeShe stifles a sniffle "She like's it. I never doubted, not once." The HeShe, smile is transfixed on the Warrior in a mesmerized daze the HeShe continues watching the Warrior eagerly, and things are left as such.

The beautiful server Racckus had slapped enters and picks up all his weapons. The WarLord Warrior has stripped him of everything. His woman, his respect, his strength. He can not move and the look of disgust registers on the circulating faces of those still alive. Her hand is warm in his, turning to see the bruised maiden he had abused makes him feel ashamed for what he did, whatever he thought he lost is restored in this gentle woman's graceful administration. She leads him back to his favored table leaving him there with his wine. Bystanders pass a look at him with pity or as a looser. With nothing more to lose, he didn't come here to leave empty handed. He must make some harsh decisions concerning the Madam. Here he observes and awaits.

The Warrior takes her last and final shot in front of the HeShe, placing the empty shot glass upon the bar counter. From her saddle bag she pulls out an enfolded cloth ball. In it is half of the dead man Big Nasty' findings, she tosses it over to the Bartender. With a quick reflex he is relieved to catch whatever the Warrior throws. Smiling he thinks nothing of it as he catches the cloth. It's very heavy, yet she tosses it like a weightless object. While the Bartender and the HeShe unravel the rolled contents she exits, to relief of many who feared they may be next to die. The Bartender rushes to see what's in it, not noticing the Warrior departure.

The rolled sack of sorts is heavy and jingles when shaken. Moving stealthy to a more private corner of the bar he does not realize the HeSheb is still behind him. Inside the package reveals what he always wanted, dreams of a house and a wife with children. The family now had enough to be taken care off properly. The HeShe eyes pops open gagged by the sight of wealth. His mouth begins to salivate at its sight and beauty.

There was no way he wasn't going to have a piece of this reward. It's only proper that he share a little piece, that's all he wanted. The HeShe plea is persistent and reasoning, it pays off. "Ohhhh! What will you do with all of that?" The plaguing trials of having to interacting with the HeShe has diminished in face of the freedom of limitless wealth. He can afford to be generous. "Get out from this damn place and not work any more. Make a life else where for myself and much more."

The picture the Bartender has drawn is an alluring one. His remark makes the HeShe, reflect about his/her own life. It only seems natural to want to be apart of the dream and why not a new adventure. "What about me. Can I come? "The Bartender has long tolerated the eccentric behavior of the HeShe. The fact that they made him uncomfortable at first has changed somewhat after witnessing the exchange between the Warrior and them. He can see the longing in the depths of his eyes now, he only wants to be accepted with equal respect. He is afraid to put himself with new people, maybe that's why he wants to go with him. Turning to look at the HeShe, he is a good match for the room." You belong here! but me no."

This man must be thinking HeShe is crazy, if he thinks he's going to walk out here, without leaving me a sizable tip of that stash he has another thing coming. I just know he wasn't trying to throw me off, oh no no that money got him drunk. "Am talking about the gold not where I belong! Are you saying one like me don't deserve any rewards? I could make it known you know! And how far do you think you can get before this bunch catches up with you." Am going to give him five seconds to realize this ain't no show, bringing out the man in me. And it doesn't take him long to come around. The cold reality of what the HeShe has said makes him cringe in disbelief, "Would you really do a thing like that to me?" One arched eyebrow perfectly sculpted raise, and with out a blink, the eccentric HeShe stands planted. "Try me!"

The Bartender looks about for the Warrior, but she is long gone and he has no horse of his own. Turning regretfully back to his nemesis its the HeShe who taunts him. "Your friend is long gone so what will it be?" Maybe if he talks sweetly to the HeShe they will let him slide. "Flowers! Would you really do that to meee?" Oh now he knows his/her name, how pathetic, "You finally called my name. Now figure out the odds!" It's not going to hurt him to give the HeShe something, if it ensures they are silent about it. For long life and peace sake, he offers over a portion of his gold bars to the HeShe in return for his/her silence. The HeShe accepts it with a vibrant smile. Taking off his uniform looking around the bar the Bartender calls it quits. Never would he have ever believed such fortune could befall him. Leaving the HeShe alone its their duties now.

The world was a new place, in which he can charter his own course and not have to worry about slaving for a living at a bar. The HeShe, asks him "Where will you find a horse? One chance meeting with a Warrior changed everything." Money talks! "Shrugging his eyebrows up and down. Walking away he knows he is going to steal one. The storm has long abated leaving only a slight wind. The Warrior is in the back barn collecting her stallion. Much of the sable has been destroyed, underway men are making repairs over head.

The Madam as usual is on the floor, trying her best to get away from a very persistence group of customers. Trying to extract herself from their advances she is hopeful to see the Warrior one last time if it must be. She was scheduled to depart at first morning light. In a short time, she is able to settle things peacefully on the floor. Calculating the Warriors departure, she knows exactly how much time it will take her to saddle up and leave. With little time left, she looks around and Racckus too is gone. That's a good thing, it works in her favor not to have him privy to what she is planning. He can't be that far the window was closing on her being able to reach the Warrior. He must have excused himself to the rest room, urgently she must act, she calls out to her favored server before he can return. In minutes the good server is there and she leaves her again to take over until she returns from the back barn.

Time is not on her side when she slips out silently through the front open door. Unexpectedly she is detained by the warrior Raackus just when she is able to make hast. Out of lurking shadows Raackus patience has paid off and he startles her. "What's the hurry at this time." Her heart flips over at the sight of him, "You startled me there." The menace in his voice is cold. "Where to?" His sudden appearance makes her itchy. Giving him a plausible excuse. "Need to check on the animals. Could we please leave this for later? Trying to pass him, he won't allow her access making her situation is most dire. Retorting sternly to him for obstructing her way, "Why are you stopping me! What do you want from me! You didn't kill him like you said you would do, but she did! So please, could we talk about this some other time! Plus, all bets are off! right now I have work to do."

How dare this woman dismiss him with no remorse, Raackus, looses his patient. The warrior he is, is incensed by her words. He tightens his grip "You owe me more than that! It's that damn Warrior isn't it? I thought, you would be on my side but you walked away. Maybe you wanted her to kill me too!" Demented reasoning takes over, and the rage is blinding. "No, Racckus don't you think like that. Its because of me she saved you so please may I pass?" Barring the path, she must out think him with her wit. "She still owes me money and I owe her the thanks. I just need to collect before she leaves, could you understand this." She does add that she pardoned the Warriors expenses.

This time he is more skeptical and he doesn't buy it. What other ploys will she have to undertake to move this idiot. The irritation of her thought is written on her facial expression, and he knows it. It angers him to see the woman he so loves, taken by another warrior. There is the fact that she is no more than a mere woman to him, he cannot accept. Even if this time wasn't different from others, this woman possesses superior skills in comparison and he dare not make the challenge.

In the heat of his burning and brutal passion for her a twisted fire lights his eyes. Madam certainly gets the foreboding feeling he may do something foolish and it happens unfolding before her eyes. Raackus, pulls out his short dagger and stabs it into the Madams upper chest, twisting it. The blood, spread, soaking through layers of her clothing. In the horror of disbelief of his own actions, she doesn't even move or make a sound. The shock and pivotal pain of her tears speaks out to him.

Even with a mortal wound the Madam words cuts Racckus deeply, "Am not the one you want to kill. How could you hurt the one you say you love so much?" The anger evaporates as surely as it expanded to entrap him. Guilty he removes the short digger out from of her chest. The blood flows more freely he watches her clutching to life. Trying to stop the bleeding, she presses her hand into the wound. Without emotion, he is void "Now you feel pain like I do."

To scoff at the pain, his foolish words anger her. Without a sound the trail of her tears flows out like water. There isn't much breath left to take and it's becoming more labored to breathe. The searing pain is so hot she's moments from passing out." I thought you were different but you warriors are all the same! When you cannot have your way. You want to kill. Is this the love you showed me?! I don' belong to anyone but me and all I want is to be me. Can you understand this! Can you?" There is no space for debate, or reconciliation, he rapidly pushes her to go for help. The blood has saturated her garment. "Go! You go and get help. Go! Go! Go back inside now! He does know who he should train his disgust at, her or himself. They have done many things together, she even convinces herself that she could love him." And I hope you will also get the help you need.

She doesn't move, the blood stain spreads against her bosom fanning out of clenched fingers, the guilt of his actions assuages him conscience, sadly all his dreams with her are over, off into the darkness he runs. Holding her injury, she watches him melt into the darkness, if the dagger had been any longer, she'd be dead. Laboring to make her way back inside heats her blood and it flows free again. Down the stairs into the basement, she makes her way without anyone ever realizing she is seriously injured. Into her private room she enters and nurses her wound to the best of her know how. Out here in the Inn Between these talents came in handy. She has lost a lot of blood still she tries to walk, the room slips away, it begins spinning and she falls out to the ground.

The Warrior hasn't left yet, still in the back barn trying to collect her stallion, the Drinking man hasn't been able to move further than he is. It has sobered him. The collapsed stable from the storm has impeded much progress for many. The sobered Drinking man had decided to have an early start looking to escape incident with Big Nasty crew. The Warrior is elated to catch up with him. No one has yet to tell him that Big Nasty, and all his men are dead. The Drinking man doesn't know the Warrior is just on the opposite side of him in the barn.

The barn is divided into two parts, larger stallions like that of the Warrior on the right and smaller ones to the left. Still there because his horse developed a shoe problem the barn keepers worked to fix it and move the collapsed stable. At the Inn Between, with man power limited, they work with what they have.

In the lower parts of the basement where her chamber is the Madam is found accidentally laying out on the floor by a thief. In his travel to and foe, looking for quick loot scouring the terrains treasure is where you find it. He remembers her, she once saved his life. Its the amount of blood covering her bosom which alarms him. Who could have done such a thing to this sweet woman. Lifting her semiconscious form gently he places her on the bed. In the room he finds a piece of cloth he uses to bind the wound properly, she doesn't even flinch. Before he leaves her, he doubles checks, she is still breathing and alive for now. There she sleeps in unconsciousness. There's nothing more he can do, if he's found with her blood on his hands, he would surely hang for it. Even though he is innocent he takes no chances escaping the way he came in with nothing.

Everything is made ready, the Drinking man can leave unhindered. The way is now cleared in the barn and the sober Drinking man horse shoe is all finished. In a strange turn of events the sober Drinking man and the Warrior both walk out from opposite sides of the barn room simultaneously. Not recognizing each are both on opposite sides of their horses and can't see the other. Walking out to the front entrance they continue side by side, parallel to each other.

It is early morning, feeling neighborly to the other unknown traveler like himself, the sober Drinking man greets, "It's good to have that early start my friend." The Warrior immediately knows whose speaking, the only difference is there is no slur. Quickly Leoha moves to the front and so does he to have a better look at his morning neighbor. In shock he is not so pleased to see her. He was trying to avoid her most of all, at all cost. The horses are made to stop and in fear for his life, he falls to his knees before the Warrior. Leoha is mystified by his actions and wonders why?

While he runs on with the litany of his confessions, she examines the sobered, Drinking man. "Yes, yes, I was wrong. I was afraid. I know I owe you an apology but I was afraid Big Nasty, and his men would have killed me. That is why I make the offer for you to stay in the room but I meant you no harm. Please let me make it up to you. Let me ride with you at lease until the next town." Every concern there ever was about the dog room is mote as she didn't use his room only that of Big Nasty instead. Its all amusing. "I think it's time you get up. The Drinking man gets up, checking over himself for a sign of blood, but there is none so he comes to a calm. Squinting, his eyes adjust to the suns rising rays, "So you're not going to kill me."

Life out here has little value, the litter of death scattered remains remind all how temporal things can be. The slightest offense could warrant a death notice. "You should give me a better reason. Further more your mumbling is just too much." She's not mad with him, it's incredible, it's more than that it's fantastic. Relief washes over him to know the Warrior is a friend. He beams out to her. The Warrior had long realized, he had some motive behind offering the room, his facial bruises told her the rest. There is no way he could have known, she would be leaving now and The Madam would never tell him of her early start. Let him be, even though he maybe telling another fib to benefit his journey ahead, its not significant.

On her travels, there's only room for one. Death rides its own horse. "And as for riding with me. That has already been reserved by death." It is not his intention to anger her. "Then its best. I wait here until the sun bring lighter." Leoha knows there's nothing threatening about the Drinking man, but just to be sure. Leoha baits her words to entrap him in his lies. "Big Nasty, and his men are looking for you." This was just what he feared would happen, he can see no recourse of escape. It's only a matter of time before they catch up to him and kill him. What can he do? Turning to the Warrior he asks for advice. "What do you suggest I do?" His reaction is honesty enough for Leoha to put him at ease.

"They are all dead so you can take your time." This can not be possible, the Drinking man can't believe his good fortune, all his concerns have been erased. "You know! Am a good person but out here one can change fast. Did you kill them?" Leoha refuses to take credit for the carnage she committed, "No death killed them." On to her stallion back she leaps duly justifying by her position. "Sometimes, good is sent as Punishment, but that I would never know. Should you see The Madam before leaving tell her thanks and good bye? Its a happy reunion to be reunited with her stallion again.

To atone for him misleading the Warrior he runs back to the inside strait into the server left in charge. "You aught to take your time!" Grabbing her by her shoulders, "Where is the Madam?" The last she saw the Madam she was en route to say her farewells. "I think she left to see the Warrior off." He had just left the Warrior and he couldn't miss her if she was coming to say her goodbyes. "She is not there and the Warrior is gone so where else would she be?" Alarmed, the server left in charge asks, "Why are you suddenly asking all these questions. Does she owe you? Does she know you? No time to explain it all, this doesn't get him any closer to the Madam. "You know! You are making this really difficult. I only want to give her a message from the Warrior. Can I not do that?" Oh she exclaims, "Why didn't you just say so. I can give her your message." He gives her the goodbye message verbatim and returns back to his horse. The server in charge sends another maiden to find the Boss lady. In minutes she is told the last place she passed was the basement.

The Drinking man finds dangerous the long road ahead. With out an escort he jumps on his horse and rides like a mad man. His hope is to catch up to the Warrior and he is blessed by the morning light. Some time after he finally glimpses her in the far distance ahead of him. He keeps his distance thinking she would not realize he is following. Along the sandy road side, he passes the two men dead bodies the Warrior had earlier let loose to the freezing temperatures. Their remains are slowly being claimed and devouring by wind, sand and scavengers just like the others before them. The Warrior has long realized she is being followed by the man she had left behind. She does nothing to detour him but keeps on moving.

The Madam has been found in the basement and with some help she is in better condition. But no one is able to say, how she got from the floor to her bed with out any one knowing. The place is now empty with the remaining travelers having all gone with the morning light. By dark another crew will pass and a new repeat shall begin again. Her favored server and friend are in with her and the other have left. She receives the Drinking mans message of the Warrior departure she shows a strained smile. Then she is given the updates by her best server and friend, that the Bartender has quit. The HeShe wants to go home for a few days.

After these reports she is then given a note, she has been through much ordeal, and is weary to be alone. The Madam asks for everyone to leave. Taking rest, she is given privacy. Opening the note and it is from the beautiful server. Thinking its a conveyance of good will, she is again surprised. The young and beautiful server has left to follow her heart and Racckus is the one. He asked to marry her and take her far away from this hell hole. She goes on to say she would always remember her teaching to follow ones heart no matter where the road leads. Remorseful the Madam weeps because now she realizes, those words spoken are the worst piece of advice one could ever give another. For the way ahead is never paved with gold and silver and even if it were, it could not make a difference. As long as life living remains it is an ever-changing process.

Three Men on Horseback

There are three men riding on horse back towards the Warrior, they are all fully armed and dangerous. With weapons drawn, it speaks trouble to any single person traveling alone. The Drinking man follows behind, remotely in the back he has a clear view of everything. Slowing down, he lingers waiting to see how things will unfold. There is but one road and the dangers are very real. In fear of loosing his life, he swallows hard but his mouth is dry. A drink would be good about now. Looking about, there's no escape route and the way back, is not in question. The narrow road only goes two ways, in and out. He watches the Warrior ride into the death zone. Her stallion trots apace, out from behind and over her shoulders she draws a blade like no other he's seen. The Black Blade, flashes in the light, set and ready for the kill.

The Drinking man weighs his options he can make it swiftly pass once the Warrior engages in battle. The tension of the situation is dire, fright brings on his asthma, he needs a pinch of Guinea-hen bush. Into his saddle bag reaching he fumbles to get it. The distance between three men on horse approaching the Warrior closes. His heart is racing as he watches.

The glistening blade captivates one of the men in the group, he's seen that blade before. He remembers her and the long line of death she left behind moons ago in the desert. Raising his hand to stay any further attack, he warns the others not to engage this one. If they do, they are all as good as dead. Ever ready for battle, this is just another confrontation for combat to Leoha. As she gets closer, they all stop pressing to one side, giving her a wide berth and safe passing. Her face is void of emotion, on passing them she stops to put away the blade.

The Drinking man has finally recovered the guinea-hen bush. It brings him to a calm. With his breathing restored, it works and he is back to normal. He knows his chances could never duplicate the like of the Warrior but he still moves forward. To the three Killers on horse back. The Warrior warns, "The messenger who follows is with me. You touch him, you die." They get the message to leave the way open.

The Drinking man is sweating profusely from fright it triggers him to have another asthma attack. He thanks the heavens for his knowledge of the Guinea-hen bush and its many uses. Later it will serve to diminish his bruises. Looking ahead he sees the way is still open. Apprehensively he continues moving ahead with grace and a calm attitude he does not exact feel. When they do nothing, his courage spikes to a new and brave level. He breathes in a breath of comfort with confidence.

The Drinking man doesn't ever realize he owes his safe passage as allowed to the Warrior. With an upright head, protruding chest and strait back, he slows his horse, just to prove a point. Sundering by he takes his time to pass by them his poor choice of attitude, arrogance and snail pace annoys the three riders but they dear not touch the Messenger. Their looks speak unmentionable harm, and a promise which tells him, they can wait until the next time. He speeds up, not realizing the Warrior has moved on ahead out of his sight. Looking around, she is gone and to compensate for lost time he quickly gathers himself. Another three whiffs of his Guinea-hen bush, and off he rides to catch up with the Warrior again.

For all his failing efforts the Sandy Hill coming up on both sides of the road he knows it to be a hot spot for sabotage killers and robbers to entrap innocent victims out of their belongings. Robbing and killing them at the curve makes it more dangerous because one cannot see ahead of the bend. His home town is within miles after the curve. The fear of death rides upon him, he reaches for the guinea-hen bush again and within minutes' quick relief follows. Swallowing deeply his mouth is dry again. Riding at will and as fast as he can, he takes his chances and he manages to keep riding on.

Little does he know that the Warrior stands watching on the top of the Hill. She already has cleared the way by killing all the robbers even the sentries at the top with those at the curb to make the Hills safe again. For the unlucky they are free to pass unmolested, once again the path for traveling is restored. The Drinking man never noticed the Warrior guarding his way. From the Sandy Hill, she jumps down mounts back up onto her stallion and rides away towards the next town.

The Drinking man is riding at high speed toward his home town and so is the Warrior. Her stallion is a special breed with ability to run twice as fast as local horses and is also much larger in size. No one in the Kingdom really knows where such stallions came, but they are found only in the north on Arawak and Carib lands owned and ruled by the superior race known as the Gouddaaians. His determination is to make it home in one piece and to forget about all others. He arrives successfully.

The children dart playfully about the street ways, slowing down so that the dust from the horse can stay settled and not annoy the by passers. The children jump up and down flocking around him, they love seeing the horse, walking alone side they touch its coat. The feel of its silky long tail swashes about evasively from their touch, causing them to giggle even harder. The children squeal out to him by name, he waves them to stay away, but it never works. The ground is dry, dusty and parched, there are no other indications of fresh horse prints he could see. It leaves him to wonder, where is the Warrior. The children continue playing, moving to reach the water well there they stop to be refreshed. Abandoning the horse, the children attentions begin a game of touch me and catch me if you can. Within minutes, they all run back up to the front.

Slowly the Drinking man descends to the ground sore from riding hard, for a long-needed drink of water at the well. Here he inquires to some passing if they have seen a Warrior of great statue, moving about in the town. His description of the Woman is odd and seems unbelievable. In mocking jeers, they tell him to give up the drinking thinking him drunk. They do not know his drinking is the only thing, that suppresses his asthma apart from the guinea-hen bush that provide him relief. The herb is not expensive but it is hard to find unlike alcohol.

The journey home has been long and hot, in the distance, he sees his uncle's brother still up to his old tricks on the outside. Into the air he tosses six blades at once, his uncle, never allowed his brother to preform his blade tricks in his restaurant anymore for fear of another accident. The Drinking man pulls up a drink of water from the well. On bringing the pail down from his mouth, the Warrior in question appears flanked by escorts of children running alongside. The sight of her rare breed of stallion is a marvel and delight they have never had the pleasure of seeing.

The children prance in awe, loving the long rich and golden look of the stallion's tail. It's the apparition dreams are made of come to life. To be sure of his fortune, he throws the remaining water over his head to help him cool down and it is the Warrior. He drops everything and runs out to meet her. Astonished the stares, and gaping mouths open to greet the Warlord Warrior and her prized steed. The town people are everywhere and her unique features and size makes her a featured attraction. The children are enthralled with the size of the large beast of a stallion.

Happily, they lead her to the front of the open tavern. There the Drinker catches up to them and he shoos away the children before taking hold of the stallion's reins. Tying the magnificent beast to the post the towns people look on. The very same people he inquired to about the Warrior stand off ashamed that they scoffed at him. Feeling bad for ridiculing him when he first asked. Stoically they stand isolate among the excited crowd who were oblivious to the earlier exchange. With a grand stand of an extended arm, haling the Warrior the Drinking man is now proud. What happened on the road is still not clear and he asks her, "So what happened to you back there? I though you got lost for a minute and that is why, you needed some one like me to lead the way. What a magnificent creature you ride!"

Leoha swings down to the ground from her mount. Because of her own training in skill of weapon, her focus is trained on his uncles amazing ability to handle seven blades in the air at once. From the surveillance of her surroundings, it's a small town from observation. It paints a quaint atmosphere, taking in the panorama. The Drinking man is elated to have the opportunity to share his community with the Warrior. She is enthralled having visited many towns like this in her travel, "This is a unique town.

As a Warlord Warrior, her travels have taken her to many places, climates and experiences. It always refreshes her to feel the spaces of diverse people, histories and lives. "Who is the man tossing up the blades." Ahh so his uncle prowls have commanded the Warriors attentions. With a little more bravado and an air of nonchalance he flicks his hand dismissing him as not important. "Come on, you don't have to worry about him. That is my uncle but he's not allowed to do that on the inside." Leoha takes her saddle bag and places it over her shoulders. With an extend palm upward in front of her, she indicates to her drinking comrade, "Lead the way."

Following in the wake of her drinking comrade steps, passing the stranger tossing up the blades she is transfixed observing his technique. The Drinking man her friend turns to see she has halted to watch his Uncle. Stepping back up to her side, "I see you are intrigued with my uncle skills. Well! He was not always that good. I remembered when he first started out, he missed once and one went straight through his big toe and from that time on, every one called him hook foot, because of the limp when he walks that big toe remains turned up, like a hook. "Come on let's go in."

The spell of the knives is broken upon entering the tavern. To the Warrior, the Drinking man beacons, "Come! Come on in. Here they always have a table reserved for me and its high time I have a drink. It helps with my asthma, you know!" The walk is not very far. He takes her to a far table in the back corner to avoid friends and questions he is unable to answer. All around there are eyes covertly watching them. On the outside there is buzz of spectators gathering hoping for a peek. The jolly peace of the atmosphere allows the Drinking man to be at at ease.

Together they take a seat facing each other. Its hard not to notice the gathering stares and mummers whispering, so purposefully he positions his back to the crowd, restricting even those at the bar from seeing him well. The Warrior rests her saddle bag on the table beside her. The showing out side still intrigues her, its not often she see's such feats performed. "Your uncle on the outside is good. Maybe you should think about taking up his skills to better protect yourself."

Having though about it before it's not without merit, but the discipline, and concentration it just wasn't him, especially after he almost split his head and toe open at one shot. Navigating around the suggestion he answers. "That would be good! If he is good at more of it. But that is the best of him there. Those things, he throws up in the air are called cutlass. A family to the sword. He along with a Black-Smith, friend, invented those things. And from the time he mastered it, the Black-Smith, called him the Black Sabbo, because that's the name of the black metal used to forge them."

The history lesson, is very impressive and he surprisingly is very informed wryly she jibes "Sabbo, the black cutlass man" and with a sense of humor the Warrior again said "I though you said his name is hook foot?." Smiling at their recollected conversation out to her he corrects. "No, no, I said, that is what they call him. The Drinking man accepts her naive response. It maybe foreign to her to have more than one name where she comes from. Her puzzled expression of face, allows him to feel a sense of superiority for once. The humor of his smile allows her to let it be.

The glow of the lantern on the tables fills the room, in comes the table server and she is very beautiful. Having served many patrons from many places, never has as a server has, she seen such a magnificent built woman like the Warrior accompanying the owner's nephew. With out words her eyes gravitate unnoticeable taking to the Warrior. With her most impressive smile, to him she comments. "Its good to see you back. Your uncle still talks about you not drinking any more. Does he know your here?" The little tart has put him on the spot again, if she wasn't so beautiful and distracting, he could easily dismiss her.

What he wouldn't have done to have a moment with her, and now here she is talking to him. To avoid further small talk with the beautiful server he slightly grins out to the Warrior before turning his eyes back to the server. "Yes! And I'll see him when am finished up," he lied. He had no need to see his Uncle, he only reminds him of his duties. "Now say something to my friend, here." Dow eyed she turns her head to the Warrior and melts, her eyes mist and she is lost in the hazel hues of the Warriors eyes glittering with specks of emerald green blazing.

Stunned she steps back, drawing in a gasp she drops the wine. It splatters, crashing to the floor. Her fingers are still trembling, a flood of color rises in her cheeks as she is embarrassed, the Warrior has her all twisted up, she can't think straight and she runs away from the table. Leoha has become accustomed to odd reactions when people first meet her, and thinks nothing much of it.

The floor manager runs over to the table after witnessing the whole affair. Leoha focus of attention is back on her comrade The Drinker. The mess is quickly cleaned up with the floor manager offering an apology to the unique looking Warrior. Looking at the Warrior up close the floor manager empathizes with the girl who dropped the wine. The Warrior has a magnetic presence this is why the girl was overwhelmed. Another server nearby takes up the slack.

The floor manager has thick black eyebrows, with a slight smile tugging at her lips, he reminds her of the HeShe, back at the Inn Between. The floor manager feels the bluster of privilege to have the Warrior smile at him with affection. Leoha likes this town and the people. There is one difference, this one, the floor manager is all man. The Drinking man humors the table atmosphere to make up for the servant girl's mistake. "You know Warrior. You do have an effect on people like that." The eyes of the many try to have a look at the Warrior, the floor manager defrays them to return to what they were doing. Others want to know where is she from?

By the time the beautiful serving girl had reached the Uncle, she is voiceless and out of breath. It takes her some time to calm, but when she does- the events in the bar are relayed. It is within minutes, the talk about the powerful Warrior in the tavern gets into the ear of the Uncle by the beautiful server. The Uncle orders her to return but she refuses to further work at the Warriors table. This is the strangest behavior his favorite worker has ever displayed, but he lets her be. The uncle is a bit confused about the server's attitude, it does prompt him to look into the matter but his duties prohibit him due to other kitchen matters.

He was once a great fighting General and has seen many natures of persons in his travels. For him, meeting another Warrior bares no significant value. It can only lead to clashing differences so he continues his work. The food order is taken by the floor manager and the Drinking man, head signals nodding to bring out the best. Food and more drinks are brought and placed down on the table. After riding for days, the Warrior is in need of a full meal. Course after course is bought out, elegant dishes of spices and a variety of meats in marinade sauces. Each dish is unique to her and so is the food. She needs her full strength only substance can provide.

In the calm easy atmosphere, she begins to take her fill, tasting at first a portion of each item offered. Small talks while eating is the way of life in these parts. Usually she eats alone, unless formally ordered to join the Kingdom table. In the company of the Drinking man, he has a lot to say. "So how do you like the wine?" It feels good to have an unpretentious exchange of conversation over good food for once. For a moment she feels comfortable enough to let her guard down, casting away the contentions of rival siblings, twisted fates of love, and challenges. "Not bad at all" she said resting the wine mug back on the table.

Now that the way is clear and given for small talk the Drinking man goes on to confess, "Now! I don't want you to think I was following you back there! And if I was! It was only to catch up to ask your name." Thinking back to him, the generous offer, the room, her eyes take a silent look around before offering him her name "Leoha!" Struck by her quick and direct respond, he thought he missed something, so he fumbles resounding the name on his lips, "Aaaaaa Leeeoooha." Clearing her throat she repeats "Yes! Leoha! And I think you're much better when you don't drink." He refuses to lie too the Warrior again, so he simply admits "I know! And you can call me Cidduss."

Leoha continues on, "Well Cidduss! What's your connection with this place?" Looking around the room he replies, "My uncle owns it! And if it hadn't been for you. I would have long been dead. No one can be that lucky." The food is wonderful. The samples on the table only encourages her appetite. He is pleased, watching her enjoying the delicious foods, he goes on. "You know back there,

I never enjoyed the food. The taste was off, don't you think?" "Its because most of the meat there is horse meat. As for the different taste it can even be human meat." Giving her his opinion. "But is that, why you left without paying your bill? she asked.

Behind her there is an elite group of women sitting and she can hear their talks. They make no excuses for wanting to touch her. They want to feel if she is all woman, but are too afraid to come over. Leoha striking features makes her a very intimidating figure. They are more afraid of being killed by her than to intrude and introduce themselves, so they continue talking among themselves knowing the chance will never come.

"No!" he answers "But I'll never eat out there again. That HeShe, came back into my room and stole my money. I only remember, that strange man like woman, fighting with me, they were trying to remove my clothes. I remembered that well, she did get them off and I took up the bed sheet, tied it tight around my ass. Then some one else come crashing into the room and I fell out across the bed from the many drinks. When I did finally come to, I myself had all the trouble undoing the number of knots in the sheet, rapped around my ass. Nooo! I wouldn't have been able to live with my self and that is why I said, no one can be that lucky, as for the bill, debt payed.

I am plagued with asthma and when I drink am ok and now you understand. So, what did you say to those killers on horse back to allow me safe passage. "Well, she did understand some of what the Drinking man said, but not all of it made sense." Nothing much, only that you are the Messenger, was that not good enough?" Surprisingly he smiles at her sense of humor. "No, no, no and they accepted that? Messenger I'll remember that for the next time. Plus, Messenger, has a ring to it. I like it, smart."

Finally, one of the elite group of women finds the courage to walk over to the Warriors table. Midway the Warrior looks at her advancing, the intensity of her gaze stops her cold. The woman reconsiders, loosing courage she turns back only to be scold by her peers. It was a bet, she lost and the thought of having to pay up doesn't make things any easier.

The Barbarians

From the outer skirts of the town Leoha, does not know, there is a group of three-armed looking Barbarian men riding into the town. On spotting the settlement in the distance they are more than pleased to stop into the small-town tavern and have a long and needed drink. There is a dark and dangerous manner to them that keeps the children from running to greet them. Instead at the sight of them many of the children run away to hide or tell their parents. By reputation, they are a group of three bullies,' vagabonds drifting about for what ever mischief and trouble they can find or cause. Their own home land has fallen and been ravished by war, vengeance is always their pursuit and they hate the word general. For it was a group of generals that gave the orders to fireball their village, killing most of their kind. They are but some of the remaining few left to eventually die out. The town people give way on seeing the trouble riding towards the Tavern.

The outdoor entertainer, the great Sabbo, upon seeing them quickly calls it quits and moves out to a safe place, home. The riders stop, they are not only big but strong as ox. Caring about nothing but themselves, they have long abandon civility. Into the Tavern they enter, pushing aside every one and those foolish to get in their way are put down so the way is made open. Up to the bar they approach. The Bartender has stepped out leaving only a single food server who is there getting water for a choking customer sitting on his station.

The Barbarians take no note of the other room occupants their primary focus is only on the one standing behind the bar counter.

With a bad attitude they call him over only for peace sake he abandons his duties to assist the three Barbarians. Without warning to the floor server one of the Barbarians reaches over the bar counter and grabs hold of him by his shirt, it frightens him. He tries to pull back, but the hand is just too strong. Trying to explain he is not the Bartender is fruitless, he doesn't realize his talks is falling on deaf ears. To the Barbarian holding him, frighten and in fear of loosing his life he rambles on pleading "Please! There is a big lady choking on my station, she claims when ever she eats too fast, it causes her to see her dead grandmother, who never really liked her but want her to come down and visit but she is still in the world of the living and it hinders her breathing and drinking water make it go away, she really needs the water, can you let me go?"

The rapid response confuses for a minute the Barbarian. Looking him in the face, wondering what is he mumbling about, it makes absolutely no sense to him. Gripping the server even more tightly into him he said. "You little man! You know what your problem is." Wide eye and frantic the young server begins twisting his head from left to right tortured because of the Barbarian's putrid breath. The Rotten teeth, grimace out at him making the Barbarians think he wants to get away. The frightened server only shakes out his head. The Barbarian cuts him off short, going on to say. "You talk too much! Three shots of cactus juice and one glass of lions milk with a froth top."

With that said, the Server is punched in one eye to be clear he get's the message. Laughing out at each other for sport, the innocent server is given another blow to his other eye. With two black eyes now, the strong Barbarian pushes him off and he falls hard to the ground. For a minute his sight is blurred as he struggles to get up, the Barbarians all laugh out at him. Taking advantage of the opportunity to escape the Barbarians clutches, with speed the Food Server grabs hold of the glass of water and high tails out of there. The commotion is heard in the kitchen, alerting the boss who is Cidduss uncle. From where the Warrior sits, she can see everything happening but not Cidduss, his back is turn to the escalating situation. Cidduss hears the noise but thinks nothing about it, this is a tavern, its just another celebration.

Ever alert Leoha wants to avert another confrontation, the last one didn't go too well. So, she let it be, the Warrior refuses to get involved. The Bartender having return from the outside, wants to know who is the vagabond serving in his place. He rushes up to confront the Barbarian serving his friends, only to be slapped and thrown back across the bar into the others. He is pummeled and punished with blows on the ground he balls up in a fetal position to protect himself.

It's at this moment the Boss comes in and on seeing the disturbance of things he jumps into action. Taking hold of the first Barbarian behind the counter he tosses him back over the bar counter to the others. Falling hard on them, they collapse under his weight. The injured Bartender creeps off to safety.

The injured Food Server with the two black eyes and swollen face has made it back to the fat lady on his station. Approaching with the glass of water, her head is in a down position. At first it appears like she is having another of her spells. In order to get her attention, he shakes her a little. She snaps up jolted as he holds out the drinking water to her, she takes it. Lifting the water to her lips, raising her head to drink she sees the blows to his face. The ghostly images begin to appear again to her. Frightened from the images, she freezes, as the water glass slides dropping from her hand, her large unbalanced size tips over to the ground, dead. This doesn't look so good to the server he doesn't know what to do now.

Gathering themselves up from the ground, the old man will pay for this. The Barbarians retaliate by throwing anything over the bar counter at The Uncle. Their actions of disrespect enrage him, people in the tavern begin to scatter. Angry, Uncle leaps to the air and over the bar out at the Barbarians teaching them a lesson in good manner. Screaming to the three idiots, the Uncle cries. "You fools! Don't you idiots, know who I am! I am the Boss of this establishment, the great General Wardoo!" So the old man is a General contemplates the Barbarians, this does nothing to endear him to the men who have disrupted his place of business. Quickly picking themselves up ready for battle, the time has come to teach this General Wardoo, the wages of war is death. Finally, a recipient worthy of wrath, for all that was done to their homeland, this General will pay the price.

Out at once the great general one to three, the Barbarians cry out. "General Wardooooo! Taste my foot! Together the three Barbarians, attack the old General and the fight ignites. In the far back, the Warrior and Cidduss are still eating. With a nod of her head, she indicates to him of things happening at the bar. Turning around at first glance in his chair he gets up to have a much closer look at things. The finesse of years of battle training on the field has honed and conditioned his reflexes. Even the years haven't diminished his agility. His uncle appears to be taking care of his business as far as he can see. It will teach them a lesson not to make trouble in his uncle place.

There is a sudden turn. The General no longer in his prime, begins to waver, his stamina is not what it once was. So, he begins to run out of steam. The odds turn against him, with the Barbarians fighting him as a one-unit force. Cidduss runs in across to help, knowing the odds are also more than probable to work against him. Hopeful, now is the time to show the Warrior his courage in view of saving his life. If all else fails, he's assured of one thing the Warrior won't let him die. Getting involve to help his injured uncle he finds out that to is another mistake. The Barbarians are strong and they make him pay with blood and everyone else stands at distance afraid of getting killed.

From the look of things, if someone doesn't do something, the boss and his nephew could be killed. Frantically thinking who would want to help, Sabbo comes to mind. Creeping off to the outside, the bartender hurries to find Sabbo, the Boss brother for aide. When Sabbo sees the Bartenders face, its evident that things in the bar have turned for the worst as he anticipated. Grabbing up his cutlasses he trudges forward with intent. Through the door welding his knives into the air, in comes the great Sabbo. Tossing his seven dangerous cutlasses through the air, the Barbarians are forced to move further back. Closer, they are pushed toward the Warriors table.

The Boss is injured and Cidduss are both elated and happy to see him. The unpredictable swords have not been used since the last situation that ended tragically. Both stumble out the way to safety. The Barbarians have never before witness seven weapons swirling in motion through the air at once, by one man. It proves he is a mighty skilled man. Moving further back away from the rotating blades, they wait for an opening to defeat the swirling blades before them. In all truth the great Sabbo has never been in a real battle before. He is an entertainer, this role he now playing is not a show but a confrontation to live. He must breathe steady if he's to pull this off, this battle is real. His remarkable skills hinder them.

The dinning crowd scatters out to safety just in time. The break comes for the Barbarians, the great Sabbo drops one of his cutlasses hard on his hook toe. The pain shoots like a fire through his body fresh as before, when he had his first accident with the knives. Still in motion the cutlass rotation is not as formidable as before. His disadvantage evident shows on his face, sweat beads pop, dripping from his left eyebrow rolling into his eye it begins to hinder his vision. Besides the shooting pain, his fear of them gives him away. Simultaneously the Barbarians look at his distorted foot and they capitalize on his big toe.

He never liked covering his foot, its was not something he was ashamed of. It was an accident and anyone who dared to treat him different because of it, well he has a thing about that. The defect has in fact helped him, changed the way he thinks. It has brought him closer together with the mother of nature. Grabbing a nearby small but heavy vase one of the Barbarians throws it, and it hits the target, the shock from the impact shakes Sabbo to the core, the throb in his big toe is excruciating and he stumbles back on his hook foot, loosing another cutlass. One by one the cutlass drops from the air, leaving Sabbo standing venerable. Black Sabbo knows he is as good as dead, still he stands firm.

Leoha is still eating the fare before her as she observes the diadem of the situation. Out of nowhere the beautiful server who never returned runs up falling to her knees before the Warrior crying out, "Yes! I do care! End my life as payment for them!" What conundrum is this? The Warrior is confused and puzzled by the servers displayed outburst. Overwrought with feelings she can't deny anymore she hangs her head without further words to her. The Warrior mind was up made long ago the actions she now takes is as a defender. She leaps from the table to the air pulling out the Black Blade.

Into the fighting zone she comes down with swift death already prepared for the three Barbarians. In an instance the mater is resolved. The ghost of speed moves her, taking her back into the air bending over in reverse she lands. She has returned to the very same spot in front of the beautiful server still on her knees. From the table she takes up the saddle bag, her time here is done. The General did not make it his business before to meet this Warrior of such great skill he has never witness in all his years of battle. The sword is unlike anything he's even seen. If she had not intervened, he and his nephew would surely be dead. He must make restitution for his earlier manner. The Drinker has yet to put it all together, everything happened so fast. On seeing the old General moving fast toward her, Leoha will not allow civilities to detain her once again. It's becoming the same with every town she is engaged.

Out through the side window Leoha leaps escaping to the outside and is gone. Limping, he is still stiff from the fight, his muscles are tight and painful from lack of use. Before the General could see out the window and follow her she's gone. He wanted to thank her, he can't let her leave without a salute of gratitude. Running with the last of his strength, quickly back up front to the outside he arrives. Not even her stallion is there, not even a lingering trail. Only the foot prints of her large beast mark the way she left. The day is soon over and the sun is low in the sky. Forlorn at the missed opportunity he returns to inside. The old General make his way around the tumble of chairs and tables being put back in place.

With the removal of the bodies, the place is soon back to normal. His brother is waiting for him, they have not spoken to each other for the first in many moons because of a family dispute. The hook foot Sabbo, and his brother hug each other, mending the breach in their estranged relation. Apologizes are forth coming from both sides, saying how sorry they are to one another. Sabbo, brother informs him, that from now on, he is no stranger to his place. He is welcome to continue his cutlass show on the inside for all to see, conditionally of course with safety measures put in place. A place to perform was all he ever wanted. He knew in his heart he could make a great act this was the chance to make it. It would go on from that time in his life where Sabbo went from making pennies on the outside to indoors where it becomes the greatest town show ever.

Cleattius and The Guardians

Cleattius is not pleased with his behavior or lack there of performance at the temple of the White Lamb. He is even more disappointed after roaming the vast wildness for a full cycle of the first moon, before finally realizing he is lost for directions. Having to return back to the only person within miles of miles, is the old man with the usual sized head sitting and laughing on the wall. He is losing even more time having to do things this way, he's not happy, but holding on to a smothering fury. Just bellow the surface simmers that hate, the laughter and jokes of the old man stretches Cleattius patience to the point.

He would find relish in the privilege of shutting the old hoot up, from chastising and scolding him for good. To exasperate things further, his mount has developed a limp, hindering their speed. Besides wanting to silence the old laughing hoot, he would like to also do away with his horse. If not for the long and treacherous trek back home killing him, the chance of meeting any body else in these parts is next to none. The few drops of water in his sac are all that's left. It would be suicide to killed his horse now.

Only after falling to his knees, the old man's earlier request to have his true name is given. The old magi have pity for him, he's given mercy and directions to the way out. Riding off he looks back and its an uneasy feeling, it causes him to tremble, no one is on the wall. Wasting no time Cleattius high tails it out from there on his horse, breathing heavily. The late evening was now upon him and he refuses to stick around any longer. Erie sounds and shadows flickers with the wind apart from feeling a little spooked, these parts groan of torments lost. The random sounds make one think they are at the end of the world. The haunting event stays with him like a heavy cloak even after he has finally reached the Kingdom.

It has been three moons of riding, the embers of the unknown still linger. The breaking of morning buds opens with a new day and he can use a good rest. His disappointment leads him directly into the Throne room. There he finds his sister Libra on the Throne. She is drafting a document of Kingdom matters more than likely. On seeing him she stops. Watching his approach, he finally comes to a stop before the Throne. He enters attired in informal garb, his face is tired and drawn. It tells her he has had a long and tedious journey. "How can I be of assistance dear brother?" she speaks. With a few words Cleattius dejection is uttered, "I just want to know, why my authority is always being undermined or should I say challenged?"

The King has no idea of his referral, so attentively she says "Am afraid am not getting you clearly Cleattius. Could you please be more precise in your words?" Looking around at the many changes in the Throne room, he confides. "What makes your authority over rule mine? You are just sitting in until father returns, are you not? You have not been announced king. Your royal seal is no greater than mine, is it?" Libra empathizes with Cleattius it's not her fault father chose her. What ever Cleattius believes she's doing her best to fulfill the role given to her. To make him better understand their positions, she proclaims. "This is not about what you think Cleattius, but about where I sit and where you stand. Are you not standing before me?" She asks.

The king stands up and again she utters "Now, how can I further be of help, brother. You look like you could use a good rest. Why don't you finish this later, I do have much to do, let's say after rest? Returning to her paper work, she waits for Cleattius to remove himself. The King knows its not of his nature to give in so easily. At first, he doesn't move, it's to satisfy himself by standing against her.

She gives him a final uncompromising demand. "By means of your royal seal brother, why don't you order the guards to arrest me and you can take up the position until father returns." Her blunt approach, unnerves him temporarily the shocking mandate ties his tongue. She dares him to put his royal seal to the ultimate test, how dare she. Her challenge lights hell fire through his lungs. Out from his garments, he shows out to the guards his supreme seal of authority before crying "Royal seal!" At attention, they all stand officially to greet the Prince, Cleattius. Never one for humor or familiarity, he is serious when he commands, "Guards, arrest her!" No one moves.

King Libra and the guards all look at Cleattius. The order should never have been stated, but he was provoked to act. Now frail and disappointed he tries to back off but it too late. The King, iron look speaks out, repeating his own words. With out emotion, Libra instructs, "Guards arrest him." In swift motion brother Cleattius finds the pointed end of lethal spears and blades at his throat, head, neck, heart, and all his lower vital body points. He dares not move, defeated he get the picture the hard way. Still looking on at him the king knows he gets the message by his lowered stance. He is much aware of the Throne guard's abilityies, to kill without the person feeling the touch. "Guards stand down," she orders, and they do.

Moving back in position as if they were never there, King Libra watches her brother Cleattius reaction. He rubs his hand up against his neck and throat taking stock of himself. Looking down at himself, there are no apparent injuries. "How is this possible, Libra?" The lack of response from the guard's compliance has wounded his image. He continues to ask not pleased with the out come. With affirmation she said "By father's orders, how else." He won't admit it but he's glad to still be alive after such a treasonous act. Turning to walk away the King calls "Cleattius!!!" In his tracks he stops, what else does she want now, she has proven her authority. Turning around makes him wonder why.

From the Throne the King reaches for what appears to be an edict. Tossing it out to him, he catches it in hand. The King, "I need you to deal with it as soon as you have rest up. You can take what you need. Please, do be most discreet." sarcastically he can't help his attitude "Any further inquiries?" She emits, "A rich merchant by light and a beggar by dark, I expect you to catch this thief and have him here to be question before the next Cycle of the wind. I want you to leave as soon as possible!"

With out further question to the edict Cleattius interjects "I hope this is not your way to refrain me from my long quest?" Cleattius is always suspicious of her intentions, not that she's not to blame. As children Libra talent to plot action didn't always end with him succeeding, even the games. With a slight smile out to him, she indicates, no harm done. "No brother, only a way to redeem you back into my sight. Maybe if you would stay around and stop following abstract dreams about this so called Fifth Element, you may know more about what goes on around here, and it's good to have you back." With spite, "Once finish with this mission, I'll do just that!", and off Cleattius goes. King Libra knows, if she can only keep him busy, it will keep him away from Dicious. With that said her father's last words resound in her consciousness. "There cannot be an inner war." Turning her attentions back to her duties the King continues reviewing circulation deeds of the Kingdom, that her father left in her care.

Valley of the Dust Storm

The open plain spread wide before her, the Warrior rides with high speed, in the vacant beauty holds treacherous conditions. Across the open plains, a large dust storm is moving in ahead of her. She must choose, go around or strait down the middle in hope to live and see out the opposite end. The magnitude of such a storm from what is visible, defiantly erupts making both considerations impossible. Varying off away from the big dust storm she pushes the mighty beast, he knows his job. To its running limit he performs. On the wind she rides on and on making every second count. They make it just in time to see the end of the sand storm pass by. In the process of evading the storm she has lost direction and now finds herself emerging into an unknown valley.

From the looks and direction of the sun this is uncharted territory, a place, heated and very dry in the middle of No Mans Land. Looming in the distance of her stands a huge old structure with high walls on all four sides. Strangely there's an abnormality flourishing as an oasis in a desert, it is green grass, twenty feet reaching out all around from the walls of the structure. The rest of the land surrounding it is barren spaces. She could tell from its large mass it was once an enormous Kingdom of some kind. Bringing the firing stallion to a trot, slowly she leads the mount around most of the outer perimeter until she comes upon a very large gate, securing the entrance.

The gate is partially open, but not enough for a rider to enter. The noise of children wafers over the far side of the outer wall. Peering to take a better look, she sees what appears to be two homeless boys throwing stones up at a large green apple tree. All they want is an apple treat. High in the large tree branches rests the objects of their desire. A branch full of green apples sits hanging over the top of the massive wall. It's much too high for the two boys to reach even with the stones. They are so engrossed, intent on getting just one, no one pays attention to her coming. Leoha smiles to herself, to be young again. Many orchards in the Kingdom received the same favorable attention when she was a child. Unlike these boys, she remembers climbing so many different sizes and shapes of trees to obtain her prizes.

When she does pulls up on them, they are so surprised they dare not run. The bulk of woman before them leaves them speechless. From her stallion looking down at them they need water as well as nourishment. To assist them better she pulls out her water bag tosses it out to the oldest of the two. Her eyes are gentle as they look to one another, and they both drink their belly's full. Kindly its given back over to her with words of thanks.

The boys find her to be different from others who just want to catch them and whip them for feeding from the apple tree. From her stallion leaping upward onto high wall she picks three apples and somersaults back down to the ground. The boys have never before seen such amazing movements and a person such as she. "What are your names?" Then the oldest of the two said. "I am called Splitt and my young friend is Ttail. So, impressed with her skills Ttail says," Lady! How did you do that? Can you teach us to fly like that?" He is so cute even with the smears of dirt on his body. She speaks their language, "Well Splitt an Ttail, that would take time." and they both smile out at the way she placed their names together. Her tone, makes them even more comfortable.

Out to each boy she throws an apple, together they eat and the two boys come to trust her. The apple does taste good and Leoha is refreshed as well. Looking to her Ttail innocent eyes stare up at her and he asks, "Lady, are you also homeless? The other quickly give him a tap to the back of his head for asking a dumb question. Obvious in conflict with intruding into her affairs, they both smile it off.

The Undaunted King Gouddaa of the Arawaks and Caribs

It isn't long before they are informing her of the surrounding condition. Splitt speaks "We live away from here and we have no way of getting a belly full so" He is interrupt by Ttail audible expression "So we are taking apples to full our belly's. Its best not to stay around here lady. The Madam doesn't like people stealing apples off their tree so we have to go." Splitt begins looking out for the danger, while saying to the Warrior, "I think you can take care of your self but we must leave before some one else comes out."

A solemn shadow covers Ttail face, with a quivering lower lip he remembers the death of their close friend. Ttail confides, "Yes! That's how we lost our friend Tulli, they killed him for stealing one apple. We take mostly, the ones on the ground! The others are just too high to reach so sometime we throw stones and knock them down but we are not thieves. If mother ever finds out, she will kill us. Our friend Tulli, did ask them to have the apples from the ground, you know. I'll kill her too if I have the chance." with tears trailing from his eyes.

Judging from the boys, they look to be no more that thirteen and fourteen. Already they talk about killing like its dinner. Splitt then cuts in adding on saying "I think, they may not have killed him. If he did not go on the inside begging to have the apples in his hand. What do you think lady?" Killing a child for fruit she finds the cruelty savage. Leoha knows by being on the outside of the Kingdom stranger things have occur and strange is an understatement because when the order of things is broken, chaos becomes the settlement.

Looking down into their pleading eyes, Leoha takes a breath first so to make the boys better understand she'll keep it as simple as possible. "Sometime, its most difficult to determine how anyone would react but what I do think, it is best you two return home before you're caught out here." If ever a time to give is given, its obligation to is bestow liberation. Reaching her hand into her bag, "Maybe there is something in my bag you can take with you, just don't open it! Give it to your parents and they would know how to use it."

What an unexpected day. At best the boys hoped for maybe finding an apple on the ground. Now after drinking from her pouch, and having an apple a piece, they have something else from the salvage. Their happy smiles couldn't be more appreciated. From her saddle bag she pulls out the remaining half of Big Nasty's lootz and she hands it over to the eldest boy. The weigh of the bag causes Splitt knees to buckle a little pulling him down. What ever is in the bag is heavy. Looking back up at the Warrior holding the bag. Leoha instructs him, "Just give it to your parents. Its for both of you." Together they begin to each feel its weight, while admiring the pretty colored red cloth. Curious and inquisitive like most children Ttail asks, "Lady! Why is it so heavy?" He wants to open it and again he is smacked to the back head by Splitt.

The prickling on her neck tingles, her Warrior instinct alerts that someone is coming from around the corner of the wall. The boys are unaware of the pending danger, she wants them out of harms way. They have already endured much. Her voice is sharp and curt, "Go now! just go." Quickly thanking her they have only the chance to make two steps. Out from around the blind corner of the high wall with a dart like weapon in hand is a young lady crying out, "You thieves! Stay where you are or I'll kill you both!" With fright in their eyes, they look to the Warrior. She tells them, "Keep moving!" That's all the encouragement they need. She didn't have to say it again. The two boys break off running. This infuriates the Young Lady even more. Because they disobeyed her words, she launches out her weapon at them.

The dart is stopped in mid air by the Warrior knocking it out from its intended target with the remaining piece of apple in her hand. The dart falls to the ground. Livid the ladies feature twist in raged and she looks into the eyes of the Warrior studying her. "You know! You should watch, where you throw those things." Leoha having been appraised of nefarious acts by the boys is primed to act. Their eyes lock on each other, Leoha waits for the young lady's next move. From what she has seen of the young lady its only a matter of when. The Young Lady ready to enforce her principal rights cry out "Thief! I don't know who you are, but you let them get away, so you have to pay for the apple! As well as those of the boys."

The Young Ladies high temper matches her red hair. From the looks of the strange unique clothing and the rare stead the Warrior rides there is every reason to pause in her tirade. Her mind flashes back to how the Warrior was able to stop a moving dart in mid-air with only a piece of apple. Without warning the Young Lady launches

The Undaunted King Gouddaa of the Arawaks and Caribs

another attack with her hidden darts, missing the Warrior by inches. Before she can act again, the Warrior kicks a small stone with her foot out at the Young Ladies hand, the shot upon impact bruises her. Wobbling she shakes her hand from the pain. The Young Lady is too ashamed to cry out, holding a breath she becomes even more puffed up. The thought of a child being killed over an apple, resurfaces in her thoughts, and she questions the Young Lady. "Tell me youngster. Does the apples value more than your life?" The Young Lady does not grasp the meaning behind the Warrior words and the spews of her rants answers, "I don't believe in answering foolish questions. Have you every known, apples to be valued more than life?"

The girl is rude and naive showing no remorse or respect, she refuses to back down. Leoha could snap her neck at any time but because she knows not what lies behind these great wall safe guards her words. "Then you should thank me for not killing you!" In a huff, the Young Lady grasps the meaning and she secures her stand "Even if you kill me! You still won't get out this Valley alive!" That's enough to warn and alert the Warrior. "Then I won't kill you and maybe you will let me out." With a proud disposition she cuts her eyes prudently at the Warrior and she whistles for help.

At the sound, the alarm is raised and a small grade of ten armed men with spears and shields comes running out from behind the blind corner of the high wall. The young lady stands smug and vindictive watching, they encircle the Warrior and her stallion taking battle formation. Leoha unsheathes her sword, pulling out the Black Blade. She realizes she is looking at a remnant of what is left of the gigantic mighty Kingdom, this could only have been the Kingdom of the Arks. Now confidence of the upper hand, the Young Lady boldly insist "You can pay and leave, or die and stay!"

Suddenly the battle formation is broken by a single man. It appears to be the leader and he walks over to the Young Lady, ever so softly he whispers but it's audible that the Warrior to hears. When the captain of small infantry answers the call, he is surprised to see the Warrior. Having believed it was just another kid caught stealing the apples. The Blade she is holding is like nothing he has seen before. "There is something, that doesn't add up about this one. I suggest we question her first. Please do not make a rash decision. That Blade she holds. I have long witness coming across the desert." She is callous and loud caring nothing about what he speaks and she makes this clear out to him. "I don't care what Desert she come from. Just follow my lead and don't you ever again break the formation!" His advice falls on deft ear and he runs returning back in line thinking what a mistake this must be.

Abrasively chastised for his opinion, from out the corner of his eyes he witnesses the venom of a poison butterfly kill a crawling beetle on a near by stone. This sign is enough to tell him the out come should they attack the Warrior. Being in charge of the nine he gives out a signal. The Young Ladies Grand Father is already on his way down to see her after hearing the alarm of an intruder on the grounds. He watched the last of the soldiers running outside and he follows at his pace. He's not as young as he once was to keep up, age has taken its toll.

The Young Lady has given the orders to attack the Warrior but not one man moves and baffled she wonders why. With her Grand Father now in sight, his eyes take to the Warriors Blade like a magnet of fire. How could it be, it's the same Blade he remembered as a young boy that brought down a whole Kingdom, his fathers Kingdom. The Ark Ones. His heart starts to race at the sight, out loud the Grand Father cries to the men. "Stand down! Stand down! Get back! And they all do.

The ill-tempered Young Lady riles in disgust, she walks up to the Headman of the nine and slaps him in front of all his men for disobeying her orders. Then she stalks across the distance to meet her grand father. The grand father knows much of the Black Blade of death dipped in black magic. The welder is not the one he remembered, plus, she is just much too young to be that one. His grand daughter is screaming out of control, he has spoiled her to his own distress. With her Grand Father behind her, she boldly walks up to the Warrior. "Don't you think this is over? She reaches out to discipline the Warrior with a slap but misses. The Warriors has quick reflex an in an instant she finds the Blade now pressed against her throat. She may not be the original welder who destroyed the Kingdom but her skills appear just as lethal.

The Grandfather, loves his Granddaughter, not wanting her to be killed, cries out. "Warrior! Please don't!" For the Grandfather sake, the Warrior removes the Blade and puts it away. The Grandfather is relieved his privileged brat of a Granddaughter runs up to him. The Granddaughter counteracts explaining how the Warrior injured her hand, and took apples from the tree, showing no respect.

Forlorn, his Granddaughter can be so exhausting, in front of the Warrior the Grandfather studies his Granddaughters countenance before emitting. "Something I should have done long ago." With force the Grandfather draws back his hand and slaps her once across the face. The startling blow stocks her. Falling to the ground from the impact wide eyed with questions, she gets up with glossy eyes. In her embarrassing madness, she looks to her grand father crying. "I hate you!"

Backing away she holds the side of her face where he hit her before running back inside. The Grandfather nods his head out to the head guard, to say thanks. The head guard nods back. The guards all hurry off back inside behind the gate. All is now clear, leaving only the Warrior and the Grandfather to face each other. The Grandfather walks up to the Warrior, the winds are churning a sudden gush strikes up the dust, taking with it the dead dry leaves from the ground. Over the open plains, dried and cracked soil serves as a reminder of the existing harsh conditions.

Apologetically the Grandfather recites. "Warrior! please forgive my Granddaughters behavior, she is still young and a little head strong. May I ask your name?" Still very alert she turns to the side "Leoha is my name." The Grandfather admires the beautiful stead, looking at the magnificent beast standing beside him. He offers, "A stallion such as this, is from the forbidden north. I am the last of the Arks family, I remember your blade very well. Where did you get it?" It's no surprise that the blade has a history, considering it once belonged to her arch rival. "From the grave!" She replies, still alert.

The Grandfathers last name rings a bell, but she says nothing of it. The Grandfather goes on to say, "Well Leoha, your name also tells me, you are from the far north. Should you ever be passing this way again. Please do stop in. It would make up for my grand daughter poor behavior." There are many questions to be answered if time permitted, but as it is enough to suffice her, the contentions have dissipated Leoha sees the old Grandfather is still strong and even stronger in his ways. His apology is enough. Looking at him admiring her stallion she settles herself returning the sentiments. "Think nothing much of it. If you are the last! It's your duty to discipline her."

For a moment the Grandfather forgets himself, stern in his ways. The biting retort of his nature answers, a signature emotion she recognized in the grand daughter's temperament "You don't have to remind me. I know what needs to be done." Searching her memories Leoha recalls the name Ark One to be that of one she once met in the gardens back in the Kingdom with her sister Libra. He was one of her fathers superior fighting Guards reserved to watch over Libra. "Thanks for your kind manner. Would you be some how related to the Ark One?" She asks.

This stranger has knowledge of his people, this colors his perception favorable toward her. Stepping in closer, the old Grandfather proudly acknowledges, "Yes! Yes! I am his Grandfather, and I am the last generation of the Arks Ones. Do you know of him? Have you seen him?" She not wanting to reveal her status and what she knows of the Ark One, she replies "We did once cross paths." Favor turns sour, his countenance darkens at the news. He pauses sensitively considering, in his time crossing path meant a challenge to the death. He moves away before having his say "Judging from the little I have seen. The Blade you carry is a Blade of death. Did he challenge you? Have you killed him?" His alarming words awakens her instincts, pulling back she corrects the perspective "No! No, Its nothing like that, so please. . ."

The Grandfather contours the conversation by saying, "Good! That's good! That's good to hear because if you did. I would not let you out of this Valley alive." Staying alive in these parts is vital to her plans, he and his Granddaughter speaks the same words, presuming she will never get out alive. Little do they know she has already figured out the place is booby trapped. Not to alarm him, she is not the least afraid of him nor his Granddaughter. "Thanks for the warning and I'll remember that for the next time,"

The Undaunted King Gouddaa of the Arawaks and Caribs

It is too late, the Grandfather realizes his mistake he has just given away, the Valley secrets. His words are harsh and direct but honest. The Grandfather and his daughter do not intimidate Leoha, her elite training and Warrior skills far surpasses the normal soldiers training. She knows what she's able of doing in a battle, the dead mass of graves in her wake are a testimony to her abilities. With a little quirk in her eyes, the curving twist of her smile warns him. "I think am able to acknowledge now! Just where your Granddaughter headstrong behavior come from."

The Grandfather ashamed of the observation, takes in a deep breath, turning to the Warrior, he concedes. "I don't mean to offend you Warrior but we the Ark Ones, have always been a headstrong family, and may be, just may be, its apart of our down fall but it is the truth. I have long heard the rumors of my Grandson, the Ark One, visiting a princess in the far north in the house of King Gouddaa. Should you ever return there, could you try and find him and tell him, his Grandmother has already passed away and he needs to come home. He was moving around with his younger sister who has already returned home with escort. What ever his motive was for carrying her behind him. I may never know but I am certain, it was for his own personal gain. When I was a fighter, I fought for gain and honor but now that am older. I no longer can see the gain or the honor for at the end of days, when the heart of a King and the heart of a beggar are laid side by side at deaths gate, will both be welcome?"

The Grandfathers illustration causes her to ask, "Can you tell me, who is the King? who is the beggar? With a solemn expression on his face, he bow's his head before saying, "If only I knew." Leoha knows better, even if he won't admit it. "But you do, know." The Warrior is shrewd she doesn't miss a thing. He ponders rephrasing the question and its connotation. Her meaning leads him no other alternative but to admit "The question is yours to ask." The experience of boys, is a lingering thought she wants answers to. "Then tell me! How did the little boy die?"

The fact that the stranger has been told information about the child that was killed puts him on the spot. Suppressed memories he wants to forget return, stumbling few steps back he places his right had over his heart, securing his pain. The situation causes him to groan, submitting honestly to her question. "I have long wanted to forget about it, but here I am and with a stranger from the far north. A traveler brings it back to me.

We are not killers here but food is. The Valley is large and dry and yet green flourishes only here. The apple tree bears fruit all year around. How? We don't really know! But that is how we out here survive. Yes! They did beat the boy and so strangely he died. I had the in-house physician look into the boy's death, it was determined, the boy had a weak heart." Leoha can't shake the image of the little boy's tear-stained face talking of what was done to his friend. "Can you make compensation?"

With remorse and regret the Grandfather peers into the eyes of the Warrior, making a pledge. "Yes! By not ever letting it happen again." The Warrior leaps to her stallion leaving parting words, "Old father! I thank you for the words of wisdom. Should I see your grand son, I shall give him your message to return home at once? The Grandfather says nothing, but watches as the Warrior rides away and disappears through the dust. The sword strapped to her back is his last vision of the Warrior. The Blade that once transformed the relations of his Kingdom departs the premises, this time thanks is given.

The Grandfather returns to the inside of the holdings only to be told by the Head Guard, that he did all he could to stop his Grand daughter from leaving. As always, his efforts are met with resistance and the Grandfather understands. He is told, she left through the back gate taking his horse and weapon. The Grandfather carefully mulls over his Granddaughter intentions. He instructs the Head Guard not to send out the men after her but to leave it until she calms down.

The Head Guard likes the young lady, but he could never appreciate her quick and volatile temper. He is most concerned and he fears the worst will come of it. He knows its important he conciliate this situation for what it is between he and the girl and help his Granddaughter from being further hurt by the Warrior or even killed. Confirming his Granddaughter action out to him, he again said "She left to ambush the Warrior at Stonebridge." This gets the Grandfathers full attention. He thinks back to the talks earlier with the Warrior and he concludes, should his Granddaughter engage battle with the Warrior, she will not kill her, but save her for his sake and he accepts things as that.

The Warrior still rides at high speed through the Dry Valley. She heightens her instincts to echo the location, with the help of her stallion they will find the way out. She is heading out of Dry Valley and directly into the Granddaughters path way on stone bridge. The Granddaughter sits ready, prepared armed with her Grandfathers Blade. Its a Stratus Blade one of the best forged, able to break the hardest of metal. She stand's in wait to split the Warrior strait down the middle.

The bridge is called Stone Bridge because of its four gigantic stone laid two on each side, a length no less than thirty feet with an open top. The width makes is only good enough for two wagons to pass at a time. Its a tight berth and a good place for ambush. Pressed for time she must reach the temple of the White Lamb before the last Sun Sleep. Having no time to engage in battle with anyone she rides. Her keen vision allows her to see the Stone Bridge in her view. A dust trail moves toward her the Granddaughter knows it is the Warrior coming in fast. The Warrior can now see her on the bridge but the Granddaughter can only see a big cloud of dust moving in fast.

The Granddaughter can now see the Warrior coming in fast and she stands ready to split anything that crosses in half. The Granddaughter miscalculates, she has never before seen a stallion move so fast. If she doesn't get out the way of its force, the speed pressure alone will hurt her. The fast-moving beast moves forward towards the crossing. The Warrior pushes the beast to ride even faster. Leoha knows the Granddaughter is out for revenge. It's time to teach the Granddaughter a lesson and give her an awaking moment she will remember for the rest of her life. The event unfolds right in front her eyes she must move or suffer injury. The beast is moving too fast, in a panic she is clipped by the side of its belly and thrown hard against the large bolder. She sees everything in slow motion, just before she passes out.

The beast front legs reach the start point of the bridge. The Warrior leaps into the air moving on the wind above the length of Stonebridge, coming down at the opposite end astride on the fast-moving stallion. A short time later, the Granddaughter comes to not realizing she had passed out not knowing the amount of time that has passed. Up from the ground, she gets up sluggishly to her feet, looking to see the Warrior riding off from her challenge. Regrettable she realizes she is all alone and not even the dust from the beast lingers. To satisfied herself. She cries out to the lonely valley wind. "Warriorrr! Warriorrrrr! I'lll get youuuuuu."

The only response she receives is the echo of her voice back. On the ground she sits disappointed with herself while pondering her next move. On arriving home her Grandfather is pleased to see she's uninjured. Out of respect to him, she asks if she could be excused to her room. This manner is so unlike her, which he finds most strange. The quiet of her nature, plagues him a little but he lets it be. It isn't until later she leaves quietly to go after the Warrior, without him or anyone knowing.

Urobeha's Visit Among the Leviathans

Much time has passed and Urobeha joy has expanded throughout the town and out to the women working in barnyards and beyond. The harvest of the village is plentiful and everything seems to be back in balance. The morning is young and Urobeha, feels the need to spend more time with the ladies working at the barn. Having developed a liking for working with her hand, on this particular morning she enters the barn house. The women are engrossed with talks about a strange looking man with muscles like a lion, long black hair down his back and with strength of a bull. No one in the barn yard knows why or when he was placed there. He is there plowing the land alongside the leviathan of the fields with whom he also sleeps alongside. In their joy, they share their conversation with Urobeha. Together they all laugh out at the thought of a man living, working, and sleeping with the great beast that plows the land.

It isn't until days after, Urobeha begins to think about the stories told and it starts to intrude with her sleep. Her curiosity takes the best of her. One early morning under the cover of darkness, she goes out and visits the fields. This is where the beast and the man work by day and slept by night. The tall grass is high, slowly she makes her way through the rice field to the other side.

Animals are sleeping everywhere in the field but she is not the least afraid of them. She keeps moving showing no fear of them, they do not take much notice of her. In the distance among the largest of animals there is the man chained by his hand and feet. There is something strange around his neck, he is naked. His hard snoring gives him away and she dare not approach any closer. A flash back of her running up into the mountain occurs and its gone, leaving her standing alone. Time passes and she make her way back before day break.

Urobeha memory is beginning to return, she remembers more of her past and fragments of what had happen in the mountain. Keeping it to herself and much time after she receives visions of herself running up the same mountain over and again and then it goes blank. She is brave and not one to be frightened easily. Many moons after, she visits the man in the fields dwelling place, without ever being seen or heard. That is until one early dark morning she gets in too close and her fragrant moved on the wind and into the man nostrils awaken him from his slumber.

The sweet smell, he remembers is the fragrance of a woman. He cannot see, but his smell senses have grown. He sniffs in the sweet scent just like the animals and knows someone is there. With a husky tone, he cries out." Who'sss there? Who'ss is there? No one answers so he returns back to rest. His husky voice is that of a person, who hasn't spoken for a while. This makes the formation of his words even more difficult to comprehend. Judging from him laying out, he is a big and strong man with a body mass to be admired. The morning after, she stayed until the beast of the field had waken to the morning light. For the first time she gets to see his face and he is without sight. Blind as paper, all the darkness which followed her flashback ceases to exist.

In the air above unnoticed a falcon flies, and no one knows why the sentry is there. It another early morning and she goes to visits the elders in roles of leadership. She questions them on the blind man out in the fields. They can tell her very little and no more than he has been given another chance and his hard labor is until death. Should he by any means be removed from the soil of the land he shall die. Something about the man in the fields troubles her. With passing time after Urobeha having seen his deep wounds she begins to pity the man. His body scars are brutal, still some how, he is able to heal and live again. Living chained is not much of a life for anyone and time after time she wonders, how can a man live with such great affliction and it saddens her. For long hours she visits, sitting and observing him but never again did she get too close for him to pick up her scent again.

The Warrior at The Temple of the White Lamb

Leoha, has ridden for many Cycles of the Wind, and its the longest journey she has ever made away from home. She finally arrives at the temple of the White Lamb. The place is quiet and peaceful with no one around. Its easy to figure why no one is out. She is at the back side of the great structure instead of arriving at the front, which is ways off. Taking matters into her own hands, she scales up the massive wall to the top and quietly descends to the inside. It is stark and dark and all around her. In the patches of light suddenly the whole place lights and she is surrounded by people dressed in white linen.

This is the Holy realm, these people are called Lamb Angels, because of their holy way of living. They are special people with abilities far beyond that of the commoners and herself. They possess the power to see into time with superior fighting skills. Cautious of them, she reaches for her Blade. Each time she is made to stop by their quick movement, to avoid the risk of endangering herself she leaps back up the massive wall escaping and returning back to the outside. It's obvious the answers she seeks will not happen today. She hurries her way to the front on her stallion, only to discover a Lamb Angels is already there awaiting her.

She descends to the ground but is halted by one of the Angels. The Lamb Angel walks up to her without any sign of guile, kindly she said. "Lady Warrior! We are sorry but no one is allowed to enter without the Lamb of the High Archives permission! We are sorry." The Warrior accepts the greeting of response. Her comments resound with her inner spirit and the surrounding nature of things, bringing the Warrior to a much deeper calm. In face of pure and true beauty the Lamb Angel, skin glows with brilliance like no other. Leoha explains her position, "I have traveled wide, and far to come here and I have only one question. May I please be allowed to see the Lamb of the High Archives? "An observation is declared by the Lamb Angel "From what I can tell, you are connected to the last Warrior who passed this way and was denied entrance." Right away the Princess Warrior recalls her conversation with her brother Cleattius who said he would be passing this way.

Not to raise any further alarm, the Warrior says nothing. She is most impressed with the Lamb Angels ability. The Lamb Angel goes on, "Forcibly, you cannot make your way to the inside. A lesson well learned! Now come with me!" and Leoha follows, at lost for her failed attempt of scaling the wall earlier. On arriving at the front colossal doors, the two Guardians allow passage giving way as the Lamb Angel speaks. "Now take your Blade and place it above the door. When you descend, do not enter or speak, just listen, and when the Lamb of the High Archives is finished, you may retrieve your Blade and leave."

It takes an instance, the Warlord Warrior Princess leaps into the air high above the massive closed door resting the Blade. Upon landing back on her feet, she discovers the Lamb Angel gone and the massive door open. The two Guardians which guard the entrance greet her with a slight bow of their heads. On the inside ahead of her a strange woman unknown to her stands. She is robed also in all white linen but with much more embellishment than the others. Her head and face are covered by a veil and there is a light of radiance about her face. To the Warrior standing on the outside in the door way. She speaks, "I am the White Lamb of the High Archives, the keeper of all things here, which remains in balance with the surrounding nature. The ground on which I stand is Holy grounds and no one carrying a weapon of the Black Arts is welcome."

For a transient moment before the Warrior could answer, behind the veil, The White Lamb of the High Archives peers closely into the Warrior eyes. There is something compelling about Leoha that makes her search the depths of inner soul. The history of Leoha unfolds suspended in mirrors of her past revealing her status out to her. "Warrior, from the Arawak and Carib Nations and Princess from the House of Gouddaa what is it, that's brings you to our door steps?" "I come only to read the writings in the book, which tells about the Fifth Element. May I please be allowed access to enter?" The Warrior is amazed by the White Lamb of the High Archives ability's and the elective accuracy of her word choices.

Speaking again, "The holy agreement, made between us and your father Gouddaa, have long been in motion and it is only for Gouddaa's name sake, that my words to you young Warrior, do not fall on deaf ear. The Holy book you seek was long taken and handed down throughout the ages of the Mighty Kings of your ancestors. Please, leave here, go and see your father for all of what you now seek is with him. This is not the place where blood should be spilled." There will be no more answers to be had here and her final statement makes that plain.

Humbled by the impressions she's witnessed, to show her fidelity of loyalty and thanks to the White Lamb of the High Archives, the brave Warlord Warrior falls to one knee in front of the open door before requesting one last inquiry. "There are many stories, both old and new. What is true?" Deserving an illustration of the question in mention, the White Lamb of the High Archives said. "Stand! Young Warrior, and retrieve your Blade." On standing the Warrior leaps into the air but before she could retrieve the Blade, it fall's up right to the earth in front of the colossal door. Leoha comes down to land, one foot touches the Blade handle before she herself somersaults back to position. She tries to retrieve the Blade but it does not move.

The White Lamb of the High Archives indicates, "Now try again." To her surprise she is able to remove the Blade. The realization comes to her therein, that there are powers out there far beyond her reach and comprehension. If they wanted her dead, her fate would have already bean sealed. Deserving of the highest respect, the Warlord Princess bows before the White Lamb of the High Archives, uttering "Great is the wisdom that lies with in you. Thank you."

The massive door closes before her and she is allowed to leave. She retrieves her stallion. Trained to respond, she whistles and the mighty beast comes running out to her. Tranquility of the moment causes her to pause, she looks around basking in the peaceful nature of things. Leoha sighs breathing in absorbing the harmonious atmosphere with eyes closed. Even though her eyes are closed, she senses the Lamb Angel is with her. Her opened eyes confirm her notion, it is, the Lamb Angel who asked her earlier to place her Blade over the massive door entrance.

There is a grace of peace that covers her like a mantle, she stands with hands pressed together in prayer. There is a kindred spirit, the Warrior can not resist or refute her utterance. "Warrior! Here all things are in balanced with nature. What do you now feel?" With out doubt, the Warrior looks to her so at peace and asserts "Regardless to my motive for being here. I feel so much at peace with this place." The Lamb Angel favors Leoha with her words "With yourself or with the surroundings?"

A silent minute allows the Warrior to ponder the peaceful surrounding in a slower motion. The compelling comforts of peace mollifies her heart and mind seeping into her soul. It brings her back to herself. "I would like to stay here, when I am in peace with myself." Pulling herself up on her stallions back, The Angel conveys departing sentiments. "May the blessing of the Lamb of the High Archives be bestowed upon you, young Warrior." It is Leoha heartfelt desire to secure a guarantee on her words to the Lamb Angel. The Princess Warrior is determined, "Should I live to return. I will leave the Blade here on your door step." Cocking her head to the side, for a minute, the Lamb Angel considers the Warrior words. She can see she is serious, and to bind her to her pledge the Lamb Angel, replies "And should you not return, then the Blade can only be returned to it's rightful owner."

The Angels premonition is graced, but Leoha will not accept nor abide by the decree. Because as long as the Blade is with her, its death to those who want it. The Warrior reassures her word with assurance and grantee. "That's not possible." The owner the Angel refers to is none other than the Black Widow herself. The Lamb Angel, knows possible is only for those who rule out the probable and predict the future. So, to give balance and credit for the Warrior words and those of her own, she amends. "The young man I earlier mentioned. A full moon he spent wondering around the barren land before finally returning to the old man sitting on the wall. In spite of his behavior, he was given direction enabling him to find his way out. "What I am saying, is the way out is far from simple."

Leoha nods her head and the Lamb Angel, goes on to say. "You came in through the Valley like he did but by means of different directions. Take the way going east, where the road ends, turn north and you will come to the Dead Tree of Skull. Its ghostly image, whistles a sound on the Wind. Follow it until you come to a large wall, sitting on the wall is an old man with an unusual size head. Have words with him and he will direct you out." This news is helpful, "Does he have a name" Leoha asks. "I do not know his name, but he lives under the earth and he comes out every day light to sit on the wall drinking and laughing, giving lost souls directions.

He is known here to us as the great saint Hummptly" Having offered this information The Lamb Angel retreats. The Warrior watches from her stallion as she turns and walks away, disappearing through the tall pine green trees. Picking up on the wind, the breeze causes the dried pine needles to fall like small sickles of snow. It's a mystical sight worthy of seeing and the Warrior rides away.

Gouddaa's Vision

The fragrance of diver's flowers scents the air. The Mighty King Gouddaa, is in his wife Laurrennius, gardens. Sitting, he awaits her return from addressing matters on the inside about work. Laurrennius garden is flood with colors of purple, yellow and pink flowers among many others. It is like no other garden in the Kingdom, even the server's uniform is an adorned sample of its magnificent colors. Alone, sitting his thoughts drift to the land of dark days ahead. The wine he drinks has lost is savor, it is not to his taste so he sets it aside on the table with orders for another fresh port to be sent.

The servant girl takes it away returning with a new port of wine and wine mug. After pouring his wine she gracefully replies, "My King, as you have ordered. I went to bring in fresh wine but your wife stopped me and she ask I bring in this taste for your liking." His countenance is silent and weary with thoughts. With few words, the King dismisses her. "Please leave it and you may go." The server hesitates, this is not of the Kings nature. His love for old vintage is without measure, the deprecation of his spirit is fallen, but not with out atonement.

Soon there after, another young servant girl comes before him, with a large silver pan. Filled with water and a wiping cloth bowing in grace she informs the King of the Mistress intentions. "My King, by orders of the mistress. She sends the waters so it may cool your feet. The King smiles to its welcome. Removing his boots, she is allowed to continue her duties. After washing and cooling the Kings feet, she requests to leave. "My King, I will now go and fetch another pail of rinsing water." From under his feet, she removes the silver pan of dirty water. On the white piece of cloth, she rests down his feet and walk away.

As quickly as she has departed, another comes in her stead before the King with the same intentions. Another silver pan is filled with water and she begins to rinse his feet. Thinking nothing of it, he lets it be, this must be a new formality set by his wife Laurrennius. Her thoughtful considerations always minister to him, so he leaves it alone. When the servant had finished, she enlightens the King on his treatment, "My King, your feet is washed in pure oil and anointed with the liquid fire of life. I am the Lamb from the High Archives." She rises removing her hood in a flood of blinding light she is gone.

For an instance King Gouddaa is stunned and puzzled by her words. Even more puzzling is when the King realizes no one is there but him. Looking around and down at his feet the King discovers the rinsing pan is still there under his feet. Again, making him wonder, how could that be? Leaning back he picks up the fresh mug of wine. The taste of the new wine is a bit strong but he hadn't drunk much of it. To be certain its not the wine he tastes it again, swashing it in his mouth he finds it to his liking.

The first young lady returns with her silver pan of rinsing water. The duplicated actions have him confused and so strangely the King looks at her. Concerned, she begins to think, what did I do? Where did I go wrong? Out from her mouth comes her concern "My King, are you not pleased with my work?" Still puzzled by it all, the King again looks down at his feet and so does the beautiful servant girl. On noticing the Kings feet have already been rinsed, wiped, oiled, and dried her head slinks to one side, leaving her puzzled and wondering how and why too? When her eyes behold beneath the King feet, the exact silver pan and white cloth in her hand.

What abnormality is this? The Servant becomes chilled and frightened, something is not right here by the evidence before her. Did she shirk or scorn to upholding her duties, why was there another pan beneath the Kings feet? Numb to the events, the silver pan of rinsing water slips out her hand dropping to the ground. The clanging of its echoing alarm get's the attention of her colleagues passing by. They run in to assist her with the duties by allowing another to take up her place. Stuttering, flabbergasted, she tries to explain and they all want to know, how could this happen in the presence of the Mighty King Gouddaa.

Taking her away becomes difficult, she can't phantom how it could have happened. The King also appeared equally disturbed by the situation, they try to calm her but it's no use. The King says nothing, he is not cognizant, lost in his own thoughts. Sadly, they pull her away. Knowing the rules, they take her to the Old Madam of conduct, who officiates the merit of their duties. The Old Madam of conduct deals with all matters concerning the King, the Princes and the Princesses. She is a very old matron, one of strict rule who doesn't waste idol time with failures. Because this is a matter concerning the King, it has top priority for the Madam.

A top servant of the King, Prince or Princess must be beautiful without blemish. They are to perform their royal duties without mistake, living only to serve. The young and beautiful servant girl is left alone with the Old Lady of Conduct. She is still very up set, upright, concern knits her features where she stands, both hands down, lock to her side. Her glossy eyes do not give her an advantage standing before the Madam of conduct. Someone is trying to unseat her she's convinced of it they want her to look bad. She only wants to know who wants her out and why. The Old Lady of Conduct walks up to the young and beautiful servant girl and with force she strikes the young girl across the face. She falls crying out, "Its not my fault. Its truly not my fault."

As a servant many have to accept the rules that is administered by their superiors. Physical discipline are a part of the work details at times of error. If she doesn't get back to her feet with in minutes she is out, they will kick her out the Kingdom leaving her to live like the commoners on the outside. She composes herself, making it up just in time. The Old Lady of Conduct look is piercing. "You are one of the best, how could this have happened?" With permission she is allowed to speak and tell her side of the story. Telling the story, she baffles even the Old Lady of Conduct. The Old Lady of Conduct knows the young servant girl well enough to say she is incapable of fabricating such a story.

A full investigation is ordered into the matter. The young and beautiful servant girl is no longer allowed to further her duties until the investigation is concluded. Assigned to the investigation is the one and only top-ranking investigator, Liammiciane.

Laurrennius's Flower Garden

Queen Laurrennius, arrives in her gardens. The confusion has garnered her attention. The investigations haven't revealed much. She orders the new servant girl to leave and have the Madam-Lady of Conduct call in Meiha. Meiha is the sister of Urobeha, and Laurrennius personal care taker. She is needed to finish up the rest of the evening. Laurrennius looks to her husband immersed in his own thoughts. Kneeling over him she notices his feet are still bare. Inclining down to one knee she gently begins to dress his feet and put back on his boots. The sight of her at his feet brings his mind back. "Let me help you with that." he maybe King but this woman, gleaming, is his dearest prize.

Together they finish dressing his feet and he helps Laurrennius up. Closely he pulls her into his arms embracing her lips with silent kisses of joy. It is late in the evening and Meiha, has not yet arrived. Queen Laurrennius she leaves message to have her follow up in the morning. On the horizon a dark cloud is moving, in the air the smell of rain swells in the clouds above staining for release. Together they walk back to Laurrennius bed chamber.

In his mighty arms, ever so gently on the bed he lays her down caressing the contours of her shapely body. Their touching lights the flames and heat of passion ignites, stripping her of every piece of garment he looks at the beautiful woman who is his wife and Queen. Her hand reaches out to him, being welcomed he himself covers her space with grace. They make passionate love to each another. When the surges heating the body peek, the over flow of energy makes

Gouddaa roar. His release groans loudly, her exhaling cry is joined with his in unison. Their exertion of their passion is consuming, it is heard as rumbling through the temple walls into the ear of Libra and many others.

Their lovemaking leaves them both spent, there is no more thought, only the relieved bodies intertwined. Outside the darkness of clouds has rolled in closer, lights flash, thinking it no more than the troughs of the storm Laurrennius falls deeply asleep. With the added patter of rain, it soothes her, she will be out for some time. The great Gouddaa tries to fall asleep but rain drops against the window keeps him wake. Disengaging himself from the warm folds of his wife, out from his bed he makes his way across to the window. Staring into the falling rain drops, each drop reminds him of the promises he has made.

In the glitter of raindrops, the promise to the the Black Widow, of the forest is foremost in his mind. In return for his wife Laurrennius awaking he must now honor the obligation of right to that promise. It is the Eight Cycle of the Wind the night is pure. Restlessly he dresses himself, occasionally looking over his slumbering wife asleep. King Gouddaa exits his chambers making his way into the Great Halls. No one questions the oddity of his movements or the time, and to his Throne he comes to rest. This maybe his last time here on the Throne, it's a possibility he won't deny considering what he has been done for the exchange.

His daughter Libra is up and passing by. On seeing her father, she stops. His head is low she walks up to him sitting almost lifeless. Mediation is not helping to relieve him, on seeing her, he comes back. He is some what surprised to see her at this time. At the motion of his lift eyebrows, she speaks. "Father, you do not look so well, I can sense its because of your thoughts about the Black Widow. Tell me father! Is it a must you face her alone? Can I not take your place?" This child of his heart has just offered herself, foolish as it may sound. If it were only possible. Her unannounced visit, not only surprises him but her words convict him and settles his heart. It hits him as a lightning bolt making him remember his once words to her. It's her sincerity that touches him the truth can break even the strongest heart of gold. Though it is not in his heart to say. I would so much love you to take my place. He chooses to defend his heart. For there is no good father who loves their child more than he. No good father who wants their child to die before they pass.

He closes his eyes to keep them dry, holding the pain in his heart, he opens them again only to say, "Please daughter, please I beg of thee, speak not of such words." She desperately wants to comfort him, but doesn't know what to do. Right now, she must be strong for him. She has an idea of what is at stake, peacefully utters speaks "Father, if it is your command. I shall order your Black Army of Death to march across the Black Forest and annihilate everything and everyone." He knows she is willing to do what ever is necessary but this was for him to do alone.

Sadly, he shakes his head out to her, as to say, no, no, that's not the way and his words rings out. "No daughter no! Understand this is not about war nor battle but about the incantations of the unknown. It is about that which passes beyond the seed of life and death. I once told you, that to believe in the unseen and the unknown, requires a certain amount of faith. Like I have said before, faith is that which hold together the feature, to correct and protect that of the past. Please daughter! I beg of you, say not more, no more. Please go to your mother, she has been awakening out from her deep coma like sleep. Go now to her for she also has been touch by it all."

To his surprise, she does not move instead she falls to her knees before the Great Throne. With grief, she said "Father, in spite of all my harsh words towards thee. Forgive me for my trespasses for they may truly be my own tomorrow. I am so afraid at times to sit in thy seat for it is now that I understand. I am not worthy of thy seat and if it's your will I go. I will leave and go to mother. I shall go to her but before I leave you, tell me father. Why do I feel, you must ride soon once again into the Black Forest." It's her words that shatters the might Kings heart like smashed rock, it hurts. Leaning slightly forward his aching heart speaks out, he so wishes he could hold her again, but to do so only makes it harder to leave. "Yes, daughter yes. When the Three Moons are in alignment with the Third Sun and its great light darkens the heavens! I shall ride once again but be not afraid for me, for your work is here where I sit!"

She remembers his pass words, and yields. "Father, you once told me, that a journey which is finished is completed, and a journey which must begin, becomes more important than a finished journey. It is only now I truly understand." The father looks upon his wise daughter, as the daughter her father. They exchange looks for what seems like ages, but it's only a minute. "Yes daughter, bring your heart to a rest, and go and see her. Go! go and see her! Go now! Now go! Just go! Go before my wrath come upon thee. You ask just too many questions of me! Now go!" He cries out. Libra bravely looks to him with restrained tears, she wishes he would not force her away.

Holding back tears, she slowly raises from her knees. Again, to his surprise instead of leaving him, she stumbles her way up to him overwhelmed with the melancholy of pain. The grief in her heart strangles the few words she holds. She reaches out to him and from his seat he opens his arms and into his embrace she is enfolded. Awash in tears of sorrow the daughter hangs her head. A Princess and a King both locked in sorrow, she can barely speak in an audible tone and whispers. "Father, please don't leave me. I will never speak out to you again. I promise, I promise father I promise." She isn't making it any easier for him, but better this than what it could become." No daughter no. I've ruled, with bronze and iron and incantations of magic. It is written in the Book of Seven Pillars and already been foretold by the highest of the White Lambs. One shall come after me to rule with knowledge not so much with bronze and iron but with that of the great lions and animals of the open fields.

The Fifth-Element is the last protector of the Throne. Remember all I have teach you and all you have read in the secret books of knowledge. You have the scrolls of the Kings, please forgive your sister Sarraha for all the wrong she had done to you, and remember I shall always be with you. Go now daughter and see your mother." Wishing he would not force her away she cries out "Please father, please don't ask me to leave you, please. . ." Weary, the Great King is left with only one option, she will abide by his word, it is the only way. "Yes daughter, I order thee from the throne to go to your mother now!" Throwing herself into his arms, she grips him hard and then rips herself out of his tight embrace leaving her tears at the Throne.

Walking away she will make him proud, so she holds her head high. Libra, always found it hard to look to her mother because of discipline. The Queen, her mother Laurrennius once wrongfully slapped her for receiving one of the Holy Crystals from the Black-Scarlet and passing it over to her father Gouddaa. It was this action that triggered all that is now in motion.

Out of all his children the balance to lead is best with his daughter Libra. He has seen the greatness of her wisdom, it shall become even greater than he the King. In his heart it is that secret he reserves. He is now alone with the quietness it makes him recall another time. His father King Aggaddaa, and his mother Uyrannius have long been from his thoughts. Long had he wanted to visit their tombs and now would be a good time. Before he can move, he is caught by an inner vision he falls into a more relax mode.

In the vision he sees from the Throne, the two colossal Pillars which guards the entrance of his mother and father's tomb. For some unknown reason the two Pillars are not in their usual position. They now stand up right but close together blocking the entrance that he doesn't get in. With both his hand on each of the colossal pillars he pushes with all his strength to divide them. Instead of dividing them both pillars fall outward tumbling to the earth.

On entering the great tomb, a white mist moves toward him. As it gets nearer the color changes from white to shadow black swiftly engulfing him ever changing. The dread there is morbid, death radiates from its center. In face of the unknown he is afraid, fear drives him piously to his knees. A blazing chariot with six stallions a blaze materializes racing strait towards him. The lone rider drawing the carriage is none other than his father King Aggaddaa. He passes him by, and Gouddaa cries out. "Oh, Immortal and eternal father let not my soul be taken across the sea of death. Let not the maggots of the earth eat away my flesh, but gather my brittle bones from falling into the hands of the Black Widow. The earth beneath my feet is soft and stained with royal blood, dripping from my veins like water taken from a fountain. Oh mother, oh father, am I awake or still at sleep?"

The vision fades and he awakens from sleep. Rising up, out from the Throne room he walks into the Halls of Battle. There he readies himself with his bright Armor of War. His firing White Stallion is on ready and without saying goodbyes to his love ones, together they ride out armed and shield with weapons of iron and bronze pieces dipped in the incantation of a lost art.

His first stop is to the colossal tomes of his mother and father. There he find's the two colossal Pillars which guard the entrance, are no longer standing up right but on the ground. The vision returns to him, he saw himself pushing them apart. Although he doesn't fully understand the vision, he descends from his stallion to the ground. Walking over to where the Great Pillars layout he drops to one knee placing his right hand on the fallen Pillars. He hopes touching them will reveal the interpretation of his vision, but instead he gets nothing. In a last and desperate hope for answers his voice cries out to the ancestors "Father, Mother, shelter and shield me form the ahead storm. Raising to his feet a silence permeates around him in this place. This is one he doesn't understand. Leaping to his stallion on the wind he ride's away.

Sheppard, Laurrennius, and The Book

At the very time Libra was having words with her father Gouddaa, on the Throne, news came to Sheppard by means of Meiha. Princess Sheppard follows the written instructions to join the Holy Mother, in her Chambers. On entering her Mother Laurrennius, greets her daughter with kisses of joy and love for all the missing time. It's a joy to see her mother finally awake. It touches her heart with fulfillment, it shows in her tears as they sit and enjoy small talk. Laurrennius looks at the beauty and the radiant brightness bestowed upon her now adult daughter. She spoke. "Child! Do not think. I no longer have informers. The echos of time, have long speak out to me from the lips of your ancestors. You are a candle unlit, believing, that love is only a dreamer's dream. My child! I could hear your cries in the distance away from me and calling out for revenge from over the heartless mountains.

Your youth and your peaceful days are all given because of the sacrifice, your sister Leoha, and your brother Dicious, and all of those called before the great Throne. Please forgive your sister Leoha, for what she has done to you and your brother Dicious, for what he cannot never be to you. So that in your youth, you may have peaceful days ahead of you."

Sheppard not knowing what to say for her surprise, is shocked by her mother's words. She drops to her knees before the Holy Mother sadly crying out. "Mother, how could you have known? How could you? Feeling her daughter emotions Laurrennius insist, "Please raise from your knees." To her feet she raises, and Laurrennius goes on to say "There is a certain brightness about you Sheppard! And when seen through the eyes of the beholder. You shall shine as bright as a star in the heavens. Your triumphs are many and still you are so blessed. Is it not I, who once told you, all in due time you will also be telepathic.""Yes mother she whispers with tears rolling down her cheeks.

Laurrennius takes from her garments a hidden book and she hands it over to her daughter, while saying, "Take this book and read it but keep it safe and return it when you are finish." Thankfully receiving the book, not knowing its contents Sheppard knows, if given by her mother it is of vital importance. Laurrennius goes on to explain "It is the Book of Thunder, written by the hand of your Grand Father King Aggadda. Learn all of its secret because you may need them in the future. There is a part in it that teaches about your Grand fathers unique fighting skills, study it well. When reading it, take time and sit out by the Caves of Arcariaa. Its a chosen spot, while out there, never leave it out in the rain."

Sheppard, thanks her mother and is allowed to leave. On her way out from her Mother's Chambers she is seen leaving with the book in hand by her sister Libra. As it so happens, she too is on her way in to see their Mother. While Sheppard walks away Libra enters. Laurrennius, gives equal greeting to Libra. The same welcome is awarded her as Sheppard for she is so pleased to see another of her daughters. Together they embrace, Laurrennius welcomes Libra to the Throne again embracing her daughter. Libra is pleased to finally see her Mother back in the world of the living. Briefly after a few small talks Libra bring her Mother up to date, "Mother, one is gone and one has returned."

Of all her children Libra always displayed the most attention for matters. Solemn Laurrennius declines her head understanding her daughters meaning but she knows not which of her sons and daughters is gone and which have returned. Sadly, she asks "Child! Where is your father?" Libra looks out to her and while thinking about her mother's pain, said "He is in the Great Halls Mother," That is exactly where she had left him.

When she had awakened from their love, Gouddaa was not there. It disturbed her at first, the weather outside foreboding produced shadows in her thoughts. It's so good to be awake to touch her loved ones and live the times. Her desire returns, with the urge to see her husband again. She cries out, "I must go to him." The Queen rises making movement to join her husband in the Throne room. At the door Libra blocks her way. She knows her Father is long gone. To save her Mother from further pain that might hinder her full recovery she came on his behalf. Again, Laurrennius tries to move, not clear of Libra restricting her path she looks at her with question.

The door is within arms reach but again she is halted by Libra and her words. "No Mother no. He is well and you should further rest for the dark is still upon us and the three moons are now in alignment and all light will soon be given back to the earth. Rest now mother and at first light, I shall return." She doesn't need to know all yet, its best this way. Libra's solemn words bring Laurrennius heart to rest. A suspended silence follows. She is still a little weary from her ill state, but Libra is owed an explanation. Laurrenniys. "I have always owed you an apology. And am sorry. I had to hit you."

The pain of that event hurt her terribly, Mother had never had cause to hit her before. Not wanting to relive the moment Libra asserts, "Mother, let's not talk about that. I understand and I too am sorry for being so distance. Please rest now Mother and I shall return later." Helping Laurrennius over to her bed side she hides away her own tears.

Libra After Leaving Her Mother

Seeing that her mother is resting comfortably, she closes the door behind her softly, pausing a moment. The guards posted outside are at attention, their presence serves to strengthen her reserve. After leaving her mothers chamber, Libra making a stop beside one of the In-house Great Pillars. There she begins to weep for the loss of her father Gouddaa. For he is the one gone and Leoha, is the one who had return.

She has spent enough time here, about to move on from the Great Pillar, Libra is met by the beautiful servant girl. From the disturbed agitation of her demeanor something troubles her. The beautiful servant girl is the same who had been disciplined by the Old Lady-Madam of conduct, some time ago. Since the Old Lady removed her from service it has been a torment, the jeers of her peers have become most unbearable. She hurries up to Libra and drops to her knees.

Libra remembers her. "Rise!" The beautiful servant rises from her knees twisting her hands in front of her. This is an unexpected and untimely occurrence, impatient to leave Libra has no choice but to admit. "This is not a good time but go ahead anyhow." How ironic, thinking back on her last words, they are those of her father. The servant is gratefully relieved to know the King grants her favor she wastes no time in her utterance. The chain of command is now with Libra, only those who know that King Gouddaa has departed are privileged to this information. Having been the last one to cool his feet, she is turning to the one person who maybe able to help her.

"You once said, should I find myself with a heavy load. I should seek you. Well! My load is heavy and I cannot take it any more. I have been removed from duties and I have search nights just to find you." Knowing of the beautiful servant girl pure innocent ways, Libra was always pleased to watch her perform the task of duties. Unknown to the girl, Libra she has always found favor in this particular servant girl. Then again it must be because she is also much liked by her brother Dicious. Stepping up to the beautiful servant girl Libra places her right hand onto the young girl chest and her heart reveals out the truth to her. The conveyance of the moments of the servant with her father replays and the omission of with is missed is also called forth. "Your heart speaks the truth. I will have words with the Madam in charge."

The young beautiful servant girl thanks Libra gracefully before walking away. Pieces of the puzzle becomes clearer, King Libra watches the servant depart mulling over what she has discovered.

Before the Last Great Shake of Time

Before the last great shake of the Arawaks and Caribs Kingdom, arched in time by the breath of the Arawaks and Caribs God Potullas, came the Caves of Arcariaa. The ancient scrolls in the library of the Great Kings speaks to its existence. Being a mythical place preserved by Four Elementals. A group of four spiritual beings are responsible for teaching the Arawaks and Caribs the art of counting and calculating mathematically. In the skies, the Moons and Suns circling each other determining the seasons and their harvest. It is also written, the four Elementals wrote the book of seasons and handed it down to the great Arawak king Haccocharaa for his people.

The Caves of Arcariaa is said to be the final resting place of the four Elementals. Their sarcophagus stands, but no one has ever found their coffins. Some say when it rains, their voices can still be heard at its peak, moving on the wind. As time evolved by, it eventually became nothing more than a Myth. The caves are said to be divided in two sections, one where water once flowed sweet as honey, it was once used by the greatest of past Kings as a Holy bath sanctuary. Now its no more than a Holy sight and the other resting home to the four Elementals.

The following morning after talks with her mother Sheppard rides out to the Caves of Arcariaa deep within the Kingdom Walls. She has yet to open the book, and the instructions she was given only makes her want to see what is really in the pages of the book. There sitting upon a white rock she begins to read the book contents secretly given to her by her Mother Laurrennius. Attentively she begins to absorb the contents in the book easily, not knowing it would be her destiny even after.

The Warrior at The Great Wall

The Warlord Warrior, Princess Leoha, has finally arrived at the Great Wall within the No Man's Land. There is nothing within miles upon miles of wall and vastness. Just like the Lamb Angel said, "you will find a man sitting on the Great Wall with an unusual size head beside his small statue, he is old and very knowledgeable." Searching the horizon, there are no dwelling places around she can see only a desolate mass of land. She moves closer toward the wall her attention is taken by a lone bird flying high to the left of her. When her focus returns to the wall, there is in front of her the Old Father stares laughing out happily to himself. She brings her mighty beast to a stop before the Old Father. In his way, he laughs out to her saying, "Another lost soul, seeking the way out."

Leoha feels the temperatures rising out here, over in the distance ripples of heat wave vapors roll continuously. This kind of heat could induce a stroke making one visualize almost anything out here. Concerned for the Old Father health the Warrior ask, "Old father, how long have you been out here and are there any others with you? Still laughing out to himself the Old Father postulates "There are no others, even the Kings men would not come out here. But who are you?" he goes on laughing like a mad man. The Lamb Angel could have warned her he was demented. This encounter is most unusual to the Warrior, remembering the Lamb Angel words she ratifies, "I am the Warrior Princess over the Arawak, and Caribs, and I am from the House of King Gouddaa. Will you accept my pardon?" The Old man echos her sentiment, "Pardon! Pardon! Well, I see no other to pardon but you! For disturbing me."

His crazy laugh splinters through the air hitting each of her nerves. The outcome of this meeting still remains to be seen. If she expects to get the answers she came for, patience may yet reward her. Looking around at the nothing, she breathes a sigh of relief, before humoring the Old man. "It is good to see one like you in such good spirit."

The Lamb Angel, said he lived under the earth but his skin tone tells a different picture making her question his true origins. Quickly tossing over to him her water sac, without effort he catches it and he laughs out. He has yet to admit it but her compassion has touched him. While she asks "Does it matter which way I go?" "You should ask the young man before you. He attempts one way taking a cycle before coming back this way. You are riding on a Ccellesstiall stallion just you keep riding and let him lead the way."

To herself she thinks, how could he have known and could it have been her brother Cleattus he is referring to. His incessant laughter continues, at this juncture turn Leoha contemplates what the wise man is saying. "Thank you, Old Father, but can you tell me, who was the young man before me?" Still in his laugh mode, he gestures with a crocked finger pointing at her, "What is he to you?" "I believe it must have been one of my brothers." The Old Father laughter becomes outrageous and he repeats," Your brother! Your brother! Regrettably it was his own temper, that caused him the long, long way back home but he will survive the harsh lands, before reaching back home.

The Old Father words or lack of confirmation, to her characterizes her brother's personality perfectly, the rider before her was her brother Cleattius. From her stallion she leaps to the earth and on her knees to paying homage before the Old Father, she said "Old father! I again thank you for your wisdom." Up to her feet she leaps back on her stallion. With eyes still on the Old man, his head turns to the right and then quickly extends to the left, he is listening to something, she hears nothing. He immediately sits at attention on the wall, to her the Old Father said. "They are all calling for me! I have to go."

Go where? The man is an enigma, for a minute she thinks his mind maybe touched by the heat, where is he planning to go out here. If he requires her to help him, she is more than able, her horse can hold both of their weight. The air churns, a surging power pulsates around them, mystically the Old Father levitates up into the air. His withered hand stretches out gripping the very air he peels open the portals of time she has heard about but never experienced until now. He steps walking and disappearing into the fabric of time and space as if never there.

The unexpected occurrence stuns the Warrior leaving her throat parched and dried. Instinctively she reaches for her water sac, strangely it is back in her saddle. Placing the bag to her mouth, she takes that long needed drink of water but the taste is off. Looking at her disposition, now is not the time to waste water. She shares a little with the beast before starting the long brutal journey ahead. Letting the horse take lead, along the way she realizes she nor the stallion are in need of water nor rest. Retracing her steps, she begins to wonder, what really did happen back there with the Old Father. It makes her realize there are things out there far beyond her understanding. In the vast reaches of the sands, this time its a gift working in her favor, silently she thanks the Old Father. It was something which will now follow her for the rest of her life.

King Libra Enters Laurrennius's Garden

It is morning and Libra, is in the garden where the incident between the young beautiful servant girl and her father Gouddaa took place days ago. Libra has only to wave out her hand across the near by flowers and she visions all that occurred, its just as she thought. If she's not mistaken the other Lady present created the confusion. She then returns back to the inside and on the Great Throne she sits to be debrief by her Adviser. The opulence and homage of respects bestowed towards her feeds her soul. At the end her mind takes her back to the last moments spent holding her father in the same seat and it saddens her. She knows he is long gone and she must now live up to his expectation and those of her own. She sends message to the Old Madam-Lady of Conduct. Which reads "By orders of the Throne. The unexplained occurrence, concerning the servant girl and my father the King is an anomaly that must be put to rest by Orders of the Throne."

Earlier the following evening, the young beautiful servant girl is summoned to stand before the Old lady of Conduct to hear her fate. She is informed by the Lady of Conduct the investigation into her matter is concluded and that she is to be reinstated by Orders of the Throne to continue her work with the King upon his return. She must report to Prince Dicious Chamber until such such time. The young lady is so pleased she walks up to the Lady of Conduct and she kisses her across the face. Saying, "Thank you! Thank you,

Madam." Concealing her fluxing emotions the Old Lady of Conduct said." The Throne has favored you. "The Old Lady of Conduct has never before received a kiss of thanks from any of the others due to her strict rules. Shes touched, trying to hide it, it's the softening of her expression gives her away. It makes the guards smile. A little embarrassed, her stern ways leave no room for cynicism such as those from the guards, she insists. "I will report you." There smiles fade and things quickly fall back to perspective.

Gouddaa Riding on the Wind

Gouddaa, has been riding on the Wind for sometime towards his direction in the Black Forest. His White Stallion requires rest so he comes to a stop beside the Great Lakes Collanney. Descending from his horse to the ground, he is pensive and his Golden Body Armor is heavy. The peaceful nature of things quiets the firing Stalling to a calm. Walking to the edge of the Great Lake there falling to one knee he fully realizes all of what he left behind is gone. Looking out over the peaceful nature of things, he lets his mind wonder. Derious, Aries, Sarraha, Libra, Black Scarlet, the Black Widow, why, can't we all live in peace. A sound from his Stallion warns him of a pending danger lurking nearby behind the tall bushes. Slowly rising to his feet, one look at his stallion pointed ears tells him the danger here is real.

Stalking him from behind the tall grass they are three, they do not know of him and his powers. To them he looks like and old and easy kill. The rewards gained from of his Shining Armor will fetch a good price on the open market and never again would they have to work. The three killers wait for the right moment to strike when he least expects it. Wary one of the killers becomes suspicious of the Stallion ears he figures now may not be a good time to strike. Desperate these men take drastic measures, together they attack him with hope of being victorious instead they find themselves on their knees begging for mercy and his forgiveness.

There request is denied and with a might wave of his hand they are instantly beheaded. No sooner the act is completed, from the corner of his eye a woman adorns in white moves toward him. Vaguely he remembers the face but her clothing reminds him of the young woman who had oiled and dried his feet back in the garden. With her an aura of a calm soothes the peace in the air. Her following words comes confirming it. "I am from the Lamb of the High Archives, and I have come to bid thee fear well Oh Great King. I am only to ask unto thee, is this the last chapter to be written in the Book of Pillars?" As the Great and Powerful King Gouddaa looks to her he foretells "Should I return from the Black Forest there shall be no end, only a new beginning."

Taking to his Stallion he rides out on the wind. It is the final hour before the separation of the three Moons in the Heavens and the Eclipse is in alignment. In the skies soon a new era in time and space. Over Hills, through Valleys and Saxon streaks he crosses riding on the wind. Finally, he has reached the Great Open Plains which he must cross to arrive at the borderline of the Black Forest. Great speed carries the white beast riding on the wind, over the great open and dry plains he brings his Firing White Stallion to a trot. In front of him the Black Forest looms.

The alarm of his arrival has already been sent out by the Watchers guarding the unseen boundary line. The alert runs spreading like wildfire through the Black Forest. The sight of his arrival is lightning into the ears of the Black Widow crackling in the diabolical strikes of each laughter's eruption. It resounds throughout the Forest scattering birds in every direction. This is the Black Forest, so much has happened here that affects what will happen today. The Black Forest is dry, every thing in it looks dead, this is its strange beauty. Whiffs of sweet fragrance remains as dew lingering in dense the air.

By the many they come out, from under the ground they slitter, creep and crawl. There isn't one alive who survived that doesn't remember the last encounter. He left behind, a trail of death and destruction equal to that of no other. Here he is now, ahead he moves, deeper and deeper inside. No one dares attack him for everyone is still afraid. His firing white stallion snorts hot steam coming to a stop and soon he is surrounded on all sides by killers. In the opening, the Black Widow, reveals herself.

At her appearance his White Stallion mounts lunging to the air closing the distance he lands down in face of the Black Widow. The hot vapor of the beast snort does not intimidate the Black Widow. In fact, she raises her hand touching its muzzle. Vengeance clashes between their eyes. Her hand falls back to her side and she turns away from her urge to desecrate his corpse to the Black-Bird. Her children. In tolerance of him her patience is limited, still she cries out "Killer of my people! Is this how you come before me, with another Armor ready to kill, that's not why your here. You have come to pay a debt. Have you not?"

Gouddaa, knows the bargain he has made with the Black Widow for the awakening of his wife Laurrennius. He dismounts from his Stallion to the ground subject to the peace of his word. Removing his Mighty Armor which protects him, it falls to the earth. His girth is removed next with his sword. Lastly his helmet comes off exposing his bared head. Now vulnerable, they move hesitantly in closer to him.

With his Armor removed, the Mighty Armor fell to the earth. It emits a sound only his Stallion can decipher. At this moment the great Beast is consistently being whipped to halt him, but all attempts fail to hold him. Finally, fast moving the Stallion breaks free. Watching the commotion, right away the Black Widow sends out a battalion of her own to track down the Mighty Beast and bring it back before it reaches the open plains. Making its way toward the boarder, the others take short cuts to cut the beast off. Some of the pursuers make it close enough to catch it but the Stallions speed is unmeasured. Making its way back and across the border onto the great open plains it runs on the Wind, making his way back to the Kingdom. The Beast open wounds are many and it has lost much blood. The stead knows it needs to slow down should it want to survive the harsh terrain ahead but like most Ccellesstiall stallions its last breath serves the command.

The Lost of a Stallion the Prize of the King

When the others report back to the Black Widow in failure, the two in charge heads are instantly cut off rolling at her feet. In a tirade of fits, she dreads losing such a great prize. The imbeciles, they had no idea how precious the fastest Stallion on earth is. The others are ordered to remove the armor on the ground out from her sight. The Mighty King Gouddaa agrees to be chained without resistance and he is carried away. He is to be the Black Widows' prisoner for the next thirty-three Eclipses of the Third moon. It's here that they will begin their afflictions upon his body and mind to break him.

King Gouddaa finds himself ensnared at the tail end of many whips. For their strife, the Great King Goudda skin is flayed with many strikes of the whip. Watching with host others, The Black Widow find's satisfaction favor in seeing her greatest adversary down to one knee. Each time, they stop the whipping, King Gouddaa would look up at them. The defiance in his stare cause many to still be afraid and watchful to come close.

The Black Widows, loathe for the Mighty King has spanned many cycles, his bad deeds against her and her people are many. It's primarily because of the principle that he is bound to his fate. If he'd been a less scrupulous King the Black Widow herself might have been dead ages ago. He is there to fulfill the bargain and to make compensation. He will never get the chance. Ignoring him, Gouddaa trys to speak out his words only to have them fall on deaf ears. She waves out her hand and the massive rushes him to the ground. Binding him with rope, they jeer, leaving him to struggle back on his feet. Roped and chained with the unbreakable chains of Gog and Magog on his hands and feet, the great King Gouddaa is truly helpless and badly injured. Yet he still is able to stand. She wants to see his legs buckling, she wants to see him bruised, cut with blood flowing screaming in agony.

Breathing heavily the Black Widow nods out her head to her Second in Command, who in return gives the orders to further afflict the Great King with many more whips. They wail upon him until the mighty King falls flat to the earth. Pouring acts of vengeance upon him until they are tired, his injuries are many. The heels of many stomp his body.

The Third Sun is moving slowly across the skies and time seems suspended, to have stopped. Unbearable, blood seeps from the deep lacerations and the scent of burned flesh permeates the camp confines. The earth beneath him is soft, soaked with his royal blood. For a minute, he remembered his vision from the throne. In the agony of his cries, he shows no shame, instead a very human spirit manifests out from the pain but they still show him no mercy.

Cutting through the red haze of pain, out loud, the Black Widow grimaces. "Now pick him up! so that he may remember my face." With force, they pick him up, he is made to stand before the Black Widow. In front of her, the great and mighty King madly cries out "Aaaaaaaa, Aaaaaaaaaa, because of his grievous pain. His outburst does not move her to emotion. Instead, she bursts out laughing. Bending over closer to study him not understanding anything from his uttering. His slobbered rambling is good enough for her, satisfied she gives the orders "Now, shut him up!"

They shuffling him as ordered, pulling him further by his ropes and chains for their own amusement. They drag, ripping him against brittle stones before finally bringing him back before the Black Widow. The Black Widow slants her head to the side. Though she is pleased with their performance her blood-lust is insatiable. To hear him crying out for mercy.

Again, she gives the orders "Now bring in his new face" On a tray two servants enter with a mask cask on a tray from molten iron.

Forcing the Mighty King Gouddaa to his knees, guards on each side take a blow to his knee caps. She relishes the agony of hearing him cry ordering them to hurry with glee for the Kings new face. Among them is one called "The Mad One." He is the craft master responsible for the metallic mask, pins and spikes. The Mask is engraved with fitting of incantation, doomed by the Black Widow. He is a Black Smith of no equal. Demented, with twisted cruelty he takes great joy in his work. Ominously he walks up to the badly injured King on his knees.

With a threatening dangerous grin spreading across his face. His empathetic concern mocks the showing of a mutual relationship. Quite friendly like an ally who helping, to the Mighty King Gouddaa he sings giggling, "Now this may sting a little! But the pain will soon go away!" With efficient and accurate precision, The Mad One clamps a metallic mask over the front of King Gouddaa face and head locking them together with two pins. The mask takes shape imprinting and sealing to the Kings face. Without remorse the Black Widows vengeance drives The Mad One he pushes the metallic rod strait through the two holes in the cheek part of the mask. Blinding and excruciating pain brings the Great King Gouddaa, up on his feet in agony it makes him wildly fling about, killing many of them.

Struggling for his life, the tides power turn if only for a moment, quickly by the ends of their whips he falls back under control. They add to his chains and ropes. He is now unable to utter a word. The shouts of spectators are almost deafening. Many deformed faces of the foul take delight in King Gouddaa torment, the Black Widow was finally successful. The Black Widow, cries out loud to her own "I am pleased to see! The Great King Gouddaa, has nothing more to say." Cackling in laughter the Black Widow orders them to bring in the Black Cross while he tastes the barbed tip of their whips again.

The massive Black Cross is laid out beside him. Lying on his back the pain is unlike anything he has experienced. Sometimes there are lulls in the pain but the beatings only compounded the throbbing fire. Harshly from the earth they pick him up, his worthless corpse is placed on it. In his helpless state, they remove his ropes and chains driving into his hands and feet the biggest of iron spikes. The piercing stakes driving into his flesh breaks bones on entry with force. Frantic he tries screaming out but the Black Widow had that fixed already. He blacks out momentarily but the strike from the next stake brings him back. He can't even move for it causes more agony.

The wood of the massive Black Cross is made from black charcoal which only grows among the gigantic Dead Trees in the Black Forest. The size of wood is two feet on all four sides and a height of two hundred feet. It takes two hundred of her men to drag the Mighty Cross. After having nailed him against the massive Black Cross, the Black Widow orders he be taken and placed in the middle of the Black Bird Corn field. She's feeling generous, its the least she can do. Why not give the Great and Mighty King Gouddaa his own private audience where justice can be served on his flesh? With chains the length of four hundred feet attached to both ends and top, they drag, the massive Black Cross away while she watches. Along the way the Mighty King is bruised pelted with stones, spit upon and showered with waste excrements. Their unpleasant words show no pity. The whip sings its answer by the many mocking him.

The Black Widow still watches from afar, she feels empty all of sudden, the pleasure of looking further upon her nemesis Gouddaa evil image will soon be at end. While they move on, she moves out to make a stop before they reach. Finally, they arrive at the Corn field, all around King Gouddaa hears the voices of thousand upon thousands of Black Birds screaming. In the center of the open massive field, they pull the massive Black Cross. It comes to rest in front of a large deep hole dig in the center of the field. The Black Widow makes good on her promise. His audience the Black Birds are all there and by far out numbered the crowd and all the dead corns stalks. Slowly many of the Black Birds take flight to the sky.

In the midst of the on lookers waiting for the lamb to be slaughtered is a Woman of Strange Behavior who is never certain of anything she does. Everyone knows of her because beside her beauty, she always carries around a pail with water and a mug on a rope attached to her side. Moving around she offers all in need of drinking water. With ways and beauty, she is treated with preference. On seeing the might King, she feels compelled to have the great and powerful King Gouddaa, drink from her water mug. Without a care she walks up to the Black Cross to Gouddaa's head kneeling, the crowd pays no attention to her. Neither do the men in uniforms but she is warned by the Head Soldier to make it quick and leave before the Black Widow shows up.

To few in the crowd surprise, she pulls out the rod from his mask and she tosses it to one side. Relieved from some of his pain the men prepare to lift the massive Cross to an upright position. They too turn a blind eye to what the Lady of Strange Behavior is doing. King Gouddaa mouth is dry and heavy, his lips swollen and cracked. From her mug she allows him two drops of water. His tears give him no comfort. He'll see those he loves no more. He swallows deeply, he is tired and his only wish is for the time to pass quickly. Its been a long, long time since he's felt such savage pain. It shows all over his battered body almost broken. From her water mug she allows the Great King a third drop of water. Which comes down into his mouth like a ball of fire melting to taste like honey. It goes down bitter.

Much of the Black Birds, have again settled on limb branches but many are still circling the sky. These Scavengers are hungry for the hunt their sensitive nose smells the stench of blood in the air. The Black Widow, readies her square of Archers. They are many, all are prepared and awaiting her orders to fire. On the hill ahead overlooking the Eight side octagon layout of the Corn field, the Black Widow arrives with the entourage of all her appointees behind her. This is a great day of victory for them. The Eight sided octagon layout of the Corn field allows sound to bend and amplify spreading out like talking to one nearby.

From where she stands, they that are bellow can hear everything said. Her keen eye-sight takes immediate notice of the shining metallic rod laying out on the ground. What is this who Ordered his Mask pin removed, her features twist into a scowl, she needs answers, and Now! The Head Soldier standing meters away from the Lady of Strange Behavior catches the Black Widow intent focus. On sensing danger to the young lady, he intercedes running over with force he pushes her hard to the ground. Its the only way to save her life from the Black Widows wrath.

Its better this than of the Black Widow and the bruises will heal. The Woman of Strange Behavior is hurt in the process, her pail and mug are scattered and damaged. She tries still to reach out for them but cannot grasp them so she pulls the mug by its cord into her. The High-Ranking Head Soldier gives the order and she is whipped over and again until, she is unable to move. Sighing in relief her anger is quench by the violence of display. This pleases the Black Widow. On eye contact by the Black Widow, the Lady of Strange Behavior is saved by his grace alone. At this moment she doesn't understand, and the scourge of the whip has never been felt on her like this. The Black Widow, nods her head to him for a job well done. He understands and gives the orders to have the massive Black Cross heist up into the air by its long chains. The massive Black Cross is made to drop into a large deep hole in the ground. This action averts the crowd and the Black Widow's attention. Quickly he orders the men to stop beating her.

The drop of the weight is so jarring it sends out an after shocking wave from his feet ripping straight up through out his body. The Mighty King Gouddaa chokes bringing up blood causing him excruciating pain. By far this was the worst of it. A glimmer of something else is happening to him beyond the pain. The massive Black Cross towers at height above the fields. He can be seen by every one in the Corn field. The beauty of Gouddaa demise brings a thrilling pleasure to the Black Widow. Slowly Gouddaa blood drips draining down the Black Cross saturating the earth beneath. Before all her subjects, the Black Widow, cries out for all to hear. No sound is heard beyond the squawks of birds spiraling above in the air. "Yes, yes Gouddaa! Now saturate the land with your blood so that life can fertilize these fields once again. Your chosen audience the Black Birds look on. And now, you may have your say." From below the crowd all laugh out at him, others scorn him still throwing stones and unforgiving words. None of the stones thrown reach the height in distance, yet still some continue to try.

There the Black Cross stands at a height above heights and from his Cross, the Great King Gouddaa, rest. Looking down from above he surveys the perimeter of his final resting place. For the first time, he regrets not killing the Black Widow, himself. The crowd beneath him are many, and they all wait for his death. His eyes are tired and blood still flows from his many deep wounds, down the Cross and into the earth. The Black Birds again take flight to the sky flying even closer to him than before. They become a dark cloud of screeching cries, ready to feed on his flesh. The Black Widow approves and the birds dangerously increase their speed all around him and below, encircling the cross. The Black Widow refuses to give him the pleasure of her seeing him die, so she turns her back to him as does all the the crowd below. With extended out stretched hands the Black Widow raises her two hands up to the sky. Forward she points signaling all below and all standing with her to move forward and they all do.

Above something strange is happening high over their heads. The clouds are closing in fast and its beginning to look like evening, nothing usual for the crowd blow, they have seen stranger things. In a rush running through the crowd below is the Lady of Strange Behavior up to the cross. Everyone back is turned from her actions. She still makes her way and there she stops and rest down another full pail of water. Taking the empty mug, she dips it full with water and offers it up to the Mighty King Gouddaa. He is unable to answer her or taste the water. A slight breeze stirs blowing in from the north and she is being grazed over and again by the fast-moving Black Birds swiftly moving around the foot of the Cross. The vortex of Black Birds screams much louder than before, it muffles out her screams and her cries. In the screeches of the Black Birds cries, they tell the Black Widow death is closing in and imminent.

The massive crowd below have all dissipated through the dry tall corn stalks in the field for shelter from the Black Birds. They are now a blur of endless numbers at her scream the Black Birds sweep down from the sky, circling the Black Cross like a pillar of black dust. Caught in the spinning flurry of black wings they pick at the flesh of the Lady of Strange Behavior. She tries to run away but instead she falls short on her steps to the hard earth, stumbling up again and again. The Birds are now pecking her even more, the shrill of her loud screams fall on deaf ears trapped in the swirling speed around the cross. He can't let her die, not everyone turned away, running in to rescue her is the same Head Guard who earlier gave the orders to have her whipped. Dashing her to the ground covering them both with his long black cape and armed head piece, they are safe.

The Undaunted King Gouddaa of the Arawaks and Caribs

In the foals of darkness under his cape he speaks "We must hurry!" Through an opening in the cape he looks up at the height of the Black Cross and out she runs to fetch her water-pail. With speed he moving quickly to protect her deflects the arched talons. Pulling her and the pail in to the cloaks cover again he covers her from the danger. Her white garments are stained with blood yet she refused to leave the pail behind. Now at the foot of the Black Cross, he manages to again look up and his eyes behold a tunnel of darkness he's never witness before swirling around the massive Black Cross. She also peeps up to witness the black veil coming down at her, they both are frightened. Suddenly and most strangely it is dark. Again, he cries out, "We have to keep moving. It will be raining soon!"

Disoriented from every thing, she does not understand when he says raining soon. He keeps her moving and into the corn field they run seeking shelter from the Black Birds. In retreat there ahead is an old wooden structure in the far corner of the corn field. They must get to it before the Black Widow gives the last orders to her General to rain down arrows from the sky. They make it just as the order is given. The Black Widow knows as well as her children. At the release of the bow cord, the high velocity sonic sound wave will reach them far before the arrows and they will scatter across the corn field to the mountains. The Black Birds now circle the massive Black Cross at sonic speed. The archers wait for the general in command order. And she gives it "Now! Black out the three moon light from the earth!"

The three great moons are now in lineament with the sun. On his command, the archers all aim high and fire. She and her appointees walk away. The arrows are many lifting into the sky they black out the three moon lights. For a full minute darkness falls up on the earth. The arrows released begins to rain down. The roof of the little barn house in the corner of the corn field is old. An arrow pierces the wall and the Head soldier is hit in his shoulder while protecting the beautiful lady. He falls over her to the ground, there's so much blood she has to help his bleeding wound. With a strange turn of events, the Black Birds all remain circling the mighty Gouddaa at sonic speed. It protects him from all danger and while the arrows fall from the sky so do the Black Birds to the ground. Now within the shelter of total darkness, the great and mighty King

Gouddaa cries out, to the heavens. "Mother, Father, into thy bosom I now come."

With the last and final arrow hitting the earth, a remaining remnant number of Black Birds fly away toward the hills and mountains. The Three moons light returns back to the earth and not one of the thousand of thousand upon thousands of arrows has touched Gouddaa's flesh. The Black Birds had given up their lives to prolong that of his own. The fallen arrows and the dead Black Birds lay about within a circumference of two miles. The number of arrows on the ground, are two million seven and the number of Black Bird's dead unknown.

The Strange Happening

The wind cycles mark the time, the Warlord Warrior Princess Leoha, has long made it out, the dry valley but the strange happening with the old father walking into the fabric of time has left her not only astounded but baffled. Minutes later she comes across a Bright Skin boy and girl running, she stopped them. Radiant and glowing they asked her to come with them to start a new world elsewhere but she decline because she is no longer pure, and her thinking would eventually destroy them all. The strange sound on the wind takes her attention and by the time she turns her focused back on them, they are gone. Could they have been a mirage, thinking about the water she makes speed to get away.

So many baffling occurrences have happened, from the lush grounds she has made it to the Lake of Geedaa. Looking to gather her thoughts, instead she finds herself in another battle of Blade supremacy. In no time she defeats her opponent coming to a rest beside one of the great stones there she falls a sleep. Some time later awakened by the sweet sound of a young ladies' voice. On the opposite side of the lake, singing so beautiful with an instrument accompaniment. The music makes her curious to see, who it is. Up on her feet she makes her way to the other side of the lake to an area unseen by many. Upon a sitting stone, there is a beautiful young dressed lady in white. Ethereally poised and beautiful as a butterfly her singing is as beautifully as she.

The Warrior is reminded to remember the old adage saying, the most beautiful can sometime be the most viscous and she approaches with guard. The young and beautiful butterfly reminds her of the Lamb Angel, back at the temple. With such calm karma she could be nothing but good. And on seeing the Warrior, the Beautiful Butterfly ends her playing and engages her, "Lady Warrior. How can I be of help to you?" The trees become animated giving a sensation whenever she speaks their leaves blows but there is no wind. "Your singing is superb. Have you also come to collect the Blade?" The Warrior asked. Standing upright, the Warrior eyes again travel over the trees.

"I am from the lamb of the High Archives, and I am sent only to speak to your heart. The Blade you carry, have brought you nothing under the darkness but more challenges, and you must believe, whosoever gave you the Blade! It was never to protect you, for the blade have brought you nothing but endless killing. Hear me Princess Leoha, from the Kingdom and house of Gouddaa! Your father needs you! He has long crossed over the boundaries into the Black Forest, and the three great moons are still in alignment, soon they will be divided to take their original place in the heavens and all lights shall be given back to the earth."

Somehow connected with the nature of trees her words just kick and troubles the Warrior's heart beat to say, "Tell me Priestess! How much time do I have and I promise! If I can save him. I shall stop the killings and bring back the Blade and leave it at your door steps but I must ride now. For I have never heard words spoken as such to my heart." Glancing at the tree leaves the Beautiful Priestess tells her, "You have only minutes left. And should the Blade not arrive at the Lamb door step, then you can be certain! It will fall back into the hands of it's rightful owner." Urgent to be about her father's business, The Warrior does not take much notice of the Lamb last words. As far as Leoha is concerned no one can take it without first dying. Leaping to the air and back across the lake into a tall tree she comes down on her Stallion and on the wind she ride's away.

The journey ahead is arduous and time is against her. Over hills, valleys, mountains, passing rivers through Saxon streaks finally she reaches the great open plains before the Black Forest. She must hurry to save her father. While riding in motion, she pats the Stallion on its neck, spurring him on, "I must get to my father before light, so

I need your all!" Taking a better hold on her saddle, the fast moving Stallion gives her it's all. Across the great open white plain, they ride on the wind. Gouddaa, is not yet dead, but he on his last breath. The earth beneath him is saturated with his blood, he finds everything around him is so quiet. The pain feels so far away, he is numb to everything in this moment.

The north winds speak out to him in silence and his tired eyes, red and heavy blood clot, his body trembles. It not so much from the cool air but from the advancing of death ready to receive him. He feels nothing now, Laurrenius is warm in his thoughts, she and his children will grieve. He so wants to sleep but the seed from all his past deeds taunt, keeping him awake. For a minute life stands still and he envisions his life reversing before him. Endorphin of death opiates surrounds the air and for the last time. A rift opens of light, he silently cries out, he sees the light of an undaunted Kingdom. He is the white knight of his people and behold his eyes now close. The life line of the mighty King Gouddaa, is pulled into eternity. With Gouddaa death, the incantation on the metallic like mask is broken reverting back to its form before melting away from his face to the earth.

To Reach the Black Forest

In order to reach the Black Forest before the sun gives day light back to the earth the Warrior Princess rides the wind across the great open plains. Quickly looking back the miles melt behind her as morning light swallows up the darkness. She's pushing the beast to it's limits and day-light rapidly approaches. She tries to compensate but the impossible cannot become possible for the beast is already at full speed. In fast moving minutes, time behind her turns night into daylight yet still she rides on, giving it her all but its not enough. As far as the eyes can see day light springs now at a distance ahead of her still, she does not give in. The life of her father depends on it, his life means more to her than her own life.

Finally, she is there at the outer limits of the Black Forest. She slows the fast moving stallion to a trot then a walk. The beast is heated, irritated, and breathing heavy huffs foam froth at his mouth. She looks at it's mouth and it is bleeding from its nostrils. Forced to bring the Beast to an even slower walk-in minutes the legs of the beast begin to buckle. Before the Stallion collapses to the earth she leaps from its back into the air onto her feet.

The Beast falls to the earth, the Stallion has exhausted himself and soon will die from the driving efforts of its Master. Time is truly not on her side, Leoha wants to save the Stallion but not at the cost of loosing her father. Taking a piece of old branch from the road side she covers the Stallion dark black eyes and with her Blade she cuts its life line. She will mourn its lost later but urgency demands she must move on, no matter the pain. In leaping strides to the air into the

Black Forest she enters. The place is too quiet no one appears to be around. She moves in deeper, she comes across pieces of her father's amour. Torn pieces from the suit, carefully looking around she does not sense him. She knows he is here. The pieces from his armor tells her so and the words of the beautiful butterfly is confirmed. Time did stands still at the exact time Gouddaa - life line is severed on the Black Cross.

A ripple in the fabric of time permeates touching all his children simultaneously. A feeling of disconnection occurs in some form or fashion. Though they are miles apart, even unto Derious, who has long been expelled to the end of the earth Gouddaa death is felt. Thousands of fresh footprints on the ground along with the impression of a dragged huge object tells her, which way to go. Eyes have lit on her and she is being followed. The foot prints lead into the wide open corn field their dead Black Birds and arrows protrude down into the ground. Never before has she witness such carnage or gore as what lies before her sight. In the center of the destruction, is a massive Black Cross towering heights. On it hangs the ravished body of what looks like her father. Or what remains of his bruised and battered body. Immobilized a chill of numbness creeps through her limbs, in a trans of surreal movement her eyes raise, taking to the very top of the Cross. She is weakened by the horrific sight of her father corpse nailed to his final resting place. With out fear for her own life, she stumbles screaming out to him. "Father!!!!"

She does not realize her cries are being heard alarming those to her presence. With warrior's speed her trots turn to sprint, she begins to run through the graveyard of the dead Black Birds. When she reaches within range of the structure, she leaps high into the air onto the Black gigantic Cross. Gripping it the best she tries to hold on, the surface is much too slippery with blood, she cannot hold on. Half the way up, she descends back to the ground for a better attempt. Walking a ways off she prepares for another attempt with dagger in hand. Taking off running with propelling force she launches it out at the half way mark up the Cross.

Into the air she leaps landing on the flat edge, she pushes from there up even higher. With two of her hands, she is able to catch up on both side of the cross bar. His eyes are closed his head is slumped to the side in the crock of his shoulder. Hanging face to face with her father, she raps her two feet around his waist to better support herself. Around his neck she holds tight with both hands hugging him tightly to her bosom. Its the first time in a long time she grievously cries. "Father, don't you dear drop me. Father, please don't leave me like this. Wake up and together we will go home and I promise never to leave again with out your approval. I will remain by your side and I shall do what is expected of me as a Princess. Is this not what you expect of me? the same as Libra. I was always so afraid of your teaching father, but I never said how frightening at times your words can be. You once said, when a good soul crosses over the sea of death It gloats over the unrighteous and it is only now, I understand the meaning. If you do not come with me. Then leave I must with you! Father."

Through the tares and ravishes of life, it doesn't matter anymore, nothing can hold back the love she has for her father. Without a care for her own life, she is willing to follow him even through the gates of death. She lets go her grip from around his strong neck falling backward only her thighs are attached around his waist. There is a breeze stirring and the sob of her tears is carried off away on the wind. Her upper body hangs morose against the lifeless corpse who is her father. Against his bared feet for a minute, she envisions the Kingdom. Releasing her legs from around his waist effortless she falls to the earth.

Unexpected, she hears him calling out to her. "Leoha, Leoha, awake for I am at the foot of the Cross awaiting you." This can't be happening again it's just like when she saw the Old Mage disappearing. It has all the components of the same probabilities. Shaking her head stunned, his thunderous voice opens her eyes restoring all hope back in her body. With super speed she somersaults in mid air out from her fall landing back on the Blade, again somersaulting she retrieves the dagger ending up at the foot of the Cross. Did she image his voice in her distress? Her father is not there and her right foot is resting on a strange like metallic like object, sinking beneath her foot. The earth beneath her feet is soft and soaked with royal blood.

Pressing into the mighty Structure with all her strength, she pulls and pushes against it. Hoping to bring it down she discovers she can't. Frustrated with all her efforts, she takes hold of the mighty structure with her two hands and falls to her knees. She rests her head against it post, oblivious to being watched. Dejected she looks up high at the mighty King Gouddaa and his final drop of blood falls on the bridge of her nose. She cries out. "Father why you? Why you father? You are at fault to have let this happen. You could have killed the Black Widow many times over. Please make me to understand why. But that's not important any more, is it father? I will kill them all father and not one shall be spared. I know father I know they are watching. I don't see them but they are there lurking at me. They must all pay in blood father, even if its at the cost of my life, I will join you! They must all pay, for in your name sake. I shall turn this place into a sea of blood. You watch me father, just you watch me." Leoaha speaks as the mad in mind.

Warning, her Warrior instinct kicks in with her back turned to the corn stalks she raises to her feet. Stealthily she reaches for her Blade hands stained with royal blood. What once was a dead corn stalk field, becomes field of life and an army of persons all armed ready to do battle with the great Warrior. Turning around to face the accusers there standing before her, is a sea of fighters and they all want her dead. With her eyes filled with blood vengeance, she smiles, its a good day to die. Her warrior speed charges into the battle zone. Death becomes her reward back to them for the death of her father. The battle is fierce, and savage, on and on the more she battles the more they press on her. In all the battles she has fought she has never killed so many at one time and in one place. The battle shows no sign of slowing down and into the night it goes on and on.

At Daybreak

At day break, she begins to show signs of fatigue. On the evening of the second day exhaustion takes a toll creeping in on her. The weight of her Blade hand grows tired, her muscles begin to lock. Weary from the slaughter, fury refuses to fuel her passion to kill. She is tired in need of rest. She must continue, rest is not an option. Her body tells differently. Her body muscles have reached their peak they tremble for lack of rest and still she will not stop.

Spent and out of breath, she stumbles in her own steps and the mighty Black Blade, is knocked out from her trembling hand. Each time she tries to reach the Blade, a blow stuns her. It is easily removed little does she know she will never get another chance to weld it up again. The Blade is taken and she is left to fight with just one dagger. She summons up the last of what strength she has left and that too fails her. Her strength is about depleted, there are just too many of them. Like the sands on the sea shore, they surge covering everywhere until finally. . . She wavers under the blows, falling to one knee first. Then on to the other she finds herself at the end, the many whips are unleashed upon her like her father. In the distance the crackle of laughter echoes.

The net has been sprung, falling face first to the earth they bind and chain her hands and feet. The sound of victory goes up letting every one knows the great Warrior has fallen. From the earth they brutally picked her up. She and the weapon are carried off before the Black Widow. That voice from her past, which is known so well to her said, "Warrior from the Arawak, and Caribs, nation and from the house of Gouddaa! You have long hold on to that which isn't yours!" The Black Widow, waved out her hand to the one who now holds the mighty Black Blade. The Blade is taken away out from sight to be locked away among others of its kind.

Then and there, the badly injured Warrior remembers the words of the Beautiful Butterfly back at the lake and the Lamb Angel back at the temple of the White Lambs. Both warned her should the blade not be left behind, then it will be returned back to its rightful it's owner. And to remind the great Warrior of their first encounter. The Black Widow said. "Now look around you! This garden may look dead but I am sure you can still smell its sweet fragrance in the air. You! Princess from the house of Gouddaa, have come to save the dead?" Out from her tiredness, the great Warrior summoned up what little of her strength remains. "Your riddles old woman! Doesn't frighten me any more. You killed my father and I shall kill. . ."

Before the great Warrior could finish she is knocked out cold with a strange piece of black cloth that turns into black smoke. Bruised and battered she has no choice other than to inhale. The Black Widow gives the orders, "None is to embrace her for she has long been poisoned and any whom ever takes her, shall surely and undoubtedly die, for she has long been touched by me. Now take her and chain he up against the dungeon walls and we shall see if the mighty Gouddaa, shall come down from his resting place and save her.

With a splash of dirty water to the Warriors face the foul smell revives her consciousness. The Black Widow waves out her hand and to the ground they push her before dragging her away. Ordered, they chain her against the dungeon wall in the exact position, she had ordered on her sister Sheppard. To further torment her they splash her washing away filth with more filth. They continue making her taste the end of the whip. For the first time in all her battles, she is at the loosing end of mercy and no one can help her because no one knows where she is. They work to break her so they continue speaking it out with their whips, until much of her clothing is torn away from her flesh.

Only then do they stop, it gives them pleasure to look upon the female naked body for it calms, and relaxes them. They know its death to touch her intimately cause the Black Widow has cursed her flesh. Her naked body makes them forget about their duties, but she wants only to kill them all. From her dungeon, darkness falls over the earth and the sounds of thunder shatters across the sky. A large storm is approaching fast and for her this is maybe a good opportunity. She can now plan her escape. The brunt of the storm is unleashing upon them and everyone scatters from the thundering sounds shaking the Under Pillars of the earth. She tries to make good on her escape but first she must calculate the strength of the chains which binds her against the dungeon walls. They are unbreakable, they are the same chains of Gog and Magog that once held her father. Trying to break away, causes her to be further whipped and punished.

The great Warrior is once again left alone in her thoughts, flashbacks of her father's body dead on the massive Cross replay. From the walls of her dungeon, she looks up, taking in the lightning in the sky. Through three small open space high above, enough only for a flying dove to enter, the brave and bold Warrior cries out apologizing to the heavens. "Father, forgive me for being so late." A great lightning bolt rips down from the sky setting ablaze the corn field devouring everything within its pathway.

The devouring fire blaze ensues circling the massive Black Cross consuming it but not burning it. Everything below it and around it is consumed in the fire. The fire becomes a great pillar engulfing the whole corn field and all the surrounding trees are burnt to ash. The Black Widow fearing the worst begins to believe, the storm is some how connected to Gouddaa. She sends out five of her own to investigate the strange like storm and report back to her by mid day. They go off into the thick dark storm, frightened, some are scared and then there are others ready to die for the cause.

The Head Soldier

The Head Soldier who saved the Lady of Strange Behavior twice made it safely out and both went their separate ways. He is much better his wound having been nursed. He is however disturbed by the strange storm or it maybe its the way he now feels after saving the Lady of Strange Behavior life. Unable to pin point the true cause of the sudden change within his body and mind, to get answers he goes in search of her. He is told by some of her close encounters, she is to be found in the feeding tents and off he goes. A small search later, the Lady of Strange Behavior takes sight of him coming toward her. Perplexed she has not forgotten his order to have her beaten. Anxious she feels the need to get away because like him she too is having issues of her own.

The feeding tent is large, able to feed thousands at a time. Up from the table she excuses herself, the others find it odd but they think nothing of. Putting it off to her strange ways they laugh. Swiftly she disappears through the standing crowd to the outside, not realizing she has been spotted. He follows at a distance, trying to evade him she misses her direction and runs straight into him. The storm leaves behind miner winds, face to face both share a sudden flash back. Looking to each other he said. "I know you remember me! But why are you running away? I only want to talk! I have a few questions for you?"

Stepping to one side, she answers. "For the same reason you are chasing me. I do remember you but I don't wish to talk." There is a change in her manner and her looks. Walking up to her, he takes her by the hand pulling her to an even more confine and secure area. She dears not scream as he lets go of her hand and takes hold of her neck. With force he slaps her once across the face dazing her, but she is stubborn and holds her ground. She wonders why would he save her just to kill her now. Turning her head to face him directly she looks into his eyes.

Much to his surprise she said, "There is no need for that." He drops his hand deflated by her response. She turning her eyes away from him, leaves him to wonder why. Concerned for both their well being he speaks, "Lady! It's because of you! Am not the man I use to be! I just want to know! What is happening to me?" She thought it was only her who felt different. So desperately she turns to him and cries out. "Please, help me?" Her sad expression touches his heart, as if she belonged there, she steps up to him and reaches out her arms enfolding them around his neck. Embracing him he feels her raged breaths on his chest as she weeps resting the side of her face. He does nothing but gently allow her to say her peace. "I don't belong here!" She cries continuing, "Would you please help me. My eyes, have seen manna falling down from the sky and I don't know why. I don't even know what to make out of it."

He stands surprised by her words because they make him better understand more about what is happening to him. Gently he begins to caress her head resting on his chest. To better make her understand, she is not alone, he asserts. "I too have seen the strange manna falling from the heavens and it led me to you. Something must have happened to the water after I got you to safe grounds. In the abandoned shack in the corn field. You offered me water and I did drink but I haven't eaten nor had need for drink since. I am a Head Soldier, one who doesn't know who he is now."

The confusion registered on his face, declares he is at odds with the changes he is experiencing. Being a soldier of war is all he's ever known. For so long, he knows strategies is what wins' wars. While he comforts her, he envisions what had occurred with the pail of water while under the Black Cross. Gently streaking his hand down her long black hair, he asks, "Tell me! Where now is your pail of water?" Slowly raising her head, she looks up at him and answers. "I left it resting on the side wall of the well." He again ponders the desperate situation. "Yes! Now I understand its his blood, it must have dripped into your pail." She too thinks back on it, she too gets the picture and from his shoulders she nods her head as to say, yes. Things now feel better. She whispers out, "I too have gathered that but I can't stay here any longer and I don't even know the way out."

Her beauty is natural, her smooth skin makes him awakens his affections, together they may not be so alone or so different. Silently she opens her heart out to him the soft touch of her finger she gently lingers tracing his lips. The tensions turn into something they both know. No more is needed to be she magnifies her feelings out to him and together they embrace in a searing kiss. The kiss is fever filled with passion, realization of what they can have offers the start of a new beginning. In his strong arms she glitters in her tears of joy. When they had finally allowed each other to breathe, she again whispers against his lips, "Please, don't leave me now." His concern is like wise is heightened with the drastic changes already in motion. He must now contend with an immense desire to protect her. Freeing her mind from doubt, he tells her more about the pending danger and how best to avoid it. "If you try to leave now. You won't make it. Wait for me and together, we along with others may have a chance. I just need you to go and continue being the way you were. I will come to you. We must search for others who may have drank the water."

The assurance of his words offers her a pillar of hope. Concerned about the others she expresses her doubts. "Can we save them all?" He knows the possibilities are dangerous and deadly. He chooses his words with confidence. "If they are like you and I! They are already saved! Now wether they live or die depends on the choices they make." The open plain beyond these lands can kill when crossing but to stay here is much worst. "I'm sorry I hit you!" Tracing her bruises tenderly causes her to shiver with desire and its promise. Go now!" Pushing her away, she walks away looking back she waves out her hand to say good bye. He watches her as she disappears out from sight, realizing his problems have just begun.

The Strange Storm

The storm is long gone and the Black Widow demands answers for the death and the lost of so many of her children, the Black Birds. Her babies lie dead all around her. Demented in her mind, the Widow tries to reason showing her people the strange storm had nothing to do with the death of King Gouddaa. They hear her but they insist its not so, she must now make commence. King Gouddaa's charred remains evaporating, leaving only the little of him laying out on his Cross. Seeking to pacify her top appointees, she gives to her four leaders, the black-flags. They must gather their troops into the corn field in front of the massive Black Cross by late evening. And by late evening the end of fearing Gouddaa and his kingdom shall be over. The last of his remains shall be the last thing they shall ever see of him. She sends them all away to prepare.

The noon day Suns ride high in the sky, and news comes to the Black Widow from all around about the strange storm and flaming pillars of fire seen by many in the corn fields. Incensed such news only serves to provoke her anger, sending them all away. Her first in command walks back in to debriefs her on the return of the five sent out during the storm. The investigation harvests an abnormal report. She demands each be sent in the order they were sent out.

From the first two allowed in she can see by the severity of their injuries something tragic has occurred to them. Heaving coughs of soot from the smoke out of their mouths. Still, she questions, "And your findings?" To stand before the Black Widow with out a favorable report is a sure sentence of death. The one with less injuries and singed hair takes the lead in hopes of saving them both. He begins with the usual formality but she has no time for that. "Forget the formality just get on with it," rushing him she wants to know now! She commands him to step up. "As you can see Great Widow, the storm was too much for us to handle, we were both injured in the process and had to turn back." They are badly banged up after all they have been through, they could use rest.

Failure is not one of the Black Widow strongest attributes but for a labor well done in Gouddaa's demise she is of more tolerance. Kindly she proceeds, "Go and take care of your wounds but bring me answers." And they both leave holding onto each other for support. Then the second two are brought in, still coughing from smoke inhalation. One has a mannerism of tapping his left foot while standing still very much annoying to her. "Report!" she requests out loud. The oldest of the two. with an up right manner speaks "Great Widow, the storm was too great and after the fire came, we were trapped but we made it back alive. We can only ask, you give us another chance." "What's his name?" She asks referring to the one with the tapping mannerism. Most proud of his old comrade he and his comrade answers "Taaperiouss." Quickly heads turn to each other then back at the Black Widow. She said "Well Taaperiouss, I have some good news for you. You both may leave but the next time you come before me with that annoying tapping. I would have to do something about that, now go." Pleased to be let off lightly the exit couldn't come sooner.

Then comes in the last man looking a bit shock and before she could ask any question to him. Out loud without fear letting loose a free tongue, the Black Knight confides out at her. "I have witnessed pillars of fire in the corn field, that burned so great around the Black Cross. It was not an ordinary fire. I believe it had a mind of its own for I looked around me and fire is burning every where. I became afraid because I couldn't see a way out, them came in the wind and I found a way out. I ran until I reached the eastern water well. There was a pail with water resting on the side wall and I took it up and I drank to quench my thirst with the rest I poured over my heated body to cool me down. As I was about to leave, I heard a mighty thunder and I looked up into the heavens and my eyes envisioned manna falling from the sky that covered over the whole corn field. Everything in the cornfield was made manna and I run back here, I waited a long period for you to hear me and interpret, what I have seen."

This is too much for the Black Widow to accept, indirectly this soldier was telling her that from beyond the grave King Gouddaa had smite her. She so much despises any type of talk of Gouddaa. She deeply looks into his eyes and she boldly calling him. "Come closer Great Knight." Thinking, of all the others he will be rewarded for his findings they remained stun at what the Black Widow does next. Apprehensively he walks up to the Black Widow and when he gets within range, she stands up pulling back her right hand with great force she let him have one full charge slap across his face. The blows magnitude and dimension is so efficacious and potent, it sends the Black Knight reeling backward over three table and chairs before hitting the ground.

When he stands up, three of his uniform buttons are snapped off his upper chest plate leaving him standing with a crooked look on his uniform and face. Backward he staggers falling out cold to the floor, all his comrades laugh loud at him, others simply hide their smiles. To the others laughing out at him like fools. She cries out. "Now throw him out!" It's with pleasure, his comrades pick him up by his hands and feet and toss him to the outside down sixty-six steps. His body rolls out and into the open street, no one passing would help and those who didn't shunned by kicking him with their heel aside.

Some time later the Black Knight, awakens on the road side standing up to his feet he realizes what has happened to him. He looks around before running off for his life. In a twisted turn of events, he accidentally runs into the Lady of Strange Behavior. He remembers her and the pail with water she carried. The pail of water, its the water vividly he remembers and is frightened by its implication. He breaks off running again but away from her. In a remote part of the Black Forest he comes to a stop not realizing she is following. She catches up to him and he being frightened drops to a stop breathless. To help him she stays until he calms and then she tells him what is happening to him has also occurred to many others like them. This helps to calm him even more.

Sheppard Back in Her Mother's Chambers

Sheppard has returned back in to her mother chamber to further discuss the content of the book given to her. After some small talks Sheppard explains her actions. "Mother! I am sorry I didn't get back to you earlier. I have been reading out by the caves of Arcariaa. The book makes mentioned of a Blade and a Capacitor used by an unknown. Is the Blade and the Capacitor one of the same and is the unknown Grandfather?" Laurrennius smiles to her and answers, "Yes! The unknown name is that of your great great Grandfather King Aggaddaa the first, and the Capacitor is the Blade, which he used to kill one hundred thousand armed men all at once. The weapon was later on used once by your father in battle to defeat eighteen hundred thousand Arawaks and Caribs warriors and it was later determined that such a weapon of the Gods, should not remain among us and the weapon was handed over to the Lamb of the High Archives and was never seen again."

This only makes Sheppard want to understand the impossible of such a weapon, she asks. "Mother how is that possible to have killed so many with only one stroke of a Blade?" Laurrennius shares what she knows with Sheppard. "Through an electrical charge, able to jump from metal to metal in less than a blink of an eye and from that time on peace rained and remained among the two nations up to this very time."

Even now Laurrennius, thoughts begin to drift on her husband, this does not go unnoticed by Sheppard. She lets her mother know of her feelings, "Mother! I know your thoughts are with Father. I too feel a separation. Maybe its just as you said! In due time I will be telepathic." Laurrennius, goes on, "The Galactic lay-line, which connects us all in some form or fashion. I feel is broken." Sheppard tries to sense her father but can not, neither can Laurrennius. Deeply worried it further saddens her but still she lets Sheppard know. "You are already telepathic. You only have to channel it and let it flow. I don't feel very well so I rather you take your leave of absence until later. . ." Sheppard knowing much about her mother's feeling leaves in hopes of returning much later to learn more from her mother about the four elementals mentioned in the book and its secrets.

The Head Soldier and the Black Knight

It's the aftermath of Gouddaa's death. The Head Soldier and the Lady of Strange Behavior, the Black Knight, and many others who drank the water from the pail have joined in meeting to hear more. They are all feeling the effects from the water. The Head Soldier has orchestrated a plan of escape, but they all want to leave now!

Meanwhile the four divisions are gathering in front of the massive Black Cross. The Head Soldier, a strategist, assures them if they do leave now, they will all die under the light for the Black Widow, will show them no mercy. He recites it is imperative they all leave when the earth is darkened again by the next eclipse. With the longer period of darkness, it should allow for a safer time in crossing the great plains. If the Black Widow ever found out they were looking to defect, they would all be killed. He already knows what pathway they must take but not before first eliminating the lookout at the boarder.

He goes on to telling them, a safe plan is all about stealth. They will divide themselves into four groups. Each with an appointed leader who knows the way to the outside caves of Dowarr shall meet. There they shall all stay before being scattered among other groups of travelers, traveling to other towns and islands. They all agreed to the plan before disbursing back into their everyday routine.

The lady of strange behavior walks up to him after he is finished talking. Pensive with excitement, there is a gleam of warmth in both their eyes. They are happy to be next to each other again. The situation is dire and grows urgently with each passing second. "Every move we now make can be dangerous and the journey out there can be even more treacherous. Should we arrive safe at the caves of Dowarr. I would never again desert you. I would like to make you my wife." Astonished by his declarations brings tears to her eyes. Nodding rapidly her doe eyes alight with joy. She too pledges her committed, assuring him no matter what the cost, live or die she will always be by his side. Into his arms she falls, this is the second time he's held her and it feels so right. All his life he has searched for the purpose in his life. This woman has come and redefined his world with one act of kindness, he can't let her go now. He embraces her as if it is the last before they separate, each returning to their positions.

Evening has come, all the Black Widow troops, have assembled in the corn field just in front of the massive Black Cross. Together, their numbers are numbers uncountable. On a great and large throne like no other, she sits high and mighty before them all with her back to the massive Cross. The throne seat is large enough for four kings it is designed to rotate. Its length is about two hundred feet with secret compartments and hidden weaponry everywhere. Its width is twelve feet with twelve up right pillars. The great goddess Sinn stands at the top of each of the cross pillars. It's a monstrosity, the rig is pulled by twelve Carrcoss each larger than a grown male elephant and family to the mammoth in rows of twos. It is protected by dark forces. This is the Black Widows' domain she rules here.

The north wind is blowing across the land, carrying within it Gouddaa's, charcoal remains to every corner of the Black Forest into everyone's nostrils below it enters. The mummers of many do not believe the mighty King is dead, they have been fooled before. To satisfy her appointees curiosity about Gouddaa being fully dead and not another of his incantations she raises out her right hand to have their silence.

Up from her mighty carrier, she stands up. To the troops she cries out. "Now look up on at the charcoal remains of the undaunted King of the Arawak and Caribs, from the mighty House of Gouddaa. He can do you no more harm! His remains are nothing but charcoal. He is dead and long gone. Now get yourselves ready for the thirteenth cycle of the second moon. For we shall ride out and claim his Kingdom and enslave all his people and all shall be ours. The house of Gouddaa, and the Kingdom of the Arawaks, and Caribs, shall all fall."

A roar of approval rises, they praise her with everlasting words. All Four Division troops cry, "Long Live! Long live the highest Black Widow. Long live! Long live, the highest Black Widow. Their adoration is a balm to her soul, she loves it. Once again, she gives the signal and one by one the four legions with their Black Flag move out further awaiting orders for the next ride of destruction.

The Disconnections

At the very time of Gouddaa's death on the Black Cross, Libra feels dread while on the throne. She not only feels it but senses her father's lifeline has been disconnected from their realm. It disturbs her heart causing it to flutter irregularly. Her stomach folds in spasms leaving her nauseous. She runs to her chamber, expelling the contents of her dinner. The moment is an empty one, there she weeps for the loss of her father before finally drifting off asleep.

On her bed curled in a fetal position, she dreams. She envisions herself standing before the great white throne of the Lamb of the High Archives. She can see the one sitting on the throne but not their face. This space frightens her giving concern she speaks to the figure. "You said! I have one question. Tell me White Lamb. Is the world of reality and the world of dreams connected?" The voice from the great white throne knows who she is. "Libra! I have long passed over the threshold of death and I now walk among you as your guide and. Your sister Leoha, life hangs in the balance of time. She is being held in a dungeon deep within the Black Forest and is in need of your help before it's too late."

The voice is that of her father, how could this be? she moves in closer for a better look at the face. She parts the veil and is shocked by the image to be that of her own. It is she sitting on the Throne of the White Lamb, out from her slumber she awakens in a cold sweat, gasping for her breath. Puzzled and afraid by the dream, she squeezes tightly to her bed pillow and there she weeps once more for the loss of her father King Gouddaa.

The End? Or is It.

The Undaunted King Gouddaa of the Arawaks and Caribs

is Written by Mr. Douglas Burns and
Mr. Eddison Alric Dame and is
based on an original book about an Arawak King named Gouddaa,
and who lived during the rise of the Arawaks and Caribs empires.

And under one rule he unites both nations which is
today called the Commonwealth of the Bahamas, and
this is his story as written as found among the native
ancient potteries hidden in a cave in Nassau,
New Providence is now known as Black Beard Caves.

The cave is now a historical sight for millions of visitors and
tourist to see and visit during their stay in
Nassau, New Providence and
each year the number grows. . .

The History Diary

In 1927, a Bahamian native Mr. Alburt Vincent, and his two sons
were exploring the caves of Arcariaa in Nassau, New Providence,
and while digging to find old treasures
and old artifacts his two sons
stumbled across two jars like potteries in a remote area of the cave
believed to have been left behind by Black Beard and his Pirates.

The boys' father took the jar like potteries
home and on opening them
he discovered two small scrolls with writings
on each of the leather-like materials
about how the Arawaks and Caribs united
under one rule to fight against
the British settlers from settling on their land.
Many of them were killed by
British settlers due to firepower falling
down upon them from the skies.

Maps of caves with tons of treasures hidden in the great Exuma keys
and information of how the Arawaks and Caribs once lived
their everyday lives were preserved by their
writings which they buried
in potteries and hid away from the English in the caves of Arcariaa
to later be found. Today the same cave is named after Black Beard
the English pirate who once sailed through the
seven entrances of the Caribbean Sea.

Mr. Alburt Vincent, diary further speaks
about how he gave the scrolls
to one of his Jamaican history teachers who were most interested
in old Caribbean artifacts, and who later told him that he had
the scrolls sent to England at the academy of historical history to
be further validated. He waited five years for a response but
sadly, his history teacher died shortly after.

www.ingramcontent.com/pod-product-compliance
Lightning Source LLC
Chambersburg PA
CBHW021437070526
44577CB00002B/198